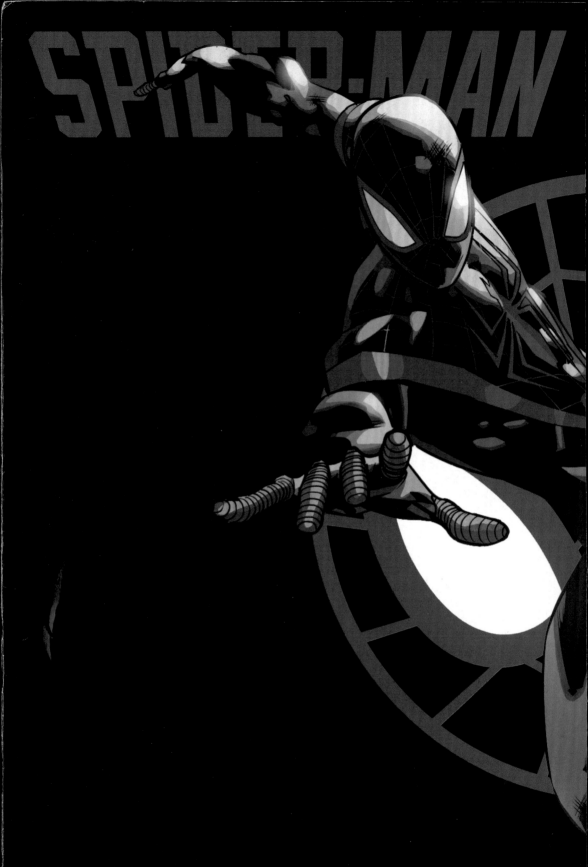

SPIDER-MAN: MILES MORALES VOL. 4. Contains material originally published in magazine form as SPIDER-MAN #234-240. First printing 2018. ISBN 978-1-302-90598-9. Published by MARVEL WORLDWIDE, INC., a subsidiary of MARVEL ENTERTAINMENT, LLC. OFFICE OF PUBLICATION: 135 West 50th Street, New York, NY 10020. Copyright © 2018 MARVEL. No similarity between any of the names, characters, persons, and/or institutions in this magazine with those of any living or dead person or institution is intended, and any such similarity which may exist is purely coincidental. Printed in Canada. DAN BUCKLEY, President, Marvel Entertainment; JOHN NEE, Publisher; JOE QUESADA, Chief Creative Officer; TOM BREVOORT, SVP of Publishing; DAVID BOGART, SVP of Business Affairs & Operations, Publishing & Partnership; DAVID GABRIEL, SVP of Sales & Marketing, Publishing; JEFF YOUNGQUIST, VP of Production & Special Projects; DAN CARR, Executive Director of Production Technology; ALEX MORALES, Director of Publishing Operations; DAN EDINGTON, Managing Editor; SUSAN CRESPI, Production Manager; STAN LEE, Chairman Emeritus. For information regarding advertising in Marvel Comics or on Marvel.com, please contact Vit DeBellis, Custom Solutions & Integrated Advertising Manager, at vdebellis@marvel.com. For Marvel subscription inquiries, please call 888-511-5480. Manufactured between 5/11/2018 and 6/12/2018 by SOLISCO PRINTERS, SCOTT, QC, CANADA.

10 9 8 7 6 5 4 3 2 1

MILES MORALES

BRIAN MICHAEL BENDIS
writer

OSCAR BAZALDUA
artist

JUSTIN PONSOR (#234),
BRIAN REBER (#235-239) &
LAURA MARTIN (#240) WITH
MATT MILLA (#240) & PETER PANTAZIS (#240)
color artists

SARA PICHELLI & JUSTIN PONSOR
art, #240, p. 20

VC's CORY PETIT
letterer

PATRICK BROWN (#234-239) AND
DAVID MARQUEZ & JUSTIN PONSOR (#240)
cover art

KATHLEEN WISNESKI
assistant editor

NICK LOWE
editor

collection editor JENNIFER GRÜNWALD
assistant editor CAITLIN O'CONNELL
associate managing editor KATERI WOODY
editor, special projects MARK D. BEAZLEY
vp production & special projects JEFF YOUNGQUIST
svp print, sales & marketing DAVID GABRIEL

book designer ADAM DEL RE

editor in chief C.B. CEBULSKI
chief creative officer JOE QUESADA
president DAN BUCKLEY
executive producer ALAN FINE

SPIDER-MAN created by
STAN LEE & STEVE DITKO

High-schooler Miles Morales was bitten by a stolen, genetically altered spider that granted him incredible arachnid-like powers. He's kept this a secret from everyone except his friends Ganke Lee and Fabio Medina, and his ex-S.H.I.E.L.D. agent father. Miles' mother recently discovered her family's secrets and left. She's forgiven Miles, but things aren't back to normal.

Actually, nothing is normal! Fabio went missing, Miles broke a rib in a huge fight with Hammerhead (who had beaten up Miles' friend Lana, A.K.A. Bombshell) and lately he's been wondering if he should keep being Spider-Man. Even one more problem might be too much for Miles to handle...

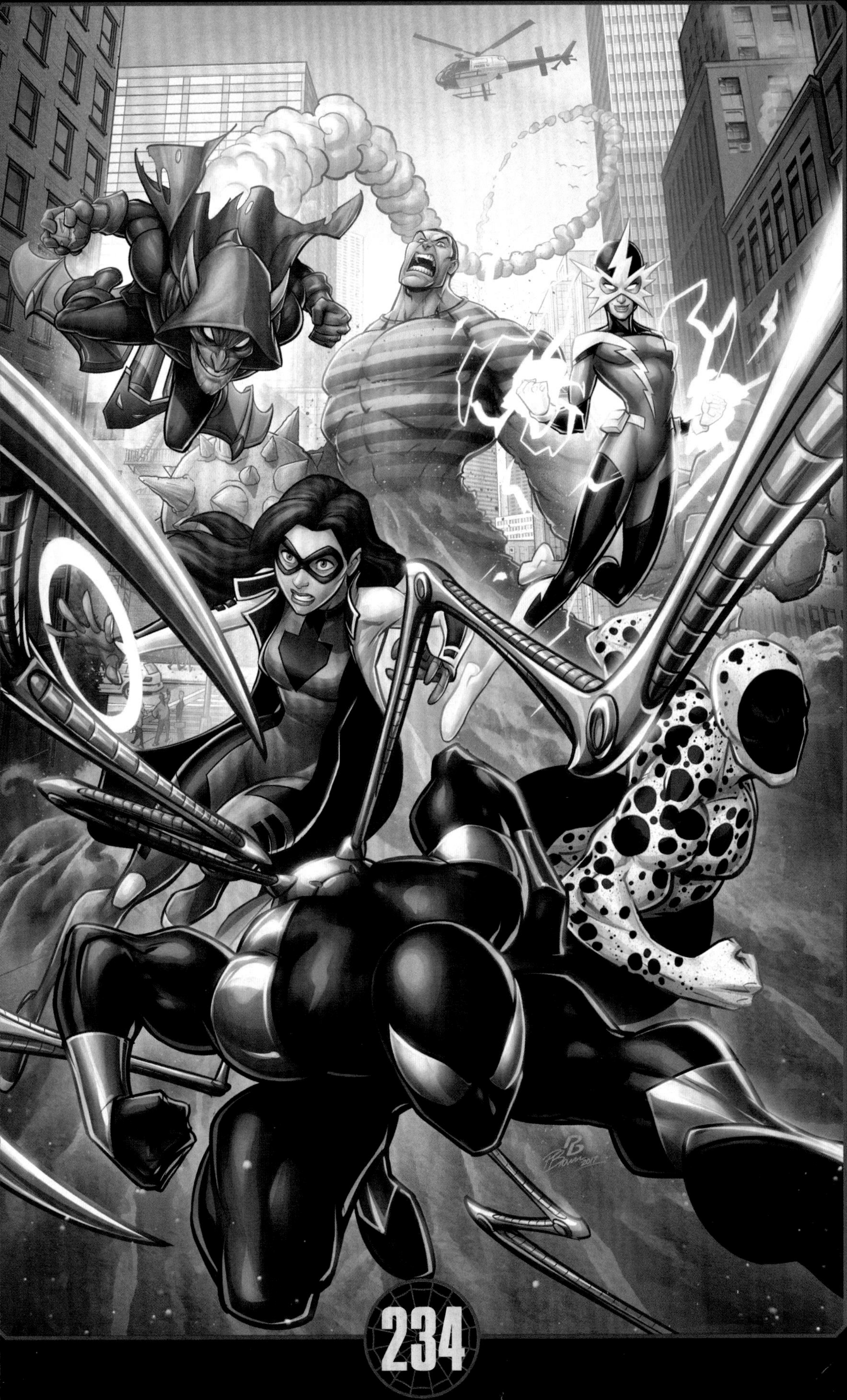
234

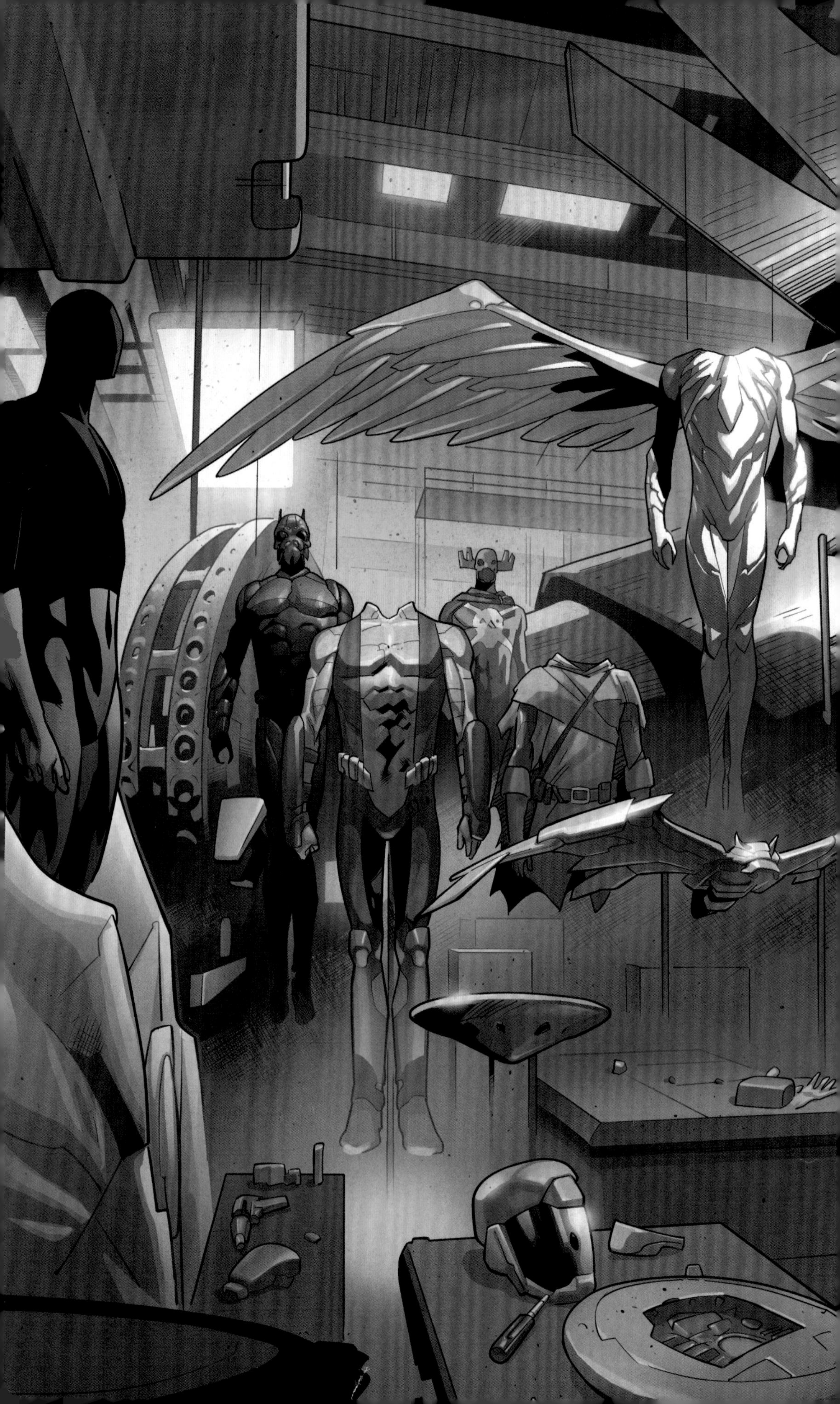

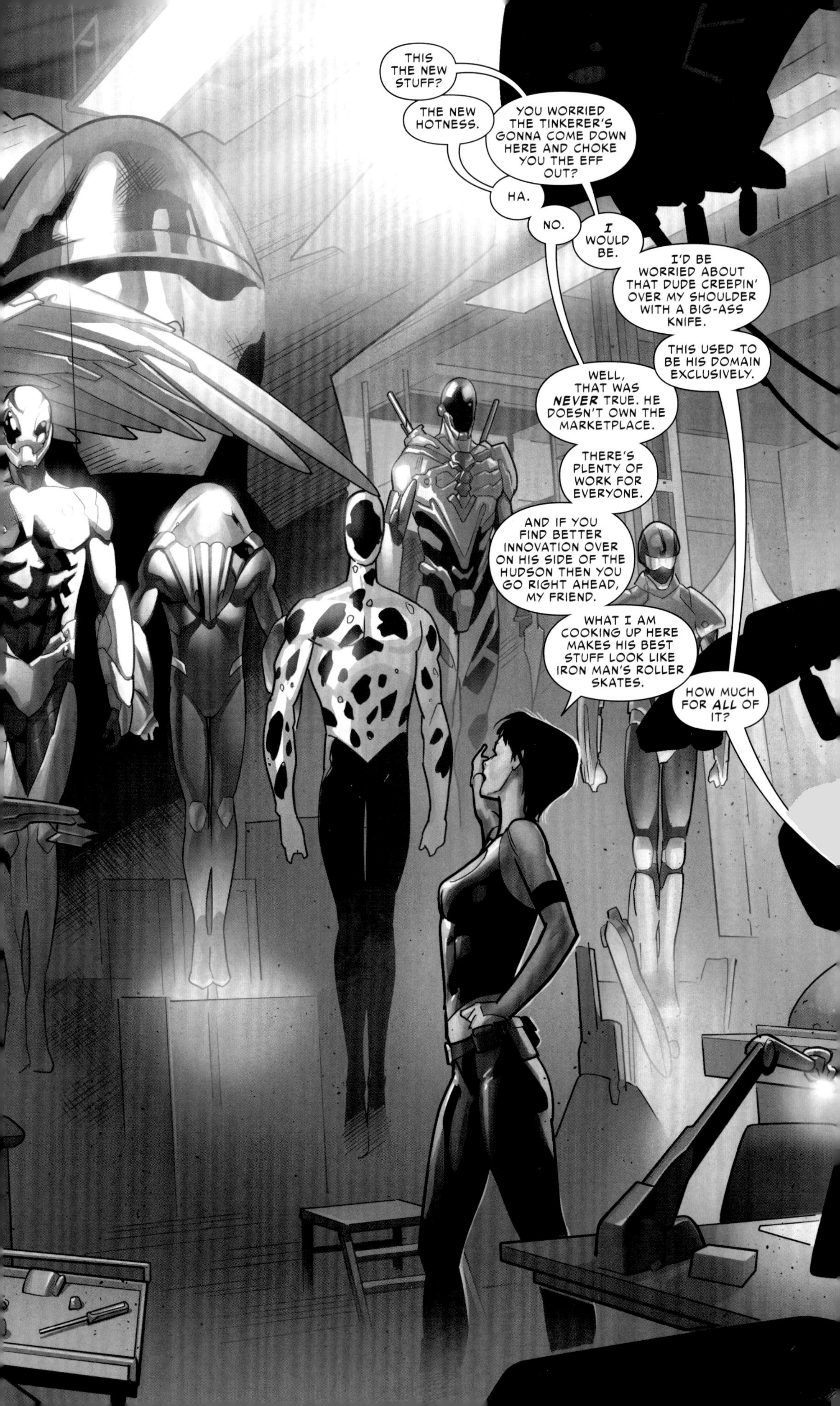
THIS THE NEW STUFF?
THE NEW HOTNESS.
YOU WORRIED THE TINKERER'S GONNA COME DOWN HERE AND CHOKE YOU THE EFF OUT?
HA.
NO.
I WOULD BE.
I'D BE WORRIED ABOUT THAT DUDE CREEPIN' OVER MY SHOULDER WITH A BIG-ASS KNIFE.
THIS USED TO BE HIS DOMAIN EXCLUSIVELY.
WELL, THAT WAS NEVER TRUE. HE DOESN'T OWN THE MARKETPLACE.
THERE'S PLENTY OF WORK FOR EVERYONE.
AND IF YOU FIND BETTER INNOVATION OVER ON HIS SIDE OF THE HUDSON THEN YOU GO RIGHT AHEAD, MY FRIEND.
WHAT I AM COOKING UP HERE MAKES HIS BEST STUFF LOOK LIKE IRON MAN'S ROLLER SKATES.
HOW MUCH FOR ALL OF IT?

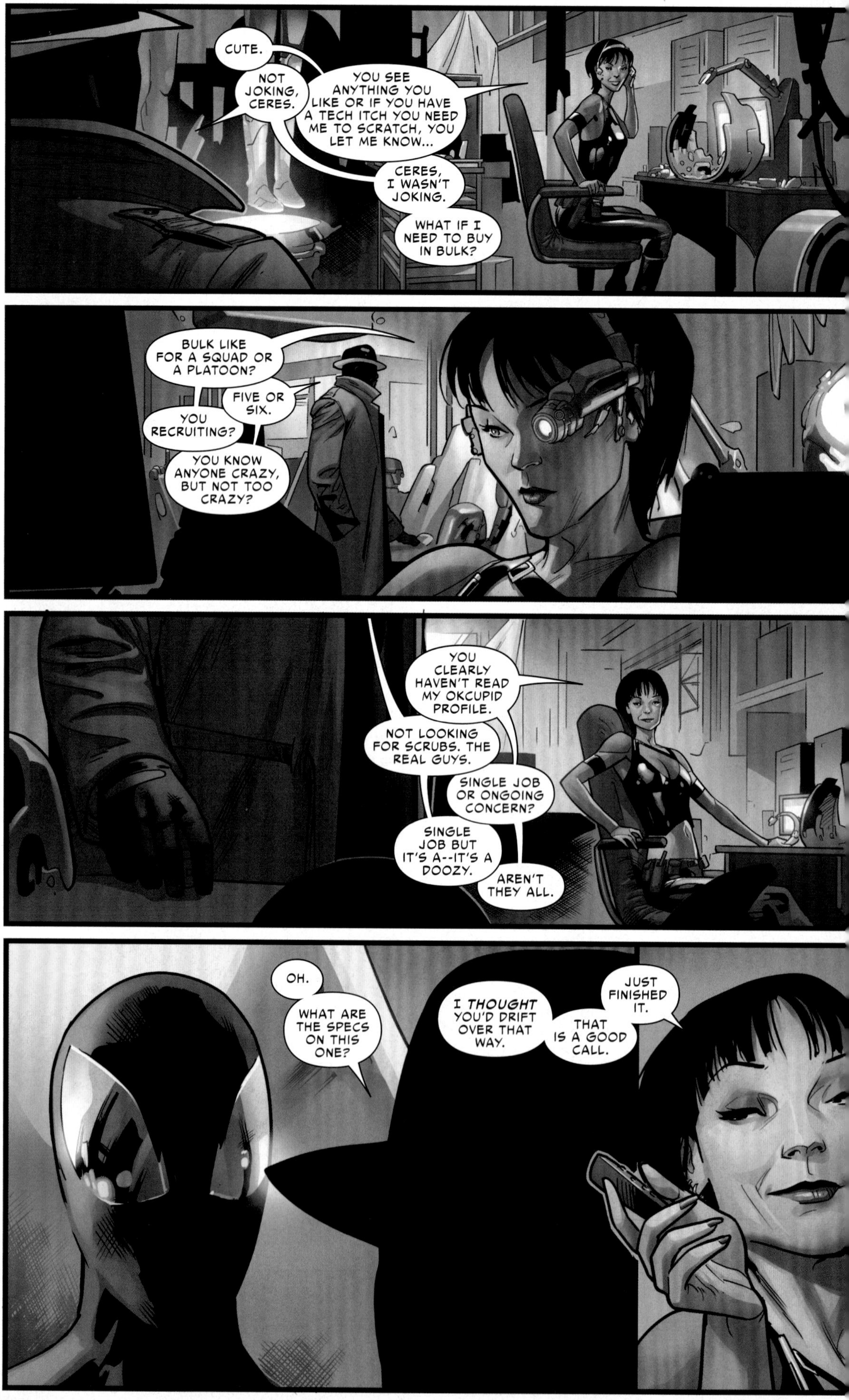
CUTE.
NOT JOKING, CERES.
YOU SEE ANYTHING YOU LIKE OR IF YOU HAVE A TECH ITCH YOU NEED ME TO SCRATCH, YOU LET ME KNOW...
CERES, I WASN'T JOKING.
WHAT IF I NEED TO BUY IN BULK?
BULK LIKE FOR A SQUAD OR A PLATOON?
FIVE OR SIX.
YOU RECRUITING?
YOU KNOW ANYONE CRAZY, BUT NOT TOO CRAZY?
YOU CLEARLY HAVEN'T READ MY OKCUPID PROFILE.
NOT LOOKING FOR SCRUBS. THE REAL GUYS.
SINGLE JOB OR ONGOING CONCERN?
SINGLE JOB BUT IT'S A--IT'S A DOOZY.
AREN'T THEY ALL.
OH.
WHAT ARE THE SPECS ON THIS ONE?
I *THOUGHT* YOU'D DRIFT OVER THAT WAY.
JUST FINISHED IT.
THAT IS A GOOD CALL.

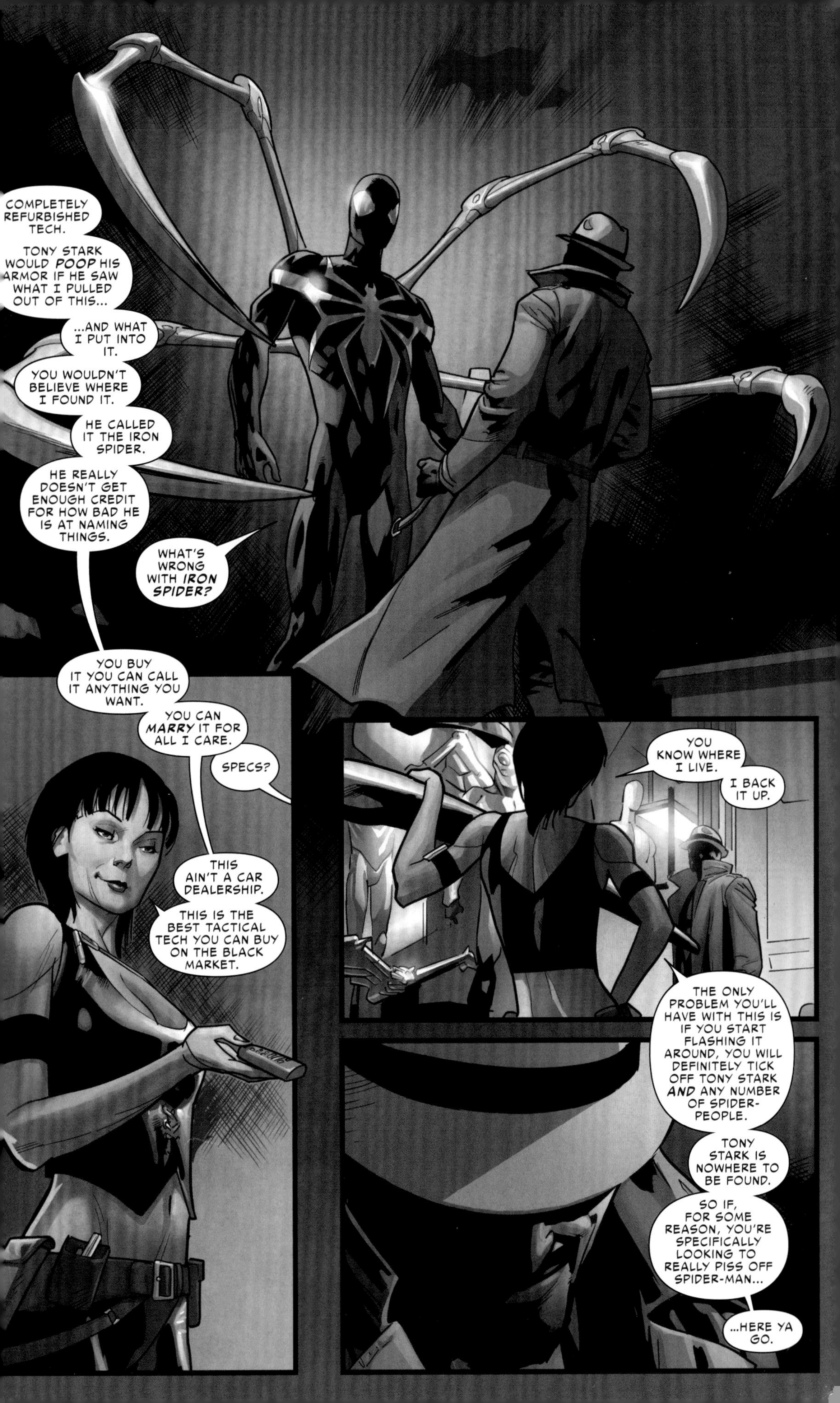

COMPLETELY REFURBISHED TECH.
TONY STARK WOULD POOP HIS ARMOR IF HE SAW WHAT I PULLED OUT OF THIS...
...AND WHAT I PUT INTO IT.
YOU WOULDN'T BELIEVE WHERE I FOUND IT.
HE CALLED IT THE IRON SPIDER.
HE REALLY DOESN'T GET ENOUGH CREDIT FOR HOW BAD HE IS AT NAMING THINGS.
WHAT'S WRONG WITH IRON SPIDER?
YOU BUY IT YOU CAN CALL IT ANYTHING YOU WANT.
YOU CAN MARRY IT FOR ALL I CARE.
SPECS?
THIS AIN'T A CAR DEALERSHIP.
THIS IS THE BEST TACTICAL TECH YOU CAN BUY ON THE BLACK MARKET.
YOU KNOW WHERE I LIVE.
I BACK IT UP.
THE ONLY PROBLEM YOU'LL HAVE WITH THIS IS IF YOU START FLASHING IT AROUND, YOU WILL DEFINITELY TICK OFF TONY STARK AND ANY NUMBER OF SPIDER-PEOPLE.
TONY STARK IS NOWHERE TO BE FOUND.
SO IF, FOR SOME REASON, YOU'RE SPECIFICALLY LOOKING TO REALLY PISS OFF SPIDER-MAN...
...HERE YA GO.

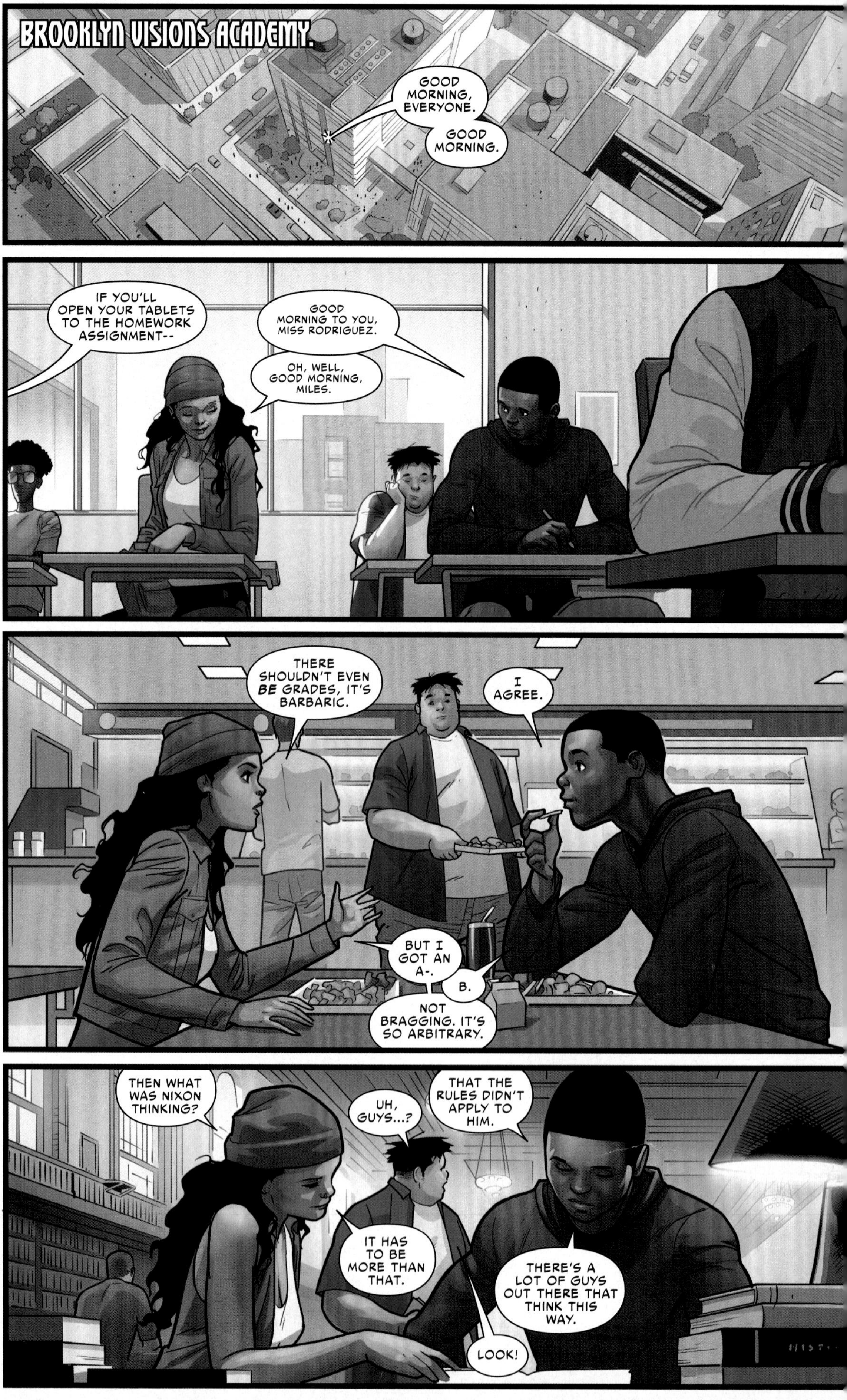
BROOKLYN VISIONS ACADEMY.
GOOD MORNING, EVERYONE.
GOOD MORNING.
IF YOU'LL OPEN YOUR TABLETS TO THE HOMEWORK ASSIGNMENT--
GOOD MORNING TO YOU, MISS RODRIGUEZ.
OH, WELL, GOOD MORNING, MILES.
THERE SHOULDN'T EVEN BE GRADES, IT'S BARBARIC.
I AGREE.
BUT I GOT AN A-.
B.
NOT BRAGGING. IT'S SO ARBITRARY.
THEN WHAT WAS NIXON THINKING?
UH, GUYS...?
THAT THE RULES DIDN'T APPLY TO HIM.
IT HAS TO BE MORE THAN THAT.
THERE'S A LOT OF GUYS OUT THERE THAT THINK THIS WAY.
LOOK!

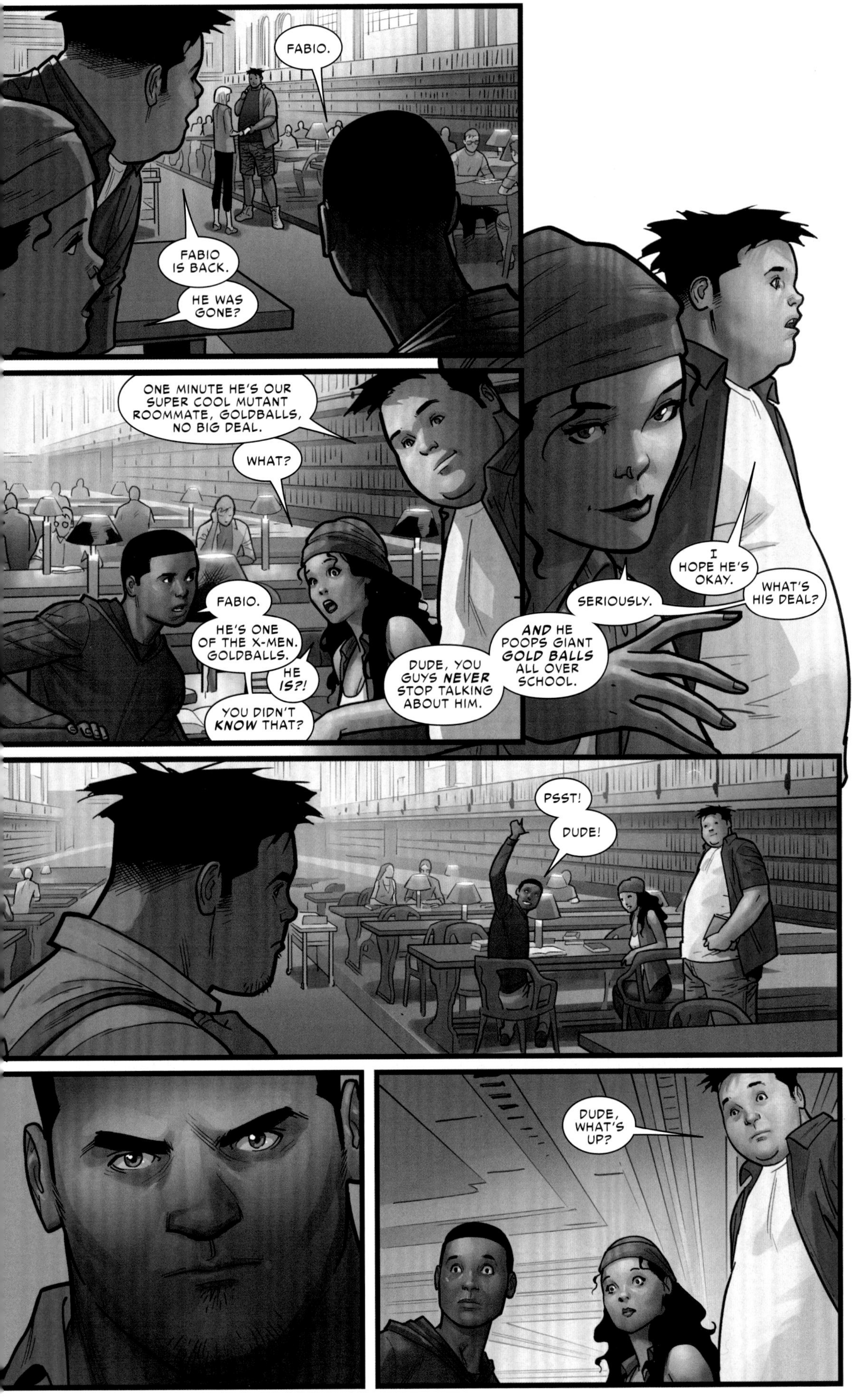
FABIO.
FABIO IS BACK.
HE WAS GONE?
ONE MINUTE HE'S OUR SUPER COOL MUTANT ROOMMATE, GOLDBALLS, NO BIG DEAL.
WHAT?
FABIO.
HE'S ONE OF THE X-MEN. GOLDBALLS.
HE IS?!
YOU DIDN'T KNOW THAT?
DUDE, YOU GUYS NEVER STOP TALKING ABOUT HIM.
AND HE POOPS GIANT GOLD BALLS ALL OVER SCHOOL.
SERIOUSLY.
I HOPE HE'S OKAY.
WHAT'S HIS DEAL?
PSST!
DUDE!
DUDE, WHAT'S UP?

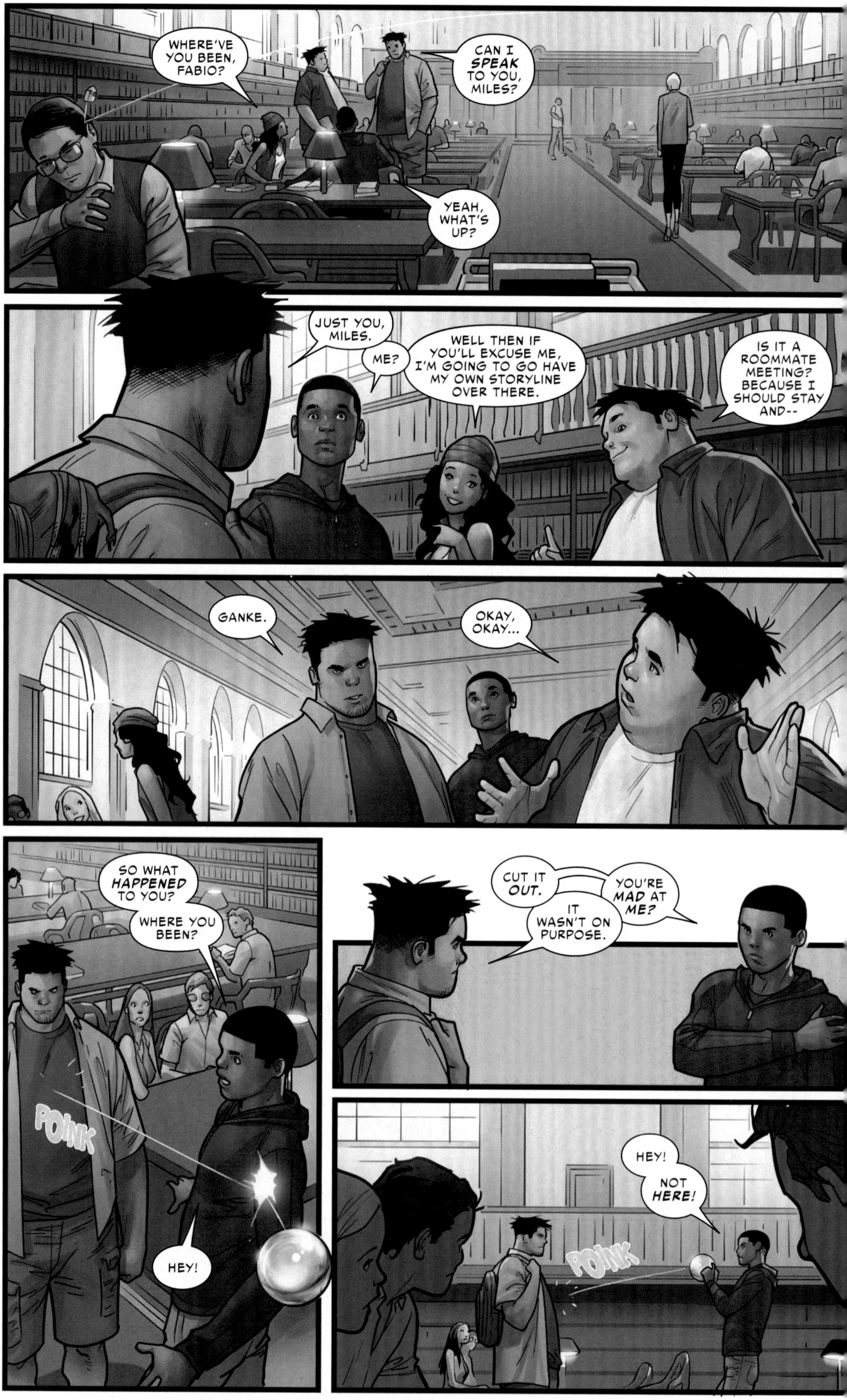
WHERE'VE YOU BEEN, FABIO?
CAN I SPEAK TO YOU, MILES?
YEAH, WHAT'S UP?
JUST YOU, MILES.
ME?
WELL THEN IF YOU'LL EXCUSE ME, I'M GOING TO GO HAVE MY OWN STORYLINE OVER THERE.
IS IT A ROOMMATE MEETING? BECAUSE I SHOULD STAY AND--
GANKE.
OKAY, OKAY...
SO WHAT HAPPENED TO YOU?
WHERE YOU BEEN?
POINK
HEY!
CUT IT OUT.
IT WASN'T ON PURPOSE.
YOU'RE MAD AT ME?
HEY!
NOT HERE!
POINK

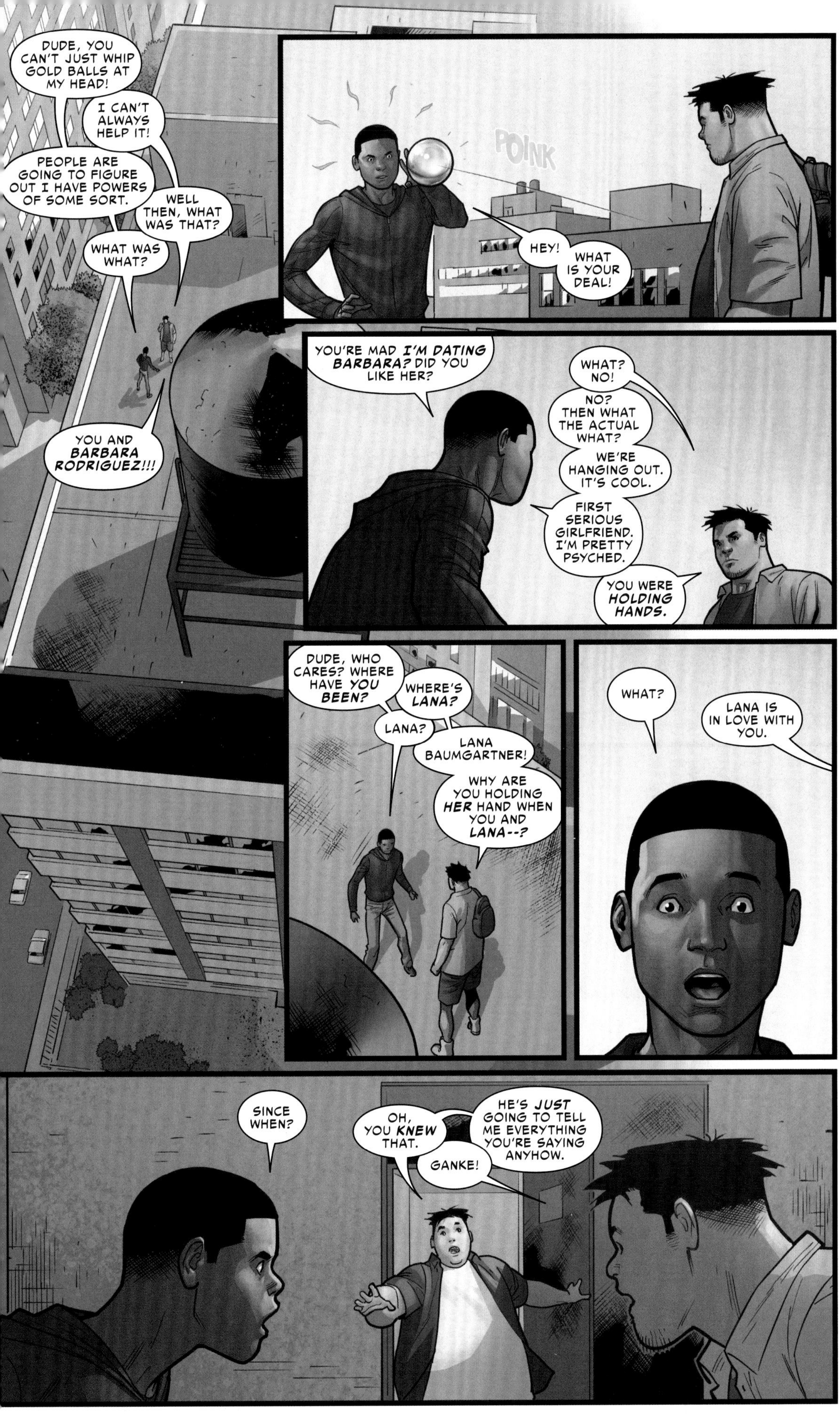

DUDE, YOU CAN'T JUST WHIP GOLD BALLS AT MY HEAD!
I CAN'T ALWAYS HELP IT!
PEOPLE ARE GOING TO FIGURE OUT I HAVE POWERS OF SOME SORT.
WELL THEN, WHAT WAS THAT?
WHAT WAS WHAT?
YOU AND BARBARA RODRIGUEZ!!!
POINK
HEY!
WHAT IS YOUR DEAL!
YOU'RE MAD I'M DATING BARBARA? DID YOU LIKE HER?
WHAT? NO!
NO? THEN WHAT THE ACTUAL WHAT?
WE'RE HANGING OUT. IT'S COOL.
FIRST SERIOUS GIRLFRIEND. I'M PRETTY PSYCHED.
YOU WERE HOLDING HANDS.
DUDE, WHO CARES? WHERE HAVE YOU BEEN?
WHERE'S LANA?
LANA?
LANA BAUMGARTNER!
WHY ARE YOU HOLDING HER HAND WHEN YOU AND LANA--?
WHAT?
LANA IS IN LOVE WITH YOU.
SINCE WHEN?
OH, YOU KNEW THAT.
HE'S JUST GOING TO TELL ME EVERYTHING YOU'RE SAYING ANYHOW.
GANKE!

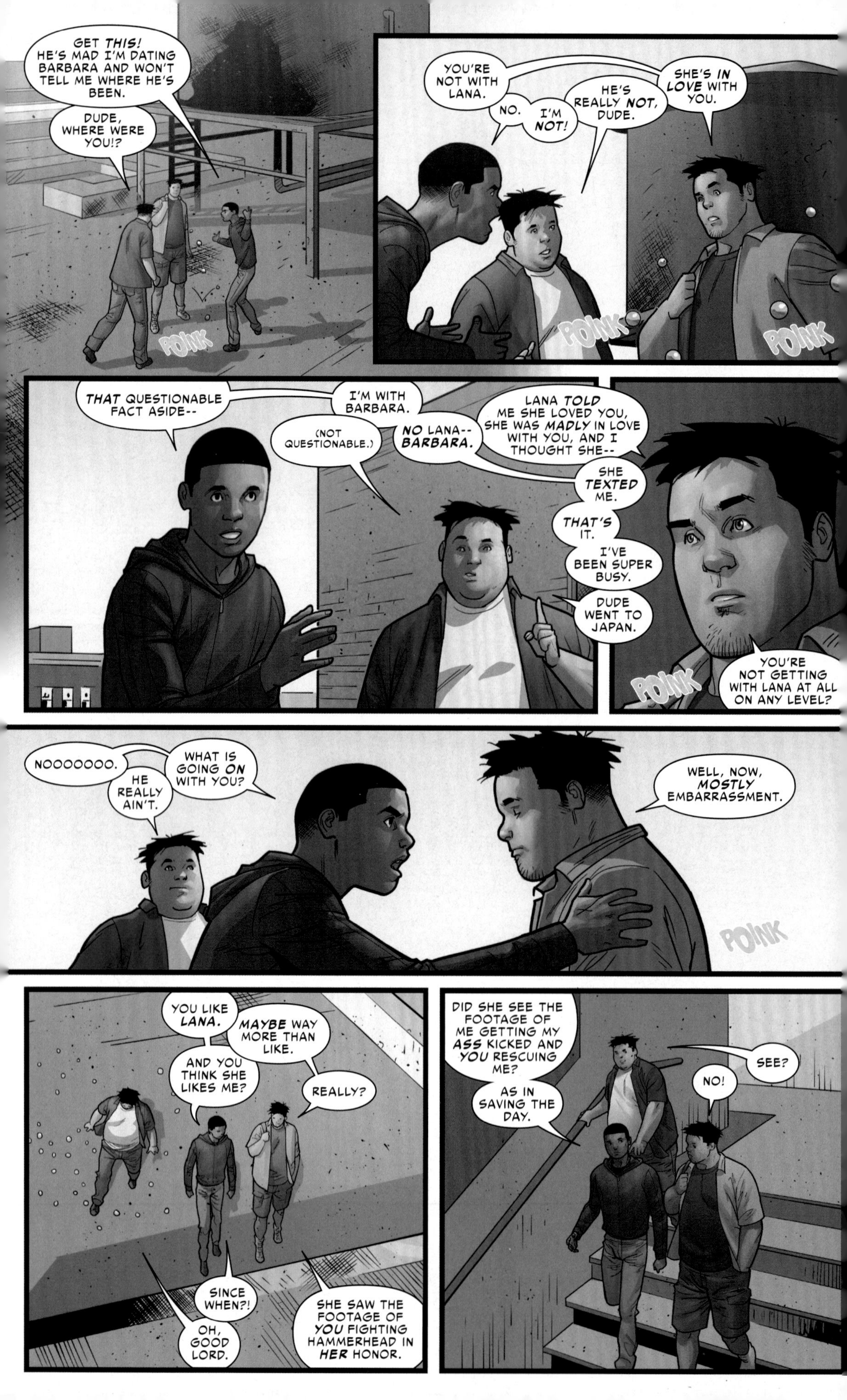
GET THIS! HE'S MAD I'M DATING BARBARA AND WON'T TELL ME WHERE HE'S BEEN.
DUDE, WHERE WERE YOU!?
POINK
YOU'RE NOT WITH LANA.
SHE'S IN LOVE WITH YOU.
NO.
I'M NOT!
HE'S REALLY NOT, DUDE.
POINK
POINK
THAT QUESTIONABLE FACT ASIDE--
I'M WITH BARBARA.
(NOT QUESTIONABLE.)
NO LANA-- BARBARA.
LANA TOLD ME SHE LOVED YOU, SHE WAS MADLY IN LOVE WITH YOU, AND I THOUGHT SHE--
SHE TEXTED ME.
THAT'S IT.
I'VE BEEN SUPER BUSY.
DUDE WENT TO JAPAN.
POINK
YOU'RE NOT GETTING WITH LANA AT ALL ON ANY LEVEL?
NOOOOOOO.
WHAT IS GOING ON WITH YOU?
HE REALLY AIN'T.
WELL, NOW, MOSTLY EMBARRASSMENT.
POINK
YOU LIKE LANA.
MAYBE WAY MORE THAN LIKE.
AND YOU THINK SHE LIKES ME?
REALLY?
SINCE WHEN?!
OH, GOOD LORD.
SHE SAW THE FOOTAGE OF YOU FIGHTING HAMMERHEAD IN HER HONOR.
DID SHE SEE THE FOOTAGE OF ME GETTING MY ASS KICKED AND YOU RESCUING ME?
AS IN SAVING THE DAY.
SEE?
NO!

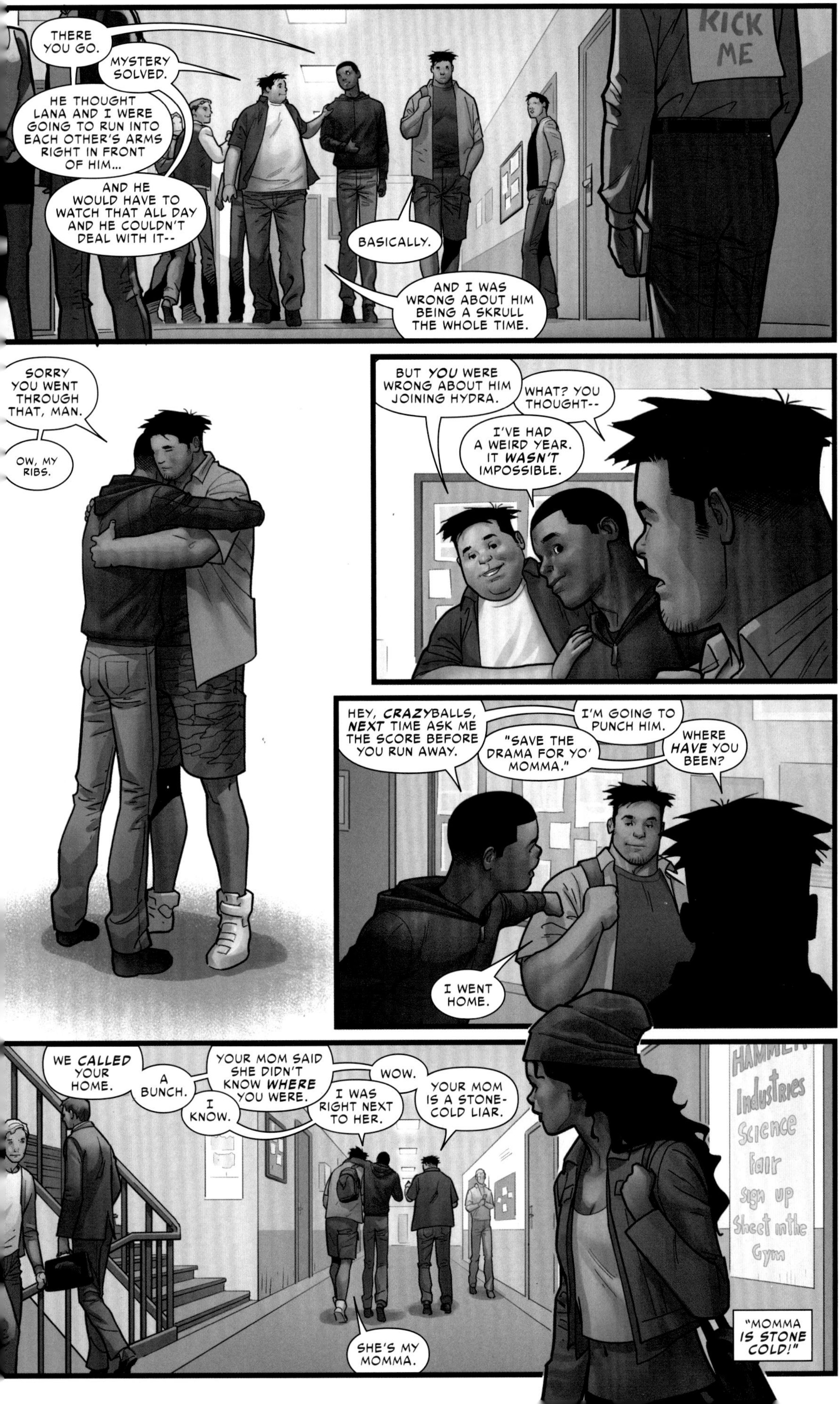
KICK ME
THERE YOU GO.
MYSTERY SOLVED.
HE THOUGHT LANA AND I WERE GOING TO RUN INTO EACH OTHER'S ARMS RIGHT IN FRONT OF HIM...
AND HE WOULD HAVE TO WATCH THAT ALL DAY AND HE COULDN'T DEAL WITH IT--
BASICALLY.
AND I WAS WRONG ABOUT HIM BEING A SKRULL THE WHOLE TIME.
SORRY YOU WENT THROUGH THAT, MAN.
OW, MY RIBS.
BUT *YOU* WERE WRONG ABOUT HIM JOINING HYDRA.
WHAT? YOU THOUGHT--
I'VE HAD A WEIRD YEAR. IT *WASN'T* IMPOSSIBLE.
HEY, *CRAZY*BALLS, *NEXT* TIME ASK ME THE SCORE BEFORE YOU RUN AWAY.
I'M GOING TO PUNCH HIM.
"SAVE THE DRAMA FOR YO' MOMMA."
WHERE *HAVE* YOU BEEN?
I WENT HOME.
WE *CALLED* YOUR HOME.
A BUNCH.
YOUR MOM SAID SHE DIDN'T KNOW *WHERE* YOU WERE.
I KNOW.
WOW.
I WAS RIGHT NEXT TO HER.
YOUR MOM IS A STONE-COLD LIAR.
HAMMER Industries Science Fair Sign up Sheet in the Gym
SHE'S MY MOMMA.
"MOMMA *IS STONE COLD!*"

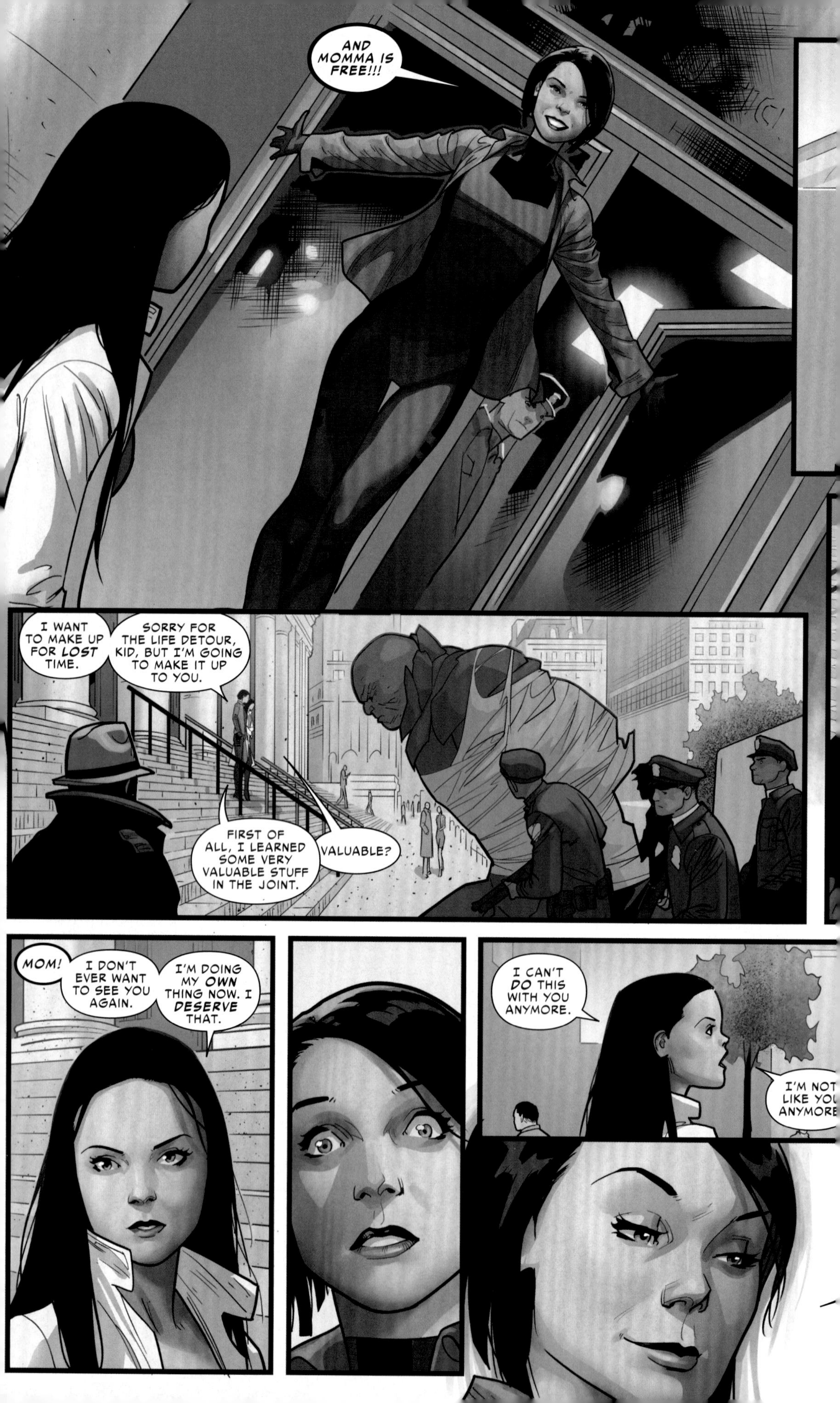
AND MOMMA IS FREE!!!
I WANT TO MAKE UP FOR LOST TIME.
SORRY FOR THE LIFE DETOUR, KID, BUT I'M GOING TO MAKE IT UP TO YOU.
FIRST OF ALL, I LEARNED SOME VERY VALUABLE STUFF IN THE JOINT.
VALUABLE?
MOM!
I DON'T EVER WANT TO SEE YOU AGAIN.
I'M DOING MY OWN THING NOW. I DESERVE THAT.
I CAN'T DO THIS WITH YOU ANYMORE.
I'M NOT LIKE YOU ANYMORE

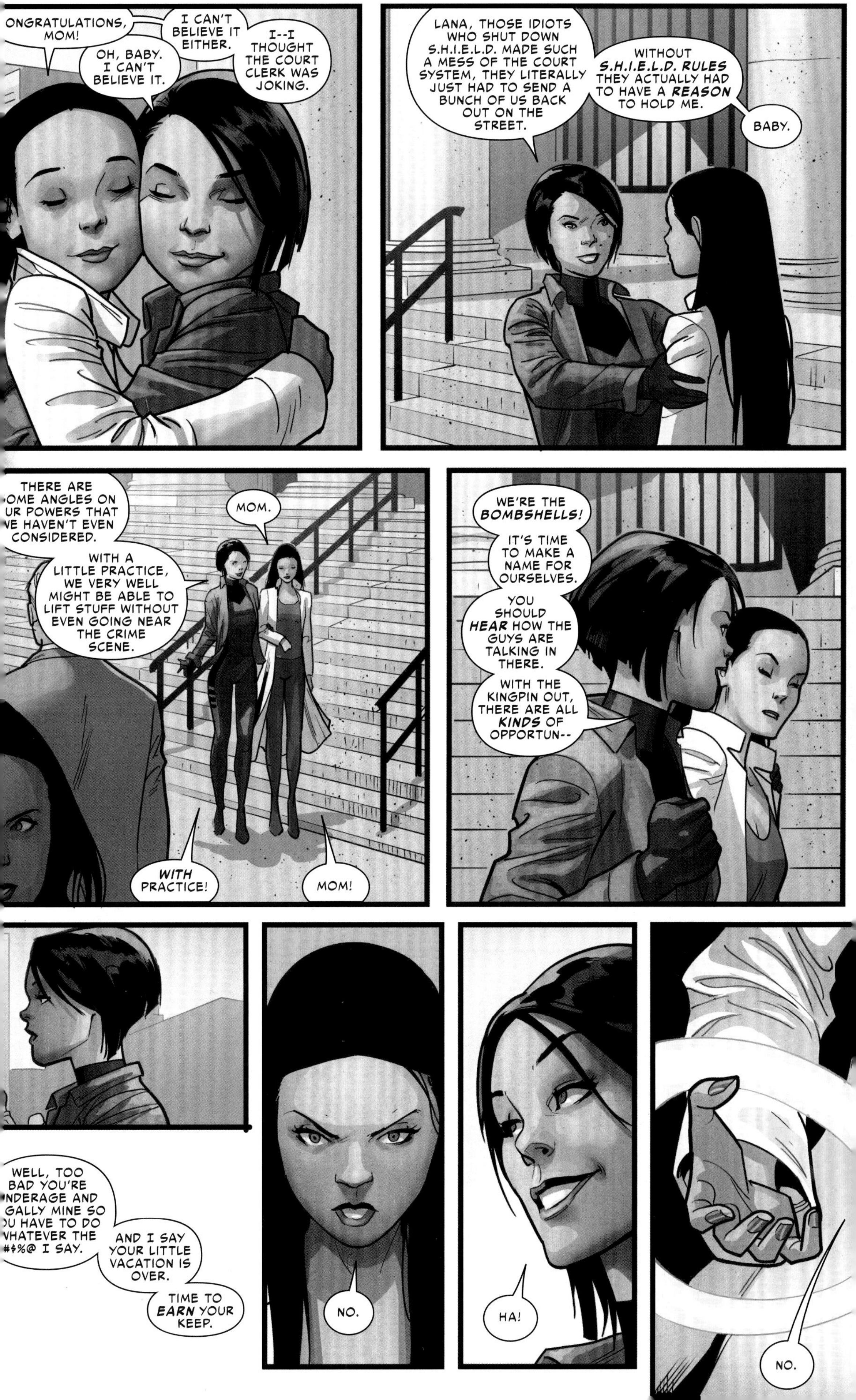

ONGRATULATIONS, MOM!
OH, BABY. I CAN'T BELIEVE IT.
I CAN'T BELIEVE IT EITHER.
I--I THOUGHT THE COURT CLERK WAS JOKING.
LANA, THOSE IDIOTS WHO SHUT DOWN S.H.I.E.L.D. MADE SUCH A MESS OF THE COURT SYSTEM, THEY LITERALLY JUST HAD TO SEND A BUNCH OF US BACK OUT ON THE STREET.
WITHOUT S.H.I.E.L.D. RULES THEY ACTUALLY HAD TO HAVE A REASON TO HOLD ME.
BABY.
THERE ARE OME ANGLES ON UR POWERS THAT E HAVEN'T EVEN CONSIDERED.
MOM.
WITH A LITTLE PRACTICE, WE VERY WELL MIGHT BE ABLE TO LIFT STUFF WITHOUT EVEN GOING NEAR THE CRIME SCENE.
WITH PRACTICE!
MOM!
WE'RE THE BOMBSHELLS!
IT'S TIME TO MAKE A NAME FOR OURSELVES.
YOU SHOULD HEAR HOW THE GUYS ARE TALKING IN THERE.
WITH THE KINGPIN OUT, THERE ARE ALL KINDS OF OPPORTUN--
WELL, TOO BAD YOU'RE NDERAGE AND GALLY MINE SO U HAVE TO DO HATEVER THE #$%@ I SAY.
AND I SAY YOUR LITTLE VACATION IS OVER.
TIME TO EARN YOUR KEEP.
NO.
HA!
NO.

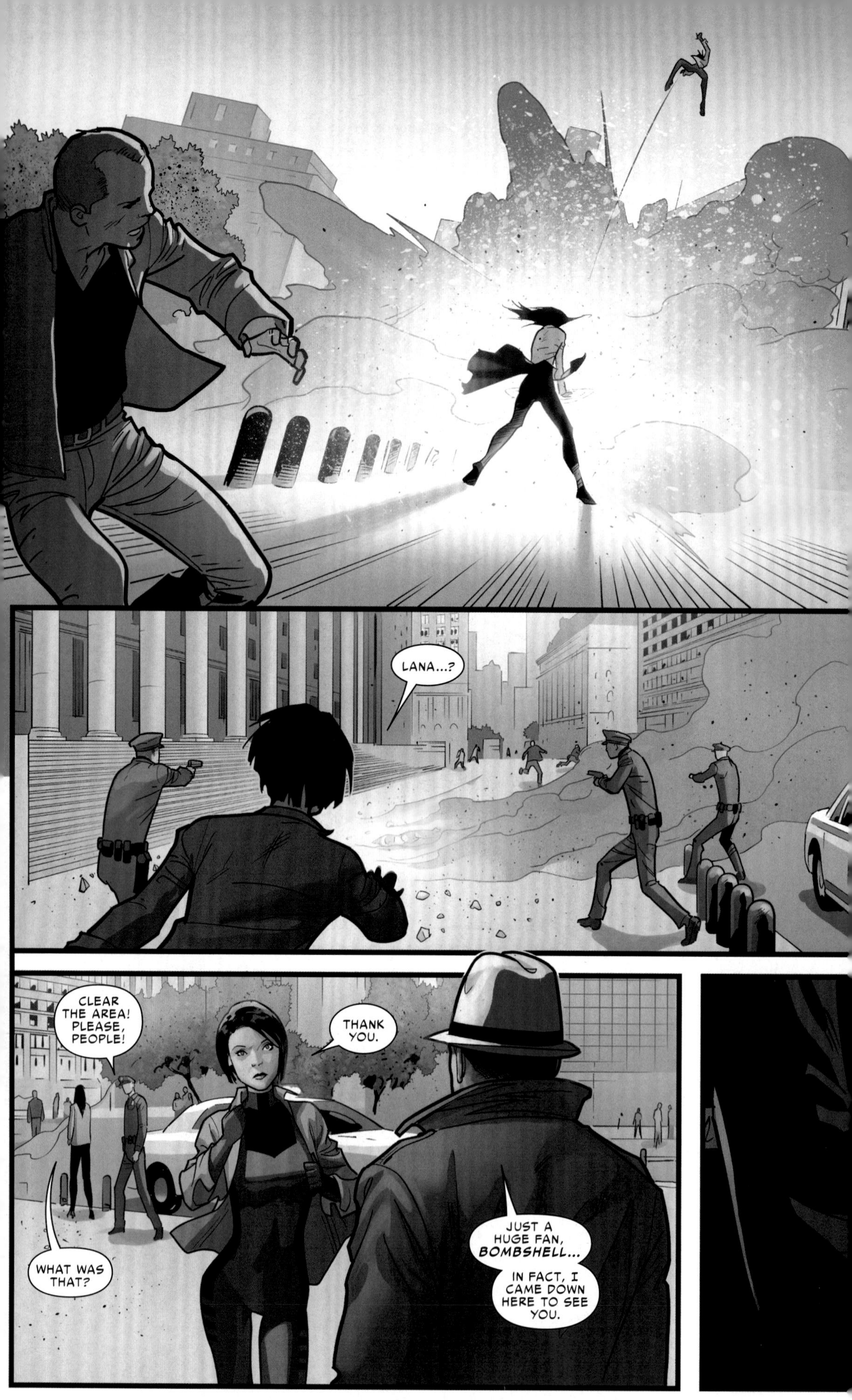
LANA...?
CLEAR THE AREA! PLEASE, PEOPLE!
THANK YOU.
WHAT WAS THAT?
JUST A HUGE FAN, BOMBSHELL...
IN FACT, I CAME DOWN HERE TO SEE YOU.

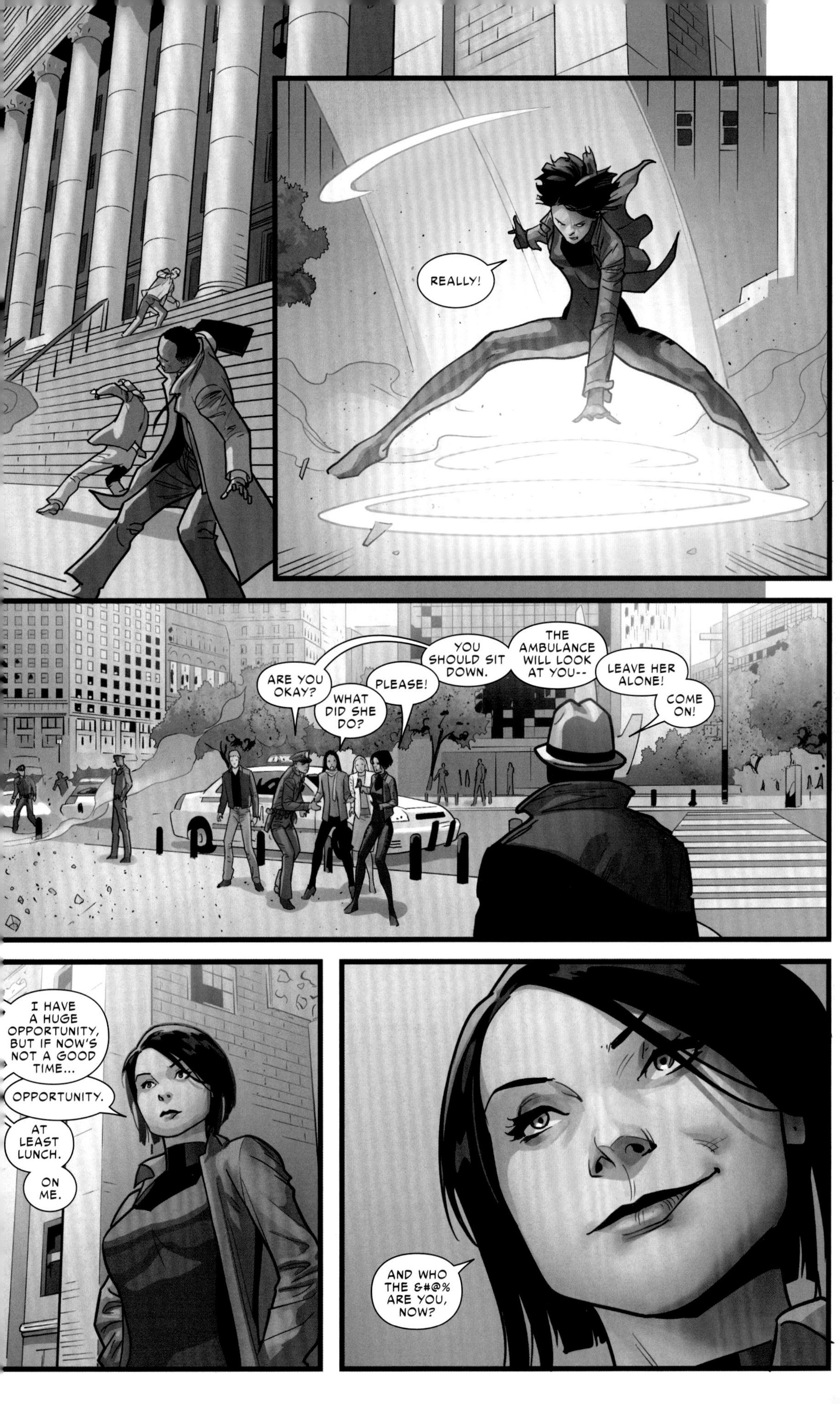
REALLY!
ARE YOU OKAY?
WHAT DID SHE DO?
PLEASE!
YOU SHOULD SIT DOWN.
THE AMBULANCE WILL LOOK AT YOU--
LEAVE HER ALONE!
COME ON!
I HAVE A HUGE OPPORTUNITY, BUT IF NOW'S NOT A GOOD TIME...
OPPORTUNITY.
AT LEAST LUNCH.
ON ME.
AND WHO THE &#@% ARE YOU, NOW?

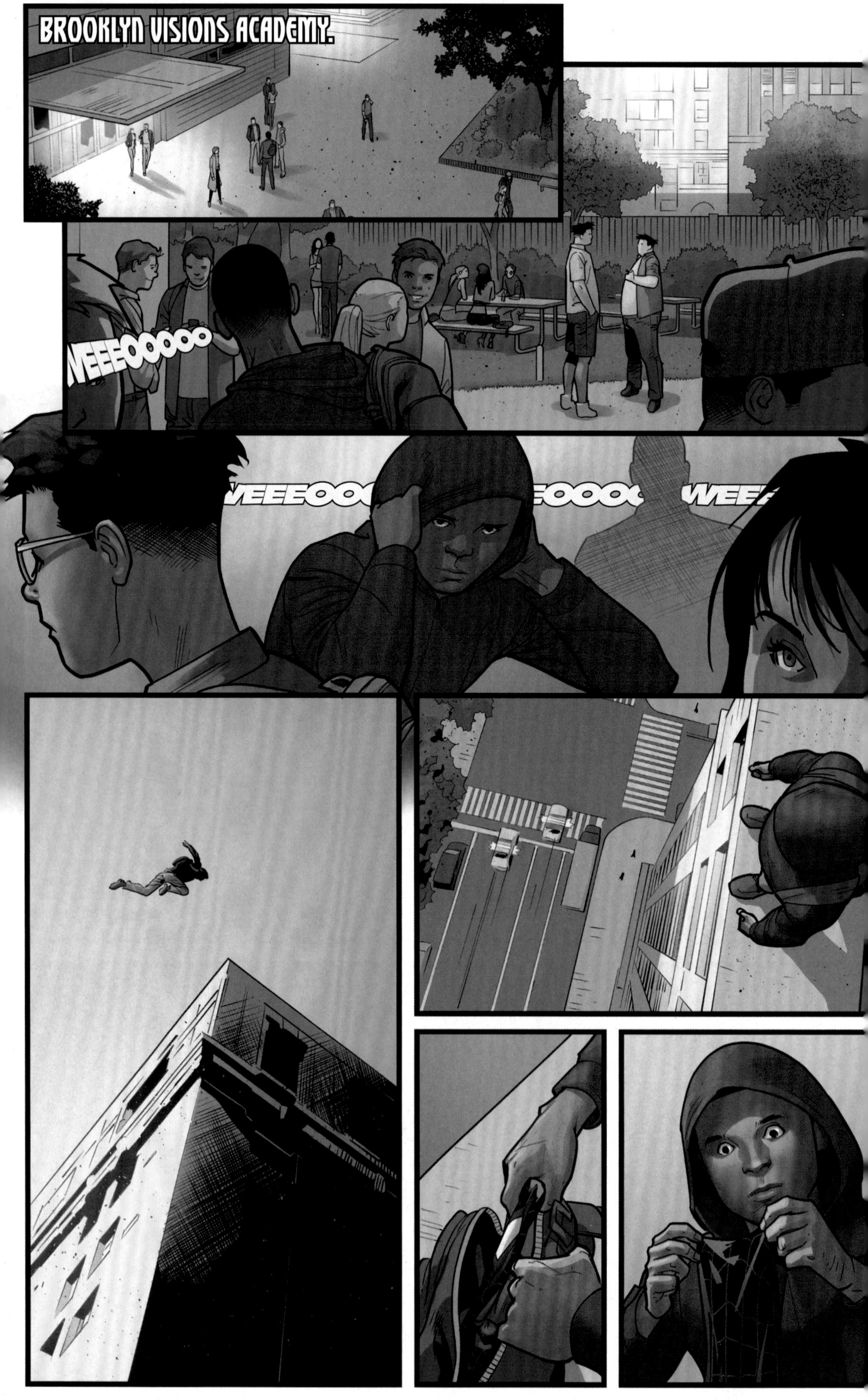
BROOKLYN VISIONS ACADEMY.
WEEEOOOOO
WEEEOOO
EOOOO
WEE

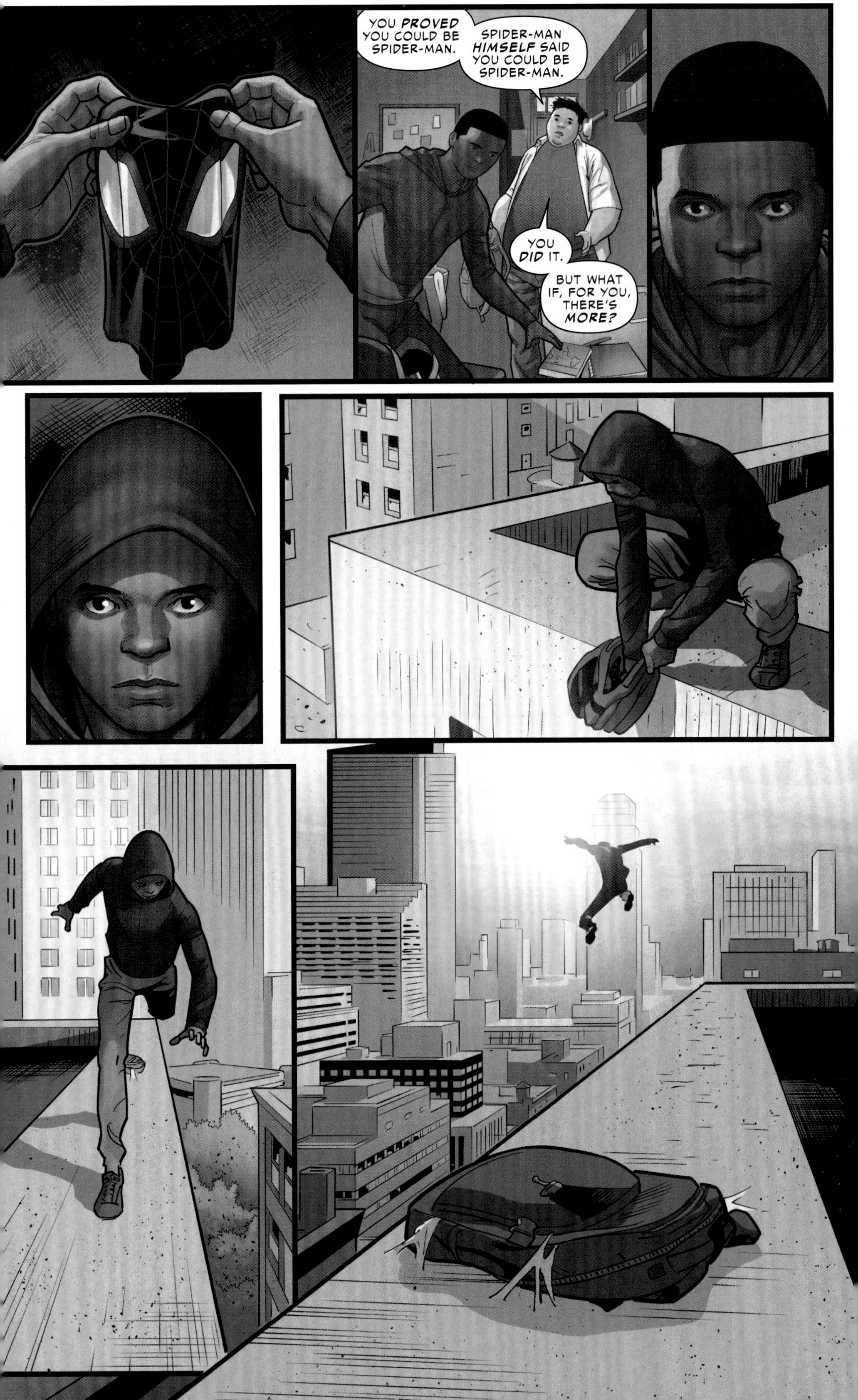
YOU PROVED YOU COULD BE SPIDER-MAN.
SPIDER-MAN HIMSELF SAID YOU COULD BE SPIDER-MAN.
YOU DID IT.
BUT WHAT IF, FOR YOU, THERE'S MORE?

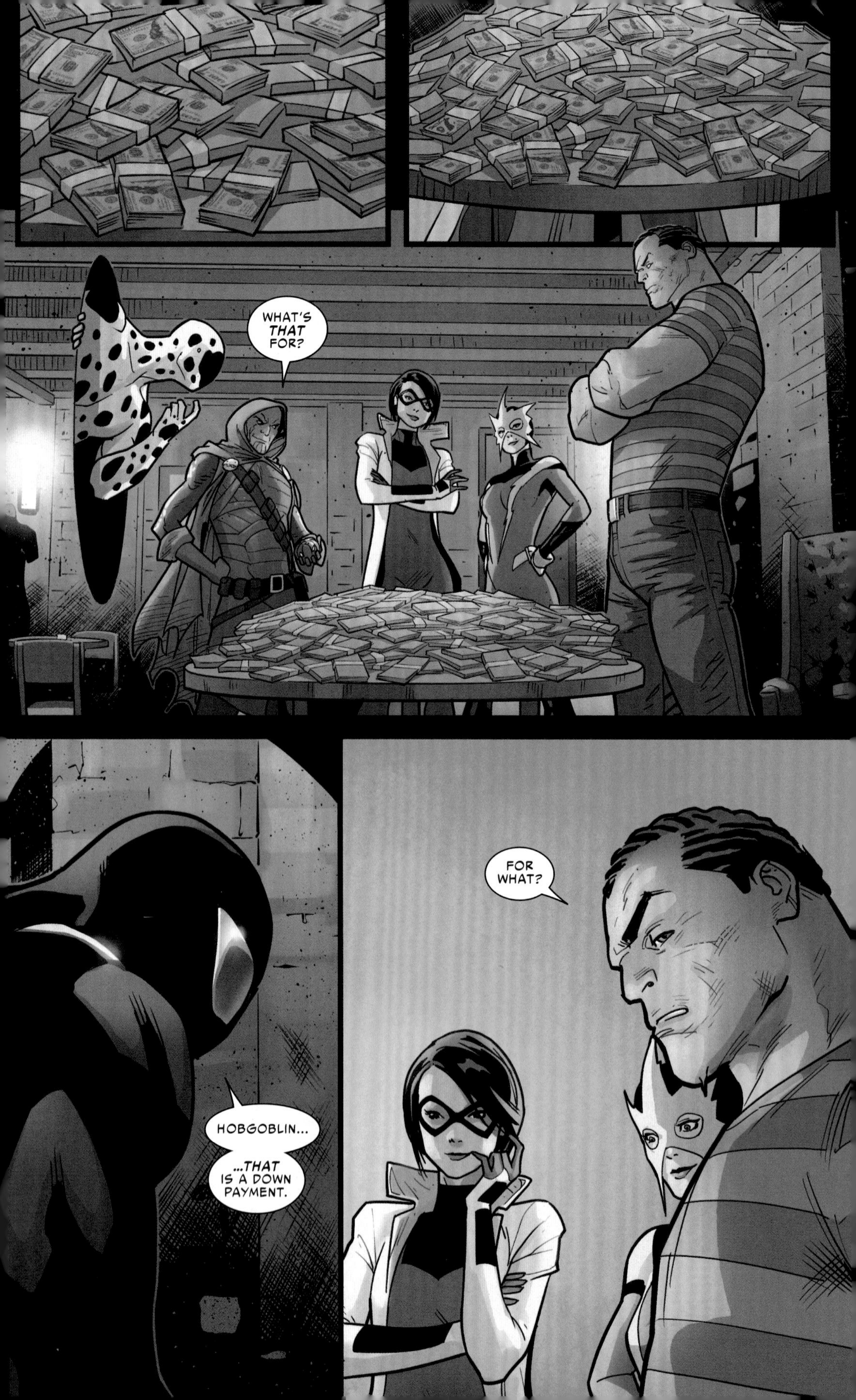
WHAT'S *THAT* FOR?
HOBGOBLIN...
...*THAT* IS A DOWN PAYMENT.
FOR WHAT?

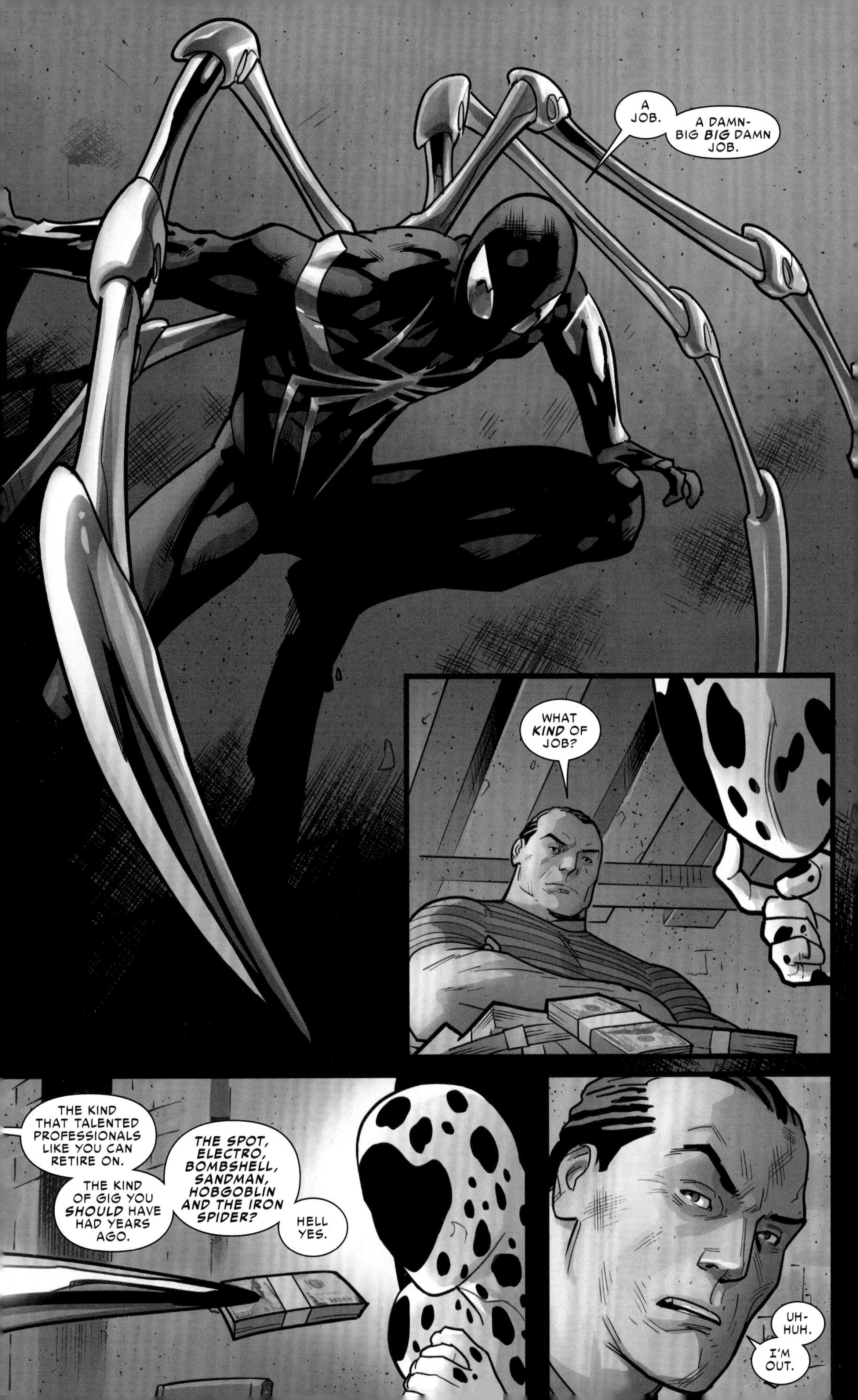

A JOB.
A DAMN-BIG BIG DAMN JOB.
WHAT KIND OF JOB?
THE KIND THAT TALENTED PROFESSIONALS LIKE YOU CAN RETIRE ON.
THE KIND OF GIG YOU SHOULD HAVE HAD YEARS AGO.
THE SPOT, ELECTRO, BOMBSHELL, SANDMAN, HOBGOBLIN AND THE IRON SPIDER?
HELL YES.
UH-HUH.
I'M OUT.

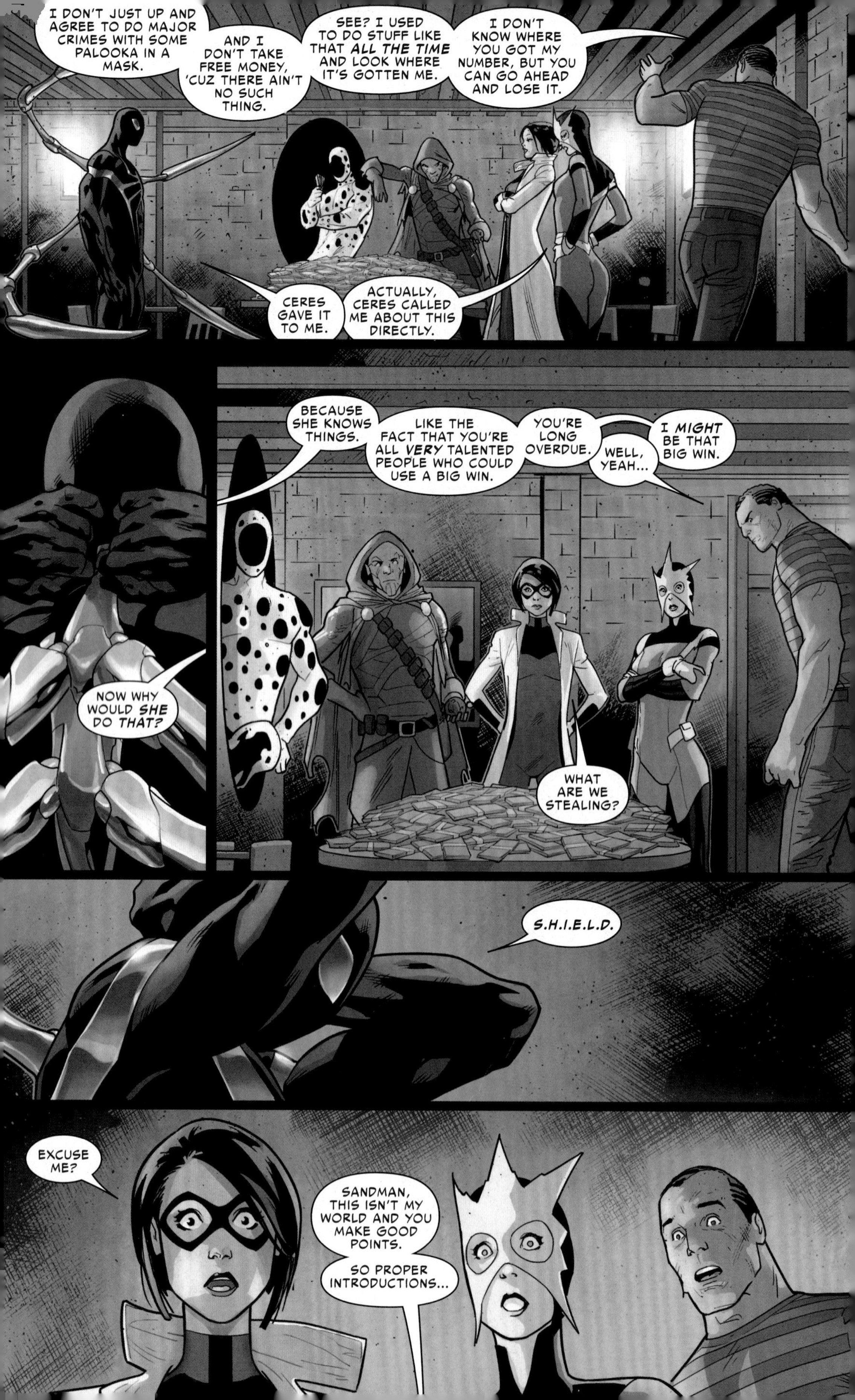

I DON'T JUST UP AND AGREE TO DO MAJOR CRIMES WITH SOME PALOOKA IN A MASK.
AND I DON'T TAKE FREE MONEY, 'CUZ THERE AIN'T NO SUCH THING.
SEE? I USED TO DO STUFF LIKE THAT ALL THE TIME AND LOOK WHERE IT'S GOTTEN ME.
I DON'T KNOW WHERE YOU GOT MY NUMBER, BUT YOU CAN GO AHEAD AND LOSE IT.
CERES GAVE IT TO ME.
ACTUALLY, CERES CALLED ME ABOUT THIS DIRECTLY.
BECAUSE SHE KNOWS THINGS.
LIKE THE FACT THAT YOU'RE ALL VERY TALENTED PEOPLE WHO COULD USE A BIG WIN.
YOU'RE LONG OVERDUE.
WELL, YEAH...
I MIGHT BE THAT BIG WIN.
NOW WHY WOULD SHE DO THAT?
WHAT ARE WE STEALING?
S.H.I.E.L.D.
EXCUSE ME?
SANDMAN, THIS ISN'T MY WORLD AND YOU MAKE GOOD POINTS.
SO PROPER INTRODUCTIONS...

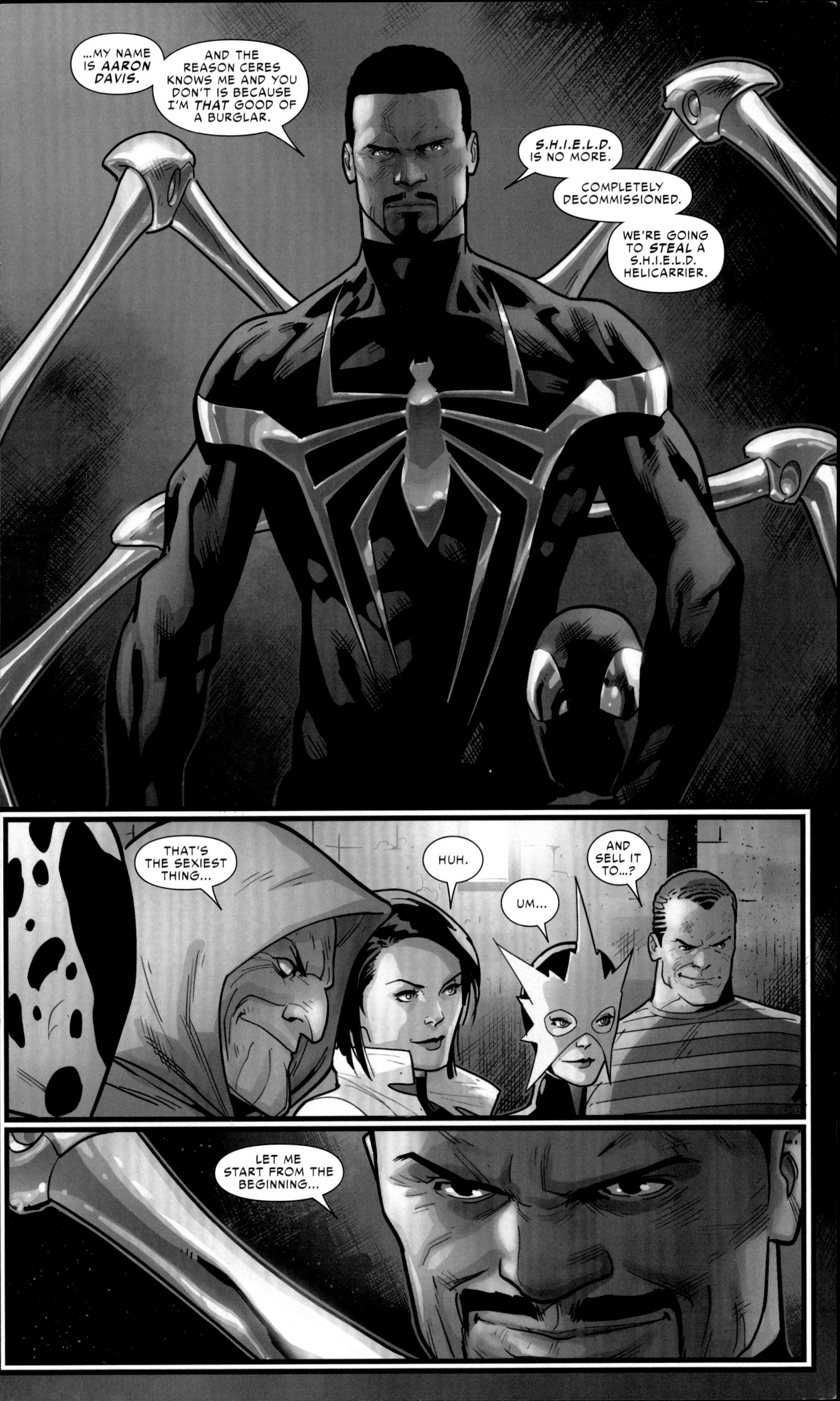
...MY NAME IS AARON DAVIS.
AND THE REASON CERES KNOWS ME AND YOU DON'T IS BECAUSE I'M THAT GOOD OF A BURGLAR.
S.H.I.E.L.D. IS NO MORE.
COMPLETELY DECOMMISSIONED.
WE'RE GOING TO STEAL A S.H.I.E.L.D. HELICARRIER.
THAT'S THE SEXIEST THING...
HUH.
UM...
AND SELL IT TO...?
LET ME START FROM THE BEGINNING...

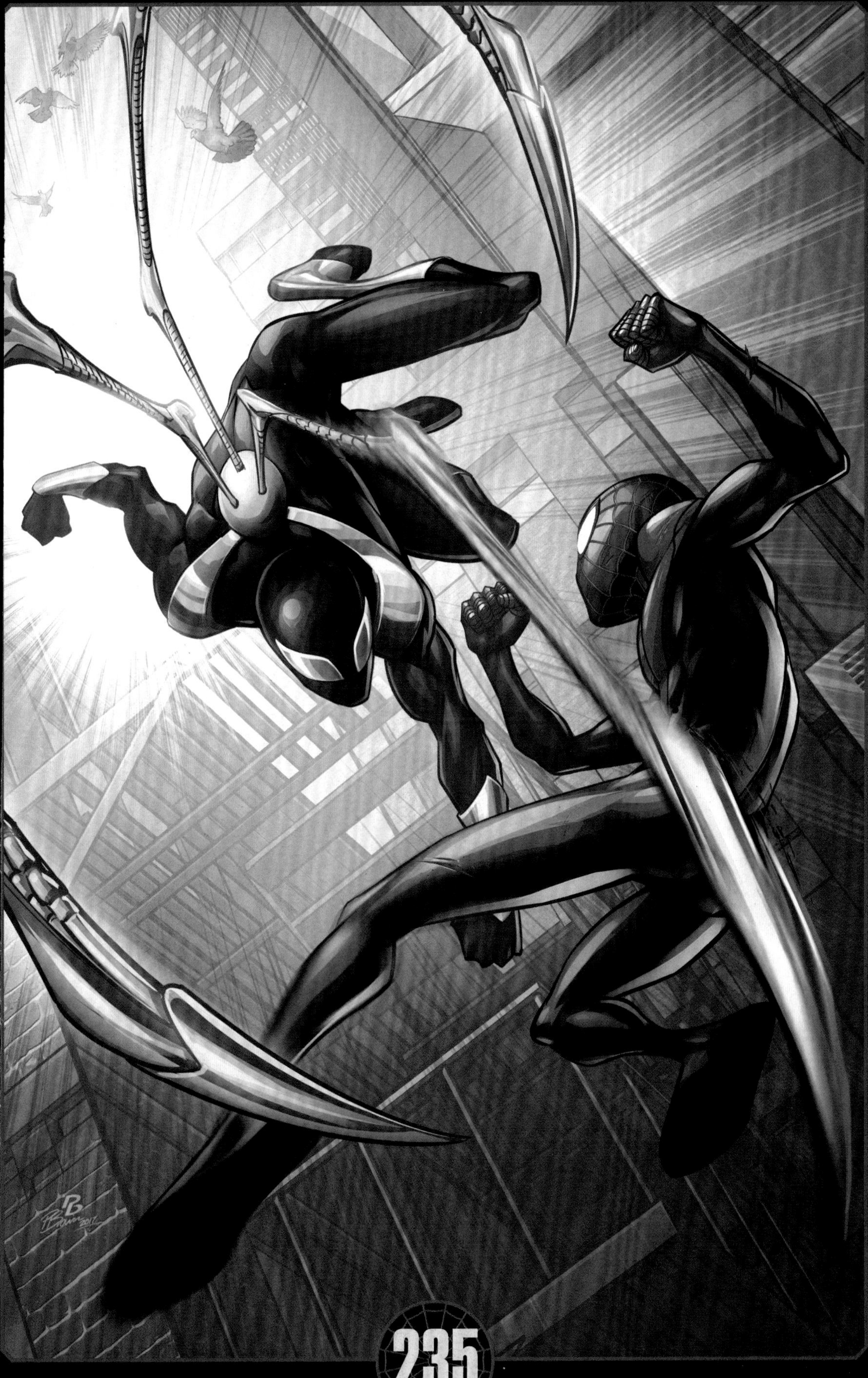

235

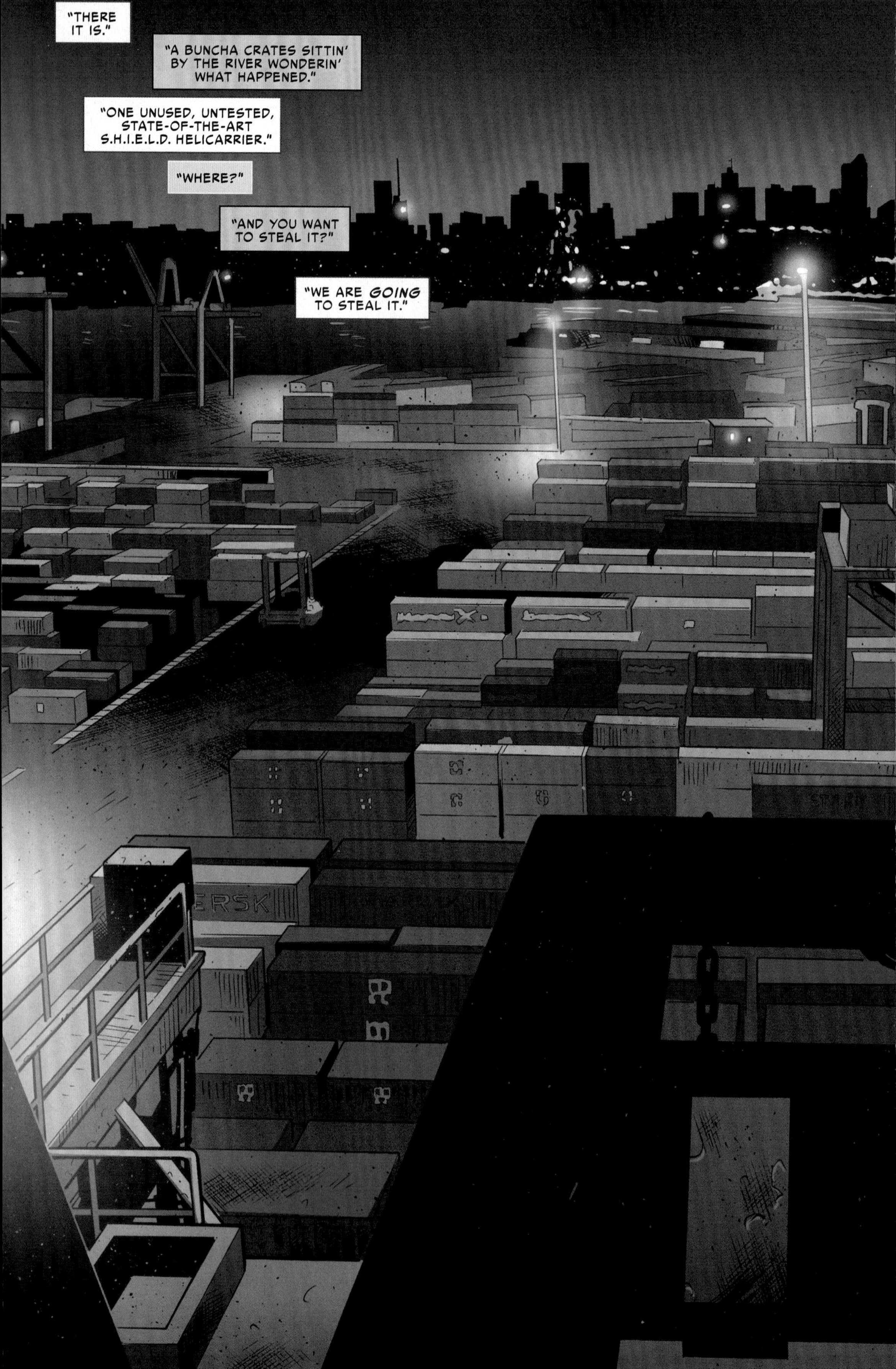
"THERE IT IS."
"A BUNCHA CRATES SITTIN' BY THE RIVER WONDERIN' WHAT HAPPENED."
"ONE UNUSED, UNTESTED, STATE-OF-THE-ART S.H.I.E.L.D. HELICARRIER."
"WHERE?"
"AND YOU WANT TO STEAL IT?"
"WE ARE *GOING* TO STEAL IT."
ERSK

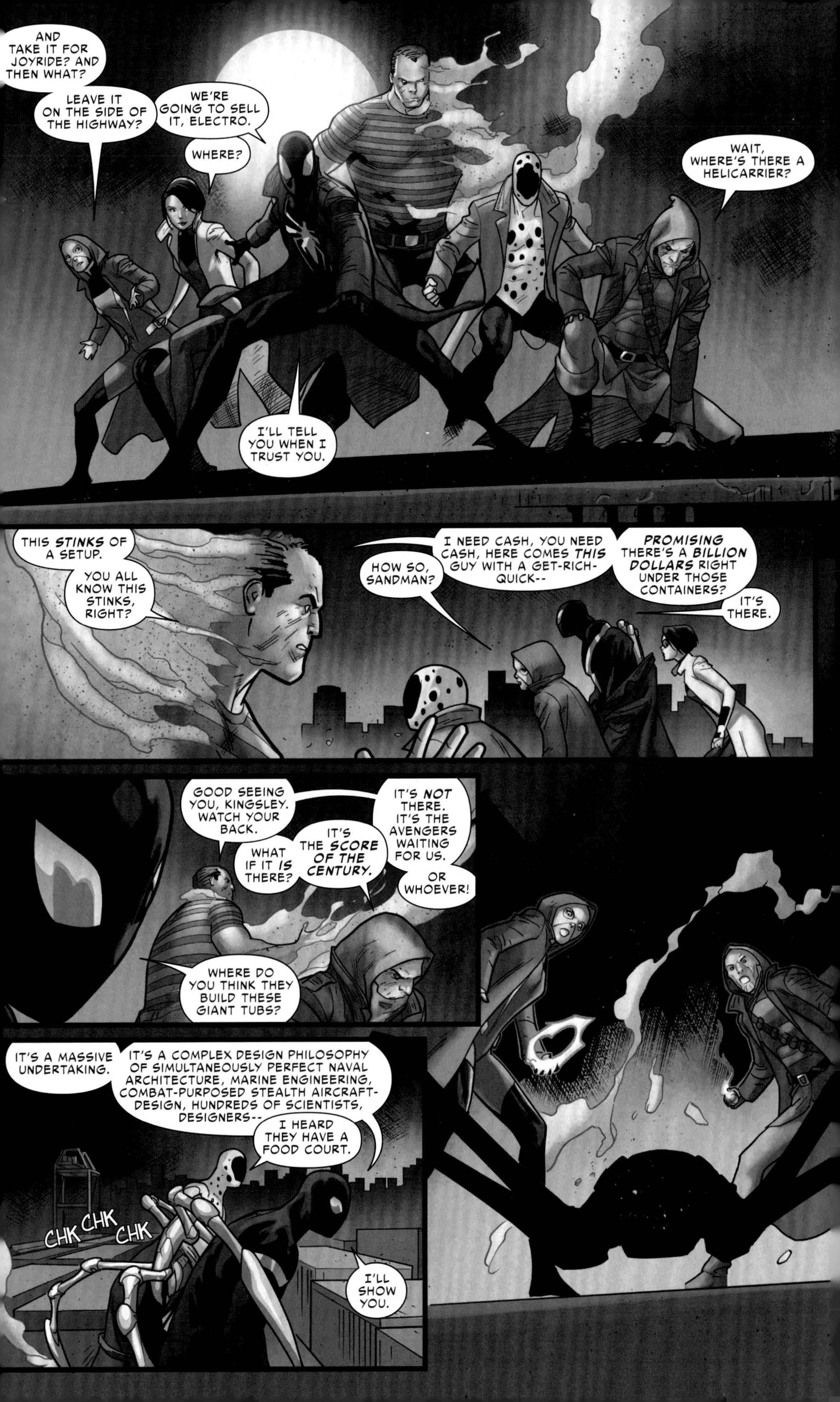
AND TAKE IT FOR JOYRIDE? AND THEN WHAT?
LEAVE IT ON THE SIDE OF THE HIGHWAY?
WE'RE GOING TO SELL IT, ELECTRO.
WHERE?
WAIT, WHERE'S THERE A HELICARRIER?
I'LL TELL YOU WHEN I TRUST YOU.
THIS STINKS OF A SETUP.
YOU ALL KNOW THIS STINKS, RIGHT?
HOW SO, SANDMAN?
I NEED CASH, YOU NEED CASH, HERE COMES THIS GUY WITH A GET-RICH-QUICK--
PROMISING THERE'S A BILLION DOLLARS RIGHT UNDER THOSE CONTAINERS?
IT'S THERE.
GOOD SEEING YOU, KINGSLEY. WATCH YOUR BACK.
WHAT IF IT IS THERE?
IT'S THE SCORE OF THE CENTURY.
IT'S NOT THERE. IT'S THE AVENGERS WAITING FOR US.
OR WHOEVER!
WHERE DO YOU THINK THEY BUILD THESE GIANT TUBS?
IT'S A MASSIVE UNDERTAKING.
IT'S A COMPLEX DESIGN PHILOSOPHY OF SIMULTANEOUSLY PERFECT NAVAL ARCHITECTURE, MARINE ENGINEERING, COMBAT-PURPOSED STEALTH AIRCRAFT-DESIGN, HUNDREDS OF SCIENTISTS, DESIGNERS--
I HEARD THEY HAVE A FOOD COURT.
CHK CHK CHK
I'LL SHOW YOU.

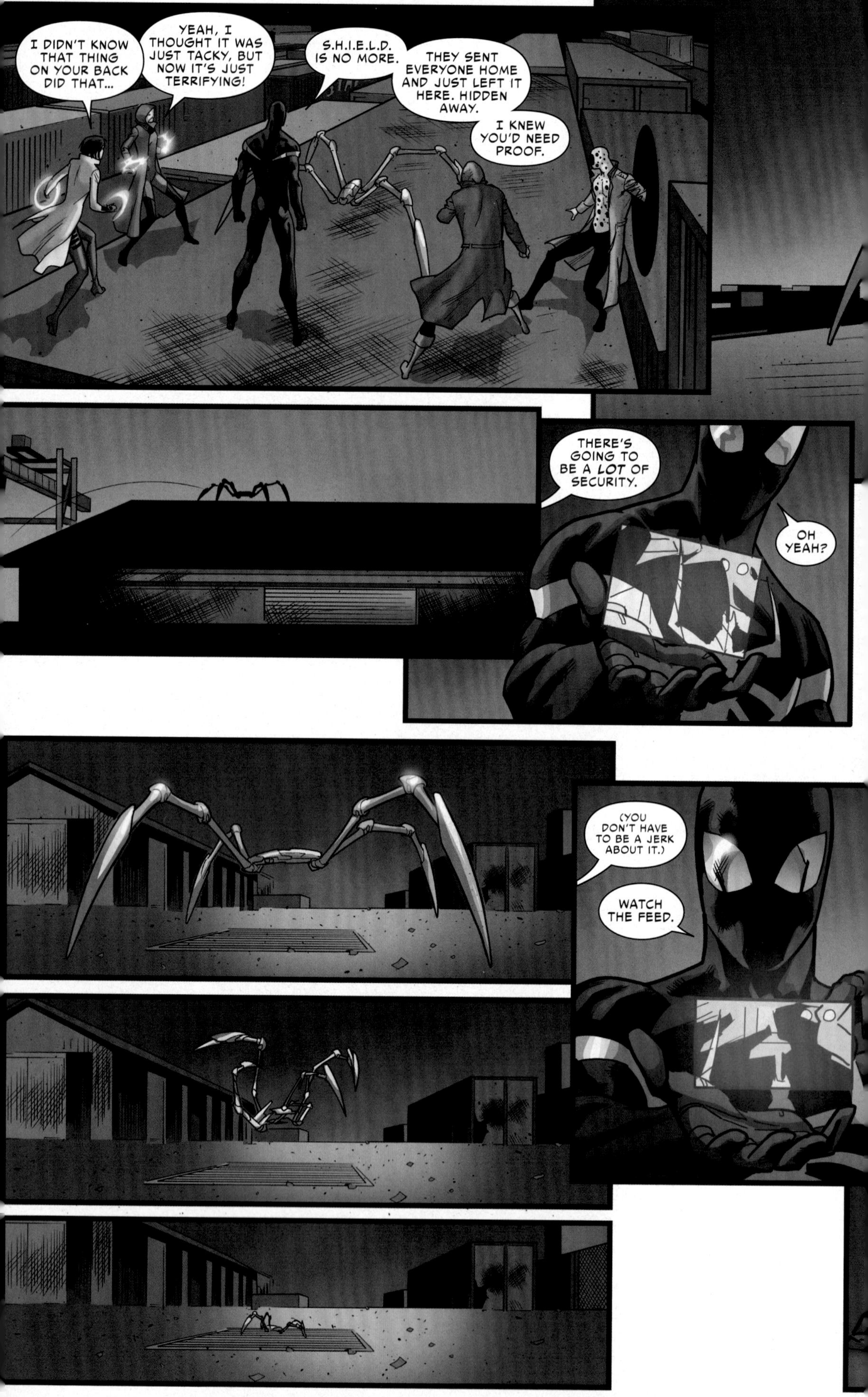

I DIDN'T KNOW THAT THING ON YOUR BACK DID THAT...
YEAH, I THOUGHT IT WAS JUST TACKY, BUT NOW IT'S JUST TERRIFYING!
S.H.I.E.L.D. IS NO MORE.
THEY SENT EVERYONE HOME AND JUST LEFT IT HERE. HIDDEN AWAY.
I KNEW YOU'D NEED PROOF.
THERE'S GOING TO BE A *LOT* OF SECURITY.
OH YEAH?
(YOU DON'T HAVE TO BE A JERK ABOUT IT.)
WATCH THE FEED.

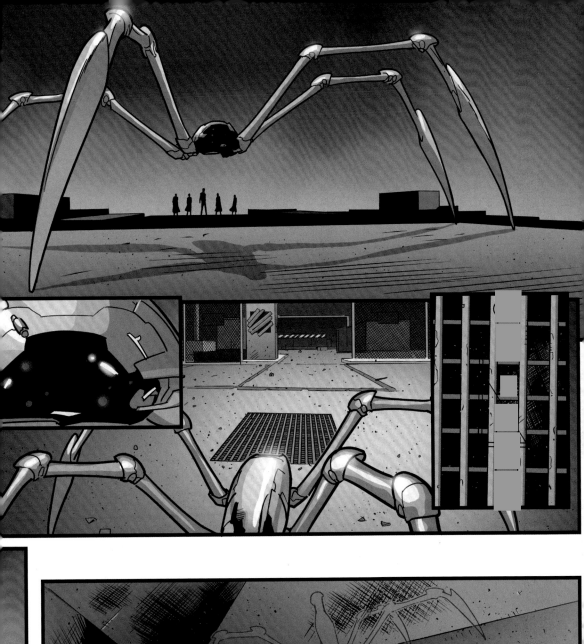

HUH.

GORGEOUS TECH.

CERES.

I LOVE HER.

GOOD, SHE'S GETTING A CUT.

IS SHE SEEING ANYONE?

TA-DAA.

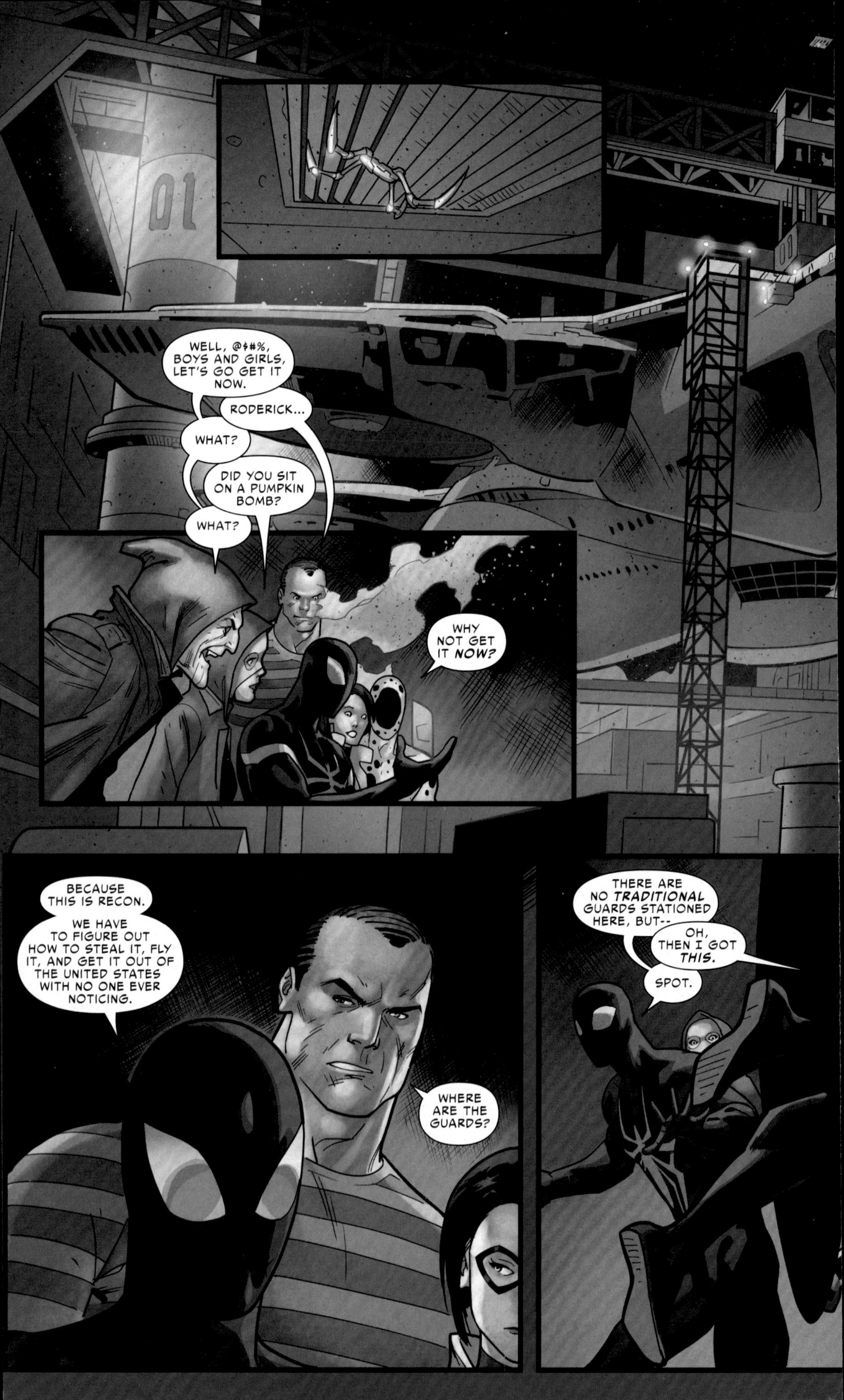
WELL, @$#%, BOYS AND GIRLS, LET'S GO GET IT NOW.
RODERICK...
WHAT?
DID YOU SIT ON A PUMPKIN BOMB?
WHAT?
WHY NOT GET IT *NOW?*
BECAUSE THIS IS RECON.
WE HAVE TO FIGURE OUT HOW TO STEAL IT, FLY IT, AND GET IT OUT OF THE UNITED STATES WITH NO ONE EVER NOTICING.
WHERE ARE THE GUARDS?
THERE ARE NO *TRADITIONAL* GUARDS STATIONED HERE, BUT--
OH, THEN I GOT *THIS.*
SPOT.

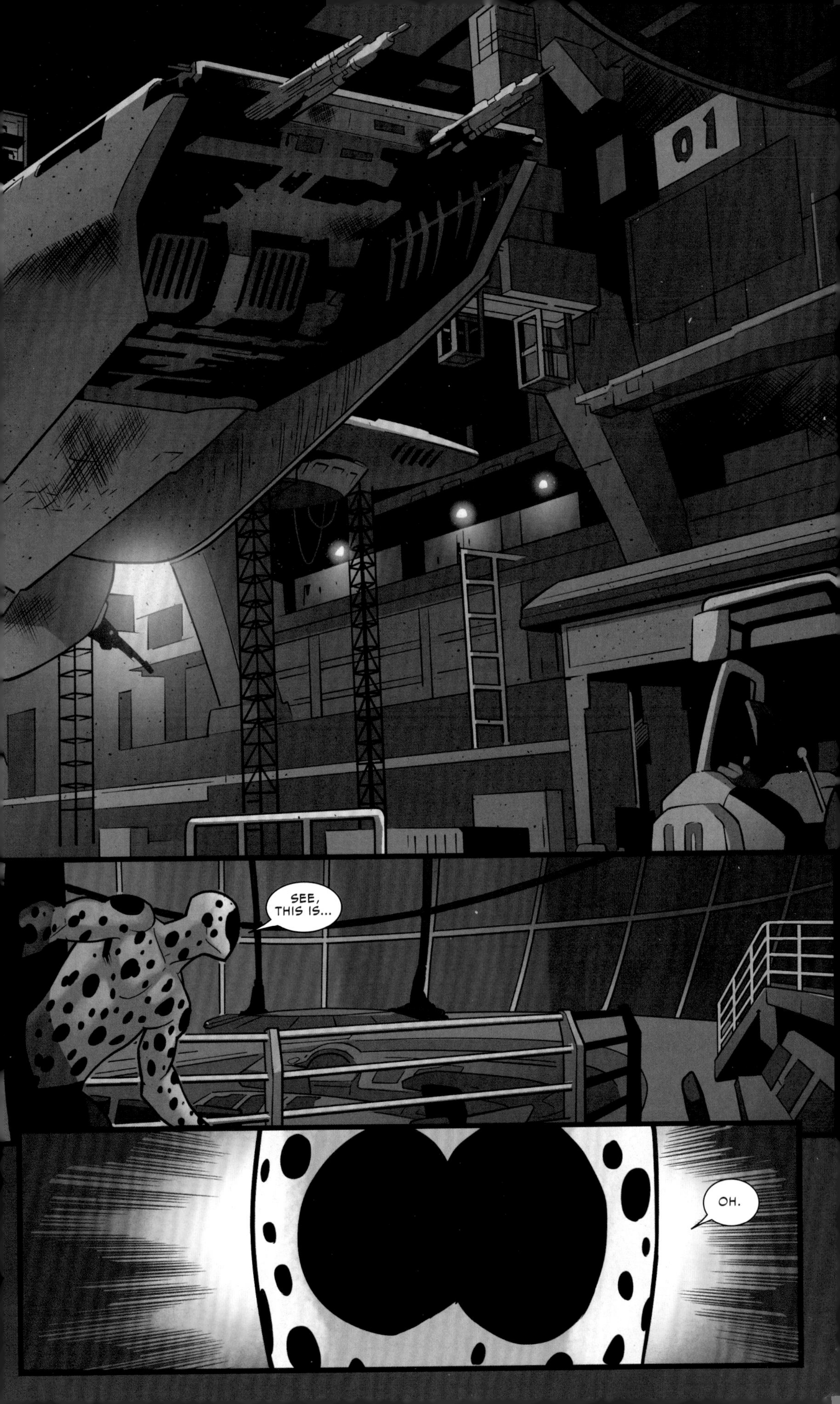
SEE, THIS IS...
OH.

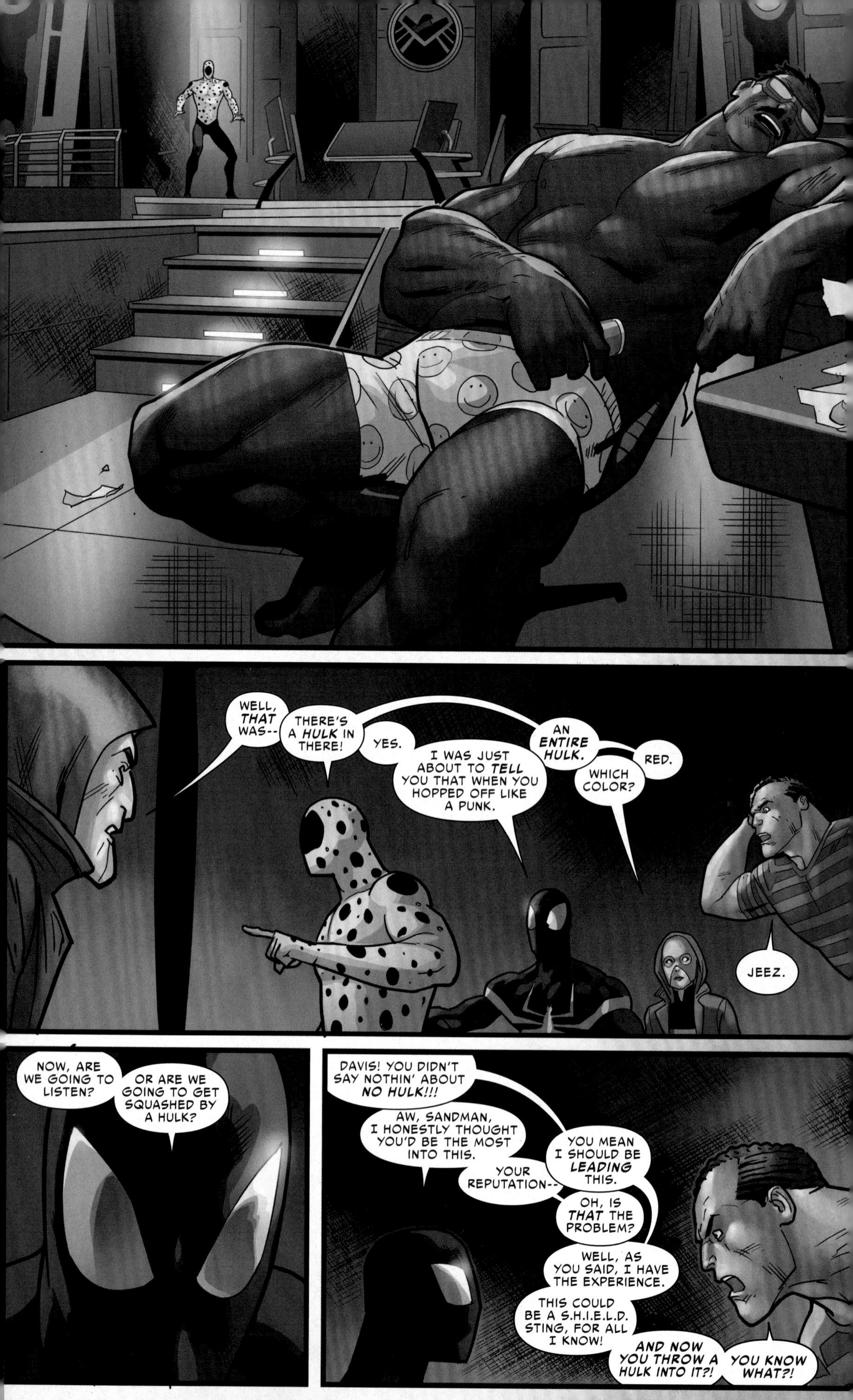

WELL, *THAT* WAS--
THERE'S A *HULK* IN THERE!
YES.
I WAS JUST ABOUT TO *TELL* YOU THAT WHEN YOU HOPPED OFF LIKE A PUNK.
AN *ENTIRE HULK.*
WHICH COLOR?
RED.
JEEZ.
NOW, ARE WE GOING TO LISTEN?
OR ARE WE GOING TO GET SQUASHED BY A HULK?
DAVIS! YOU DIDN'T SAY NOTHIN' ABOUT *NO HULK!!!*
AW, SANDMAN, I HONESTLY THOUGHT YOU'D BE THE MOST INTO THIS.
YOUR REPUTATION--
YOU MEAN I SHOULD BE *LEADING* THIS.
OH, IS *THAT* THE PROBLEM?
WELL, AS YOU SAID, I HAVE THE EXPERIENCE.
THIS COULD BE A S.H.I.E.L.D. STING, FOR ALL I KNOW!
AND NOW YOU THROW A HULK INTO IT?!
YOU KNOW WHAT?!

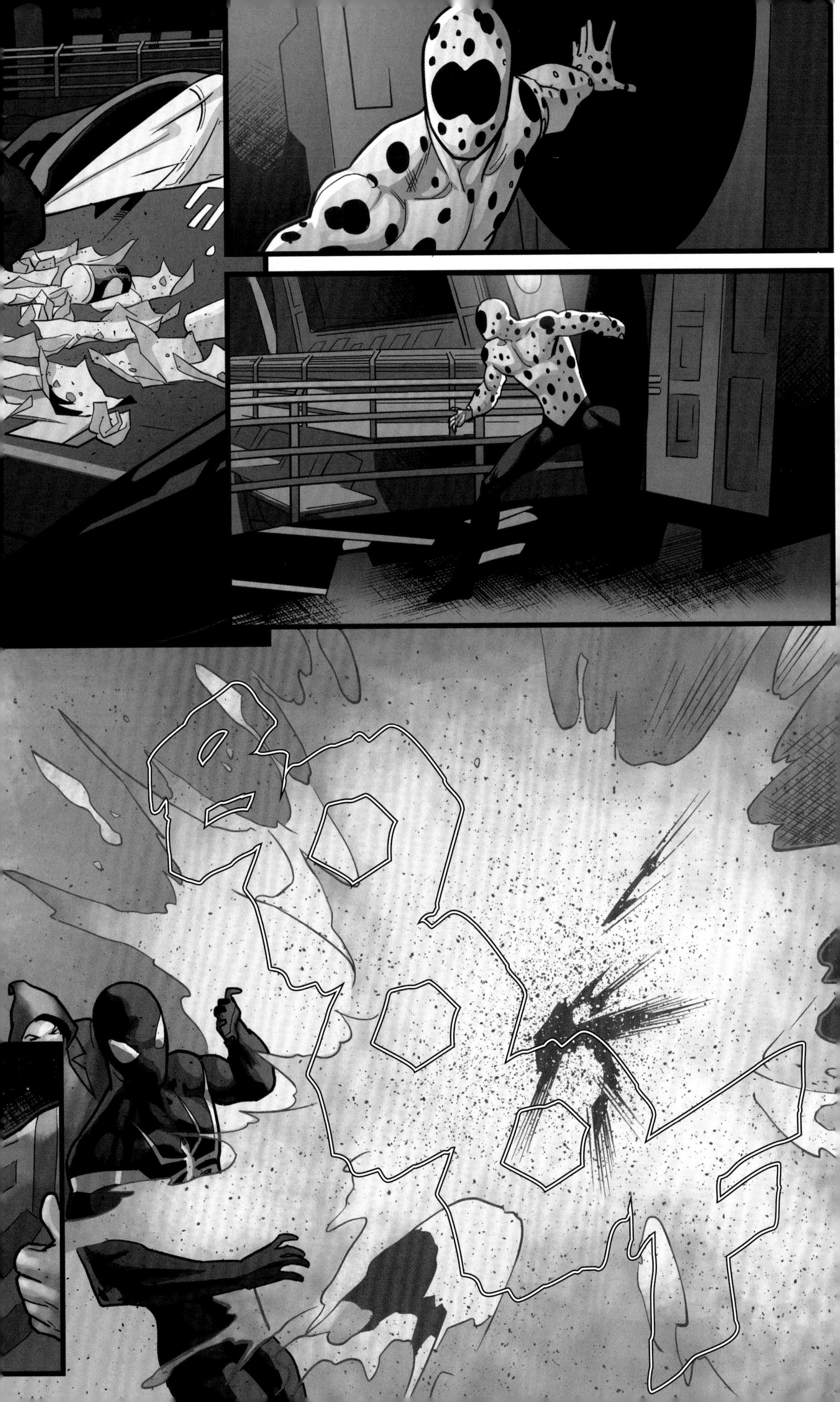

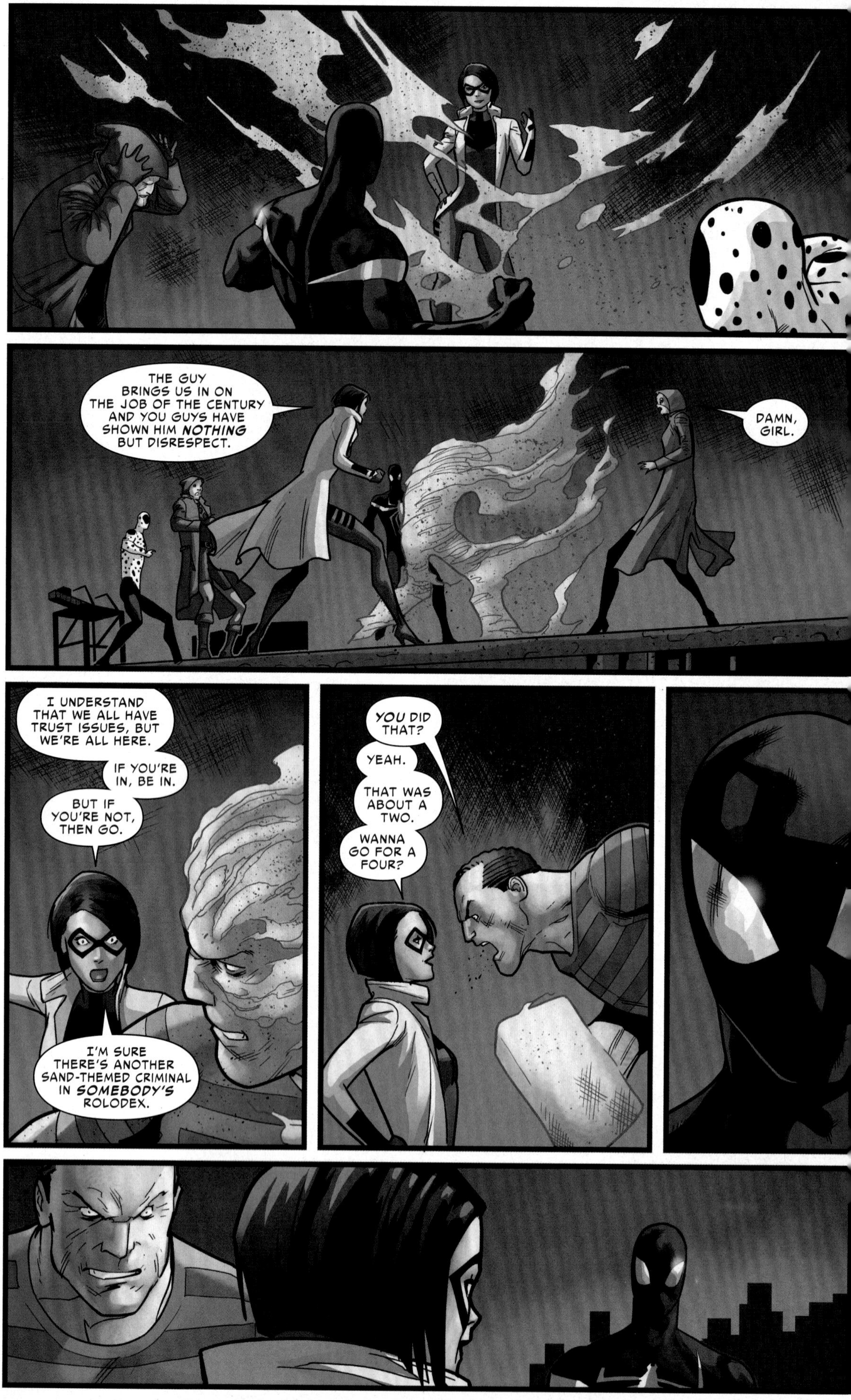
THE GUY BRINGS US IN ON THE JOB OF THE CENTURY AND YOU GUYS HAVE SHOWN HIM NOTHING BUT DISRESPECT.
DAMN, GIRL.
I UNDERSTAND THAT WE ALL HAVE TRUST ISSUES, BUT WE'RE ALL HERE.
IF YOU'RE IN, BE IN.
BUT IF YOU'RE NOT, THEN GO.
I'M SURE THERE'S ANOTHER SAND-THEMED CRIMINAL IN SOMEBODY'S ROLODEX.
YOU DID THAT?
YEAH.
THAT WAS ABOUT A TWO.
WANNA GO FOR A FOUR?

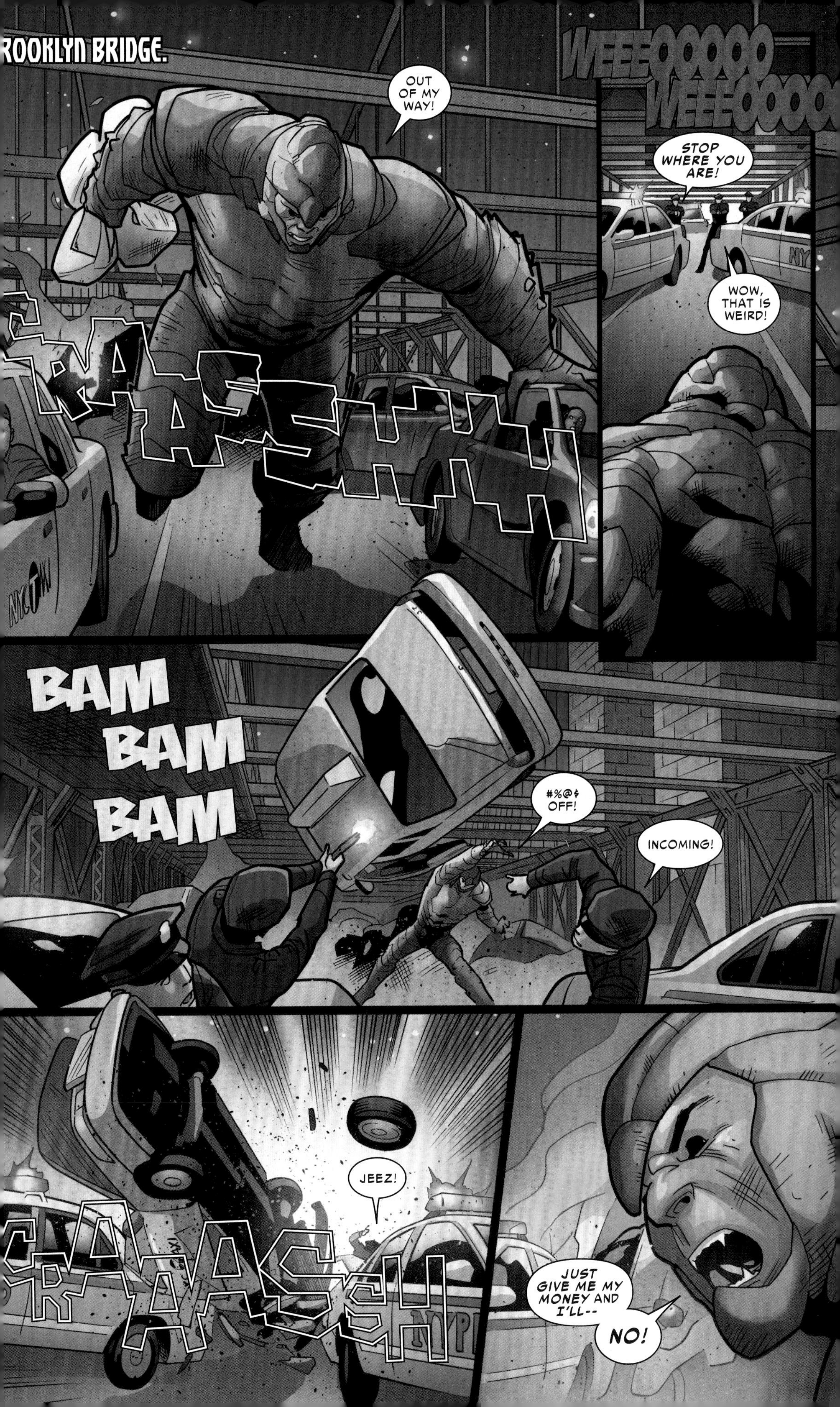

BROOKLYN BRIDGE.
OUT OF MY WAY!
WEEEOOOOO WEEEOOOOO
STOP WHERE YOU ARE!
WOW, THAT IS WEIRD!
KRASHHH
BAM BAM BAM
#%@$ OFF!
INCOMING!
JEEZ!
CRAAASHH
JUST GIVE ME MY MONEY AND I'LL--
NO!

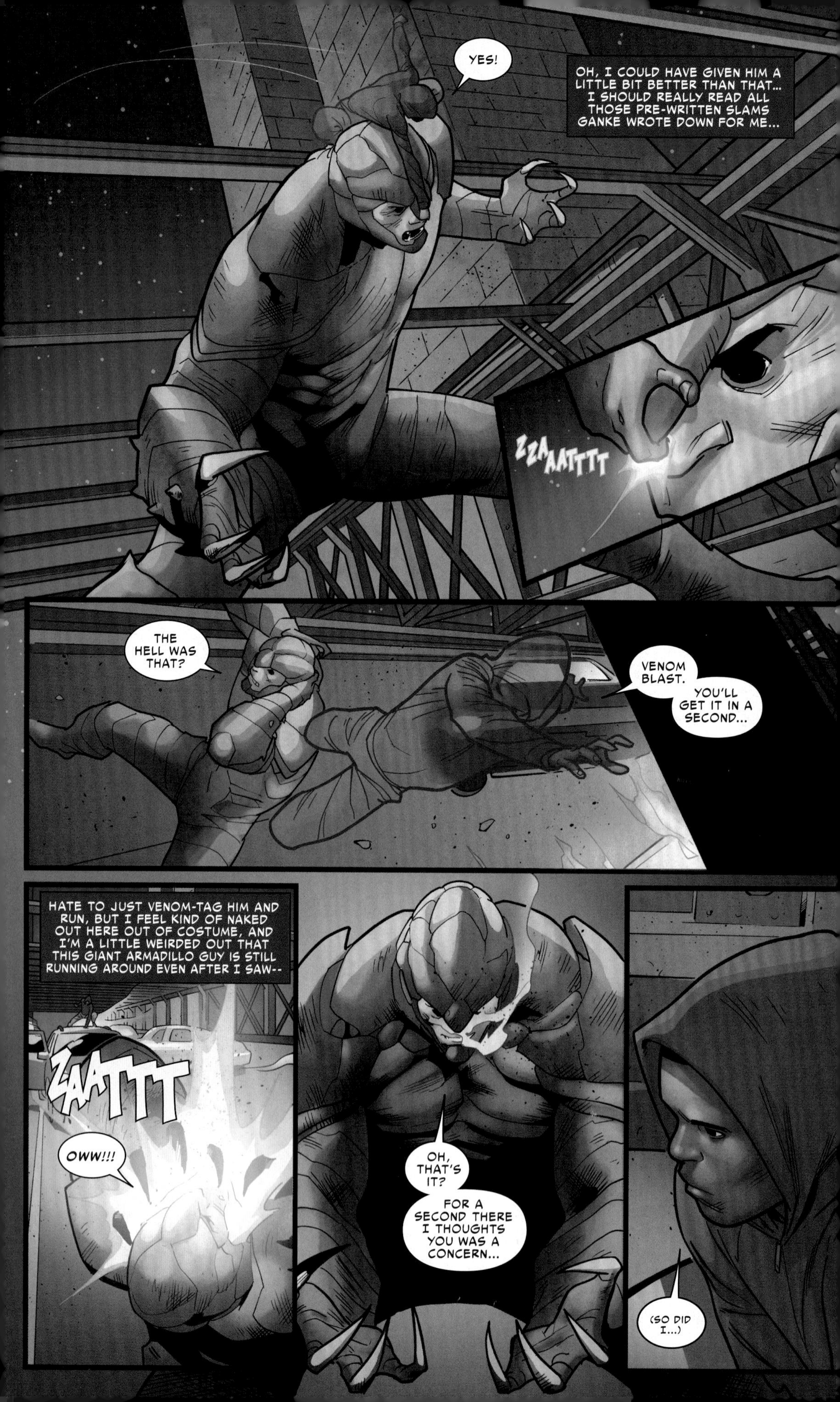
YES!
OH, I COULD HAVE GIVEN HIM A LITTLE BIT BETTER THAN THAT... I SHOULD REALLY READ ALL THOSE PRE-WRITTEN SLAMS GANKE WROTE DOWN FOR ME...
ZZAAATTTT
THE HELL WAS THAT?
VENOM BLAST.
YOU'LL GET IT IN A SECOND...
HATE TO JUST VENOM-TAG HIM AND RUN, BUT I FEEL KIND OF NAKED OUT HERE OUT OF COSTUME, AND I'M A LITTLE WEIRDED OUT THAT THIS GIANT ARMADILLO GUY IS STILL RUNNING AROUND EVEN AFTER I SAW--
ZAATTTT
OWW!!!
OH, THAT'S IT?
FOR A SECOND THERE I THOUGHTS YOU WAS A CONCERN...
(SO DID I...)

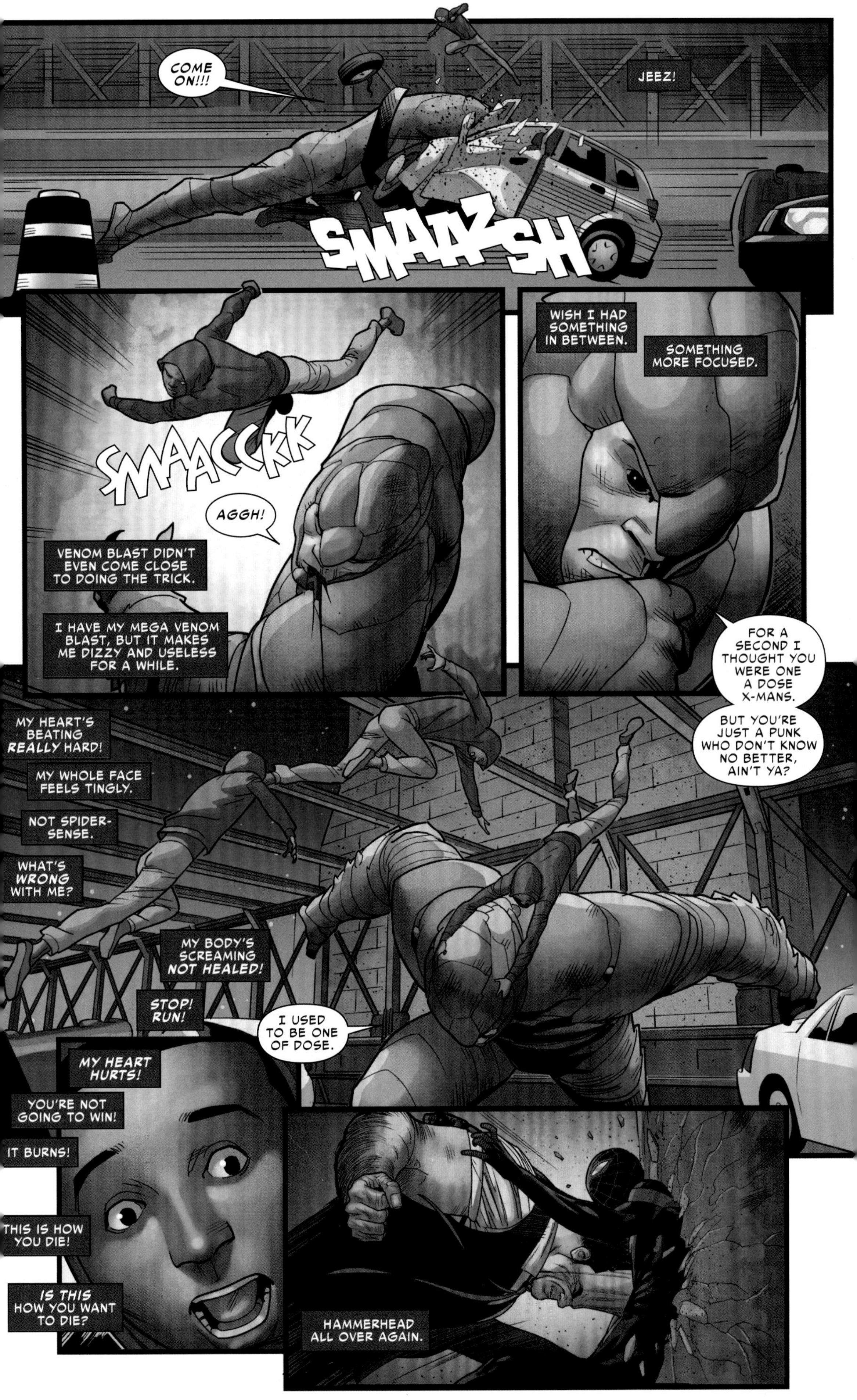
COME ON!!!
JEEZ!
SMAAZSH
SMAACCKK
AGGH!
VENOM BLAST DIDN'T EVEN COME CLOSE TO DOING THE TRICK.
I HAVE MY MEGA VENOM BLAST, BUT IT MAKES ME DIZZY AND USELESS FOR A WHILE.
WISH I HAD SOMETHING IN BETWEEN.
SOMETHING MORE FOCUSED.
FOR A SECOND I THOUGHT YOU WERE ONE A DOSE X-MANS.
BUT YOU'RE JUST A PUNK WHO DON'T KNOW NO BETTER, AIN'T YA?
MY HEART'S BEATING *REALLY* HARD!
MY WHOLE FACE FEELS TINGLY.
NOT SPIDER-SENSE.
WHAT'S *WRONG* WITH ME?
MY BODY'S SCREAMING *NOT HEALED!*
STOP! RUN!
I USED TO BE ONE OF DOSE.
MY HEART HURTS!
YOU'RE NOT GOING TO WIN!
IT BURNS!
THIS IS HOW YOU DIE!
IS THIS HOW YOU WANT TO DIE?
HAMMERHEAD ALL OVER AGAIN.

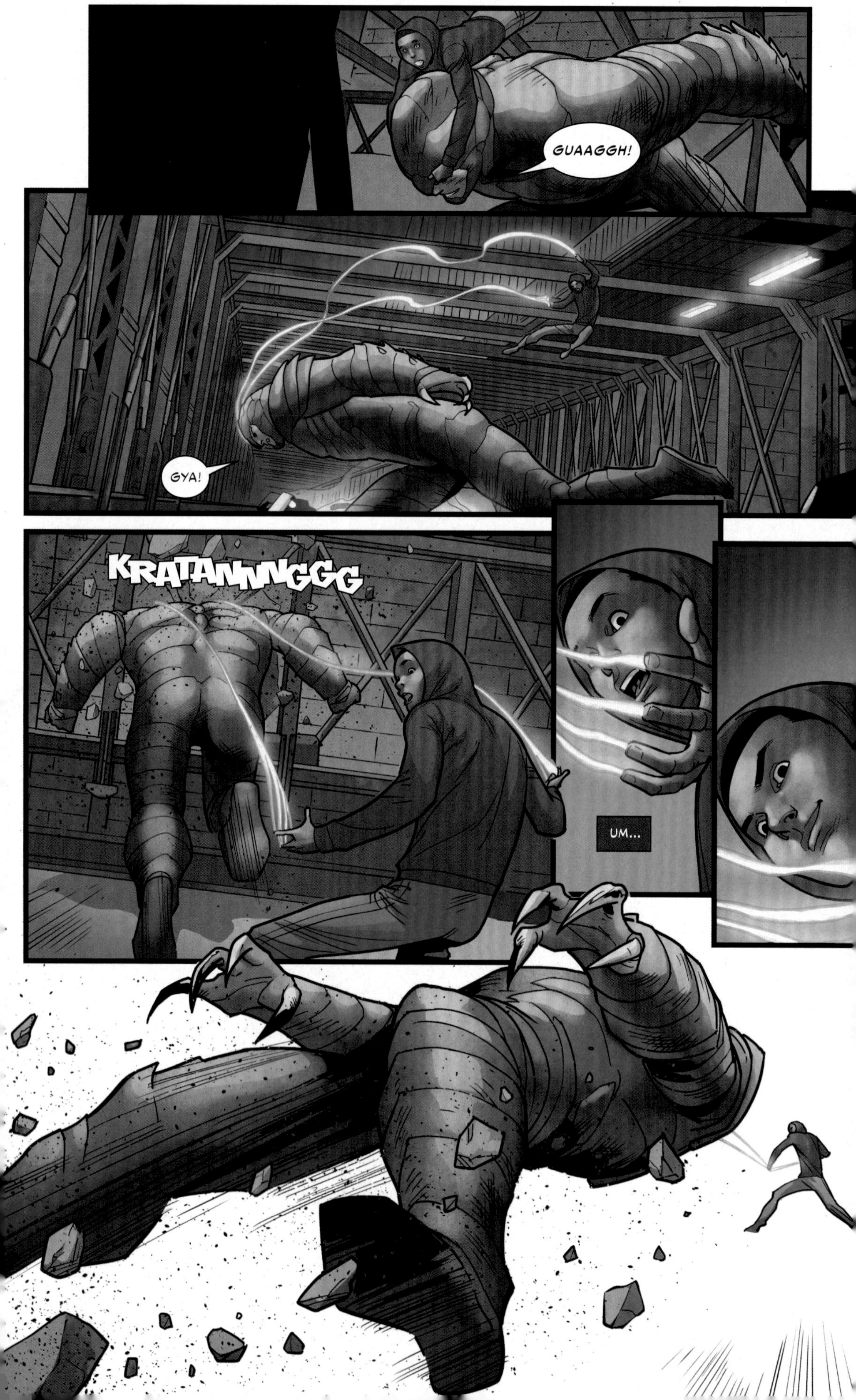
GUAAGGH!
GYA!
KRATANNNGGG
UM...

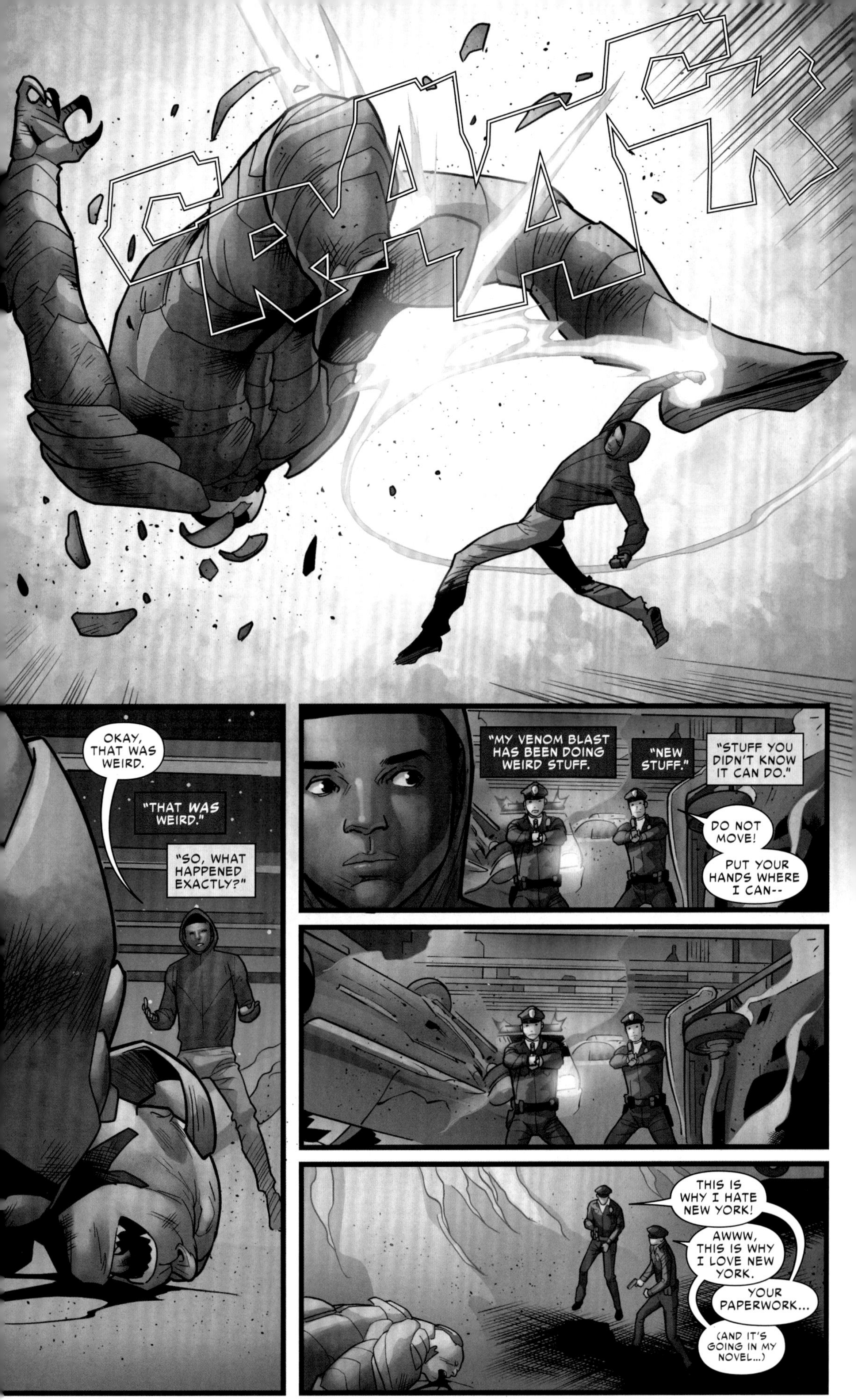
CRACK
OKAY, THAT WAS WEIRD.
"THAT WAS WEIRD."
"SO, WHAT HAPPENED EXACTLY?"
"MY VENOM BLAST HAS BEEN DOING WEIRD STUFF.
"NEW STUFF."
"STUFF YOU DIDN'T KNOW IT CAN DO."
DO NOT MOVE!
PUT YOUR HANDS WHERE I CAN--
THIS IS WHY I HATE NEW YORK!
AWWW, THIS IS WHY I LOVE NEW YORK.
YOUR PAPERWORK...
(AND IT'S GOING IN MY NOVEL...)

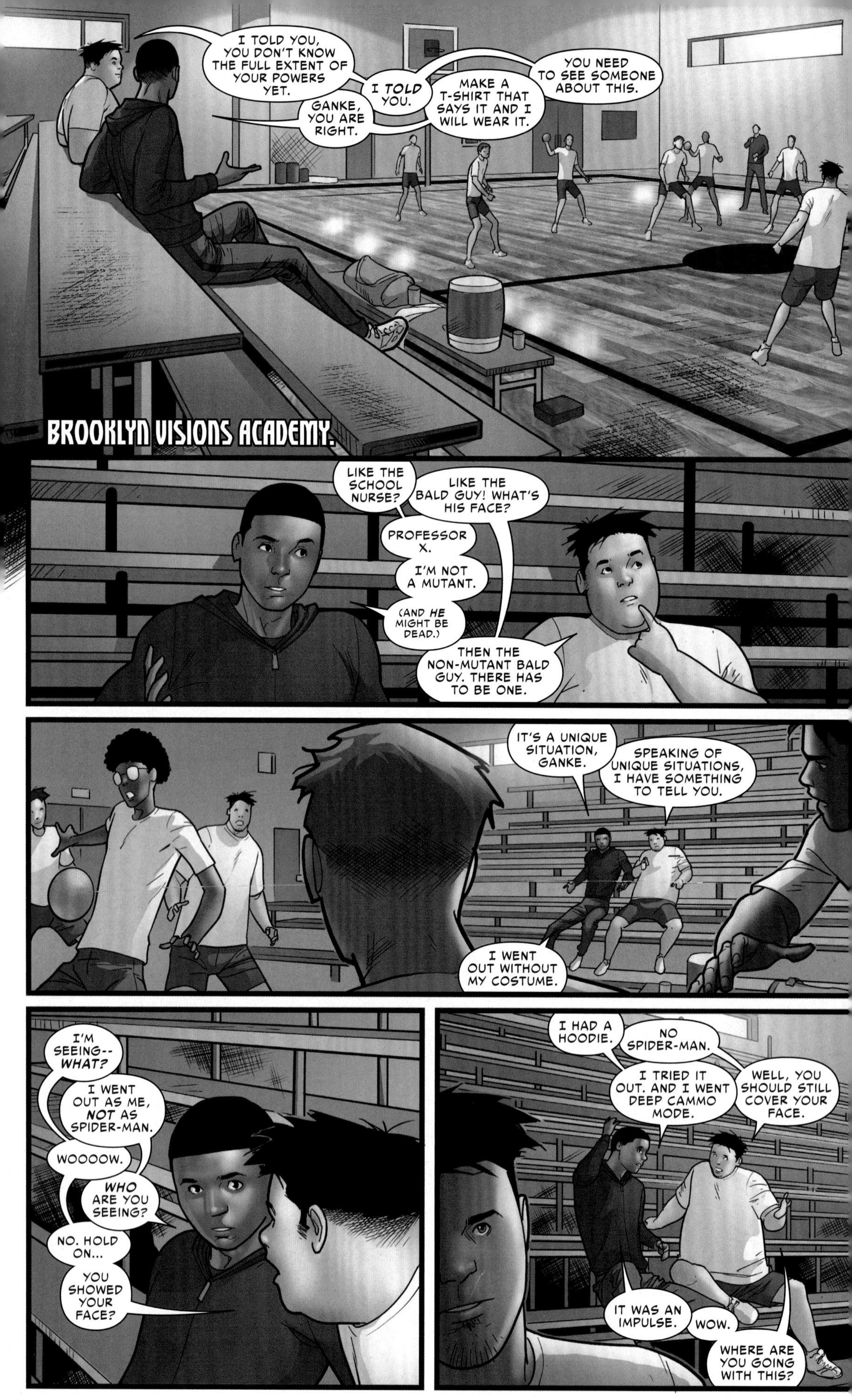
I TOLD YOU, YOU DON'T KNOW THE FULL EXTENT OF YOUR POWERS YET.
GANKE, YOU ARE RIGHT.
I *TOLD* YOU.
MAKE A T-SHIRT THAT SAYS IT AND I WILL WEAR IT.
YOU NEED TO SEE SOMEONE ABOUT THIS.
BROOKLYN VISIONS ACADEMY.
LIKE THE SCHOOL NURSE?
LIKE THE BALD GUY! WHAT'S HIS FACE?
PROFESSOR X.
I'M NOT A MUTANT.
(AND *HE* MIGHT BE DEAD.)
THEN THE NON-MUTANT BALD GUY. THERE HAS TO BE ONE.
IT'S A UNIQUE SITUATION, GANKE.
SPEAKING OF UNIQUE SITUATIONS, I HAVE SOMETHING TO TELL YOU.
I WENT OUT WITHOUT MY COSTUME.
I'M SEEING-- *WHAT?*
I WENT OUT AS ME, *NOT* AS SPIDER-MAN.
WOOOOW.
WHO ARE YOU SEEING?
NO. HOLD ON...
YOU SHOWED YOUR FACE?
I HAD A HOODIE.
NO SPIDER-MAN.
I TRIED IT OUT. AND I WENT DEEP CAMMO MODE.
WELL, YOU SHOULD STILL COVER YOUR FACE.
IT WAS AN IMPULSE.
WOW.
WHERE ARE YOU GOING WITH THIS?

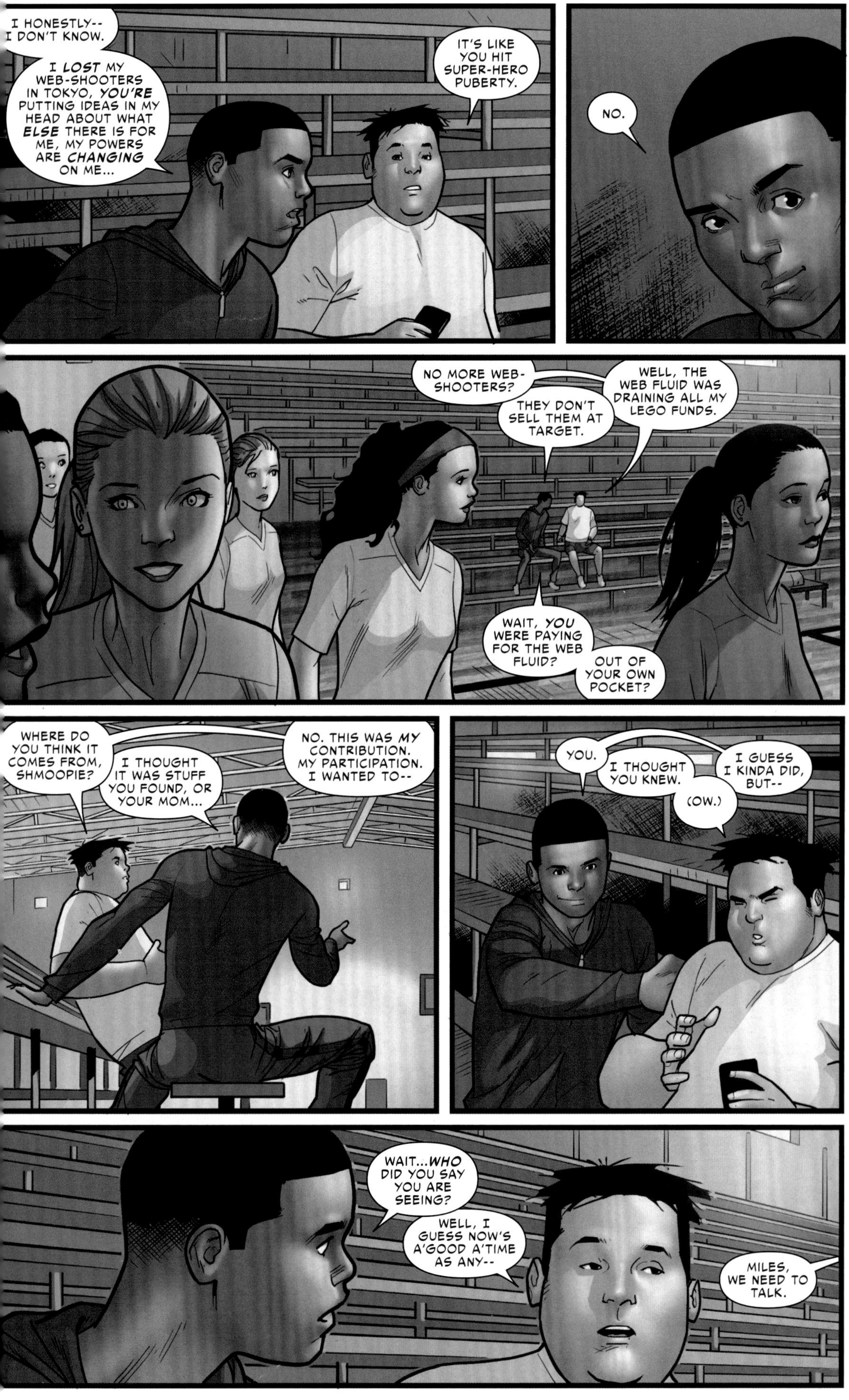
I HONESTLY-- I DON'T KNOW.
I LOST MY WEB-SHOOTERS IN TOKYO, YOU'RE PUTTING IDEAS IN MY HEAD ABOUT WHAT ELSE THERE IS FOR ME, MY POWERS ARE CHANGING ON ME...
IT'S LIKE YOU HIT SUPER-HERO PUBERTY.
NO.
NO MORE WEB-SHOOTERS?
THEY DON'T SELL THEM AT TARGET.
WELL, THE WEB FLUID WAS DRAINING ALL MY LEGO FUNDS.
WAIT, YOU WERE PAYING FOR THE WEB FLUID?
OUT OF YOUR OWN POCKET?
WHERE DO YOU THINK IT COMES FROM, SHMOOPIE?
I THOUGHT IT WAS STUFF YOU FOUND, OR YOUR MOM...
NO. THIS WAS MY CONTRIBUTION. MY PARTICIPATION. I WANTED TO--
YOU.
I THOUGHT YOU KNEW.
I GUESS I KINDA DID, BUT--
(OW.)
WAIT...WHO DID YOU SAY YOU ARE SEEING?
WELL, I GUESS NOW'S A'GOOD A'TIME AS ANY--
MILES, WE NEED TO TALK.

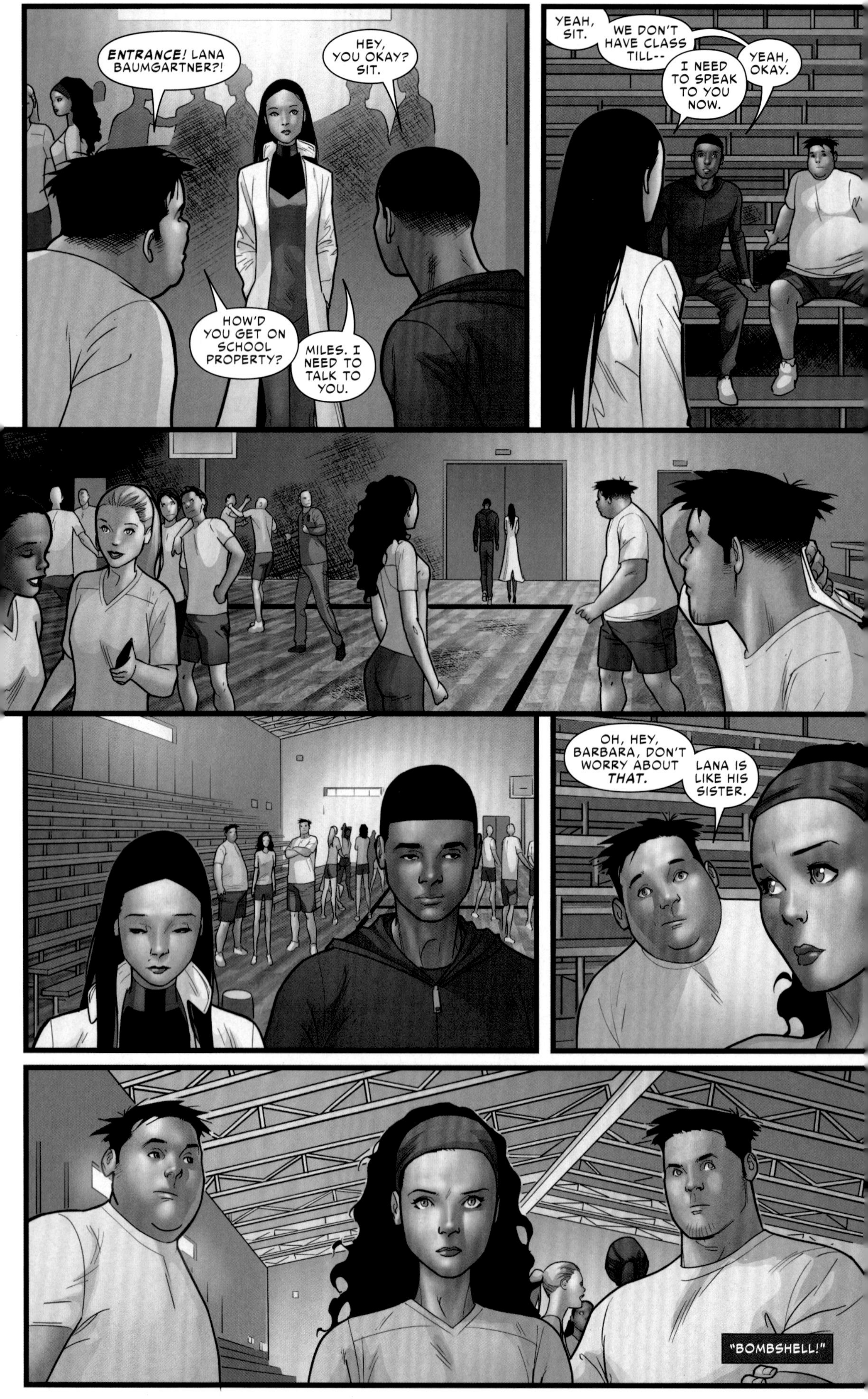
ENTRANCE! LANA BAUMGARTNER?!
HEY, YOU OKAY? SIT.
HOW'D YOU GET ON SCHOOL PROPERTY?
MILES. I NEED TO TALK TO YOU.
YEAH, SIT.
WE DON'T HAVE CLASS TILL--
I NEED TO SPEAK TO YOU NOW.
YEAH, OKAY.
OH, HEY, BARBARA, DON'T WORRY ABOUT THAT.
LANA IS LIKE HIS SISTER.
"BOMBSHELL!"

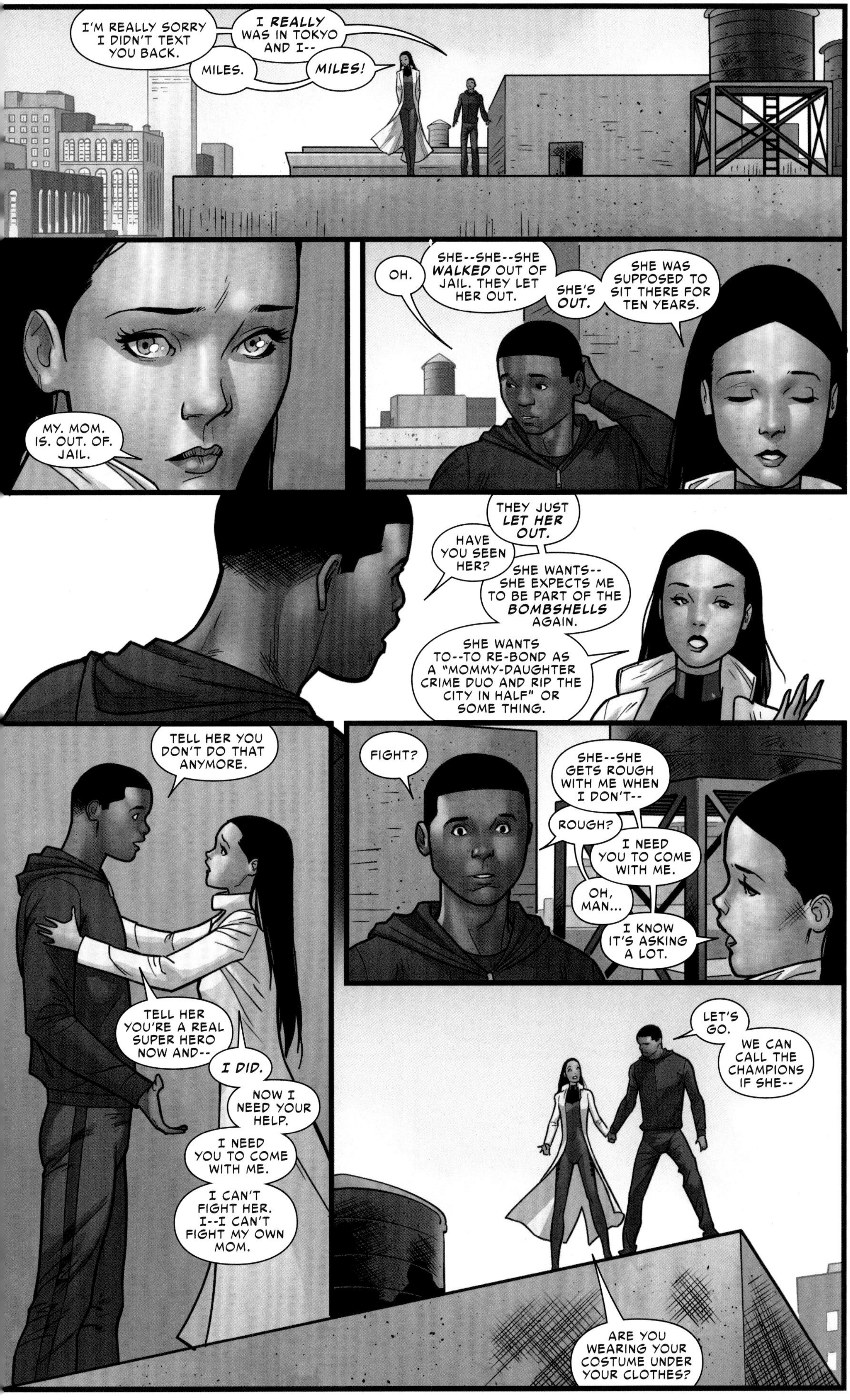
I'M REALLY SORRY I DIDN'T TEXT YOU BACK.
I *REALLY* WAS IN TOKYO AND I--
MILES.
MILES!
MY. MOM. IS. OUT. OF. JAIL.
OH.
SHE--SHE--SHE *WALKED* OUT OF JAIL. THEY LET HER OUT.
SHE'S *OUT.*
SHE WAS SUPPOSED TO SIT THERE FOR TEN YEARS.
THEY JUST *LET HER OUT.*
HAVE YOU SEEN HER?
SHE WANTS-- SHE EXPECTS ME TO BE PART OF THE *BOMBSHELLS* AGAIN.
SHE WANTS TO--TO RE-BOND AS A "MOMMY-DAUGHTER CRIME DUO AND RIP THE CITY IN HALF" OR SOME THING.
TELL HER YOU DON'T DO THAT ANYMORE.
TELL HER YOU'RE A REAL SUPER HERO NOW AND--
I DID.
NOW I NEED YOUR HELP.
I NEED YOU TO COME WITH ME.
I CAN'T FIGHT HER. I--I CAN'T FIGHT MY OWN MOM.
FIGHT?
SHE--SHE GETS ROUGH WITH ME WHEN I DON'T--
ROUGH?
I NEED YOU TO COME WITH ME.
OH, MAN...
I KNOW IT'S ASKING A LOT.
LET'S GO.
WE CAN CALL THE CHAMPIONS IF SHE--
ARE YOU WEARING YOUR COSTUME UNDER YOUR CLOTHES?

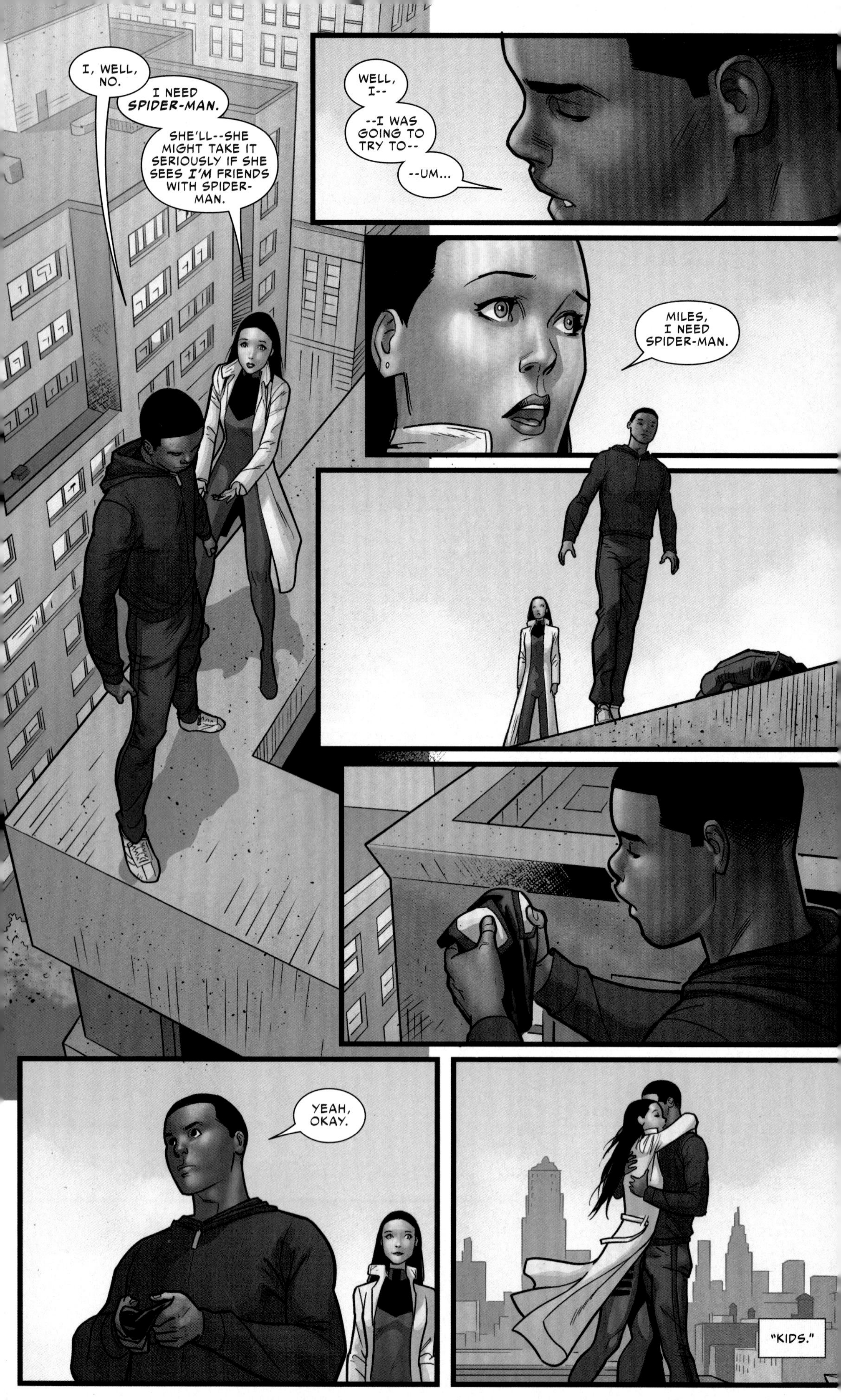
I, WELL, NO.
I NEED SPIDER-MAN.
SHE'LL--SHE MIGHT TAKE IT SERIOUSLY IF SHE SEES I'M FRIENDS WITH SPIDER-MAN.
WELL, I--
--I WAS GOING TO TRY TO--
--UM...
MILES, I NEED SPIDER-MAN.
YEAH, OKAY.
"KIDS."

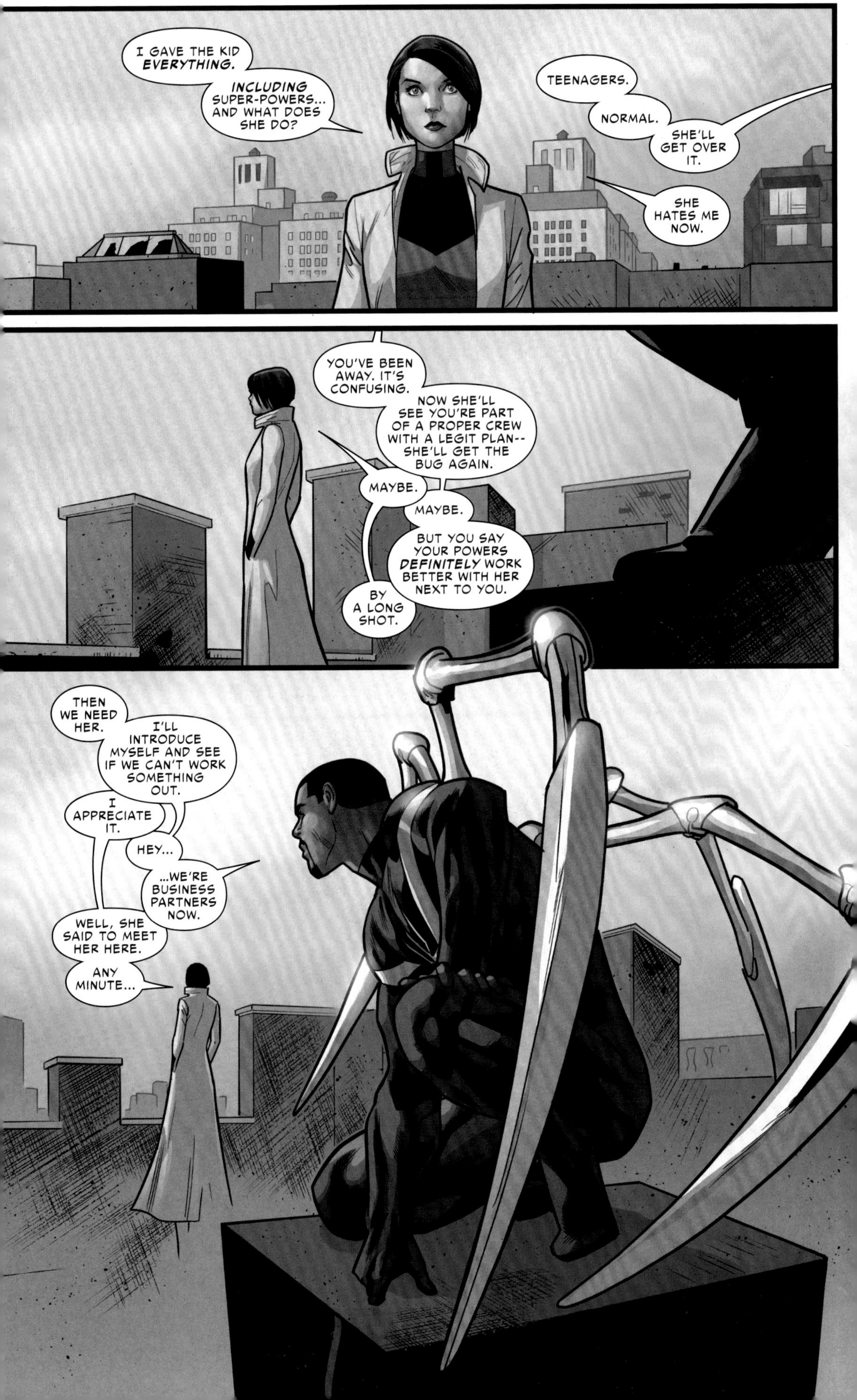
I GAVE THE KID *EVERYTHING.*
INCLUDING SUPER-POWERS... AND WHAT DOES SHE DO?
TEENAGERS.
NORMAL.
SHE'LL GET OVER IT.
SHE HATES ME NOW.
YOU'VE BEEN AWAY. IT'S CONFUSING.
NOW SHE'LL SEE YOU'RE PART OF A PROPER CREW WITH A LEGIT PLAN-- SHE'LL GET THE BUG AGAIN.
MAYBE.
MAYBE.
BUT YOU SAY YOUR POWERS *DEFINITELY* WORK BETTER WITH HER NEXT TO YOU.
BY A LONG SHOT.
THEN WE NEED HER.
I'LL INTRODUCE MYSELF AND SEE IF WE CAN'T WORK SOMETHING OUT.
I APPRECIATE IT.
HEY...
...WE'RE BUSINESS PARTNERS NOW.
WELL, SHE SAID TO MEET HER HERE.
ANY MINUTE...

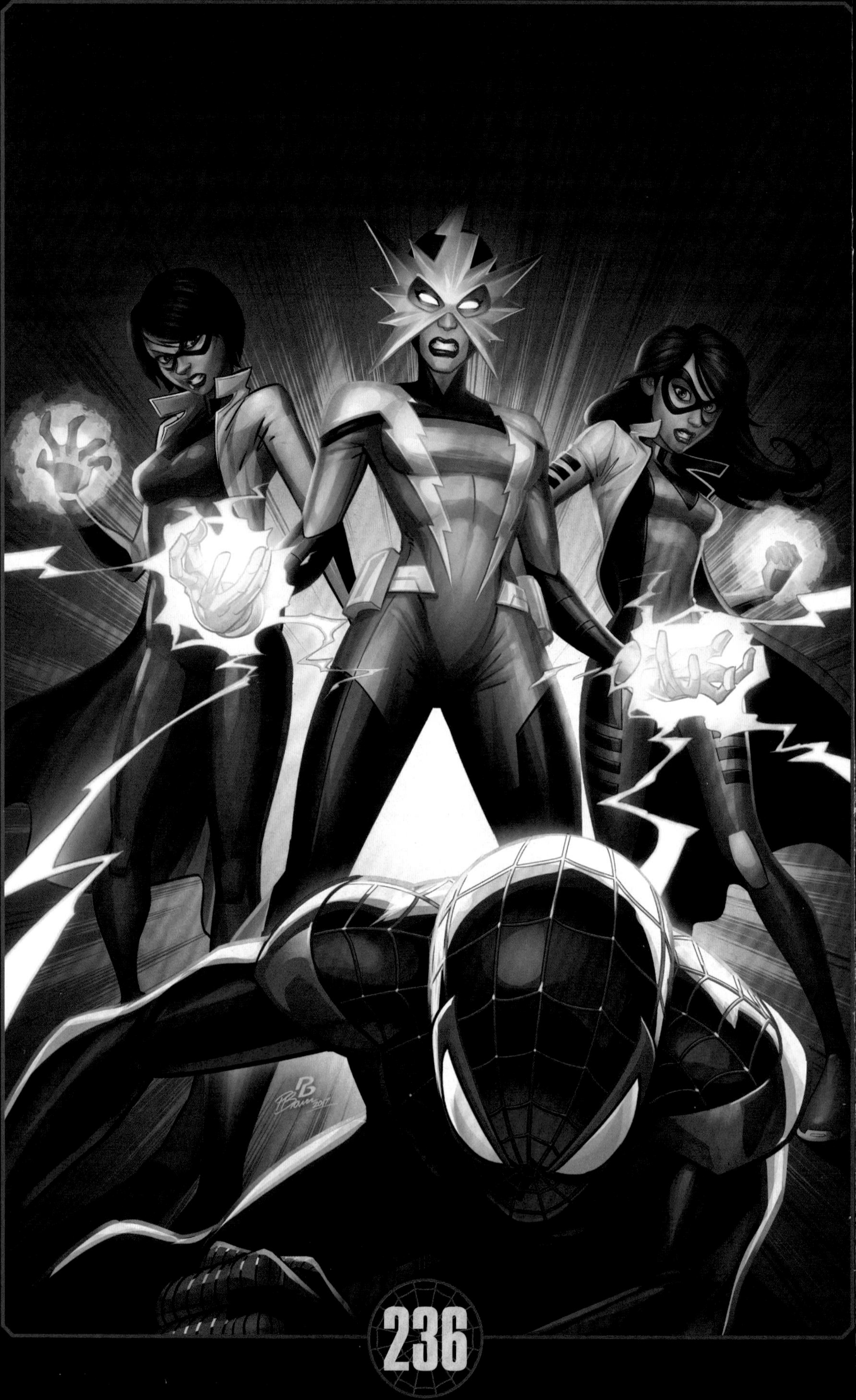
236

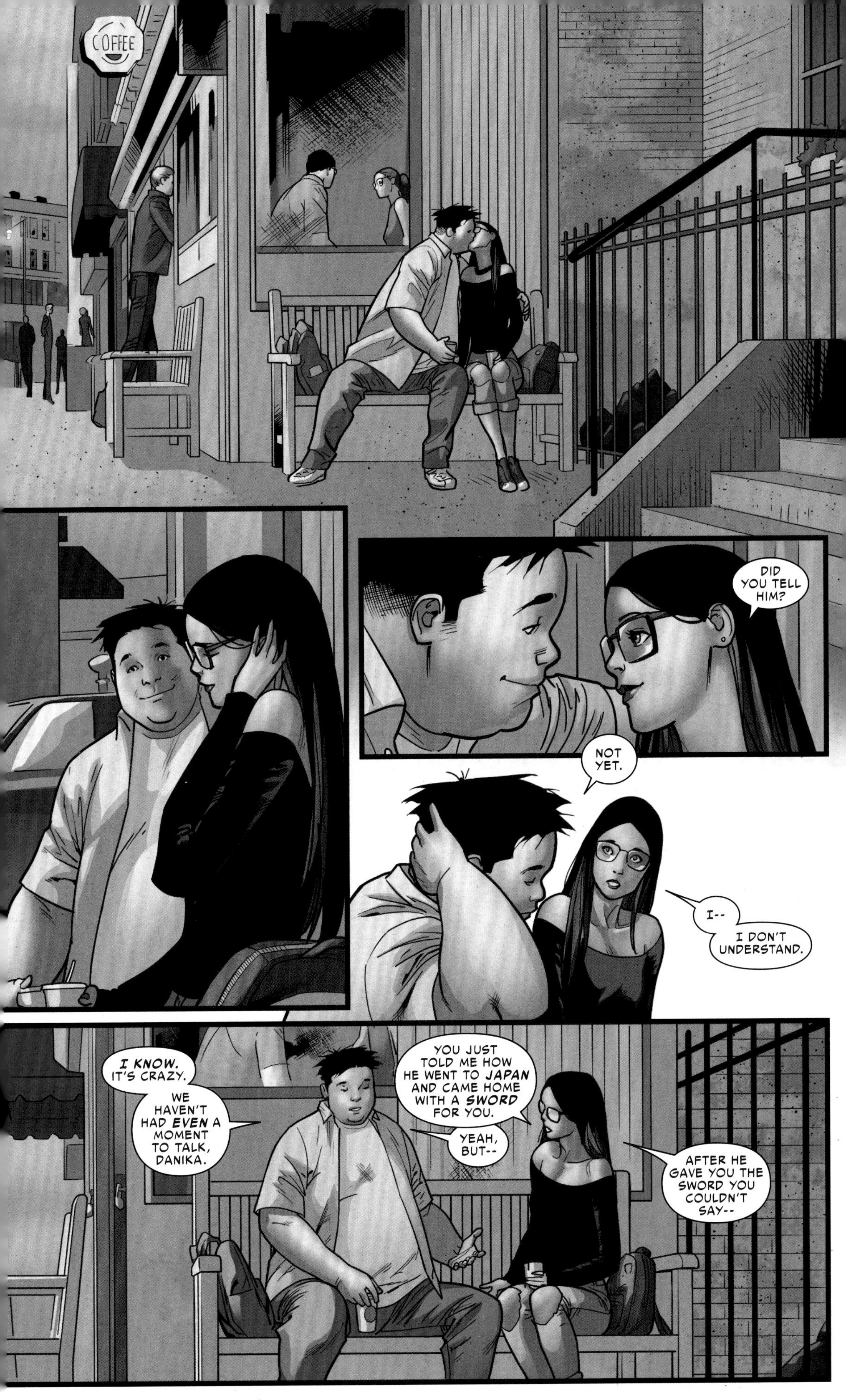
COFFEE
DID YOU TELL HIM?
NOT YET.
I--
I DON'T UNDERSTAND.
I KNOW. IT'S CRAZY.
WE HAVEN'T HAD EVEN A MOMENT TO TALK, DANIKA.
YOU JUST TOLD ME HOW HE WENT TO JAPAN AND CAME HOME WITH A SWORD FOR YOU.
YEAH, BUT--
AFTER HE GAVE YOU THE SWORD YOU COULDN'T SAY--

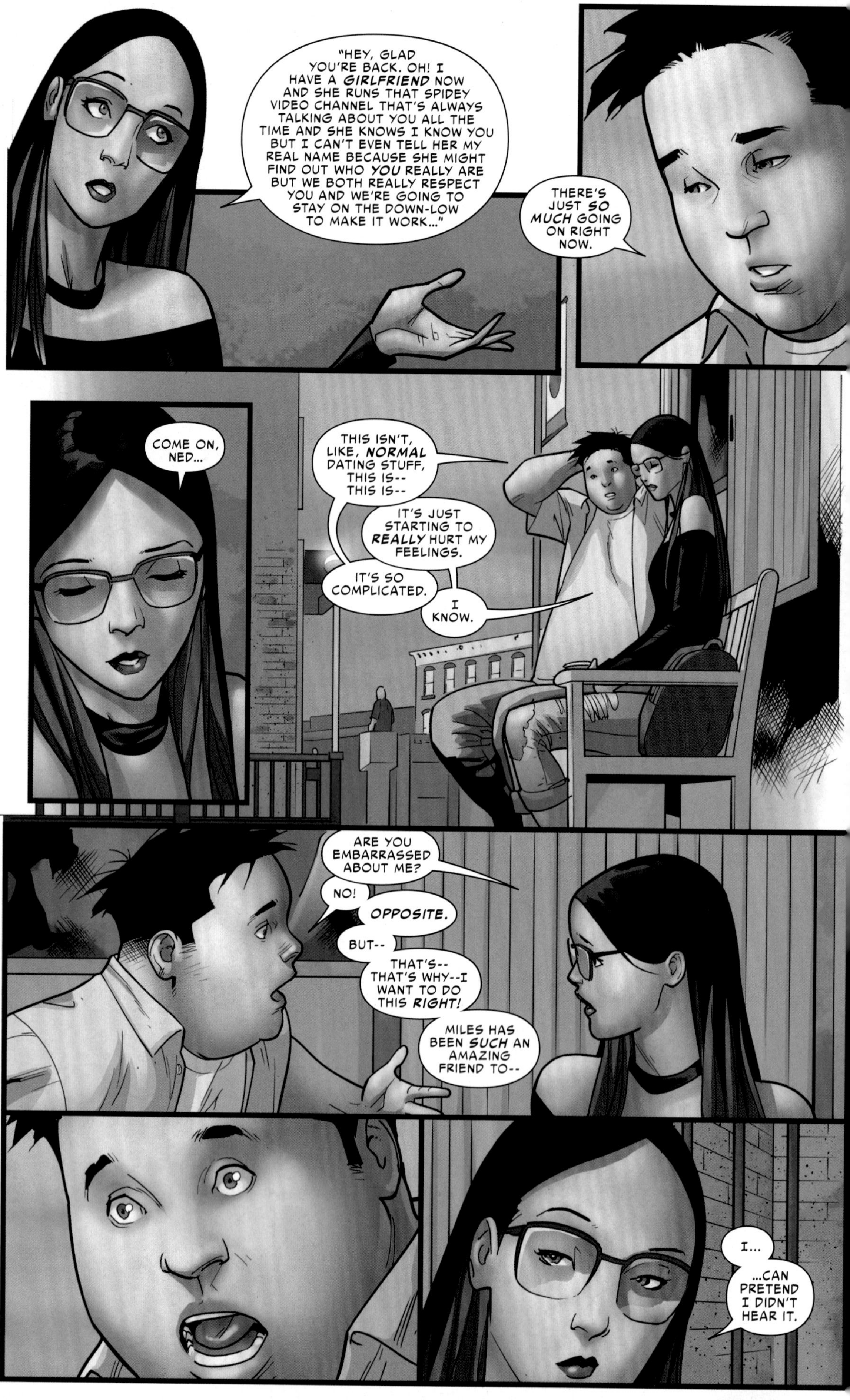
"HEY, GLAD YOU'RE BACK. OH! I HAVE A GIRLFRIEND NOW AND SHE RUNS THAT SPIDEY VIDEO CHANNEL THAT'S ALWAYS TALKING ABOUT YOU ALL THE TIME AND SHE KNOWS I KNOW YOU BUT I CAN'T EVEN TELL HER MY REAL NAME BECAUSE SHE MIGHT FIND OUT WHO YOU REALLY ARE BUT WE BOTH REALLY RESPECT YOU AND WE'RE GOING TO STAY ON THE DOWN-LOW TO MAKE IT WORK..."
THERE'S JUST SO MUCH GOING ON RIGHT NOW.
COME ON, NED...
THIS ISN'T, LIKE, NORMAL DATING STUFF, THIS IS-- THIS IS--
IT'S SO COMPLICATED.
IT'S JUST STARTING TO REALLY HURT MY FEELINGS.
I KNOW.
ARE YOU EMBARRASSED ABOUT ME?
NO!
OPPOSITE.
BUT--
THAT'S-- THAT'S WHY--I WANT TO DO THIS RIGHT!
MILES HAS BEEN SUCH AN AMAZING FRIEND TO--
I...
...CAN PRETEND I DIDN'T HEAR IT.

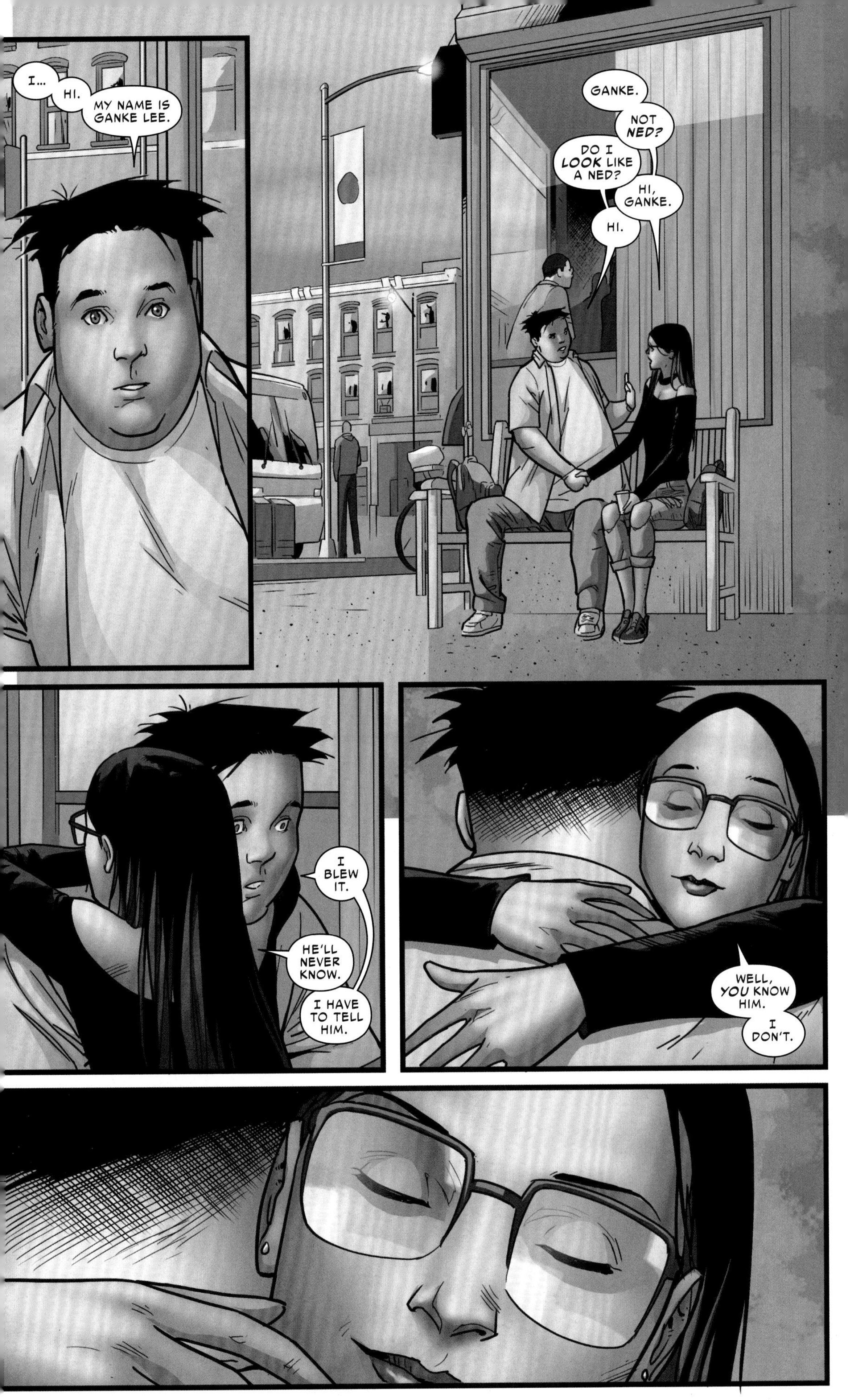

I...
HI.
MY NAME IS GANKE LEE.
GANKE.
NOT NED?
DO I LOOK LIKE A NED?
HI, GANKE.
HI.
I BLEW IT.
HE'LL NEVER KNOW.
I HAVE TO TELL HIM.
WELL, YOU KNOW HIM.
I DON'T.

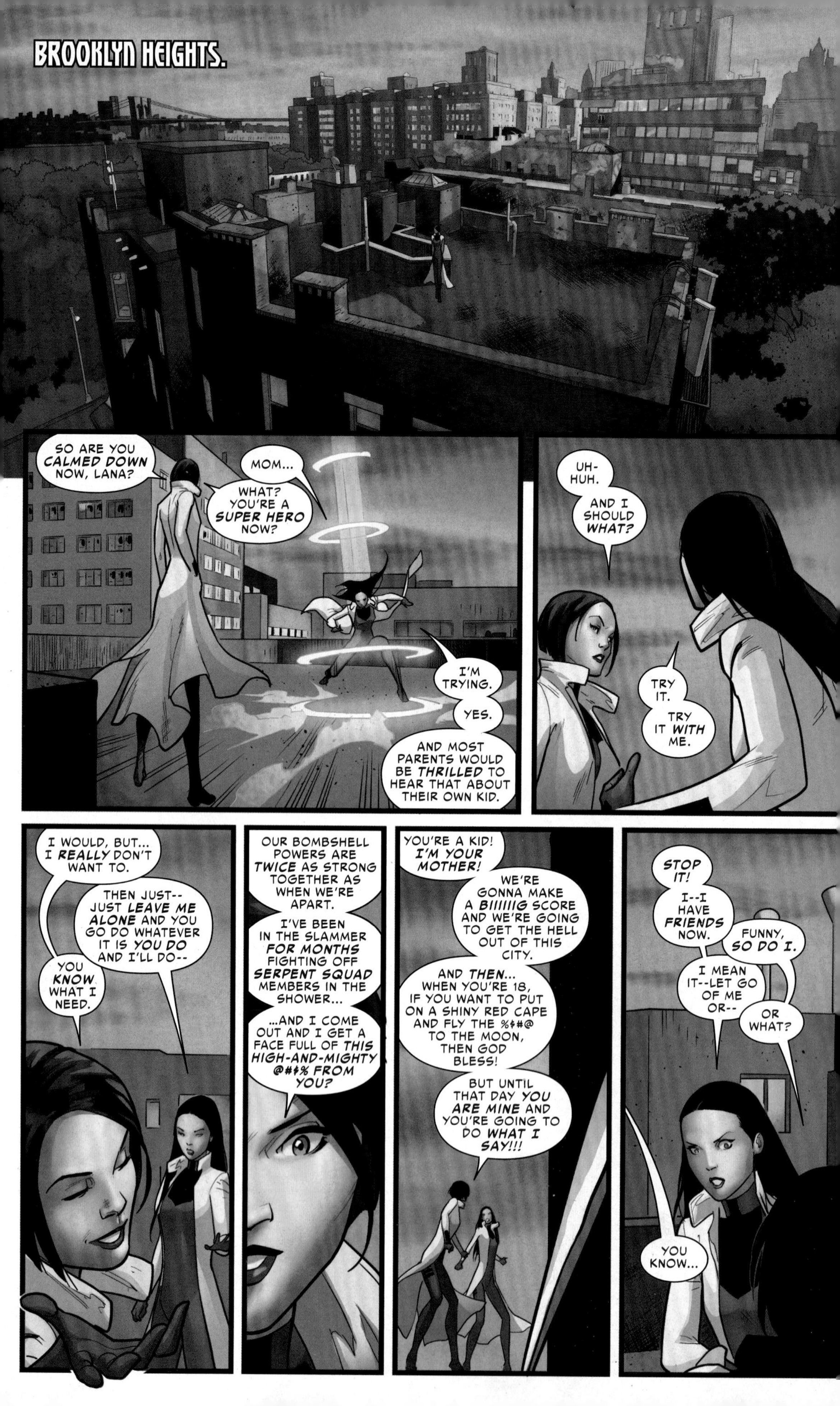
BROOKLYN HEIGHTS.
SO ARE YOU CALMED DOWN NOW, LANA?
MOM...
WHAT? YOU'RE A SUPER HERO NOW?
I'M TRYING.
YES.
AND MOST PARENTS WOULD BE THRILLED TO HEAR THAT ABOUT THEIR OWN KID.
UH-HUH.
AND I SHOULD WHAT?
TRY IT.
TRY IT WITH ME.
I WOULD, BUT... I REALLY DON'T WANT TO.
THEN JUST-- JUST LEAVE ME ALONE AND YOU GO DO WHATEVER IT IS YOU DO AND I'LL DO--
YOU KNOW WHAT I NEED.
OUR BOMBSHELL POWERS ARE TWICE AS STRONG TOGETHER AS WHEN WE'RE APART.
I'VE BEEN IN THE SLAMMER FOR MONTHS FIGHTING OFF SERPENT SQUAD MEMBERS IN THE SHOWER...
...AND I COME OUT AND I GET A FACE FULL OF THIS HIGH-AND-MIGHTY @#$% FROM YOU?
YOU'RE A KID! I'M YOUR MOTHER!
WE'RE GONNA MAKE A BIIIIIIG SCORE AND WE'RE GOING TO GET THE HELL OUT OF THIS CITY.
AND THEN... WHEN YOU'RE 18, IF YOU WANT TO PUT ON A SHINY RED CAPE AND FLY THE %$#@ TO THE MOON, THEN GOD BLESS!
BUT UNTIL THAT DAY YOU ARE MINE AND YOU'RE GOING TO DO WHAT I SAY!!!
STOP IT!
I--I HAVE FRIENDS NOW.
FUNNY, SO DO I.
I MEAN IT--LET GO OF ME OR--
OR WHAT?
YOU KNOW...

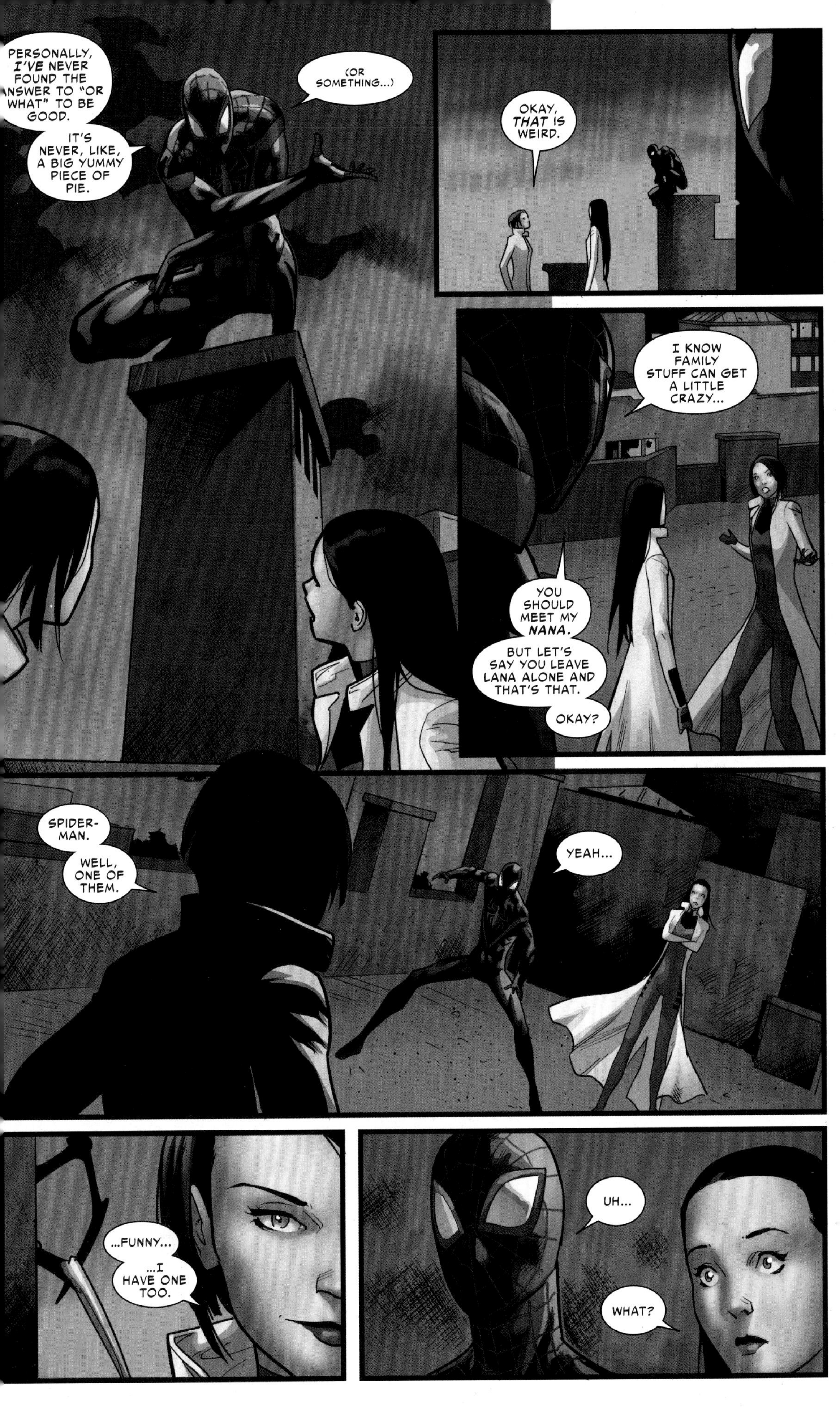
PERSONALLY, I'VE NEVER FOUND THE ANSWER TO "OR WHAT" TO BE GOOD.
IT'S NEVER, LIKE, A BIG YUMMY PIECE OF PIE.
(OR SOMETHING...)
OKAY, THAT IS WEIRD.
I KNOW FAMILY STUFF CAN GET A LITTLE CRAZY...
YOU SHOULD MEET MY NANA.
BUT LET'S SAY YOU LEAVE LANA ALONE AND THAT'S THAT.
OKAY?
SPIDER-MAN.
WELL, ONE OF THEM.
YEAH...
...FUNNY...
...I HAVE ONE TOO.
UH...
WHAT?

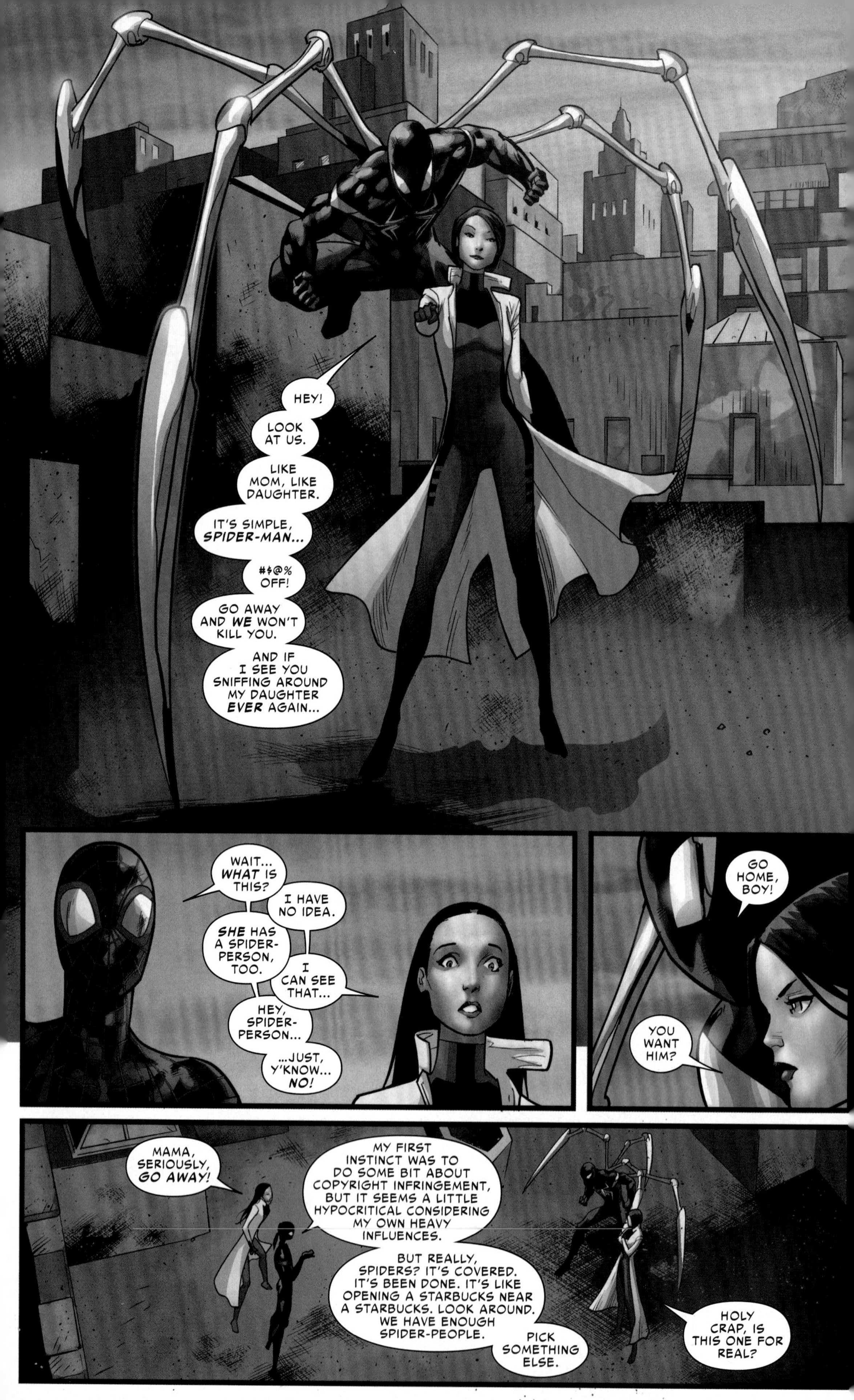
HEY!
LOOK AT US.
LIKE MOM, LIKE DAUGHTER.
IT'S SIMPLE, SPIDER-MAN...
#$@% OFF!
GO AWAY AND WE WON'T KILL YOU.
AND IF I SEE YOU SNIFFING AROUND MY DAUGHTER EVER AGAIN...
WAIT... WHAT IS THIS?
I HAVE NO IDEA.
SHE HAS A SPIDER-PERSON, TOO.
I CAN SEE THAT...
HEY, SPIDER-PERSON...
...JUST, Y'KNOW... NO!
GO HOME, BOY!
YOU WANT HIM?
MAMA, SERIOUSLY, GO AWAY!
MY FIRST INSTINCT WAS TO DO SOME BIT ABOUT COPYRIGHT INFRINGEMENT, BUT IT SEEMS A LITTLE HYPOCRITICAL CONSIDERING MY OWN HEAVY INFLUENCES.
BUT REALLY, SPIDERS? IT'S COVERED. IT'S BEEN DONE. IT'S LIKE OPENING A STARBUCKS NEAR A STARBUCKS. LOOK AROUND. WE HAVE ENOUGH SPIDER-PEOPLE.
PICK SOMETHING ELSE.
HOLY CRAP, IS THIS ONE FOR REAL?

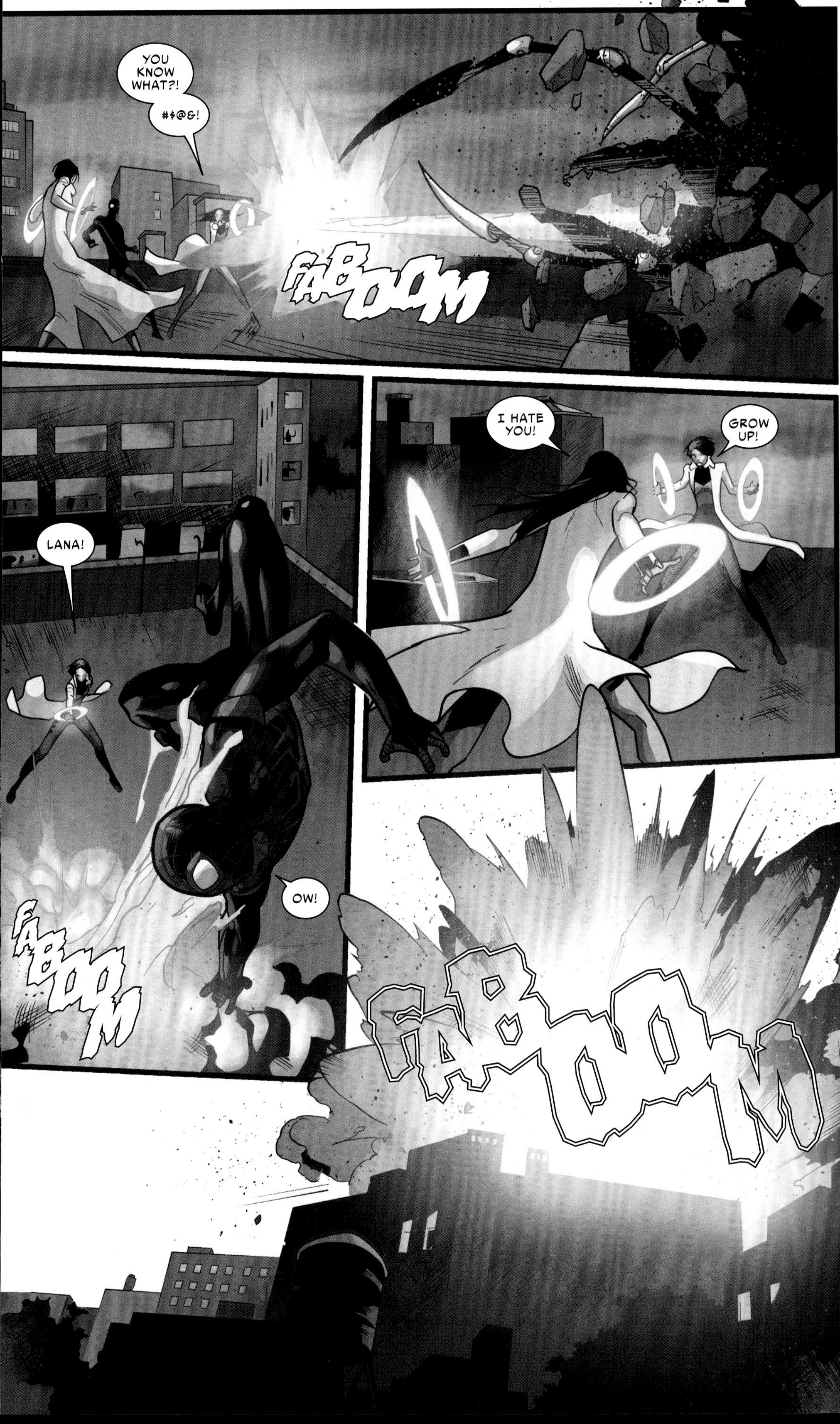
YOU KNOW WHAT?!
#$@&!
FABOOM
LANA!
OW!
FABOOM
I HATE YOU!
GROW UP!
FABOOM

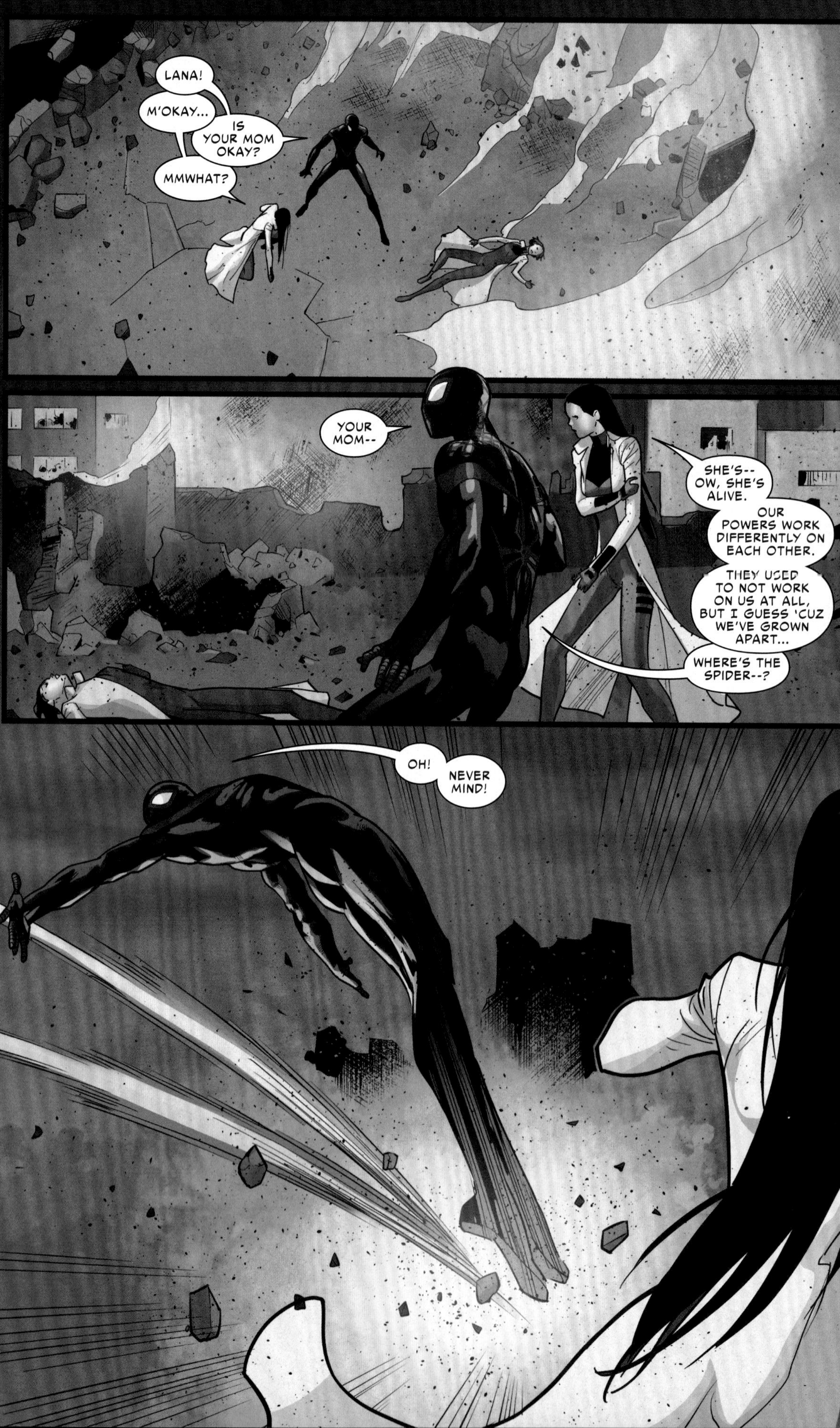

LANA!
M'OKAY...
IS YOUR MOM OKAY?
MMWHAT?
YOUR MOM--
SHE'S-- OW, SHE'S ALIVE.
OUR POWERS WORK DIFFERENTLY ON EACH OTHER.
THEY USED TO NOT WORK ON US AT ALL, BUT I GUESS 'CUZ WE'VE GROWN APART...
WHERE'S THE SPIDER--?
OH!
NEVER MIND!

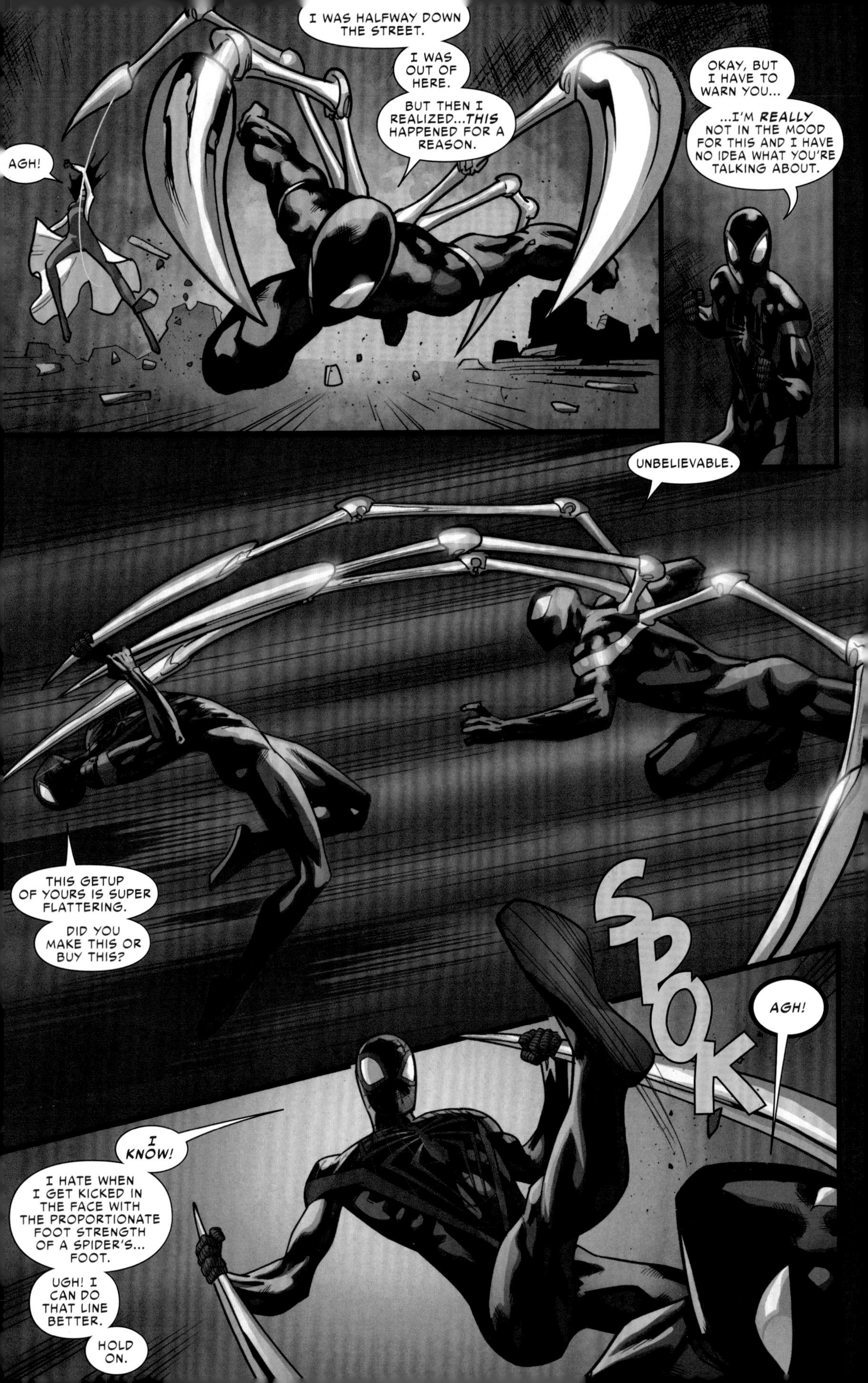
I WAS HALFWAY DOWN THE STREET.
AGH!
I WAS OUT OF HERE.
BUT THEN I REALIZED...*THIS* HAPPENED FOR A REASON.
OKAY, BUT I HAVE TO WARN YOU...
...I'M *REALLY* NOT IN THE MOOD FOR THIS AND I HAVE NO IDEA WHAT YOU'RE TALKING ABOUT.
UNBELIEVABLE.
THIS GETUP OF YOURS IS SUPER FLATTERING.
DID YOU MAKE THIS OR BUY THIS?
SPOK
AGH!
I KNOW!
I HATE WHEN I GET KICKED IN THE FACE WITH THE PROPORTIONATE FOOT STRENGTH OF A SPIDER'S... FOOT.
UGH! I CAN DO THAT LINE BETTER.
HOLD ON.

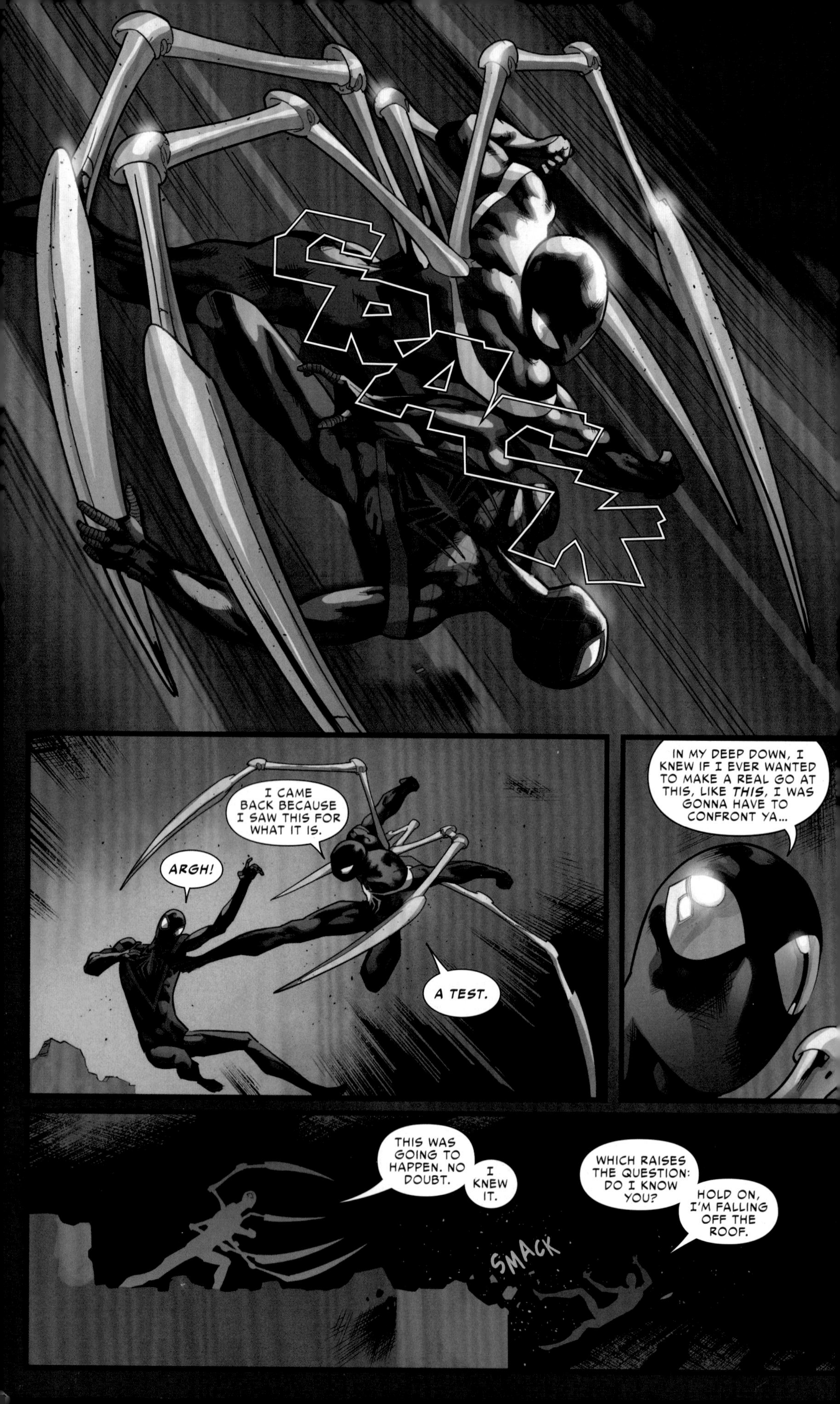
CRACK
I CAME BACK BECAUSE I SAW THIS FOR WHAT IT IS.
ARGH!
A TEST.
IN MY DEEP DOWN, I KNEW IF I EVER WANTED TO MAKE A REAL GO AT THIS, LIKE *THIS*, I WAS GONNA HAVE TO CONFRONT YA...
THIS WAS GOING TO HAPPEN. NO DOUBT.
I KNEW IT.
WHICH RAISES THE QUESTION: DO I KNOW YOU?
HOLD ON, I'M FALLING OFF THE ROOF.
SMACK

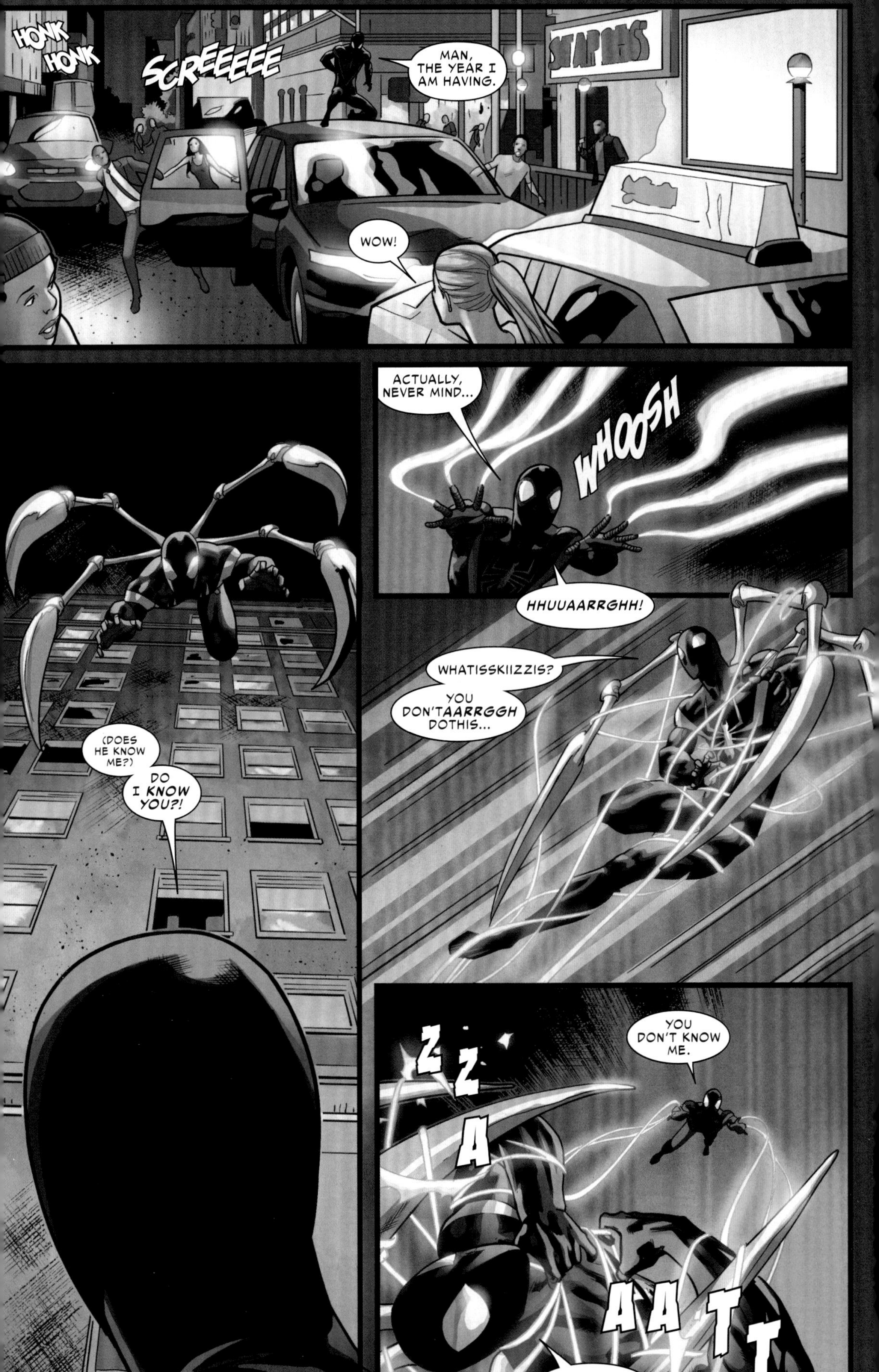
HONK HONK
SCREEEEEE
MAN, THE YEAR I AM HAVING.
WOW!
ACTUALLY, NEVER MIND...
WHOOSH
(DOES HE KNOW ME?)
DO I KNOW YOU?!
HHUUAARRGHH!
WHATISSKIIZZIS?
YOU DON'TAARRGGH DOTHIS...
ZZA
YOU DON'T KNOW ME.
AATT
YAAAGGHH!!!

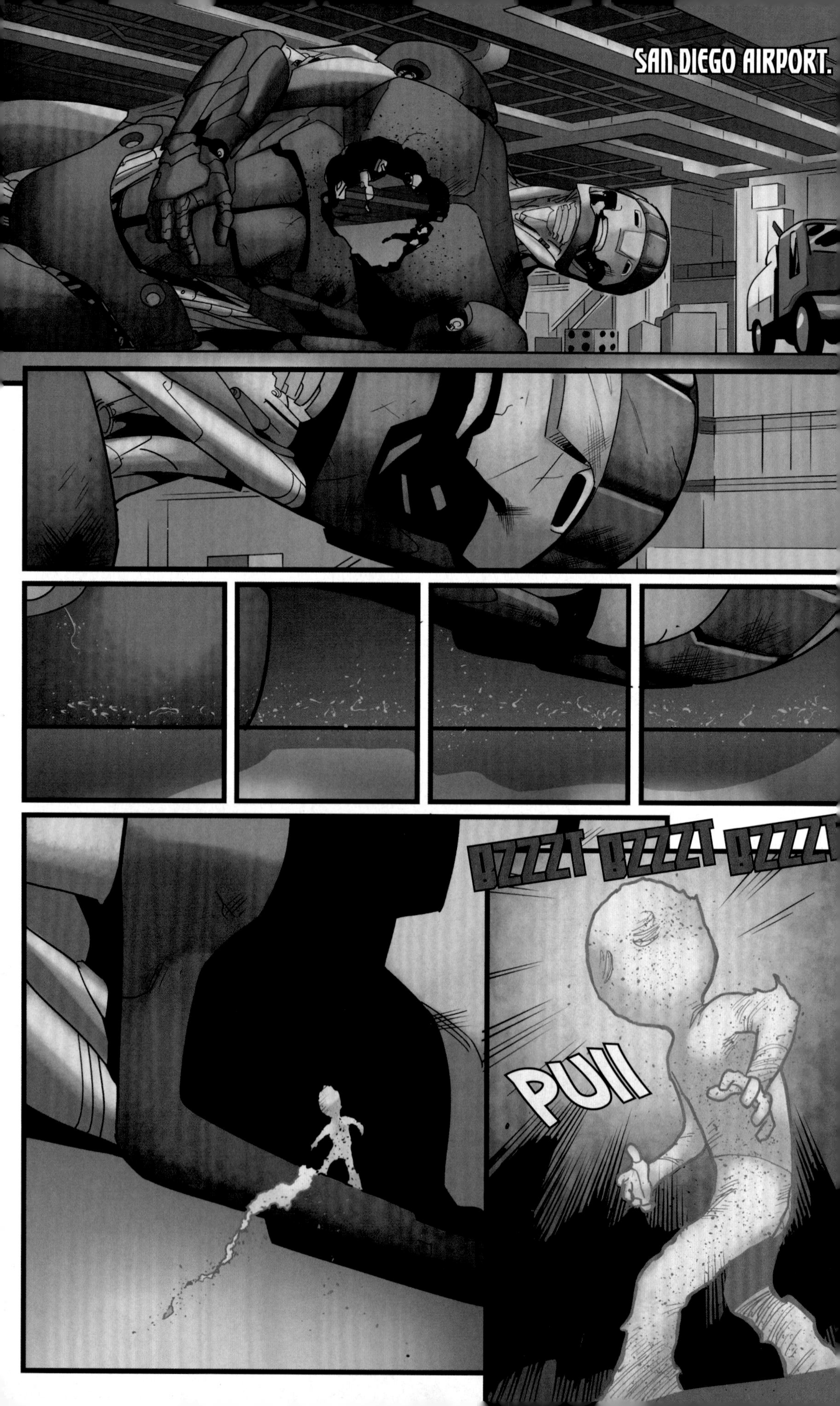
SAN DIEGO AIRPORT.
BZZZT BZZZT BZZZT
PUII

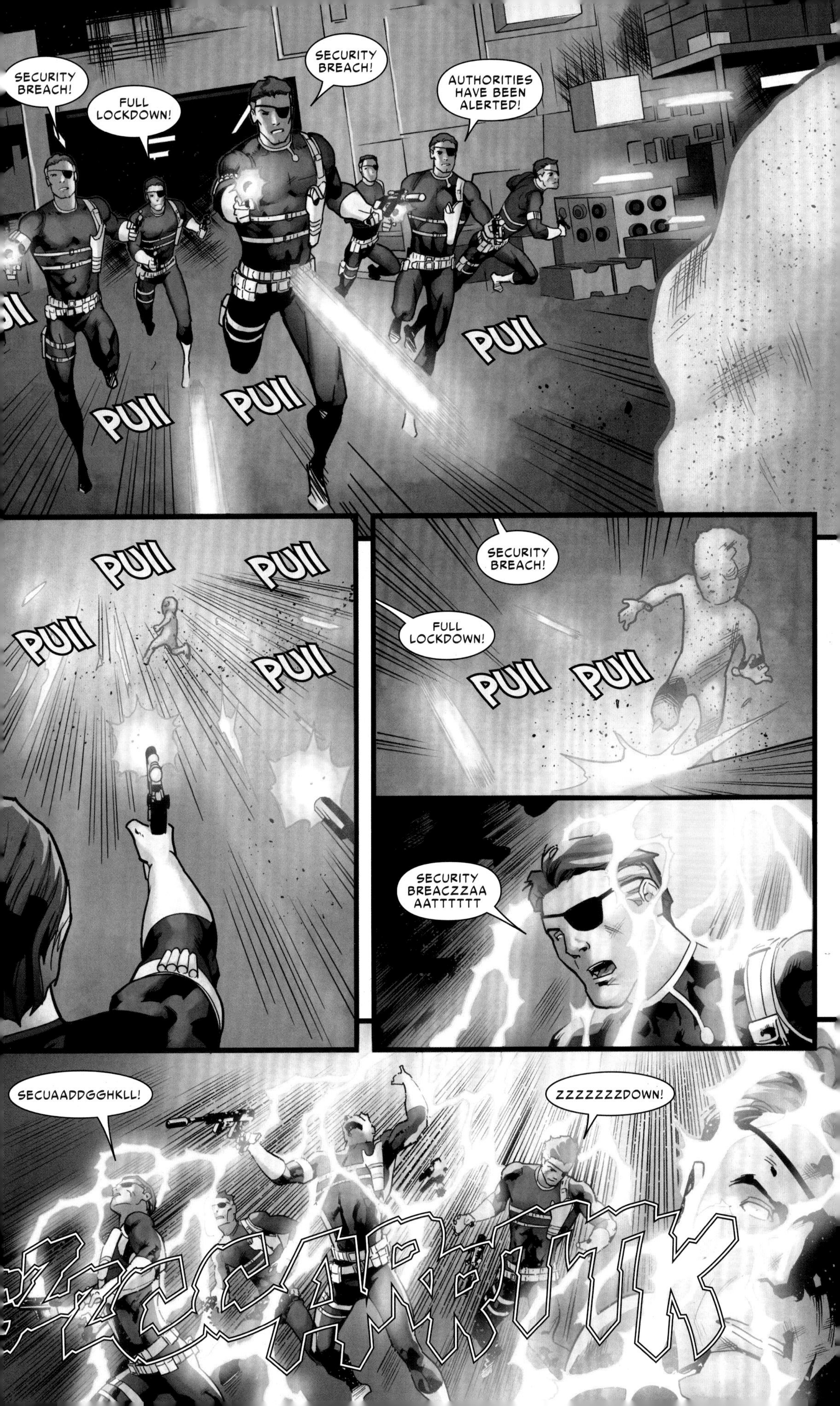
SECURITY BREACH!
FULL LOCKDOWN!
SECURITY BREACH!
AUTHORITIES HAVE BEEN ALERTED!
PUII
PUII
PUII
PUII
PUII
PUII
PUII
PUII
SECURITY BREACH!
FULL LOCKDOWN!
PUII
PUII
SECURITY BREACZZAA AATTTTTT
SECUAADDGGHKLL!
ZZZZZZZDOWN!

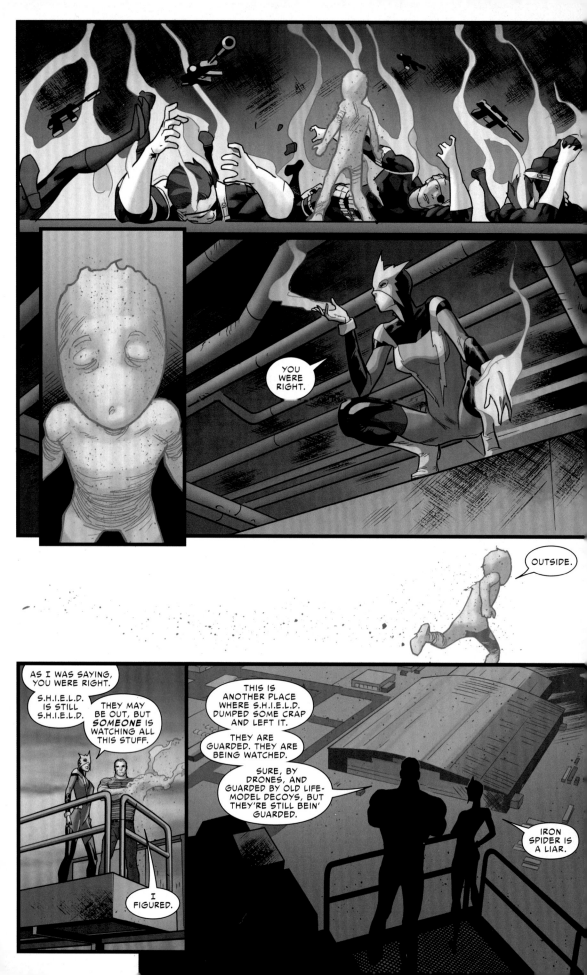

YOU WERE RIGHT.

OUTSIDE.

AS I WAS SAYING, YOU WERE RIGHT.

S.H.I.E.L.D. IS STILL S.H.I.E.L.D.

THEY MAY BE OUT, BUT *SOMEONE* IS WATCHING ALL THIS STUFF.

I FIGURED.

THIS IS ANOTHER PLACE WHERE S.H.I.E.L.D. DUMPED SOME CRAP AND LEFT IT.

THEY ARE GUARDED. THEY ARE BEING WATCHED.

SURE, BY DRONES, AND GUARDED BY OLD LIFE-MODEL DECOYS, BUT THEY'RE STILL BEIN' GUARDED.

IRON SPIDER IS A LIAR.

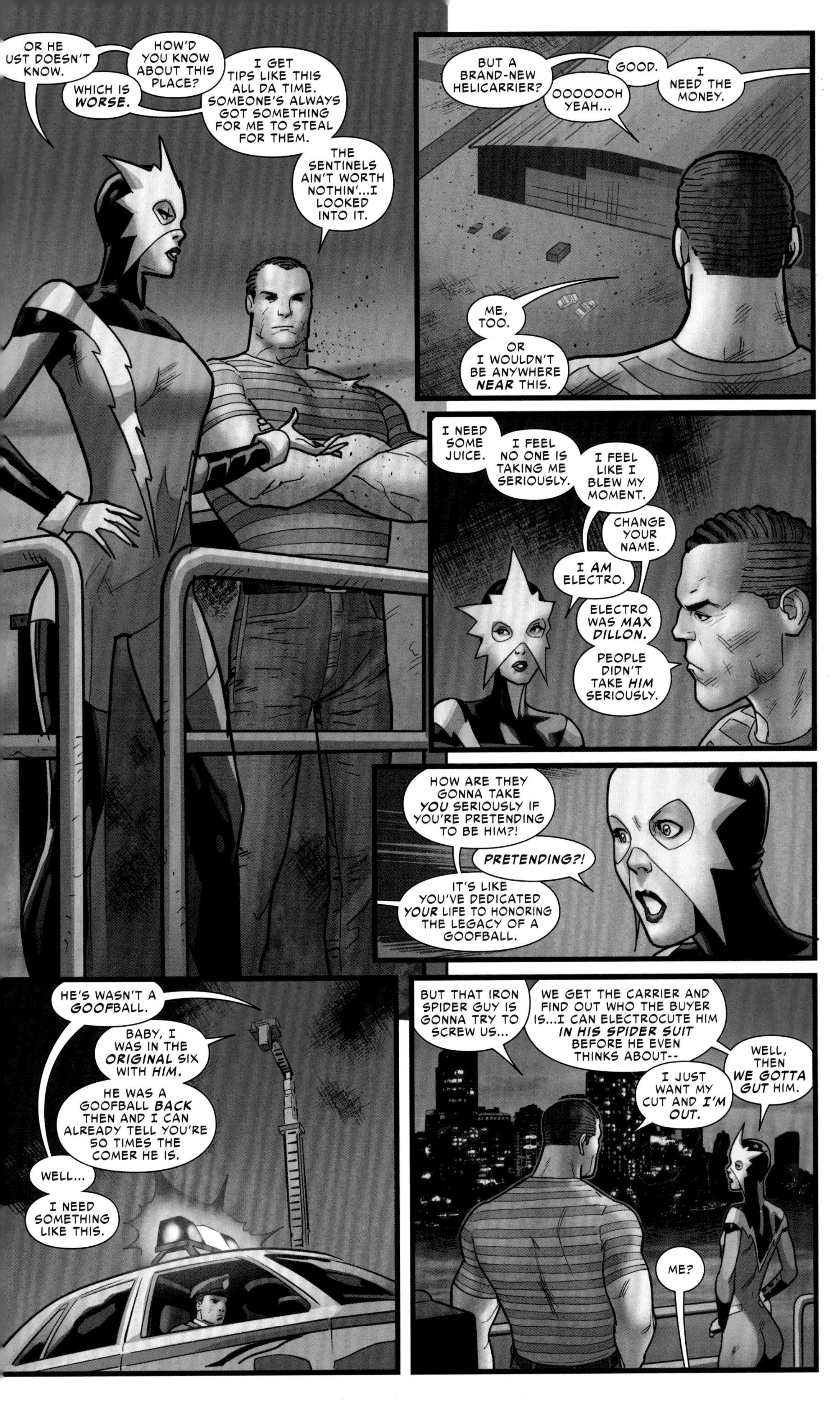
OR HE UST DOESN'T KNOW.
WHICH IS WORSE.
HOW'D YOU KNOW ABOUT THIS PLACE?
I GET TIPS LIKE THIS ALL DA TIME. SOMEONE'S ALWAYS GOT SOMETHING FOR ME TO STEAL FOR THEM.
THE SENTINELS AIN'T WORTH NOTHIN'...I LOOKED INTO IT.
BUT A BRAND-NEW HELICARRIER?
OOOOOOH YEAH...
GOOD.
I NEED THE MONEY.
ME, TOO.
OR I WOULDN'T BE ANYWHERE NEAR THIS.
I NEED SOME JUICE.
I FEEL NO ONE IS TAKING ME SERIOUSLY.
I FEEL LIKE I BLEW MY MOMENT.
CHANGE YOUR NAME.
I AM ELECTRO.
ELECTRO WAS MAX DILLON.
PEOPLE DIDN'T TAKE HIM SERIOUSLY.
HOW ARE THEY GONNA TAKE YOU SERIOUSLY IF YOU'RE PRETENDING TO BE HIM?!
PRETENDING?!
IT'S LIKE YOU'VE DEDICATED YOUR LIFE TO HONORING THE LEGACY OF A GOOFBALL.
HE'S WASN'T A GOOFBALL.
BABY, I WAS IN THE ORIGINAL SIX WITH HIM.
HE WAS A GOOFBALL BACK THEN AND I CAN ALREADY TELL YOU'RE 50 TIMES THE COMER HE IS.
WELL...
I NEED SOMETHING LIKE THIS.
BUT THAT IRON SPIDER GUY IS GONNA TRY TO SCREW US...
WE GET THE CARRIER AND FIND OUT WHO THE BUYER IS...I CAN ELECTROCUTE HIM IN HIS SPIDER SUIT BEFORE HE EVEN THINKS ABOUT--
I JUST WANT MY CUT AND I'M OUT.
WELL, THEN WE GOTTA GUT HIM.
ME?

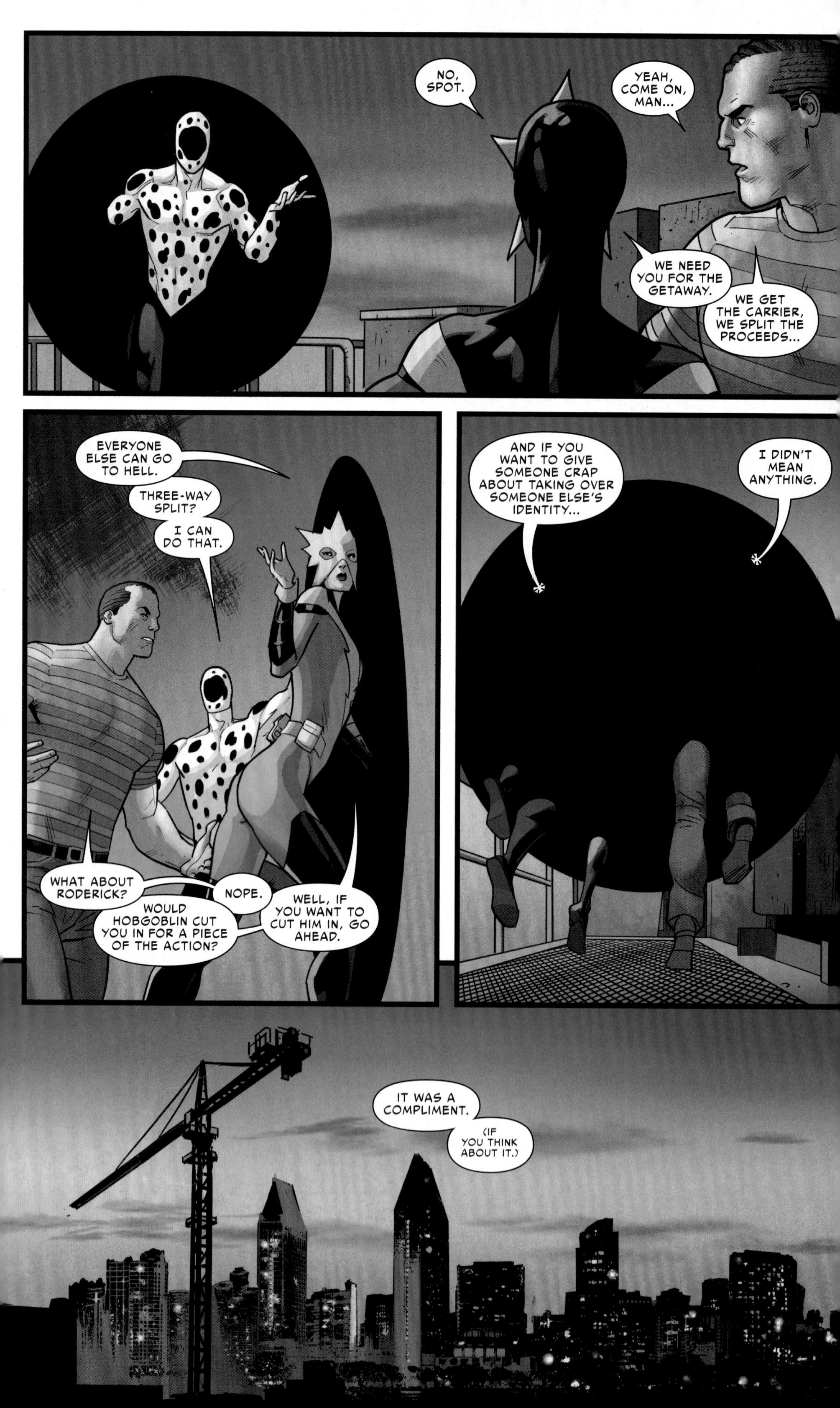
NO, SPOT.
YEAH, COME ON, MAN...
WE NEED YOU FOR THE GETAWAY.
WE GET THE CARRIER, WE SPLIT THE PROCEEDS...
EVERYONE ELSE CAN GO TO HELL.
THREE-WAY SPLIT?
I CAN DO THAT.
WHAT ABOUT RODERICK?
NOPE.
WOULD HOBGOBLIN CUT YOU IN FOR A PIECE OF THE ACTION?
WELL, IF YOU WANT TO CUT HIM IN, GO AHEAD.
AND IF YOU WANT TO GIVE SOMEONE CRAP ABOUT TAKING OVER SOMEONE ELSE'S IDENTITY...
I DIDN'T MEAN ANYTHING.
IT WAS A COMPLIMENT.
(IF YOU THINK ABOUT IT.)

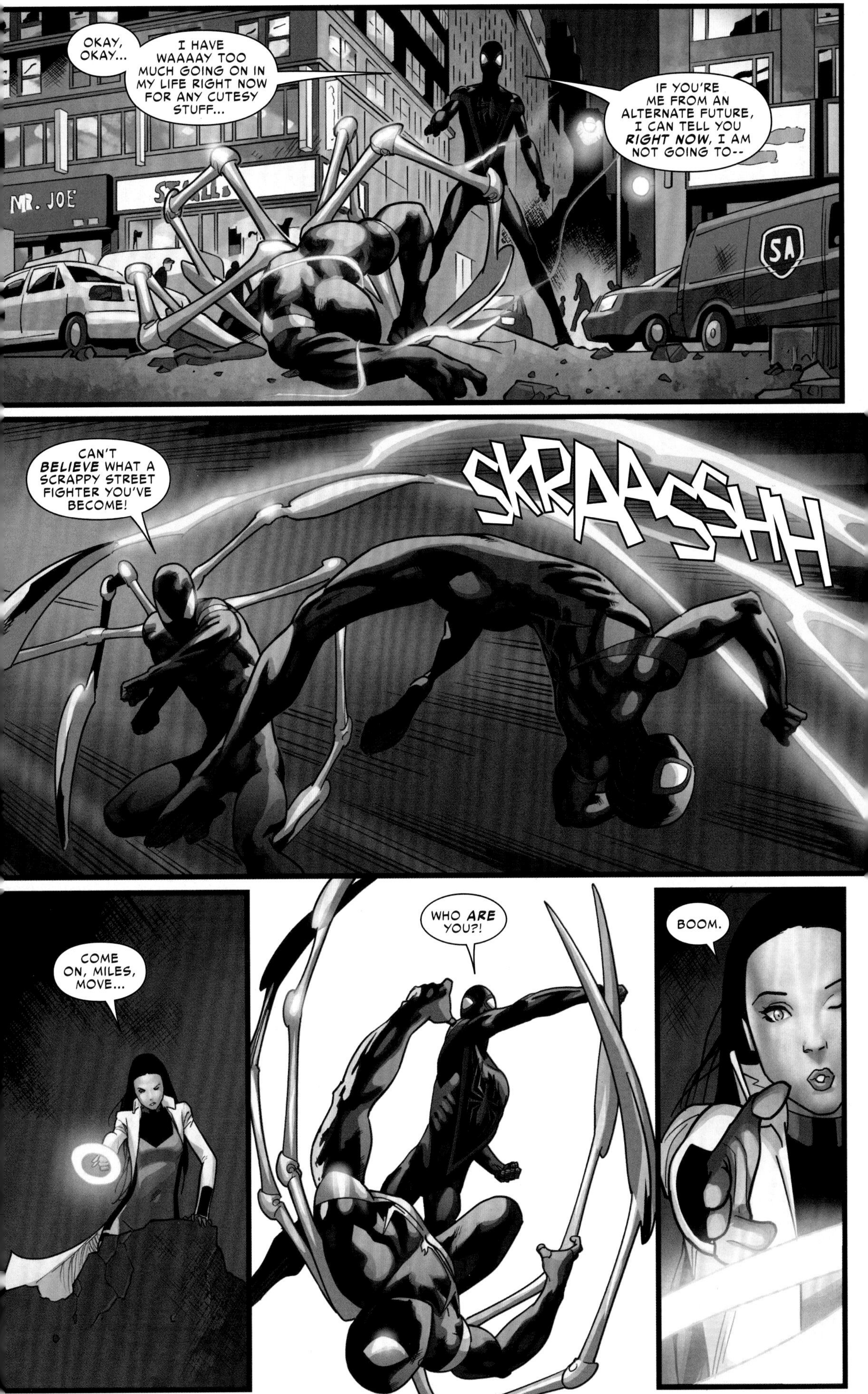
OKAY, OKAY...
I HAVE WAAAAY TOO MUCH GOING ON IN MY LIFE RIGHT NOW FOR ANY CUTESY STUFF...
IF YOU'RE ME FROM AN ALTERNATE FUTURE, I CAN TELL YOU RIGHT NOW, I AM NOT GOING TO--
MR. JOE
SA
CAN'T BELIEVE WHAT A SCRAPPY STREET FIGHTER YOU'VE BECOME!
SKRAASSHH
COME ON, MILES, MOVE...
WHO ARE YOU?!
BOOM.

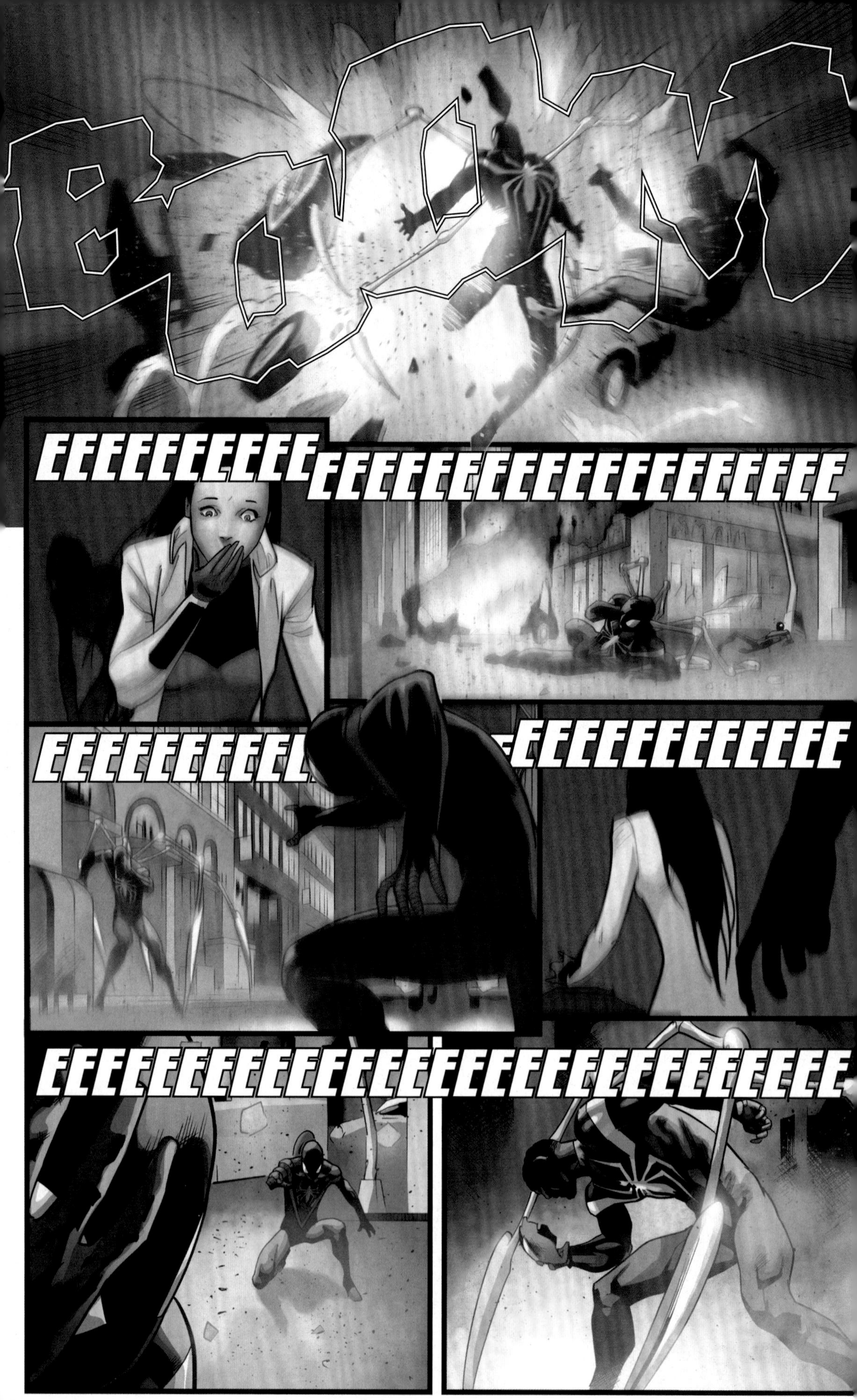
BOOM
EEEEEEEEEE
EEEEEEEEEEEEEEEEEEEE
EEEEEEEEEE
EEEEEEEEEEEE
EEEEEEEEEEEEEE
EEEEEEEEEEEEEEE

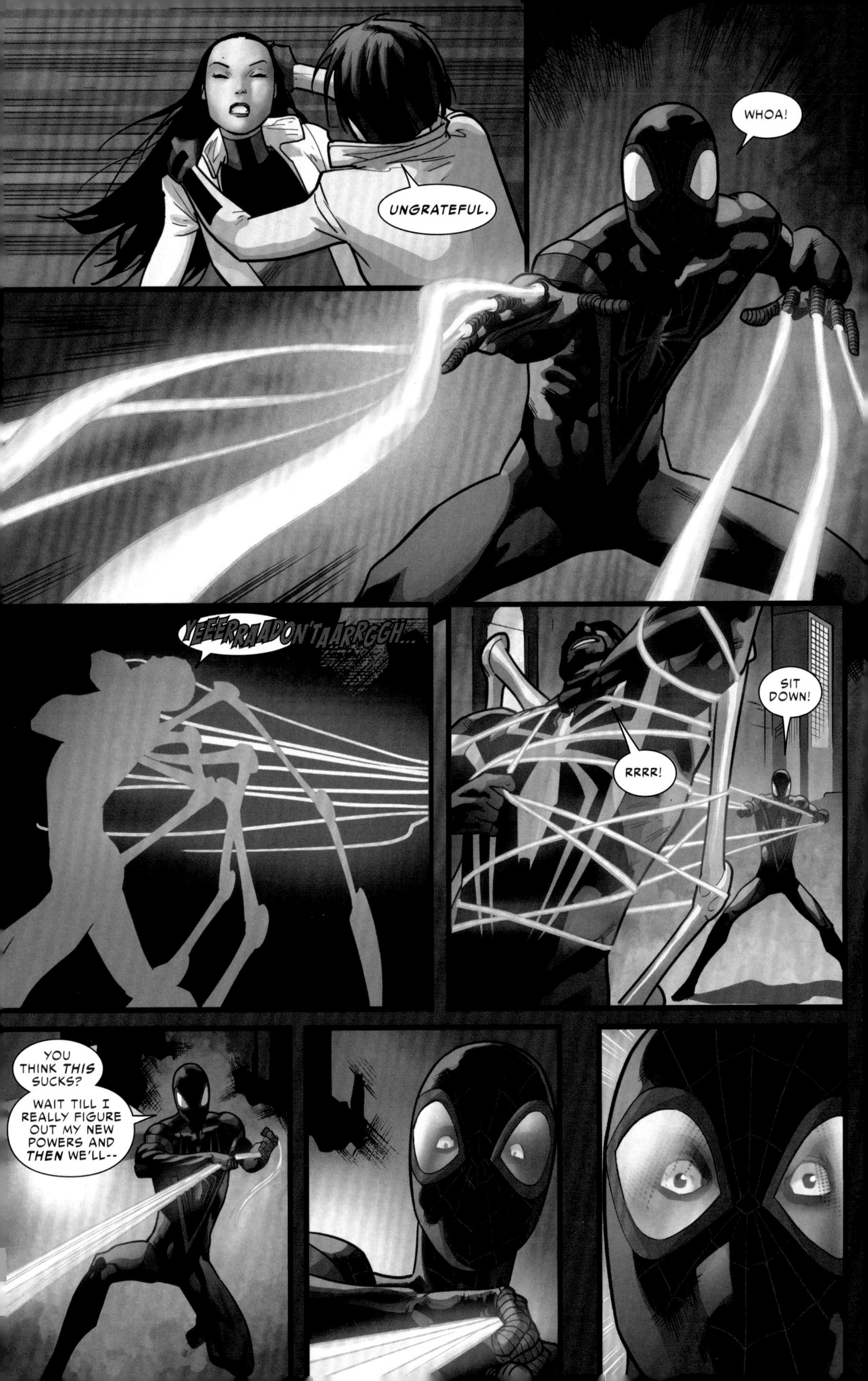
UNGRATEFUL.
WHOA!
YEEERRAADON'TAARRGGH...
SIT DOWN!
RRRR!
YOU THINK *THIS* SUCKS?
WAIT TILL I REALLY FIGURE OUT MY NEW POWERS AND *THEN* WE'LL--

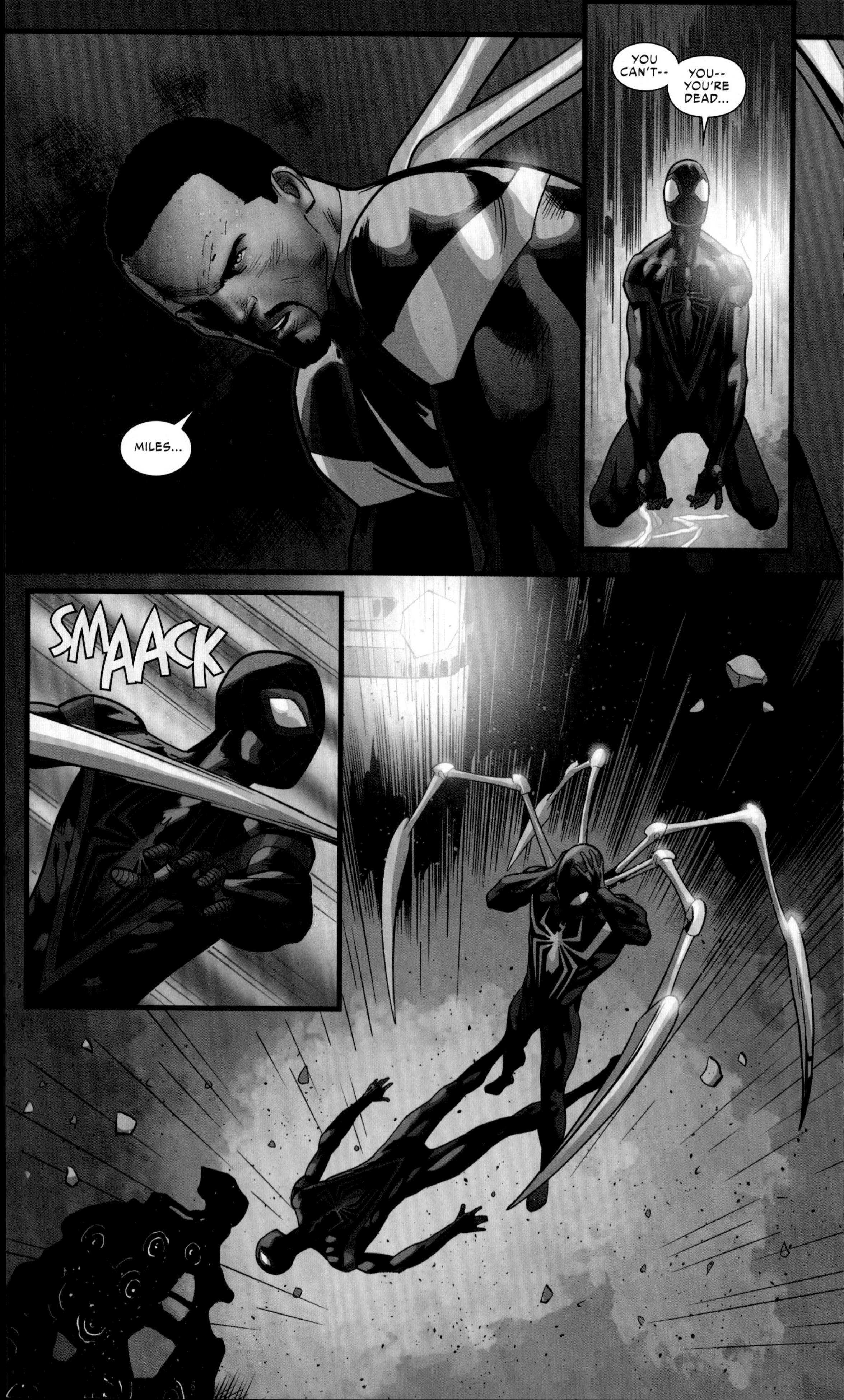
MILES...
YOU CAN'T--
YOU--
YOU'RE DEAD...
SMAACK

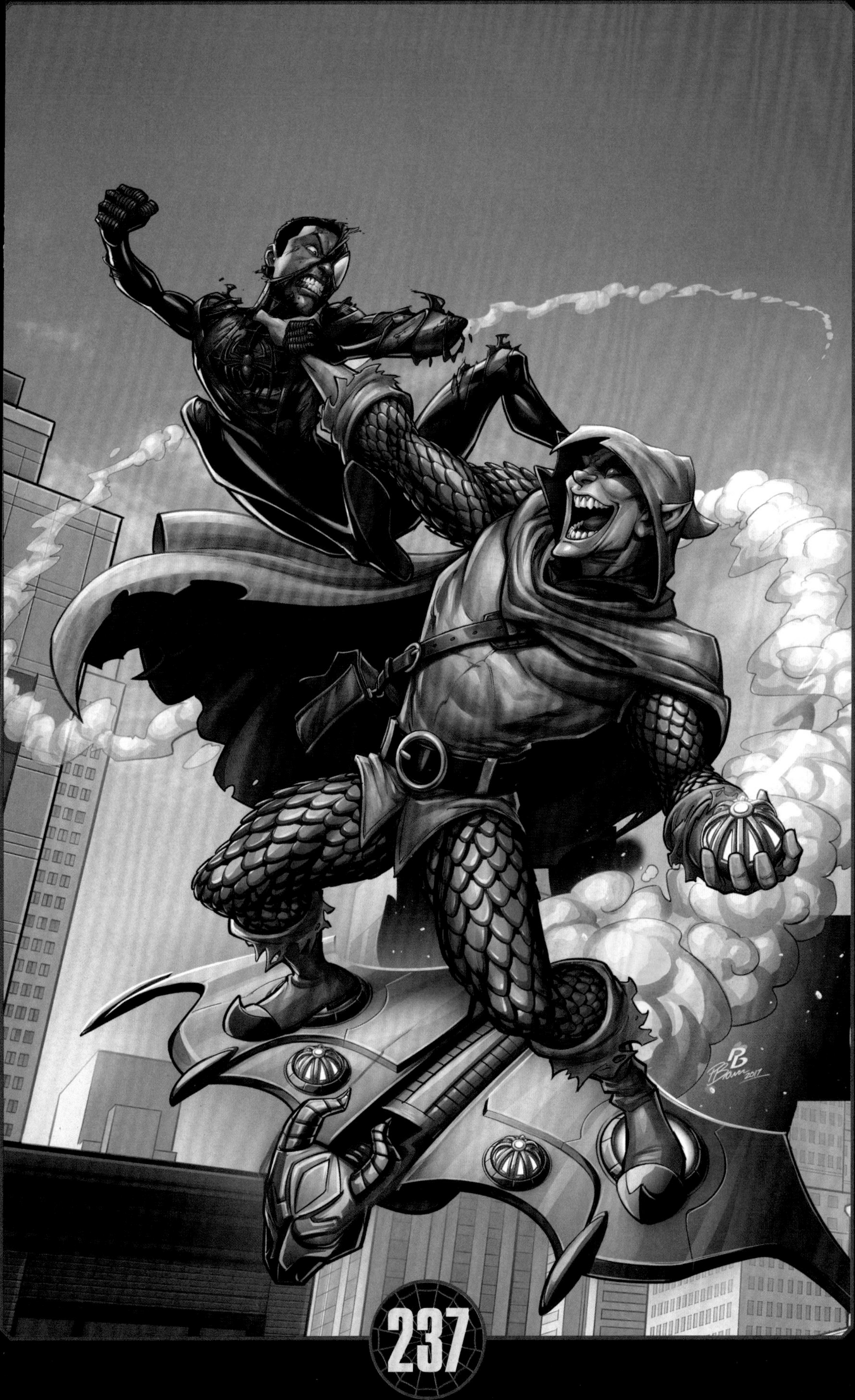
237

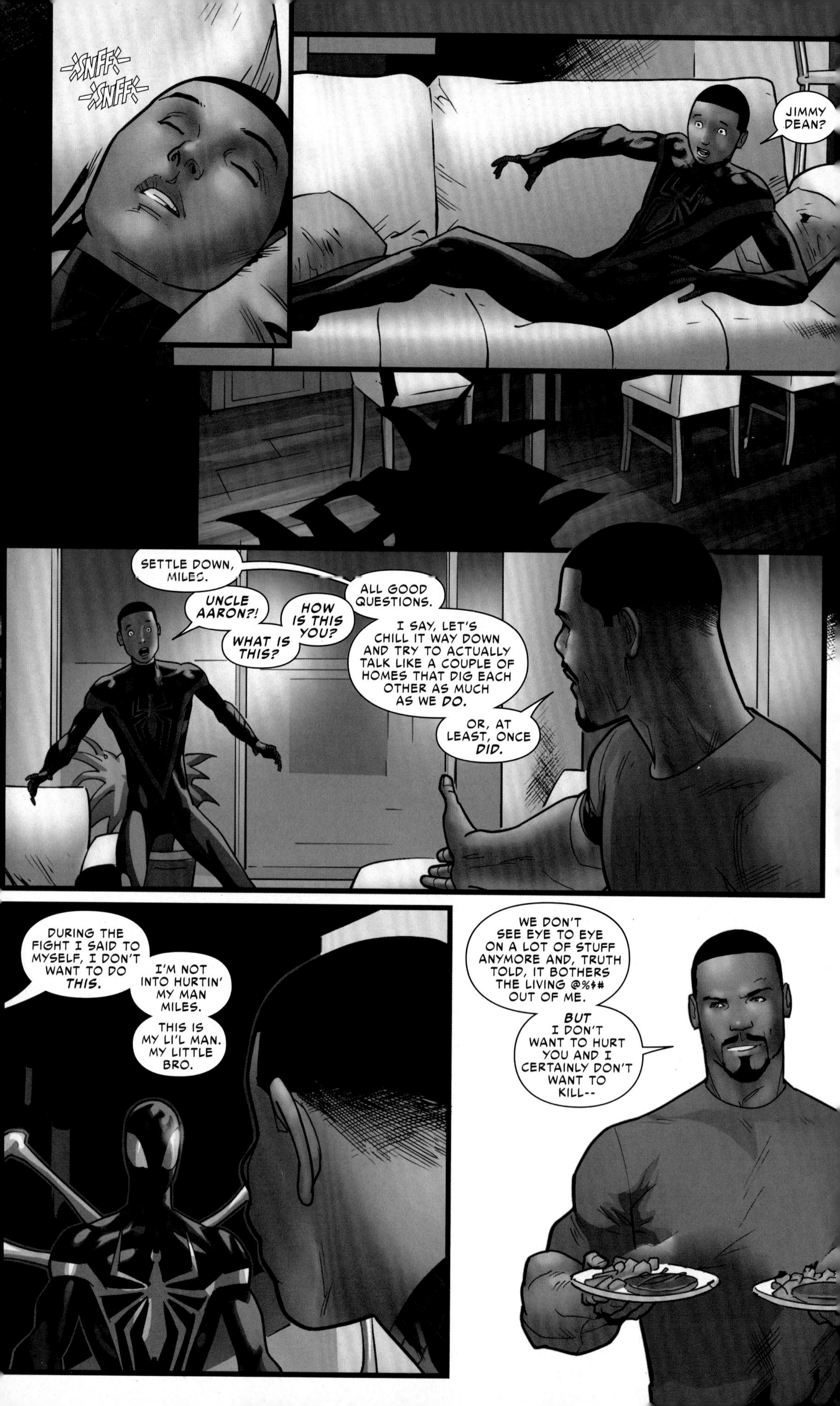

SNFF
SNFF
JIMMY DEAN?
SETTLE DOWN, MILES.
UNCLE AARON?!
WHAT IS THIS?
HOW IS THIS YOU?
ALL GOOD QUESTIONS.
I SAY, LET'S CHILL IT WAY DOWN AND TRY TO ACTUALLY TALK LIKE A COUPLE OF HOMES THAT DIG EACH OTHER AS MUCH AS WE DO.
OR, AT LEAST, ONCE DID.
DURING THE FIGHT I SAID TO MYSELF, I DON'T WANT TO DO THIS.
I'M NOT INTO HURTIN' MY MAN MILES.
THIS IS MY LI'L MAN. MY LITTLE BRO.
WE DON'T SEE EYE TO EYE ON A LOT OF STUFF ANYMORE AND, TRUTH TOLD, IT BOTHERS THE LIVING @%$# OUT OF ME.
BUT I DON'T WANT TO HURT YOU AND I CERTAINLY DON'T WANT TO KILL--

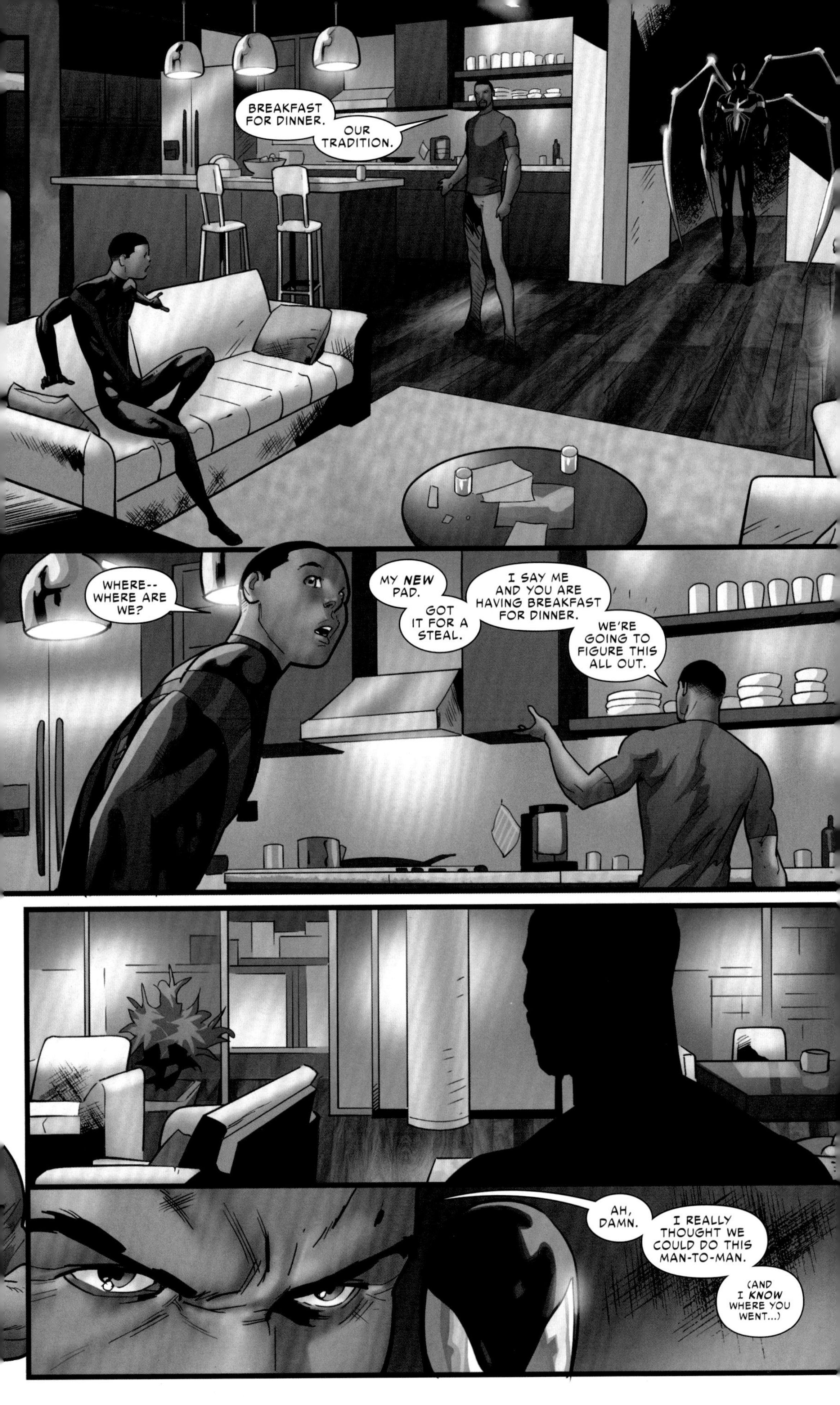
BREAKFAST FOR DINNER.
OUR TRADITION.
WHERE-- WHERE ARE WE?
MY **NEW** PAD.
GOT IT FOR A STEAL.
I SAY ME AND YOU ARE HAVING BREAKFAST FOR DINNER.
WE'RE GOING TO FIGURE THIS ALL OUT.
AH, DAMN.
I REALLY THOUGHT WE COULD DO THIS MAN-TO-MAN.
(AND I **KNOW** WHERE YOU WENT...)

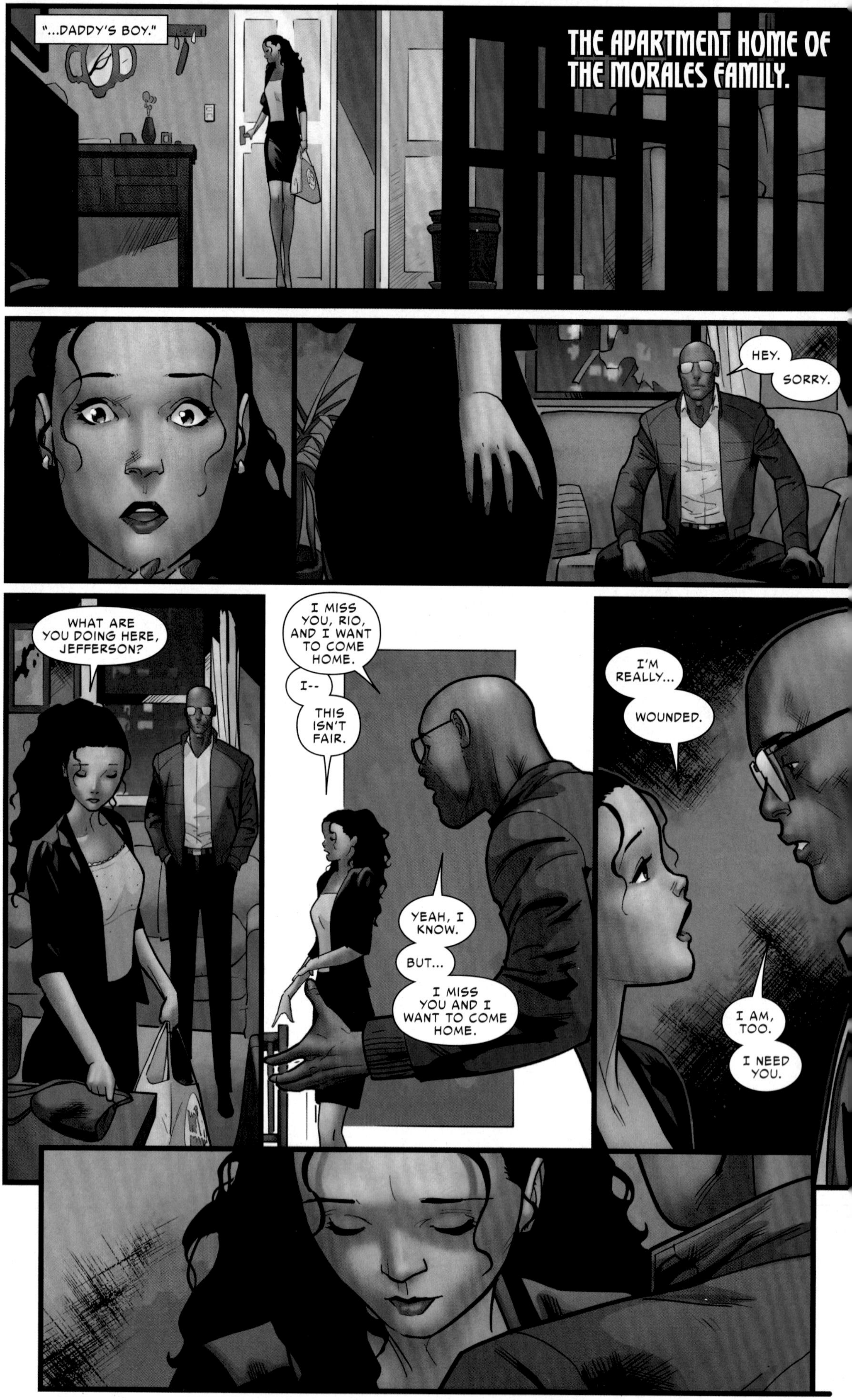

"...DADDY'S BOY."
THE APARTMENT HOME OF THE MORALES FAMILY.
HEY.
SORRY.
WHAT ARE YOU DOING HERE, JEFFERSON?
I MISS YOU, RIO, AND I WANT TO COME HOME.
I--
THIS ISN'T FAIR.
YEAH, I KNOW.
BUT...
I MISS YOU AND I WANT TO COME HOME.
I'M REALLY...
WOUNDED.
I AM, TOO.
I NEED YOU.

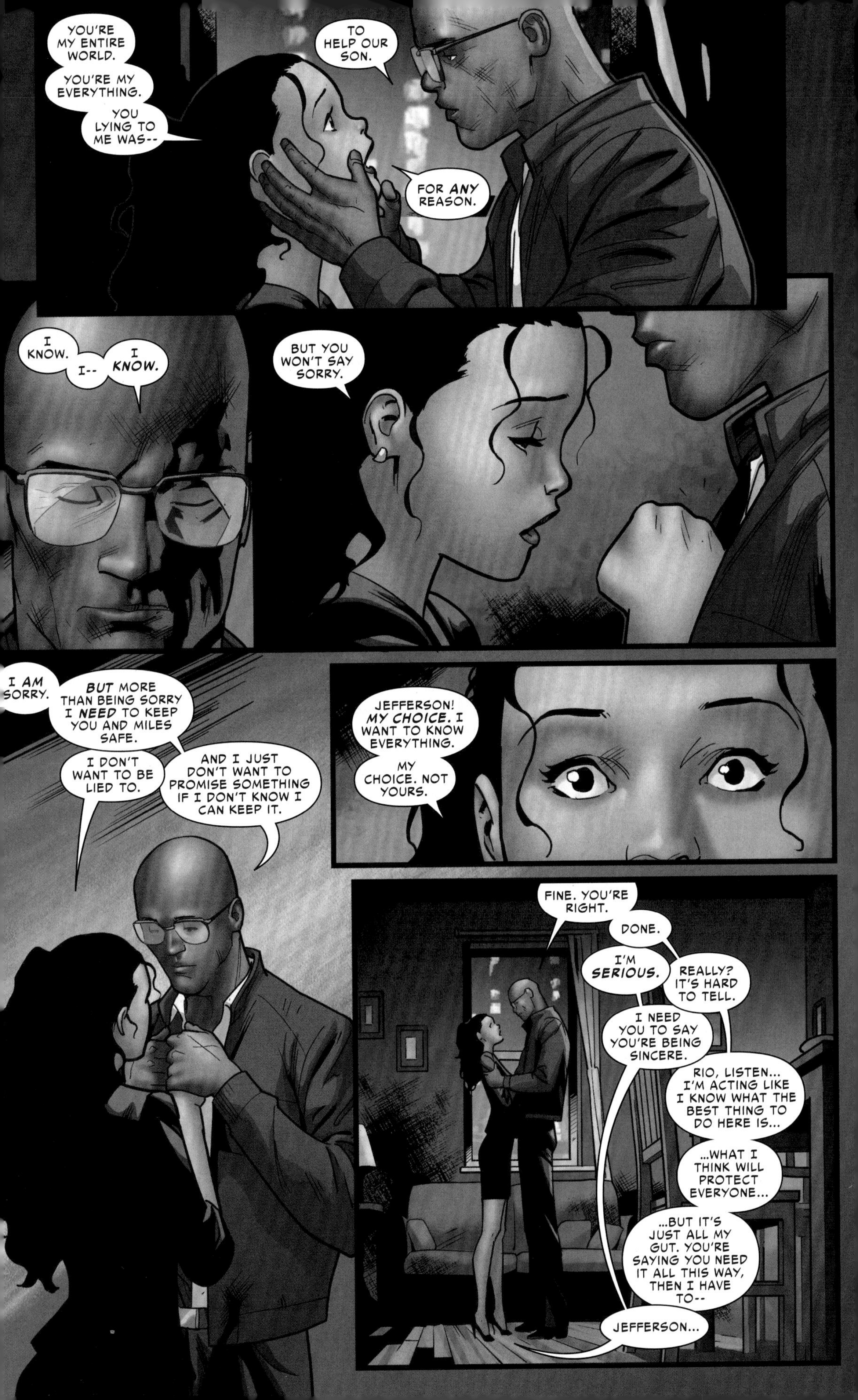
YOU'RE MY ENTIRE WORLD.
YOU'RE MY EVERYTHING.
YOU LYING TO ME WAS--
TO HELP OUR SON.
FOR ANY REASON.
I KNOW.
I--
I KNOW.
BUT YOU WON'T SAY SORRY.
I AM SORRY.
BUT MORE THAN BEING SORRY I NEED TO KEEP YOU AND MILES SAFE.
I DON'T WANT TO BE LIED TO.
AND I JUST DON'T WANT TO PROMISE SOMETHING IF I DON'T KNOW I CAN KEEP IT.
JEFFERSON! MY CHOICE. I WANT TO KNOW EVERYTHING.
MY CHOICE. NOT YOURS.
FINE. YOU'RE RIGHT.
DONE.
I'M SERIOUS.
REALLY? IT'S HARD TO TELL.
I NEED YOU TO SAY YOU'RE BEING SINCERE.
RIO, LISTEN... I'M ACTING LIKE I KNOW WHAT THE BEST THING TO DO HERE IS...
...WHAT I THINK WILL PROTECT EVERYONE...
...BUT IT'S JUST ALL MY GUT. YOU'RE SAYING YOU NEED IT ALL THIS WAY, THEN I HAVE TO--
JEFFERSON...

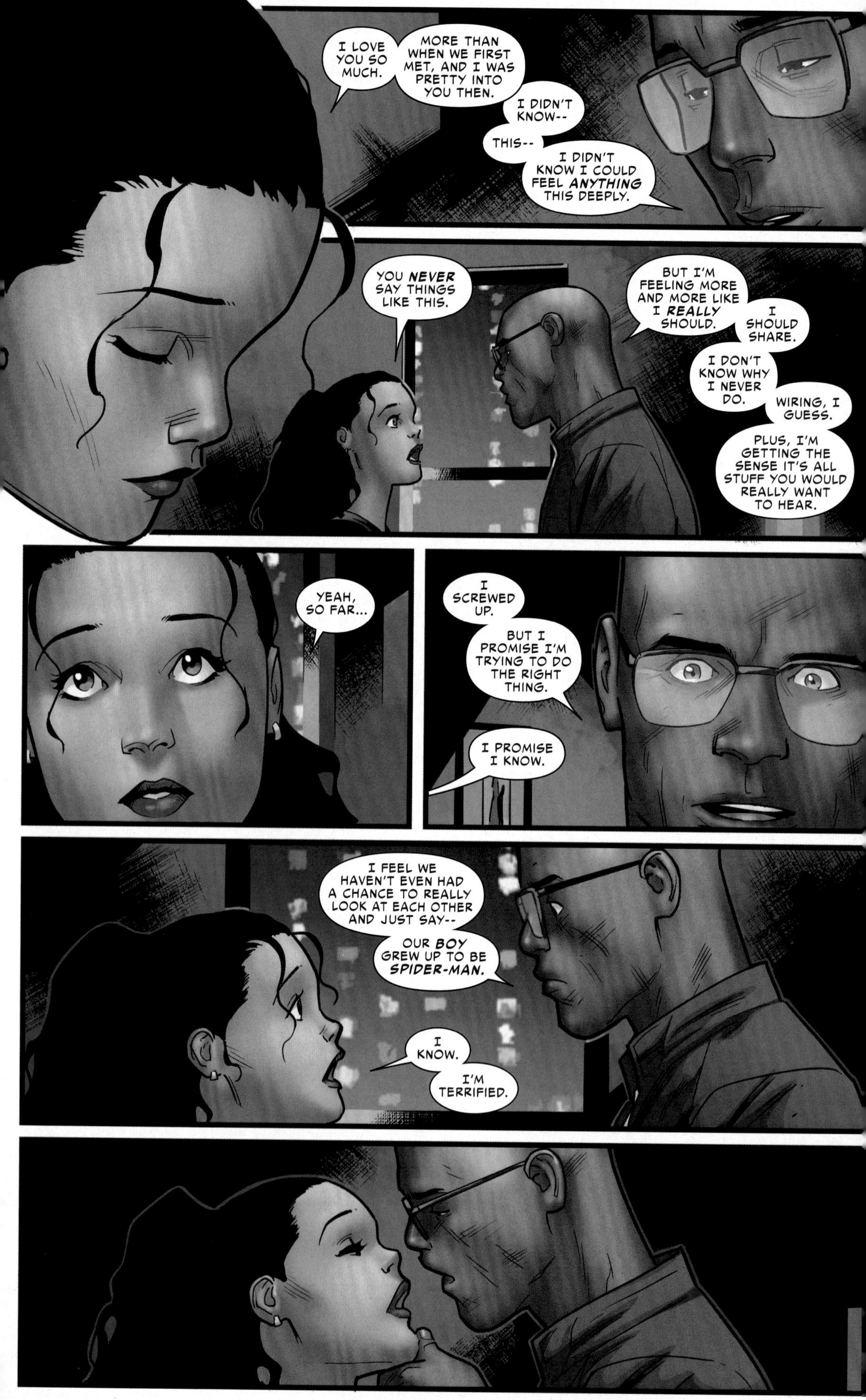

I LOVE YOU SO MUCH.
MORE THAN WHEN WE FIRST MET, AND I WAS PRETTY INTO YOU THEN.
I DIDN'T KNOW--
THIS--
I DIDN'T KNOW I COULD FEEL *ANYTHING* THIS DEEPLY.
YOU *NEVER* SAY THINGS LIKE THIS.
BUT I'M FEELING MORE AND MORE LIKE I *REALLY* SHOULD.
I SHOULD SHARE.
I DON'T KNOW WHY I NEVER DO.
WIRING, I GUESS.
PLUS, I'M GETTING THE SENSE IT'S ALL STUFF YOU WOULD REALLY WANT TO HEAR.
YEAH, SO FAR...
I SCREWED UP.
BUT I PROMISE I'M TRYING TO DO THE RIGHT THING.
I PROMISE I KNOW.
I FEEL WE HAVEN'T EVEN HAD A CHANCE TO REALLY LOOK AT EACH OTHER AND JUST SAY--
OUR *BOY* GREW UP TO BE *SPIDER-MAN.*
I KNOW.
I'M TERRIFIED.

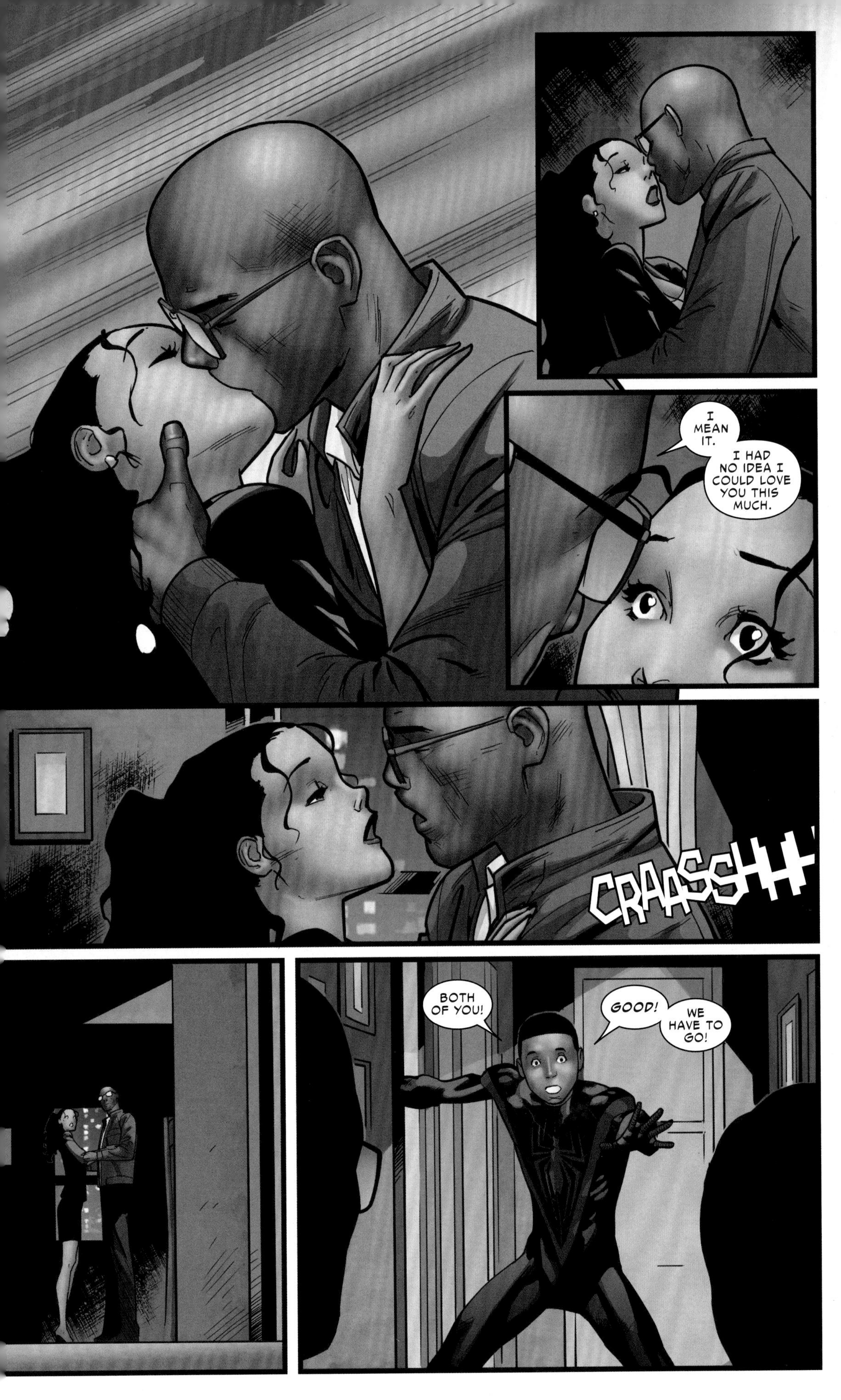

I MEAN IT.
I HAD NO IDEA I COULD LOVE YOU THIS MUCH.
CRAASSHH
BOTH OF YOU!
GOOD!
WE HAVE TO GO!

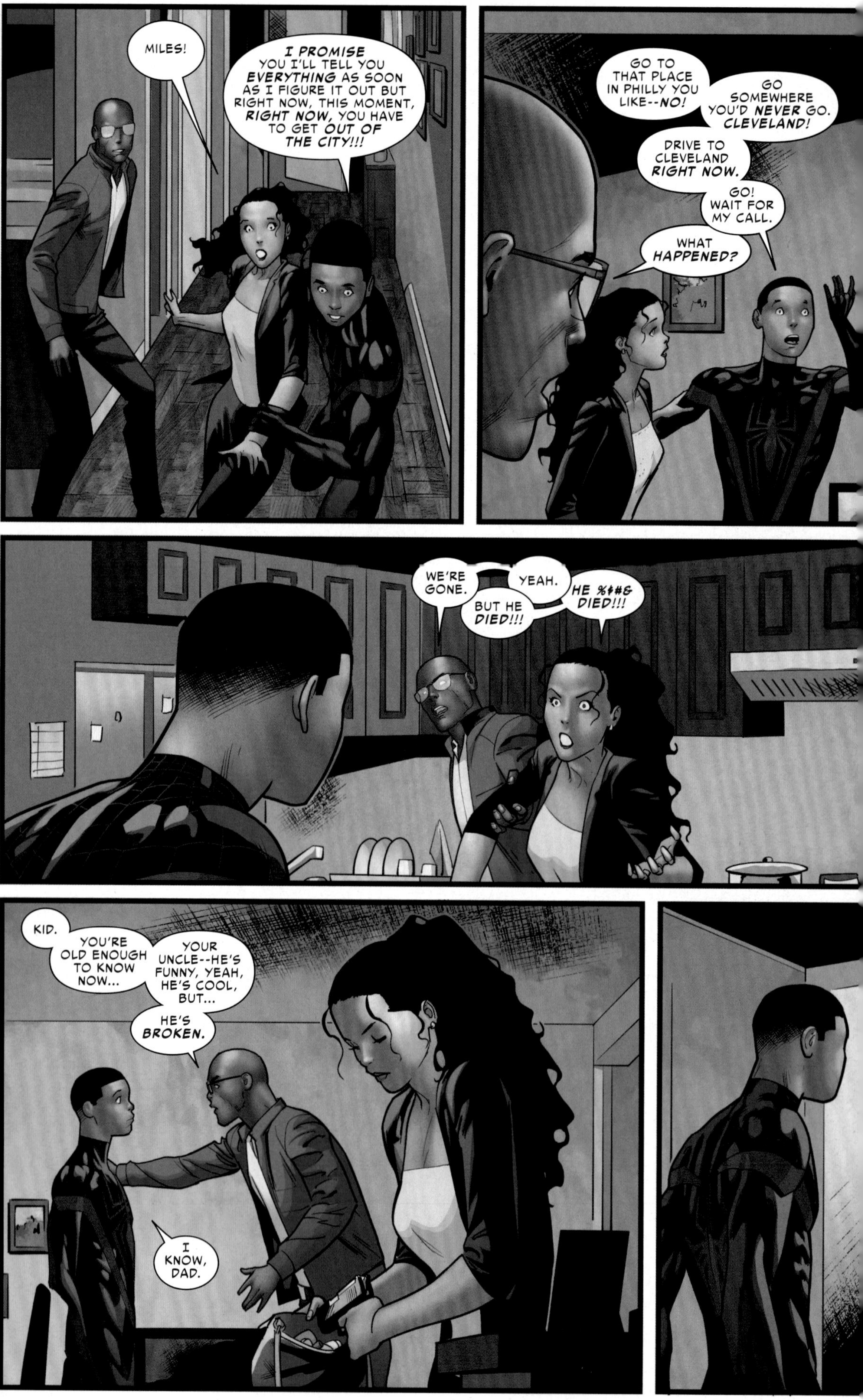

MILES!
I PROMISE YOU I'LL TELL YOU EVERYTHING AS SOON AS I FIGURE IT OUT BUT RIGHT NOW, THIS MOMENT, RIGHT NOW, YOU HAVE TO GET OUT OF THE CITY!!!
GO TO THAT PLACE IN PHILLY YOU LIKE--NO!
GO SOMEWHERE YOU'D NEVER GO. CLEVELAND!
DRIVE TO CLEVELAND RIGHT NOW.
GO! WAIT FOR MY CALL.
WHAT HAPPENED?
WE'RE GONE.
YEAH.
BUT HE DIED!!!
HE %$#& DIED!!!
KID.
YOU'RE OLD ENOUGH TO KNOW NOW...
YOUR UNCLE--HE'S FUNNY, YEAH, HE'S COOL, BUT...
HE'S BROKEN.
I KNOW, DAD.

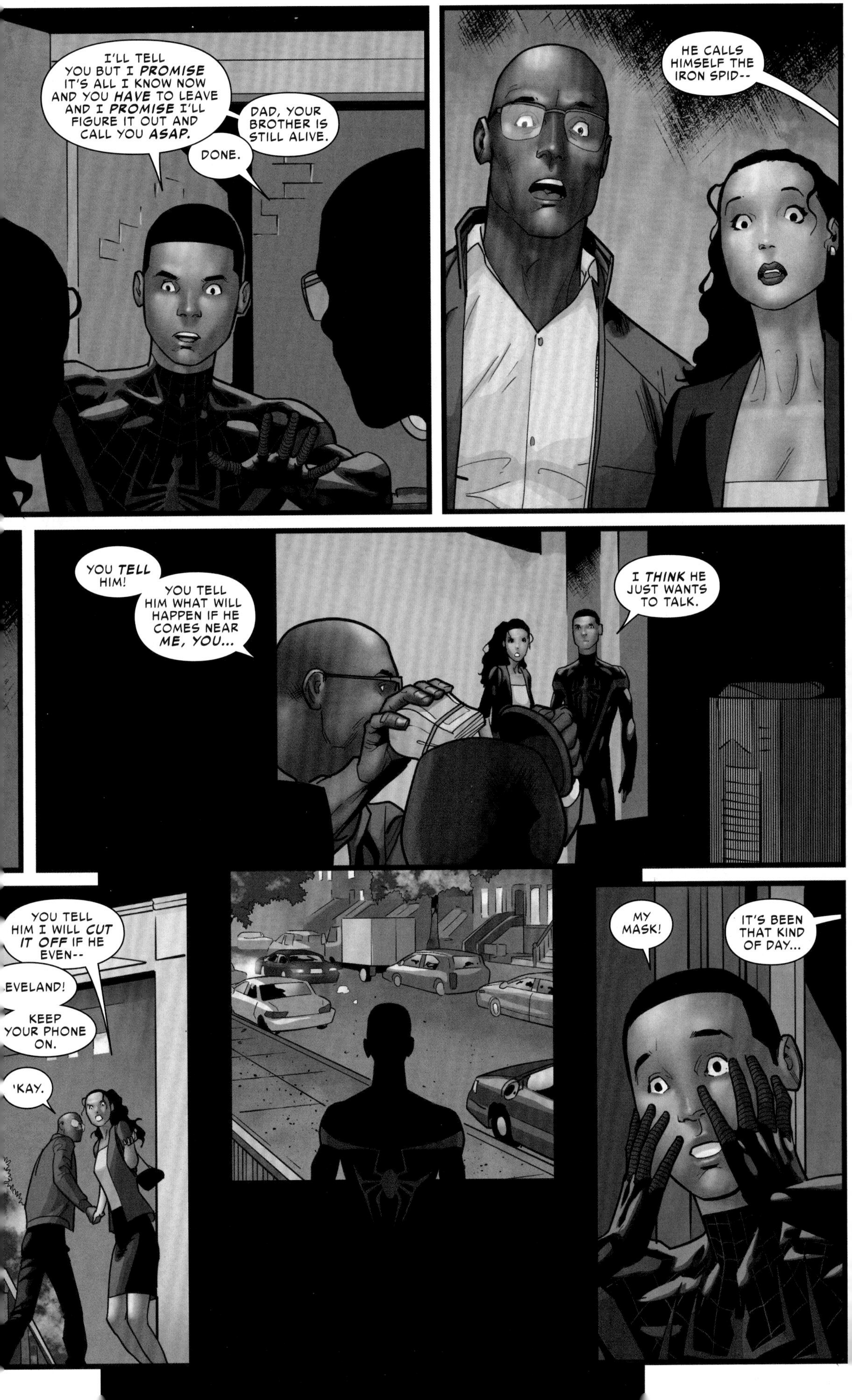
I'LL TELL YOU BUT I PROMISE IT'S ALL I KNOW NOW AND YOU HAVE TO LEAVE AND I PROMISE I'LL FIGURE IT OUT AND CALL YOU ASAP.
DONE.
DAD, YOUR BROTHER IS STILL ALIVE.
HE CALLS HIMSELF THE IRON SPID--
YOU TELL HIM!
YOU TELL HIM WHAT WILL HAPPEN IF HE COMES NEAR ME, YOU...
I THINK HE JUST WANTS TO TALK.
YOU TELL HIM I WILL CUT IT OFF IF HE EVEN--
EVELAND!
KEEP YOUR PHONE ON.
'KAY.
MY MASK!
IT'S BEEN THAT KIND OF DAY...

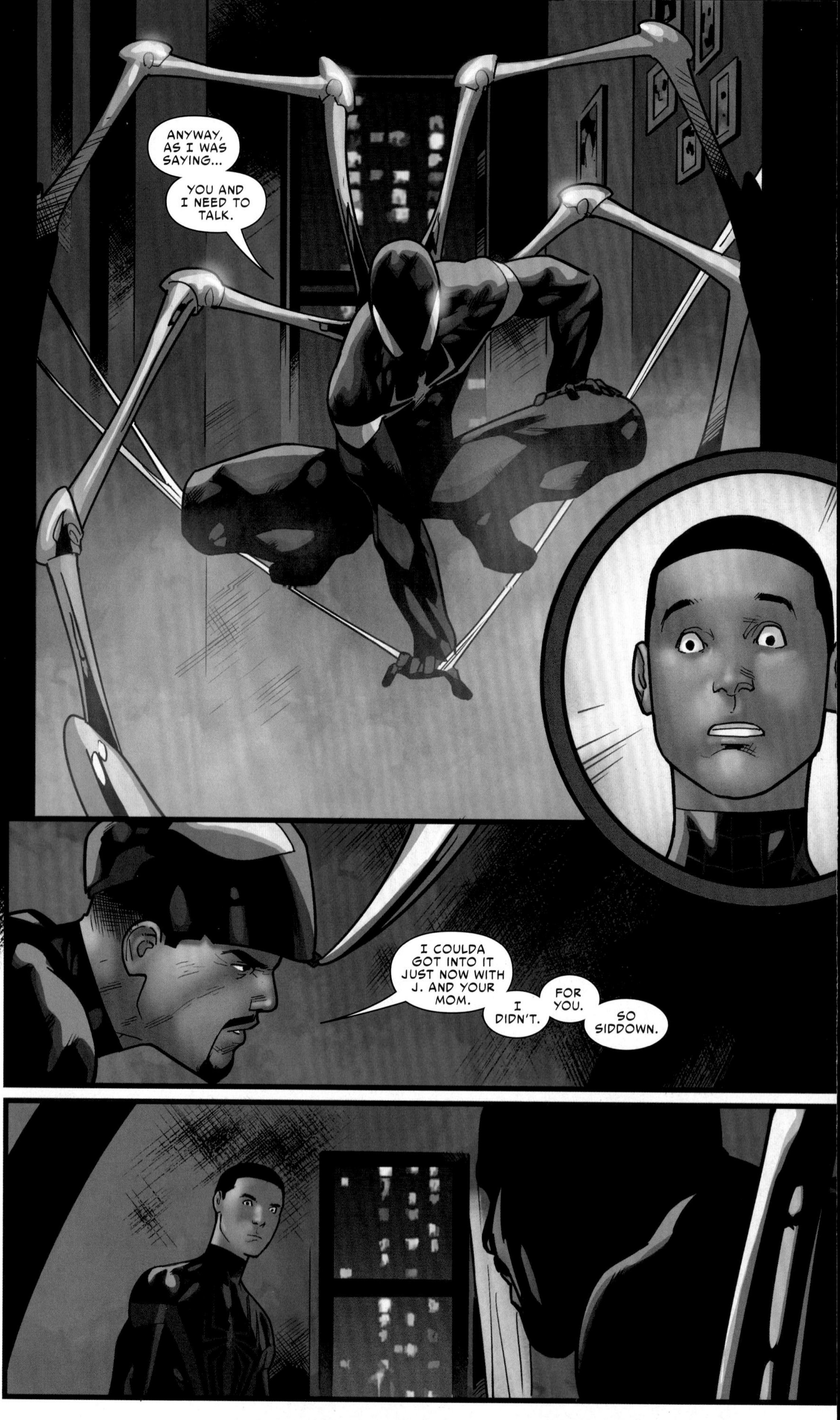

ANYWAY, AS I WAS SAYING...
YOU AND I NEED TO TALK.
I COULDA GOT INTO IT JUST NOW WITH J. AND YOUR MOM.
I DIDN'T.
FOR YOU.
SO SIDDOWN.

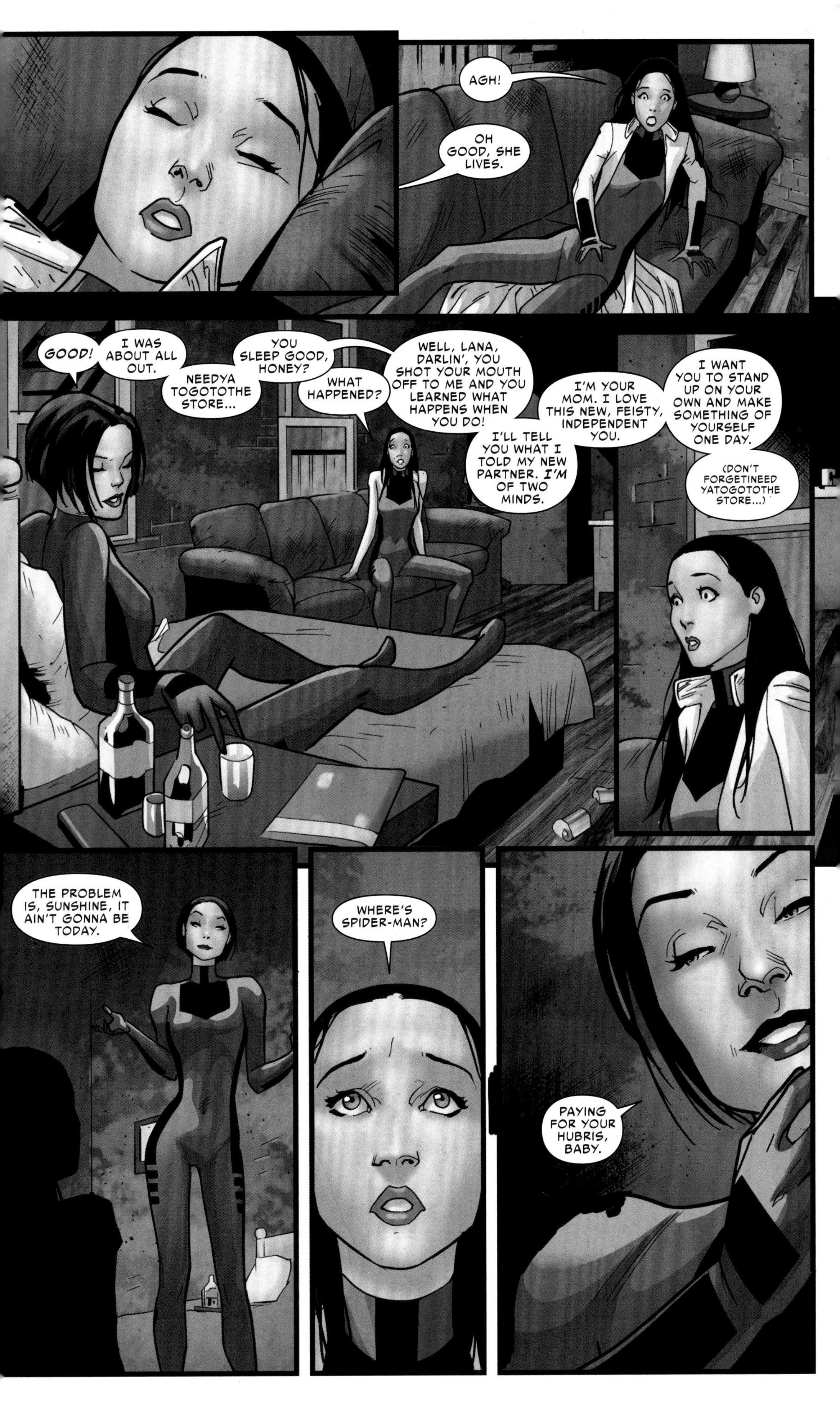
AGH!
OH GOOD, SHE LIVES.
GOOD!
I WAS ABOUT ALL OUT.
YOU SLEEP GOOD, HONEY?
NEEDYA TOGOTOTHE STORE...
WHAT HAPPENED?
WELL, LANA, DARLIN', YOU SHOT YOUR MOUTH OFF TO ME AND YOU LEARNED WHAT HAPPENS WHEN YOU DO!
I'LL TELL YOU WHAT I TOLD MY NEW PARTNER. I'M OF TWO MINDS.
I'M YOUR MOM. I LOVE THIS NEW, FEISTY, INDEPENDENT YOU.
I WANT YOU TO STAND UP ON YOUR OWN AND MAKE SOMETHING OF YOURSELF ONE DAY.
(DON'T FORGETINEED YATOGOTOTHE STORE...)
THE PROBLEM IS, SUNSHINE, IT AIN'T GONNA BE TODAY.
WHERE'S SPIDER-MAN?
PAYING FOR YOUR HUBRIS, BABY.

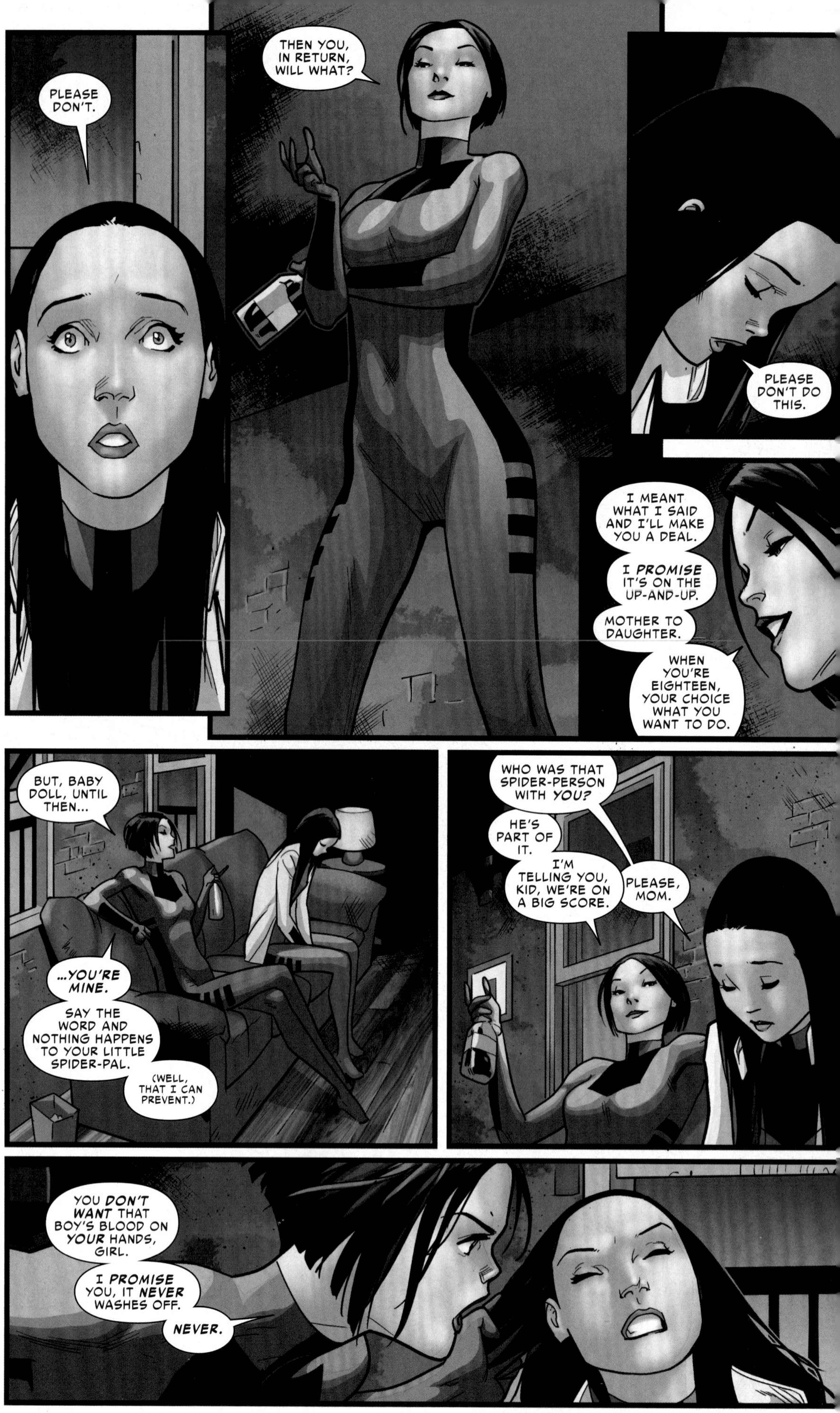

PLEASE DON'T.
THEN YOU, IN RETURN, WILL WHAT?
PLEASE DON'T DO THIS.
I MEANT WHAT I SAID AND I'LL MAKE YOU A DEAL.
I PROMISE IT'S ON THE UP-AND-UP.
MOTHER TO DAUGHTER.
WHEN YOU'RE EIGHTEEN, YOUR CHOICE WHAT YOU WANT TO DO.
BUT, BABY DOLL, UNTIL THEN...
...YOU'RE MINE.
SAY THE WORD AND NOTHING HAPPENS TO YOUR LITTLE SPIDER-PAL.
(WELL, THAT I CAN PREVENT.)
WHO WAS THAT SPIDER-PERSON WITH YOU?
HE'S PART OF IT.
I'M TELLING YOU, KID, WE'RE ON A BIG SCORE.
PLEASE, MOM.
YOU DON'T WANT THAT BOY'S BLOOD ON YOUR HANDS, GIRL.
I PROMISE YOU, IT NEVER WASHES OFF.
NEVER.

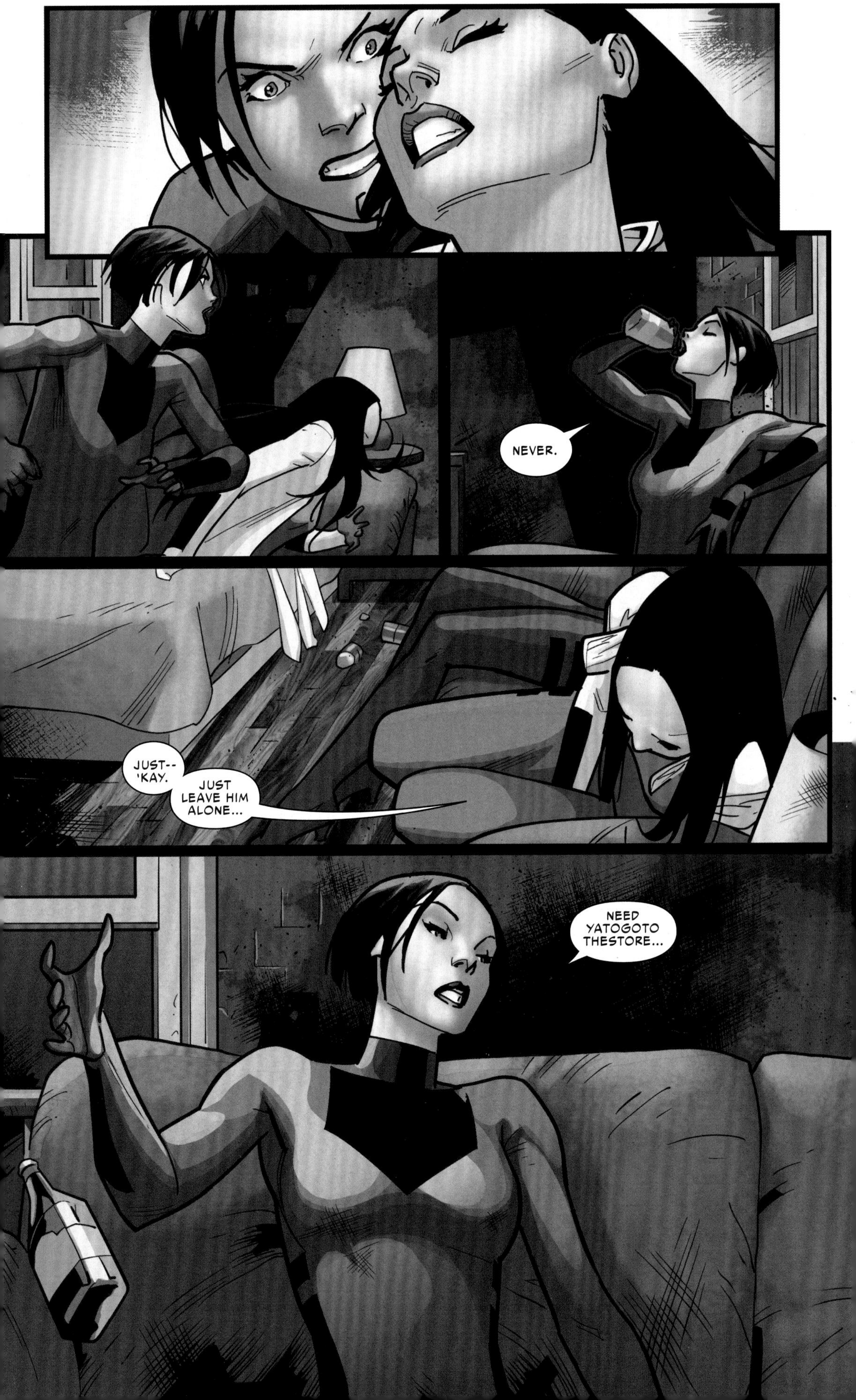
NEVER.
JUST--
'KAY.
JUST LEAVE HIM ALONE...
NEED YATOGOTO THESTORE...

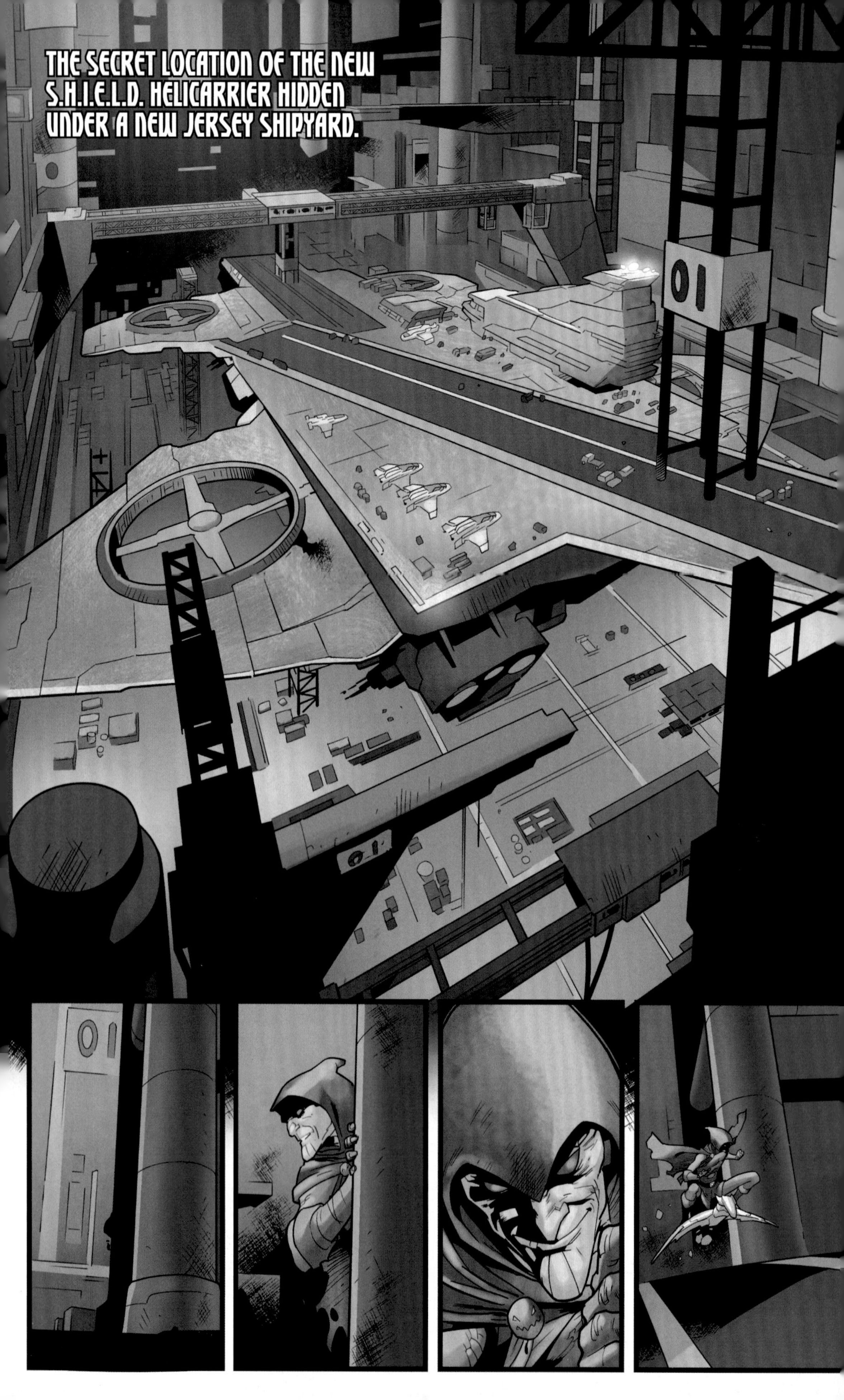
THE SECRET LOCATION OF THE NEW S.H.I.E.L.D. HELICARRIER HIDDEN UNDER A NEW JERSEY SHIPYARD.
01

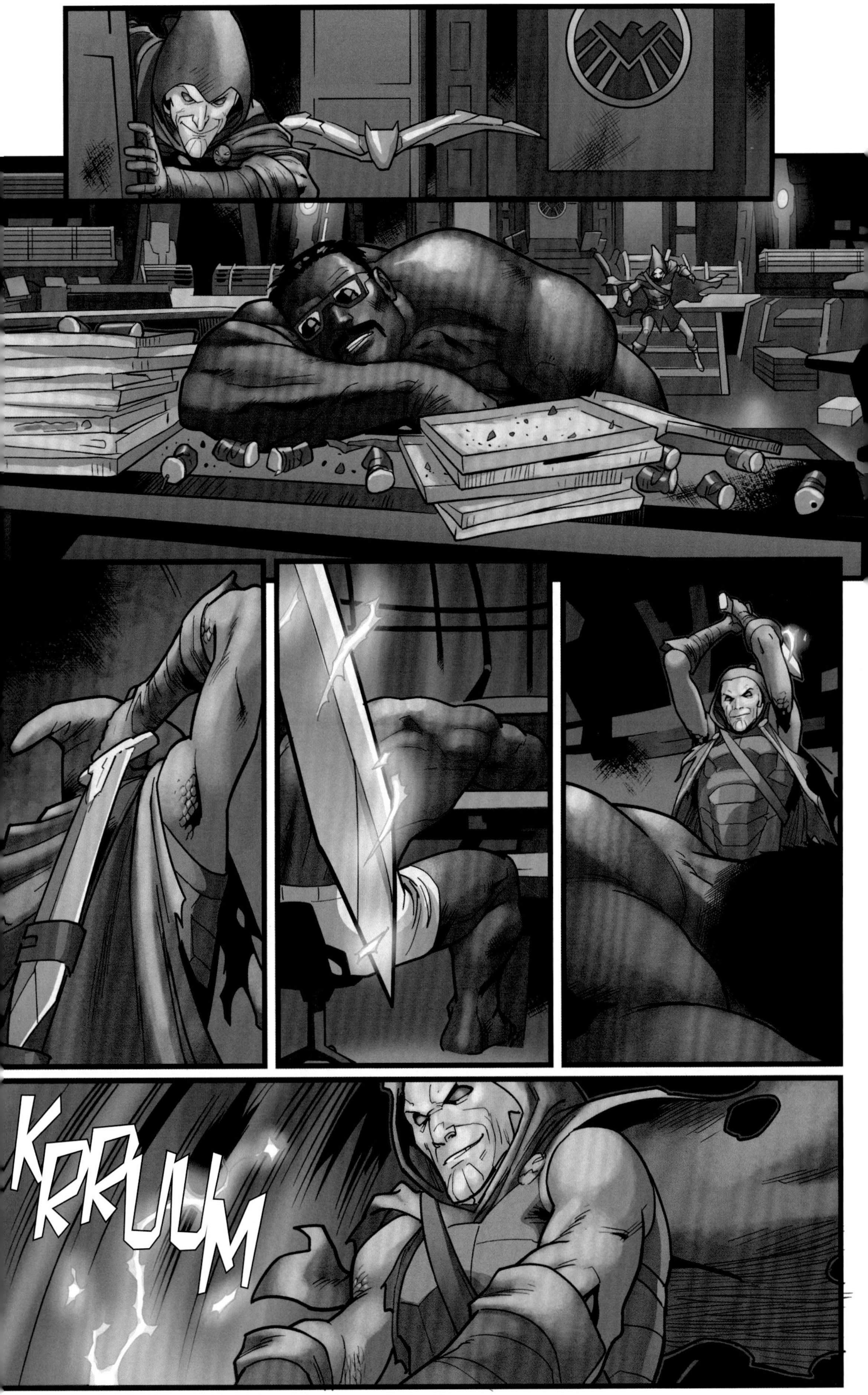
KRRUUM

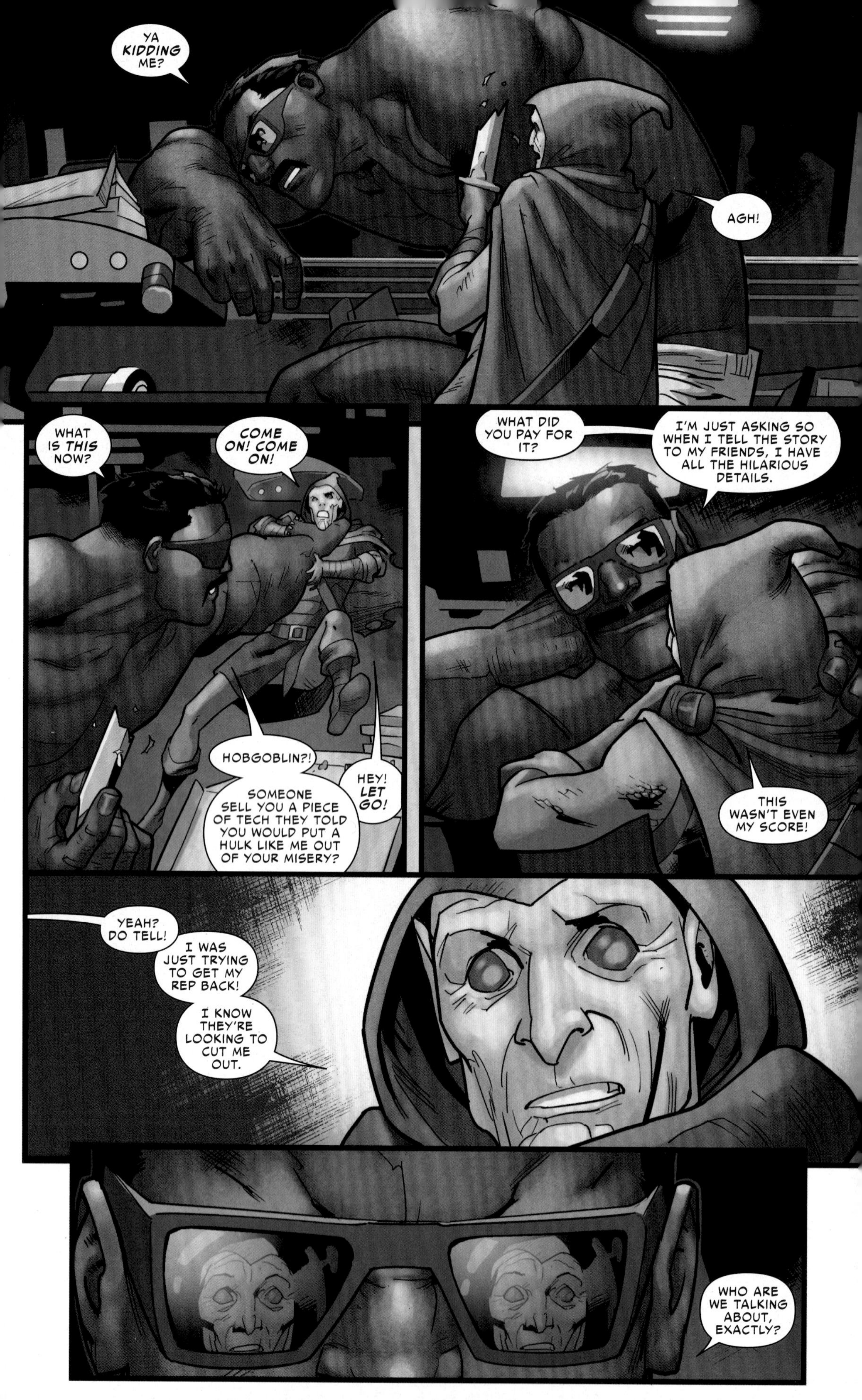
YA KIDDING ME?
AGH!
WHAT IS THIS NOW?
COME ON! COME ON!
HOBGOBLIN?!
SOMEONE SELL YOU A PIECE OF TECH THEY TOLD YOU WOULD PUT A HULK LIKE ME OUT OF YOUR MISERY?
HEY! LET GO!
WHAT DID YOU PAY FOR IT?
I'M JUST ASKING SO WHEN I TELL THE STORY TO MY FRIENDS, I HAVE ALL THE HILARIOUS DETAILS.
THIS WASN'T EVEN MY SCORE!
YEAH? DO TELL!
I WAS JUST TRYING TO GET MY REP BACK!
I KNOW THEY'RE LOOKING TO CUT ME OUT.
WHO ARE WE TALKING ABOUT, EXACTLY?

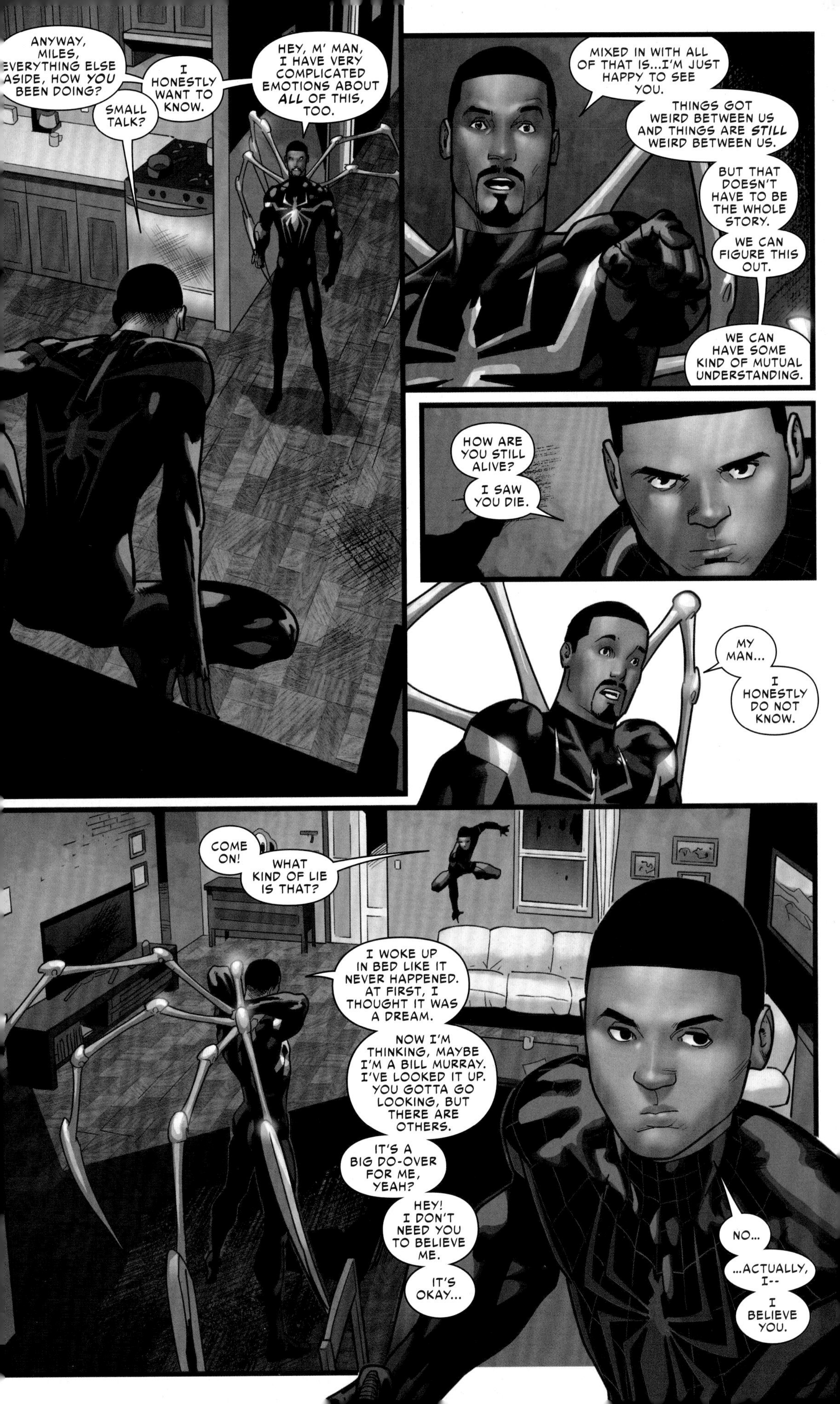
ANYWAY, MILES, EVERYTHING ELSE ASIDE, HOW YOU BEEN DOING?
SMALL TALK?
I HONESTLY WANT TO KNOW.
HEY, M' MAN, I HAVE VERY COMPLICATED EMOTIONS ABOUT ALL OF THIS, TOO.
MIXED IN WITH ALL OF THAT IS...I'M JUST HAPPY TO SEE YOU.
THINGS GOT WEIRD BETWEEN US AND THINGS ARE STILL WEIRD BETWEEN US.
BUT THAT DOESN'T HAVE TO BE THE WHOLE STORY.
WE CAN FIGURE THIS OUT.
WE CAN HAVE SOME KIND OF MUTUAL UNDERSTANDING.
HOW ARE YOU STILL ALIVE?
I SAW YOU DIE.
MY MAN...
I HONESTLY DO NOT KNOW.
COME ON!
WHAT KIND OF LIE IS THAT?
I WOKE UP IN BED LIKE IT NEVER HAPPENED. AT FIRST, I THOUGHT IT WAS A DREAM.
NOW I'M THINKING, MAYBE I'M A BILL MURRAY. I'VE LOOKED IT UP. YOU GOTTA GO LOOKING, BUT THERE ARE OTHERS.
IT'S A BIG DO-OVER FOR ME, YEAH?
HEY! I DON'T NEED YOU TO BELIEVE ME.
IT'S OKAY...
NO...
...ACTUALLY, I--
I BELIEVE YOU.

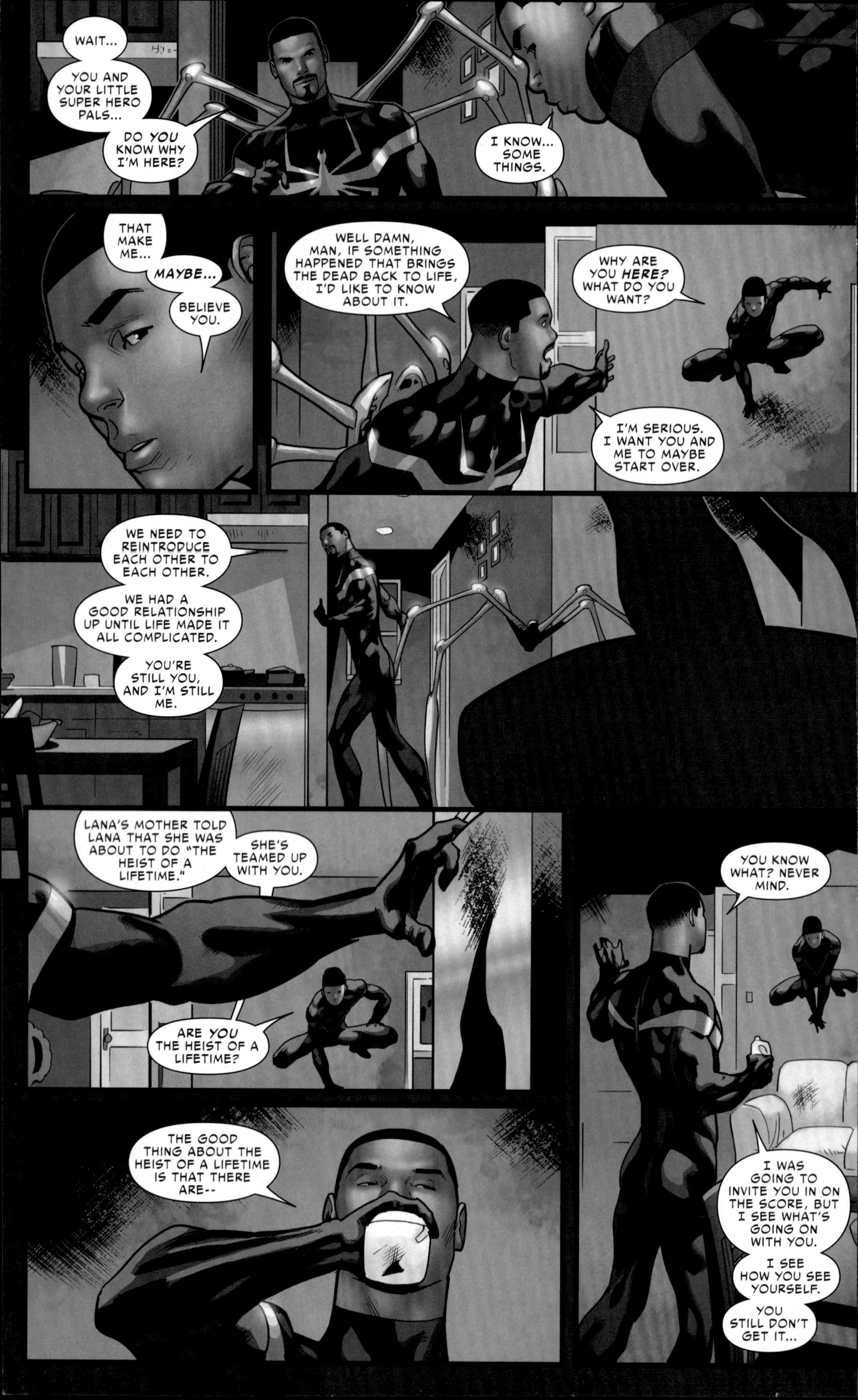
WAIT...
YOU AND YOUR LITTLE SUPER HERO PALS...
DO *YOU* KNOW WHY I'M HERE?
I KNOW... SOME THINGS.
THAT MAKE ME...
MAYBE...
BELIEVE YOU.
WELL DAMN, MAN, IF SOMETHING HAPPENED THAT BRINGS THE DEAD BACK TO LIFE, I'D LIKE TO KNOW ABOUT IT.
WHY ARE YOU *HERE?* WHAT DO YOU WANT?
I'M SERIOUS. I WANT YOU AND ME TO MAYBE START OVER.
WE NEED TO REINTRODUCE EACH OTHER TO EACH OTHER.
WE HAD A GOOD RELATIONSHIP UP UNTIL LIFE MADE IT ALL COMPLICATED.
YOU'RE STILL YOU, AND I'M STILL ME.
LANA'S MOTHER TOLD LANA THAT SHE WAS ABOUT TO DO "THE HEIST OF A LIFETIME."
SHE'S TEAMED UP WITH YOU.
ARE *YOU* THE HEIST OF A LIFETIME?
THE GOOD THING ABOUT THE HEIST OF A LIFETIME IS THAT THERE ARE--
YOU KNOW WHAT? NEVER MIND.
I WAS GOING TO INVITE YOU IN ON THE SCORE, BUT I SEE WHAT'S GOING ON WITH YOU.
I SEE HOW YOU SEE YOURSELF.
YOU STILL DON'T GET IT...

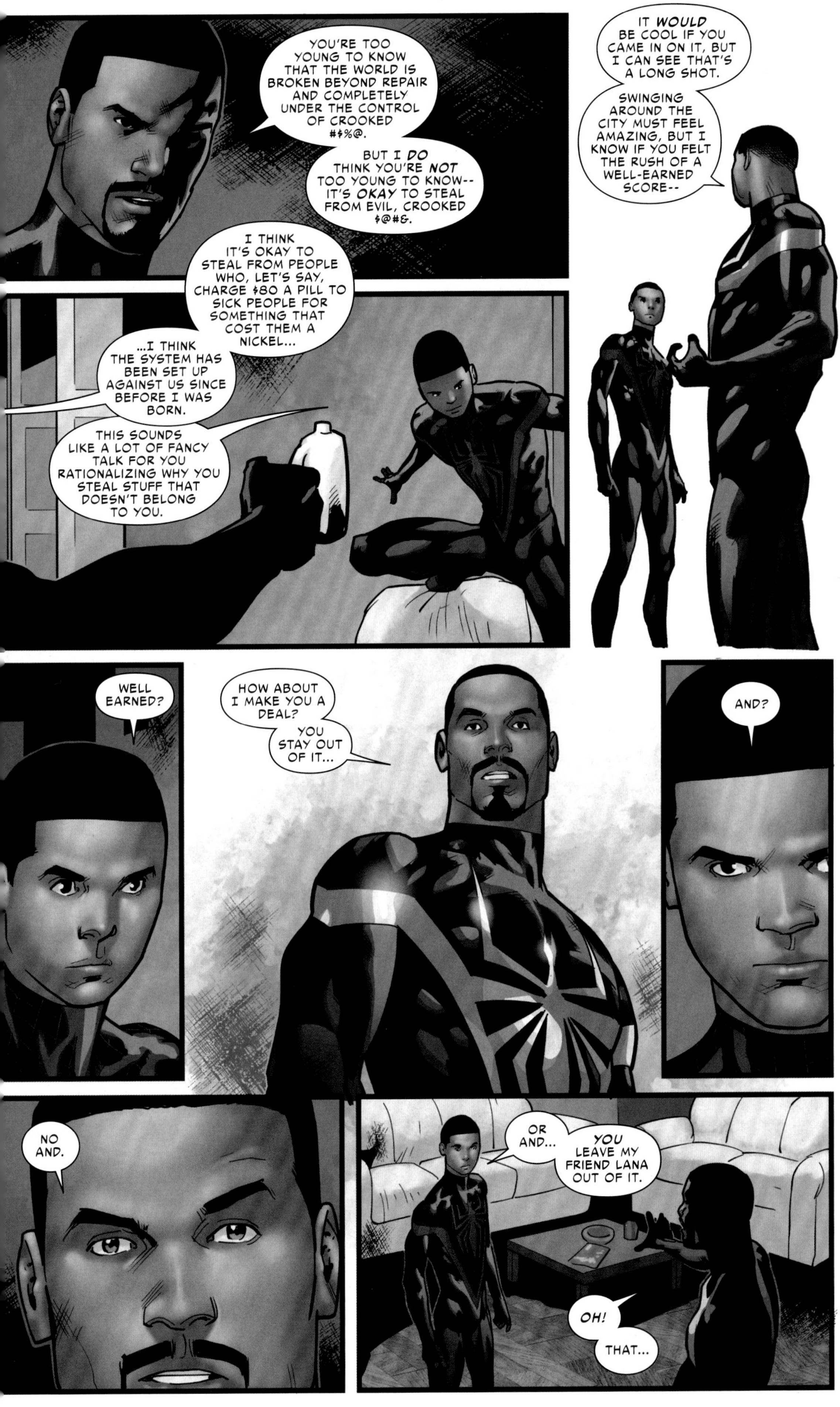
YOU'RE TOO YOUNG TO KNOW THAT THE WORLD IS BROKEN BEYOND REPAIR AND COMPLETELY UNDER THE CONTROL OF CROOKED #$%@.
BUT I *DO* THINK YOU'RE *NOT* TOO YOUNG TO KNOW-- IT'S *OKAY* TO STEAL FROM EVIL, CROOKED $@#&.
IT *WOULD* BE COOL IF YOU CAME IN ON IT, BUT I CAN SEE THAT'S A LONG SHOT.
SWINGING AROUND THE CITY MUST FEEL AMAZING, BUT I KNOW IF YOU FELT THE RUSH OF A WELL-EARNED SCORE--
I THINK IT'S OKAY TO STEAL FROM PEOPLE WHO, LET'S SAY, CHARGE $80 A PILL TO SICK PEOPLE FOR SOMETHING THAT COST THEM A NICKEL...
...I THINK THE SYSTEM HAS BEEN SET UP AGAINST US SINCE BEFORE I WAS BORN.
THIS SOUNDS LIKE A LOT OF FANCY TALK FOR YOU RATIONALIZING WHY YOU STEAL STUFF THAT DOESN'T BELONG TO YOU.
WELL EARNED?
HOW ABOUT I MAKE YOU A DEAL?
YOU STAY OUT OF IT...
AND?
NO AND.
OR AND...
YOU LEAVE MY FRIEND LANA OUT OF IT.
OH!
THAT...

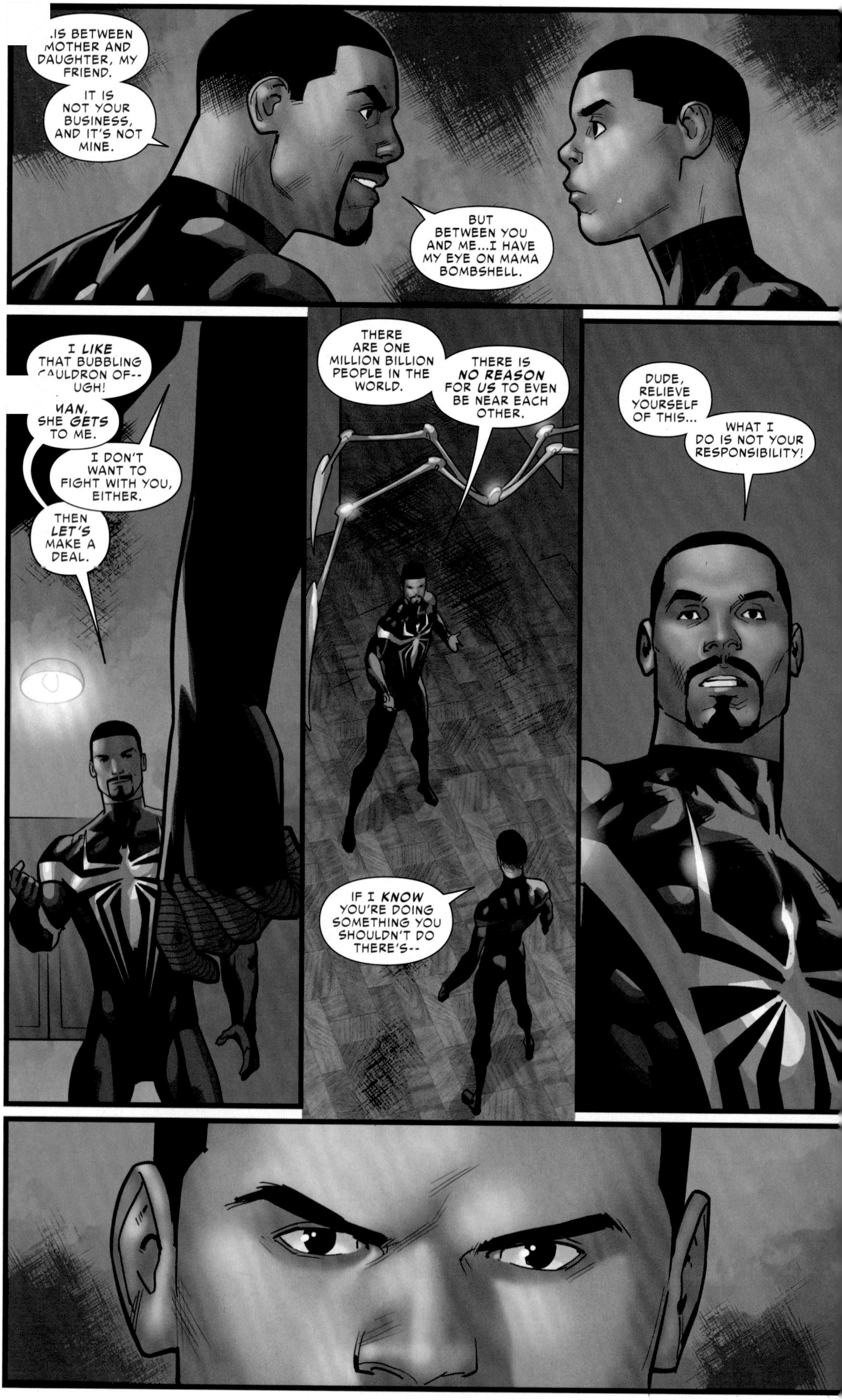

.IS BETWEEN MOTHER AND DAUGHTER, MY FRIEND.
IT IS NOT YOUR BUSINESS, AND IT'S NOT MINE.
BUT BETWEEN YOU AND ME...I HAVE MY EYE ON MAMA BOMBSHELL.
I LIKE THAT BUBBLING CAULDRON OF-- UGH!
MAN, SHE GETS TO ME.
I DON'T WANT TO FIGHT WITH YOU, EITHER.
THEN LET'S MAKE A DEAL.
THERE ARE ONE MILLION BILLION PEOPLE IN THE WORLD.
THERE IS NO REASON FOR US TO EVEN BE NEAR EACH OTHER.
IF I KNOW YOU'RE DOING SOMETHING YOU SHOULDN'T DO THERE'S--
DUDE, RELIEVE YOURSELF OF THIS...
WHAT I DO IS NOT YOUR RESPONSIBILITY!

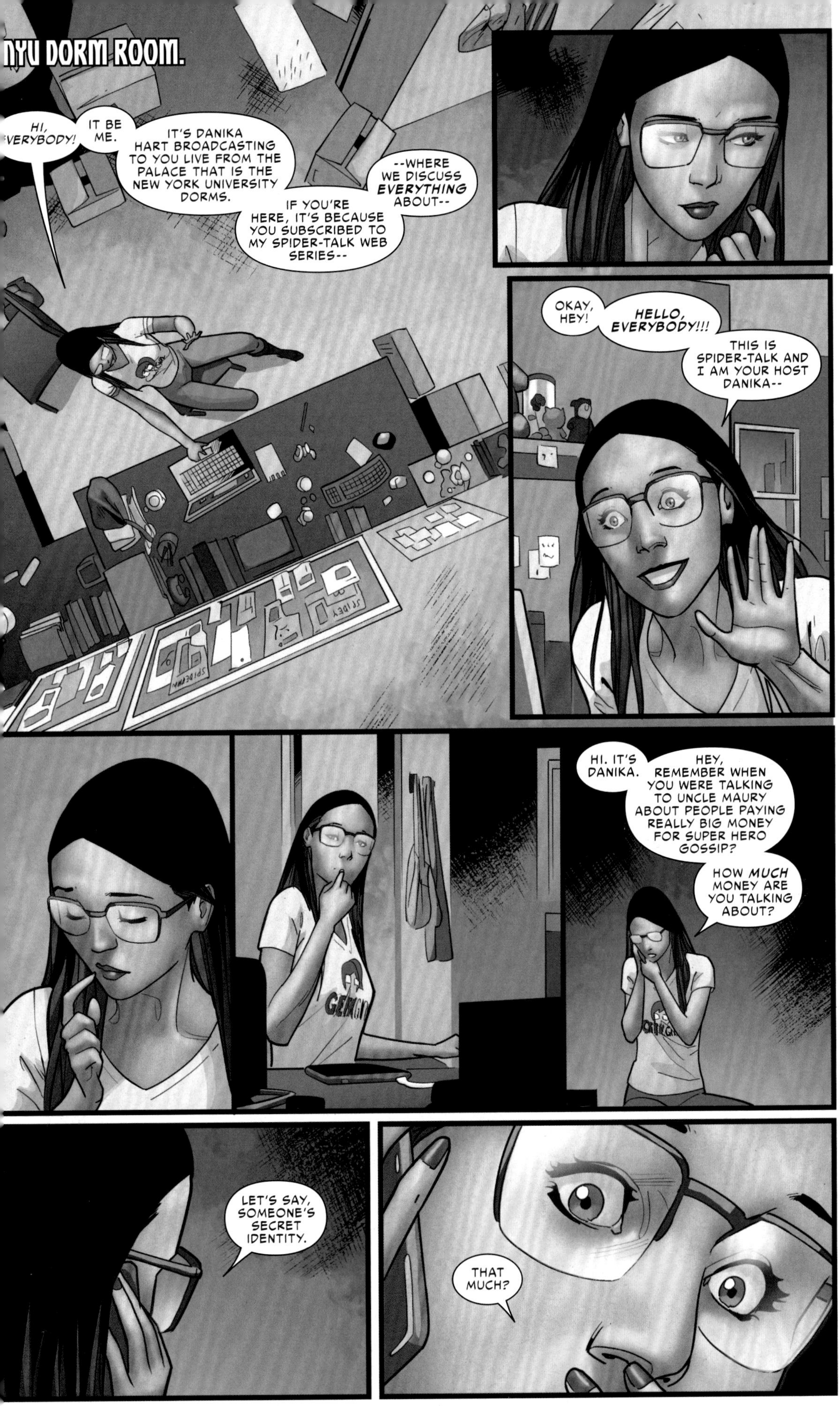
NYU DORM ROOM.
HI, EVERYBODY!
IT BE ME.
IT'S DANIKA HART BROADCASTING TO YOU LIVE FROM THE PALACE THAT IS THE NEW YORK UNIVERSITY DORMS.
IF YOU'RE HERE, IT'S BECAUSE YOU SUBSCRIBED TO MY SPIDER-TALK WEB SERIES--
--WHERE WE DISCUSS EVERYTHING ABOUT--
SPIDEY
SPIDERMAN
OKAY, HEY!
HELLO, EVERYBODY!!!
THIS IS SPIDER-TALK AND I AM YOUR HOST DANIKA--
HI. IT'S DANIKA.
HEY, REMEMBER WHEN YOU WERE TALKING TO UNCLE MAURY ABOUT PEOPLE PAYING REALLY BIG MONEY FOR SUPER HERO GOSSIP?
HOW MUCH MONEY ARE YOU TALKING ABOUT?
LET'S SAY, SOMEONE'S SECRET IDENTITY.
THAT MUCH?

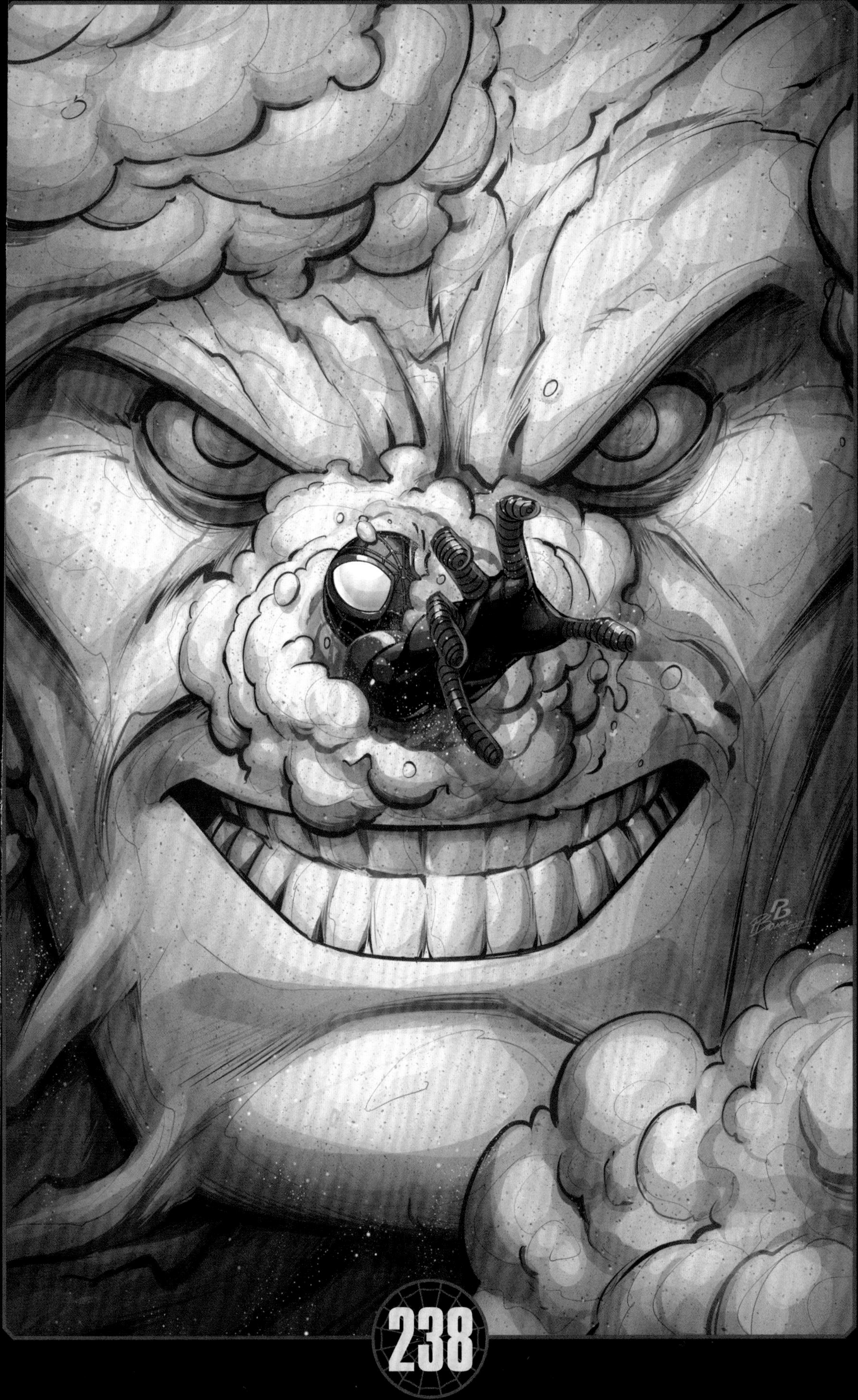
238

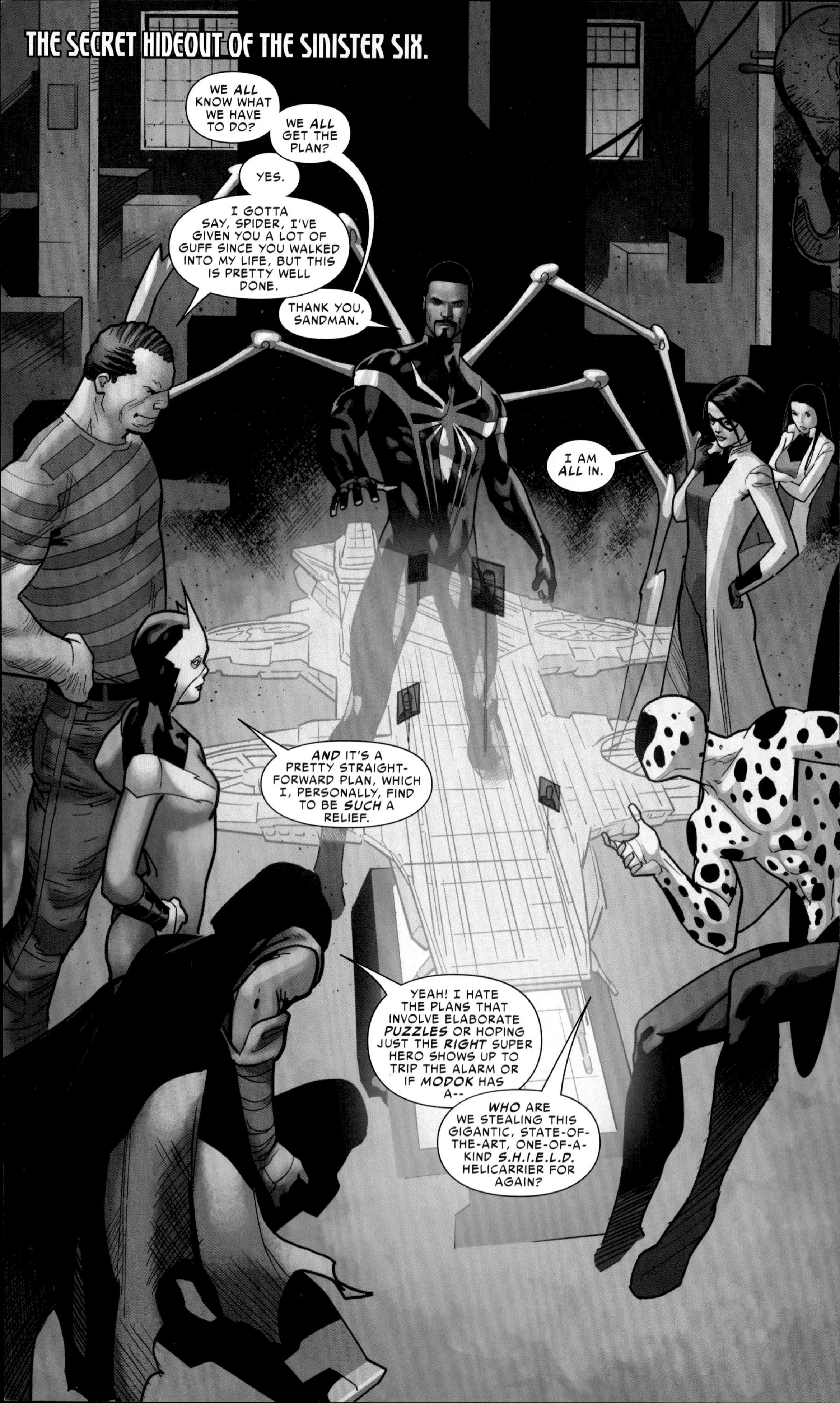
THE SECRET HIDEOUT OF THE SINISTER SIX.
WE ALL KNOW WHAT WE HAVE TO DO?
WE ALL GET THE PLAN?
YES.
I GOTTA SAY, SPIDER, I'VE GIVEN YOU A LOT OF GUFF SINCE YOU WALKED INTO MY LIFE, BUT THIS IS PRETTY WELL DONE.
THANK YOU, SANDMAN.
I AM ALL IN.
AND IT'S A PRETTY STRAIGHT-FORWARD PLAN, WHICH I, PERSONALLY, FIND TO BE SUCH A RELIEF.
YEAH! I HATE THE PLANS THAT INVOLVE ELABORATE PUZZLES OR HOPING JUST THE RIGHT SUPER HERO SHOWS UP TO TRIP THE ALARM OR IF MODOK HAS A--
WHO ARE WE STEALING THIS GIGANTIC, STATE-OF-THE-ART, ONE-OF-A-KIND S.H.I.E.L.D. HELICARRIER FOR AGAIN?

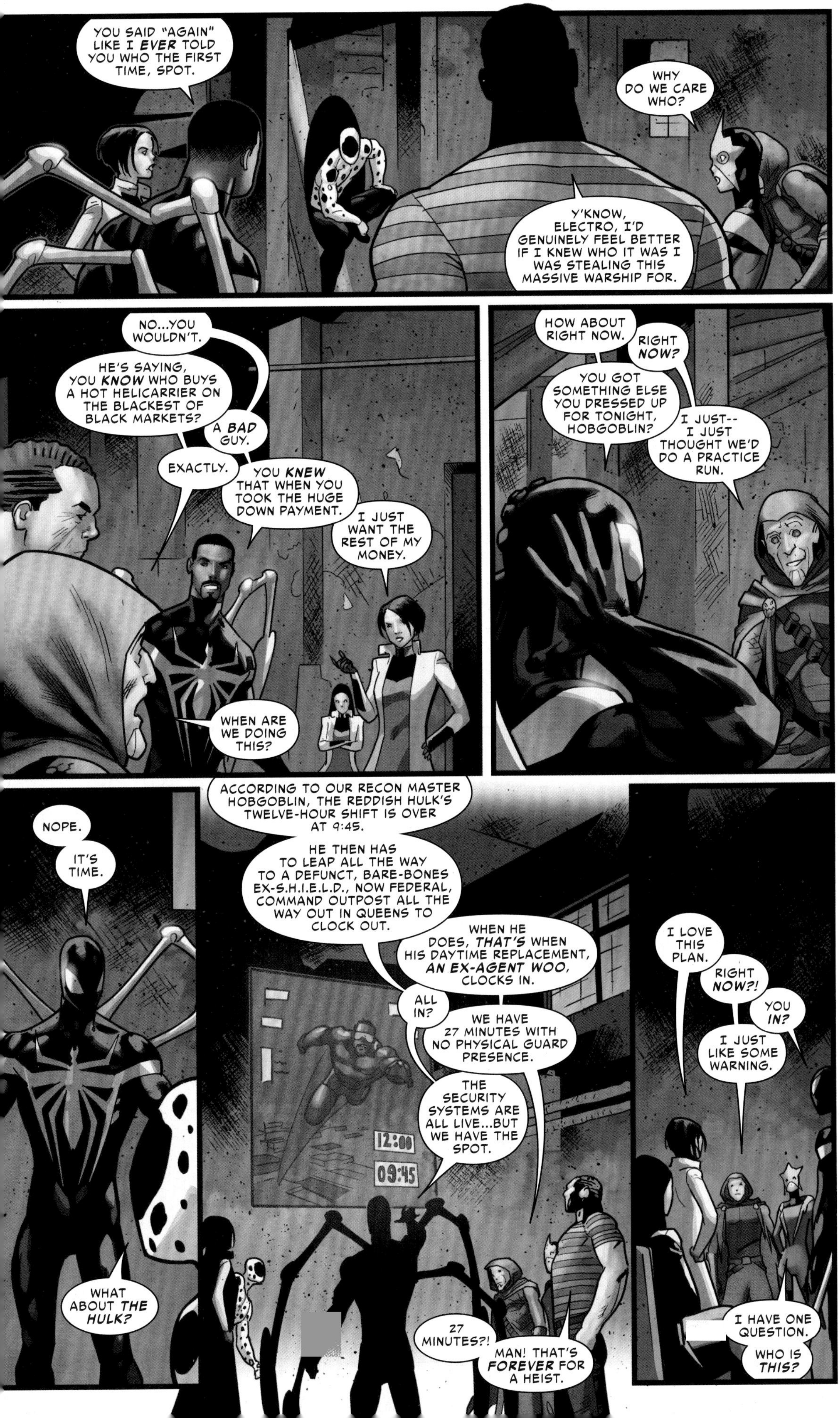
YOU SAID "AGAIN" LIKE I EVER TOLD YOU WHO THE FIRST TIME, SPOT.
WHY DO WE CARE WHO?
Y'KNOW, ELECTRO, I'D GENUINELY FEEL BETTER IF I KNEW WHO IT WAS I WAS STEALING THIS MASSIVE WARSHIP FOR.
NO...YOU WOULDN'T.
HE'S SAYING, YOU KNOW WHO BUYS A HOT HELICARRIER ON THE BLACKEST OF BLACK MARKETS?
A BAD GUY.
EXACTLY.
YOU KNEW THAT WHEN YOU TOOK THE HUGE DOWN PAYMENT.
I JUST WANT THE REST OF MY MONEY.
WHEN ARE WE DOING THIS?
HOW ABOUT RIGHT NOW.
RIGHT NOW?
YOU GOT SOMETHING ELSE YOU DRESSED UP FOR TONIGHT, HOBGOBLIN?
I JUST-- I JUST THOUGHT WE'D DO A PRACTICE RUN.
NOPE.
IT'S TIME.
WHAT ABOUT THE HULK?
ACCORDING TO OUR RECON MASTER HOBGOBLIN, THE REDDISH HULK'S TWELVE-HOUR SHIFT IS OVER AT 9:45.
HE THEN HAS TO LEAP ALL THE WAY TO A DEFUNCT, BARE-BONES EX-S.H.I.E.L.D., NOW FEDERAL, COMMAND OUTPOST ALL THE WAY OUT IN QUEENS TO CLOCK OUT.
WHEN HE DOES, THAT'S WHEN HIS DAYTIME REPLACEMENT, AN EX-AGENT WOO, CLOCKS IN.
ALL IN?
WE HAVE 27 MINUTES WITH NO PHYSICAL GUARD PRESENCE.
THE SECURITY SYSTEMS ARE ALL LIVE...BUT WE HAVE THE SPOT.
12:00
09:45
27 MINUTES?!
MAN! THAT'S FOREVER FOR A HEIST.
I LOVE THIS PLAN.
RIGHT NOW?!
YOU IN?
I JUST LIKE SOME WARNING.
I HAVE ONE QUESTION.
WHO IS THIS?

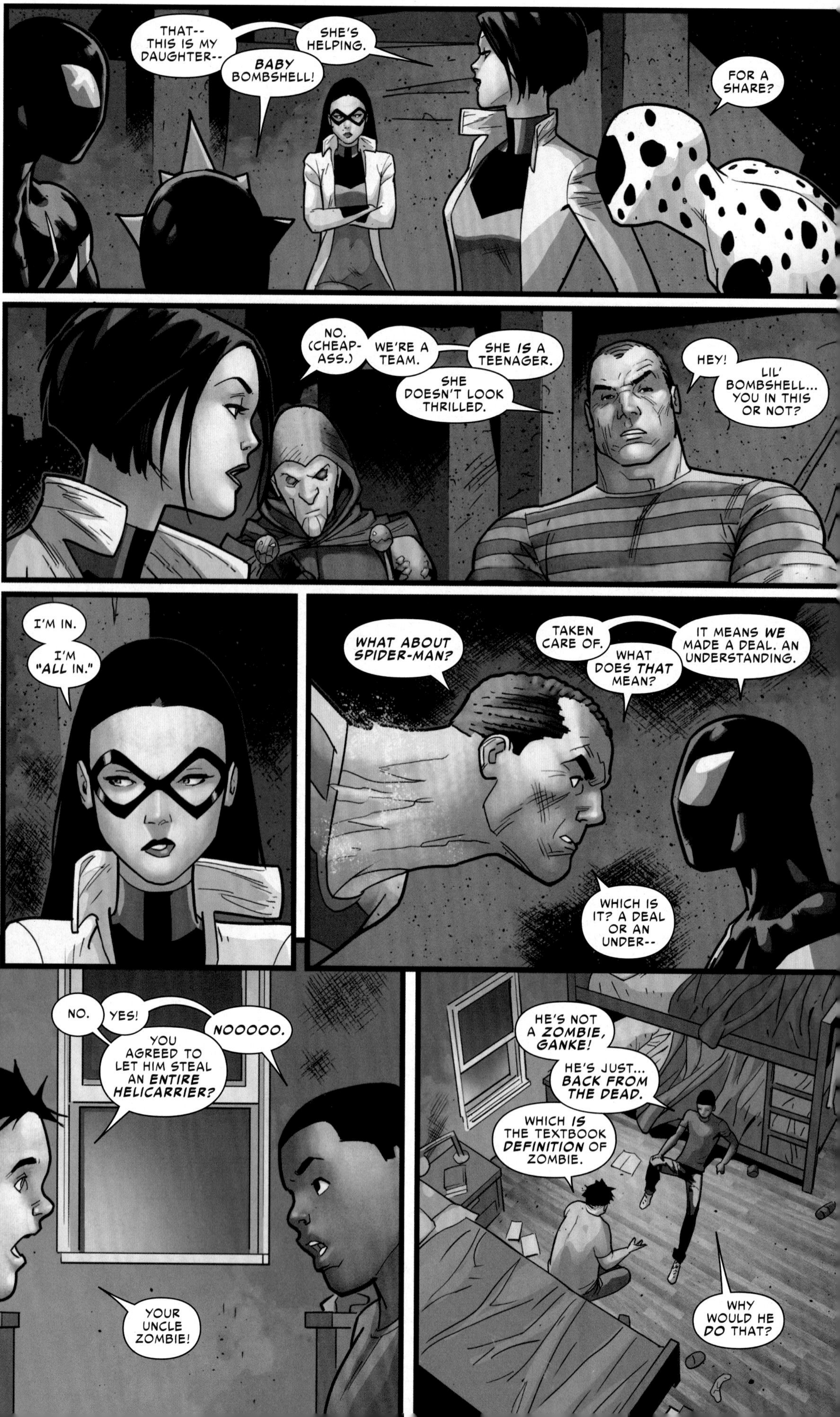
THAT-- THIS IS MY DAUGHTER--
BABY BOMBSHELL!
SHE'S HELPING.
FOR A SHARE?
NO. (CHEAP-ASS.)
WE'RE A TEAM.
SHE IS A TEENAGER.
SHE DOESN'T LOOK THRILLED.
HEY!
LIL' BOMBSHELL... YOU IN THIS OR NOT?
I'M IN.
I'M "ALL IN."
WHAT ABOUT SPIDER-MAN?
TAKEN CARE OF.
WHAT DOES THAT MEAN?
IT MEANS WE MADE A DEAL. AN UNDERSTANDING.
WHICH IS IT? A DEAL OR AN UNDER--
NO.
YES!
YOU AGREED TO LET HIM STEAL AN ENTIRE HELICARRIER?
NOOOOO.
YOUR UNCLE ZOMBIE!
HE'S NOT A ZOMBIE, GANKE!
HE'S JUST... BACK FROM THE DEAD.
WHICH IS THE TEXTBOOK DEFINITION OF ZOMBIE.
WHY WOULD HE DO THAT?

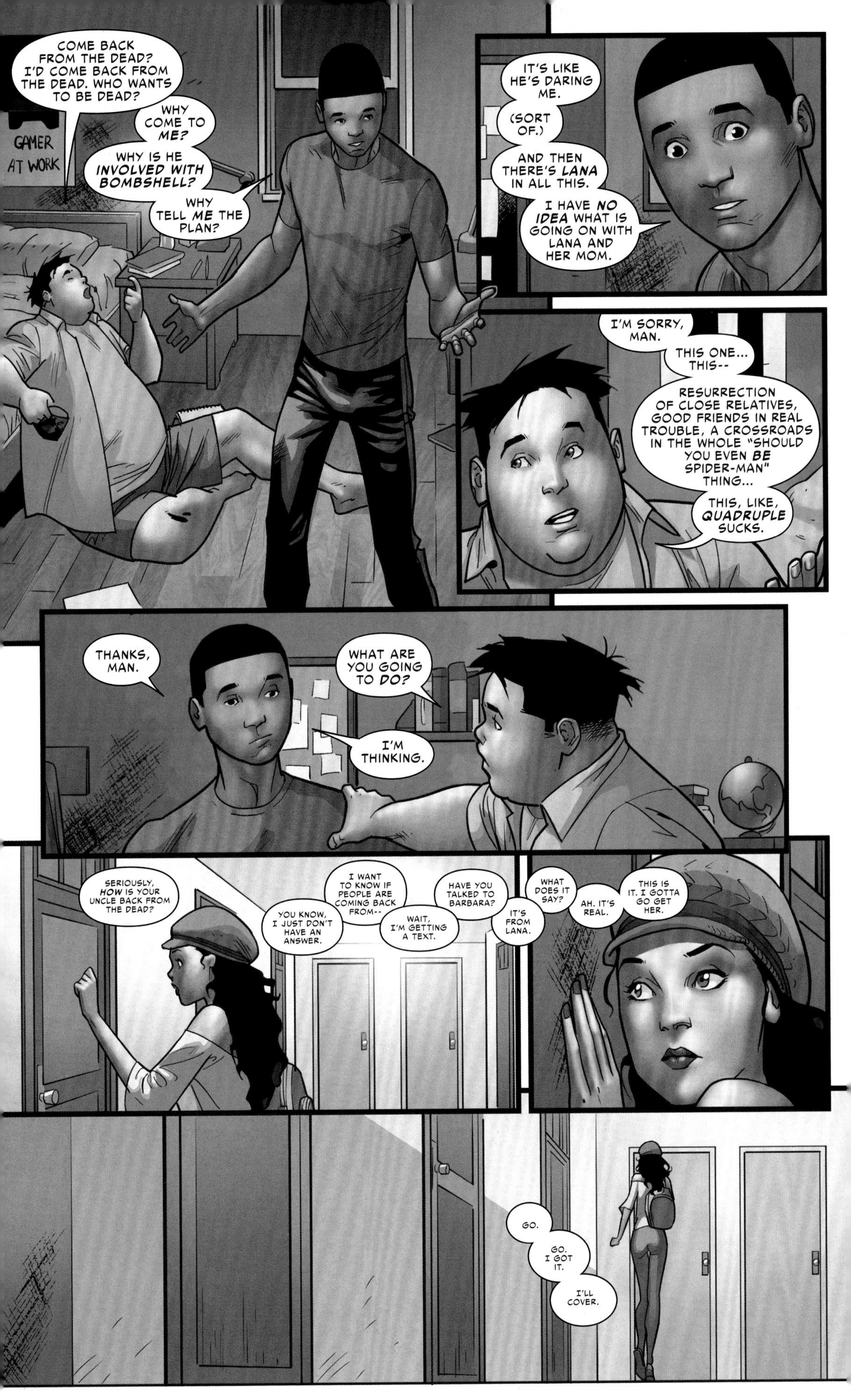
COME BACK FROM THE DEAD? I'D COME BACK FROM THE DEAD. WHO WANTS TO BE DEAD?
GAMER AT WORK
WHY COME TO *ME?*
WHY IS HE *INVOLVED WITH BOMBSHELL?*
WHY TELL *ME* THE PLAN?
IT'S LIKE HE'S DARING ME.
(SORT OF.)
AND THEN THERE'S *LANA* IN ALL THIS.
I HAVE *NO IDEA* WHAT IS GOING ON WITH LANA AND HER MOM.
I'M SORRY, MAN.
THIS ONE... THIS--
RESURRECTION OF CLOSE RELATIVES, GOOD FRIENDS IN REAL TROUBLE, A CROSSROADS IN THE WHOLE "SHOULD YOU EVEN *BE* SPIDER-MAN" THING...
THIS, LIKE, *QUADRUPLE* SUCKS.
THANKS, MAN.
WHAT ARE YOU GOING TO *DO?*
I'M THINKING.
SERIOUSLY, *HOW* IS YOUR UNCLE BACK FROM THE DEAD?
YOU KNOW, I JUST DON'T HAVE AN ANSWER.
I WANT TO KNOW IF PEOPLE ARE COMING BACK FROM--
WAIT, I'M GETTING A TEXT.
HAVE YOU TALKED TO BARBARA?
IT'S FROM LANA.
WHAT DOES IT SAY?
AH. IT'S REAL.
THIS IS IT. I GOTTA GO GET HER.
GO.
GO. I GOT IT.
I'LL COVER.

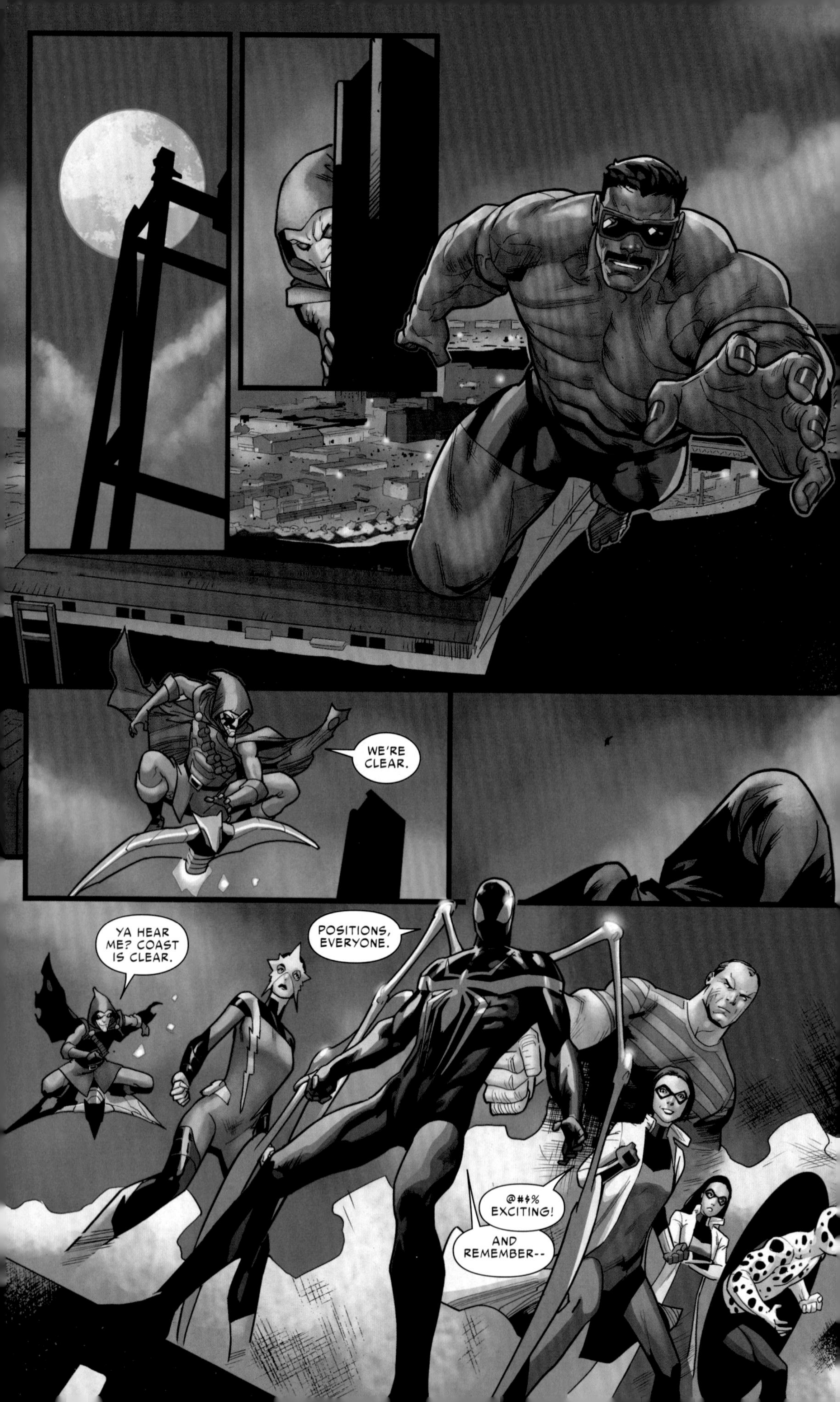
WE'RE CLEAR.
YA HEAR ME? COAST IS CLEAR.
POSITIONS, EVERYONE.
@#$% EXCITING!
AND REMEMBER--

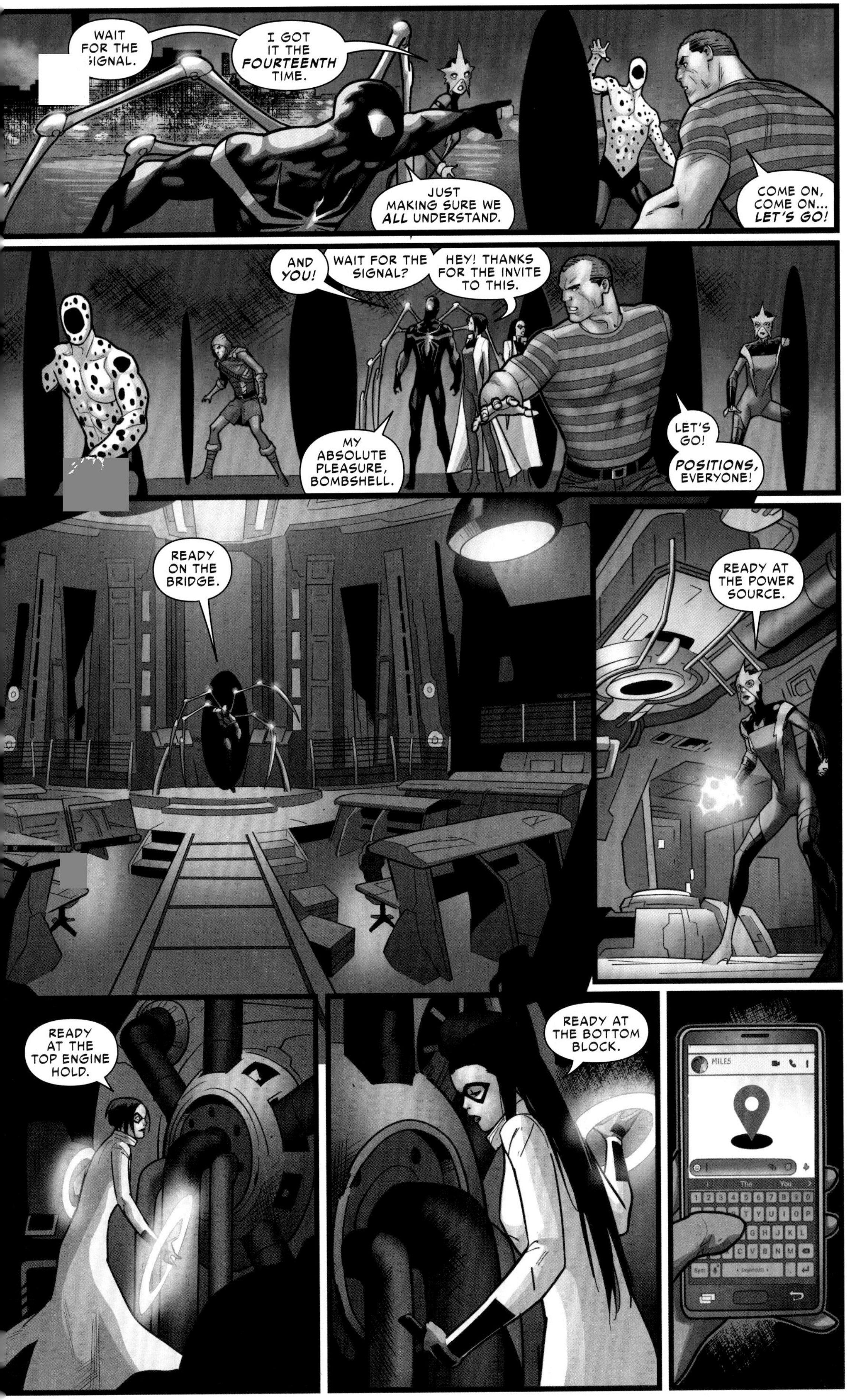

WAIT FOR THE SIGNAL.
I GOT IT THE FOURTEENTH TIME.
JUST MAKING SURE WE ALL UNDERSTAND.
COME ON, COME ON... LET'S GO!
AND YOU!
WAIT FOR THE SIGNAL?
HEY! THANKS FOR THE INVITE TO THIS.
MY ABSOLUTE PLEASURE, BOMBSHELL.
LET'S GO!
POSITIONS, EVERYONE!
READY ON THE BRIDGE.
READY AT THE POWER SOURCE.
READY AT THE TOP ENGINE HOLD.
READY AT THE BOTTOM BLOCK.
MILES

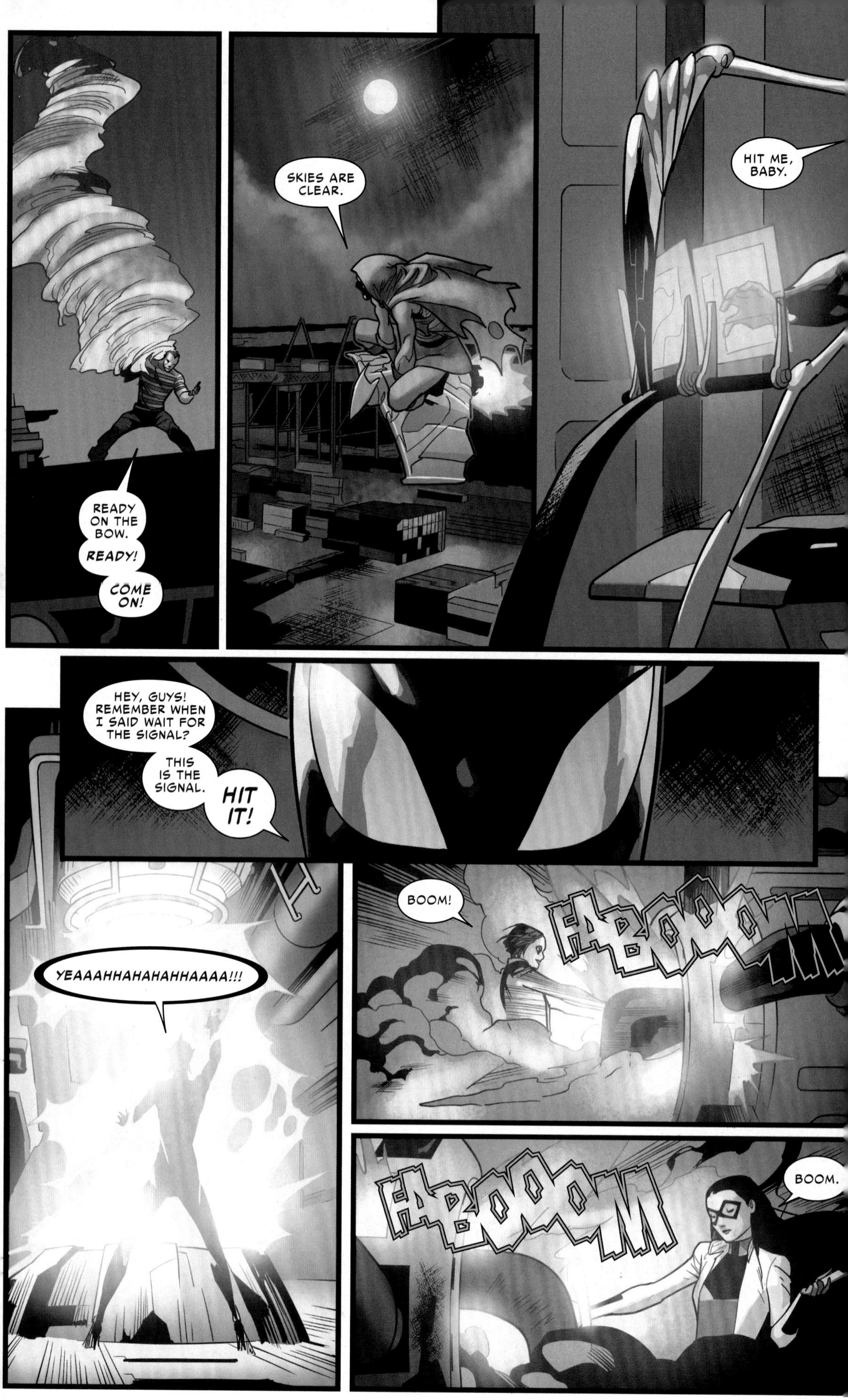

READY ON THE BOW.
READY!
COME ON!
SKIES ARE CLEAR.
HIT ME, BABY.
HEY, GUYS! REMEMBER WHEN I SAID WAIT FOR THE SIGNAL?
THIS IS THE SIGNAL.
HIT IT!
YEAAAHHAHAHAHHAAAA!!!
BOOM!
FABOOOM
FABOOOM
BOOM.

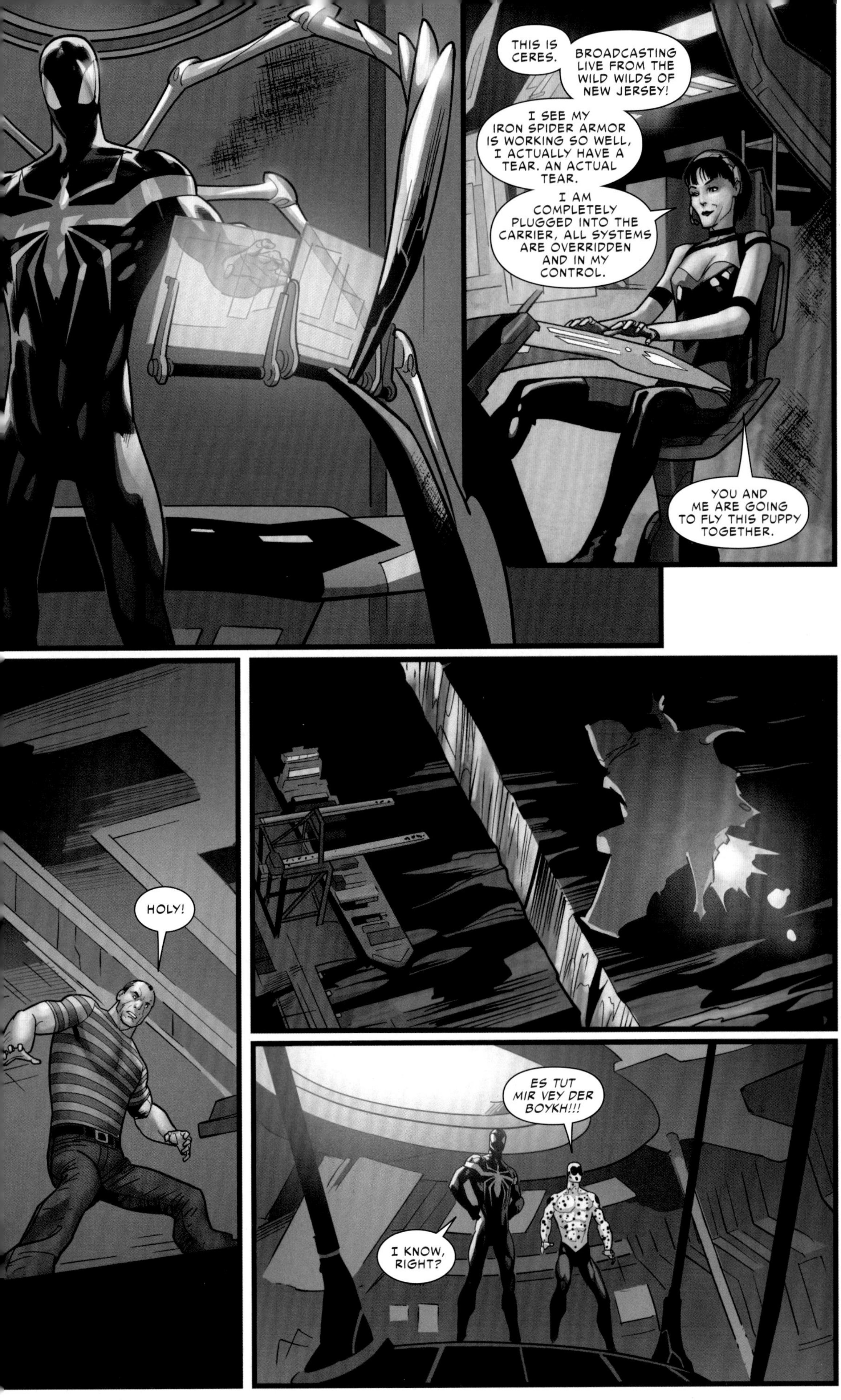
THIS IS CERES.
BROADCASTING LIVE FROM THE WILD WILDS OF NEW JERSEY!
I SEE MY IRON SPIDER ARMOR IS WORKING SO WELL, I ACTUALLY HAVE A TEAR. AN ACTUAL TEAR.
I AM COMPLETELY PLUGGED INTO THE CARRIER, ALL SYSTEMS ARE OVERRIDDEN AND IN MY CONTROL.
YOU AND ME ARE GOING TO FLY THIS PUPPY TOGETHER.
HOLY!
ES TUT MIR VEY DER BOYKH!!!
I KNOW, RIGHT?

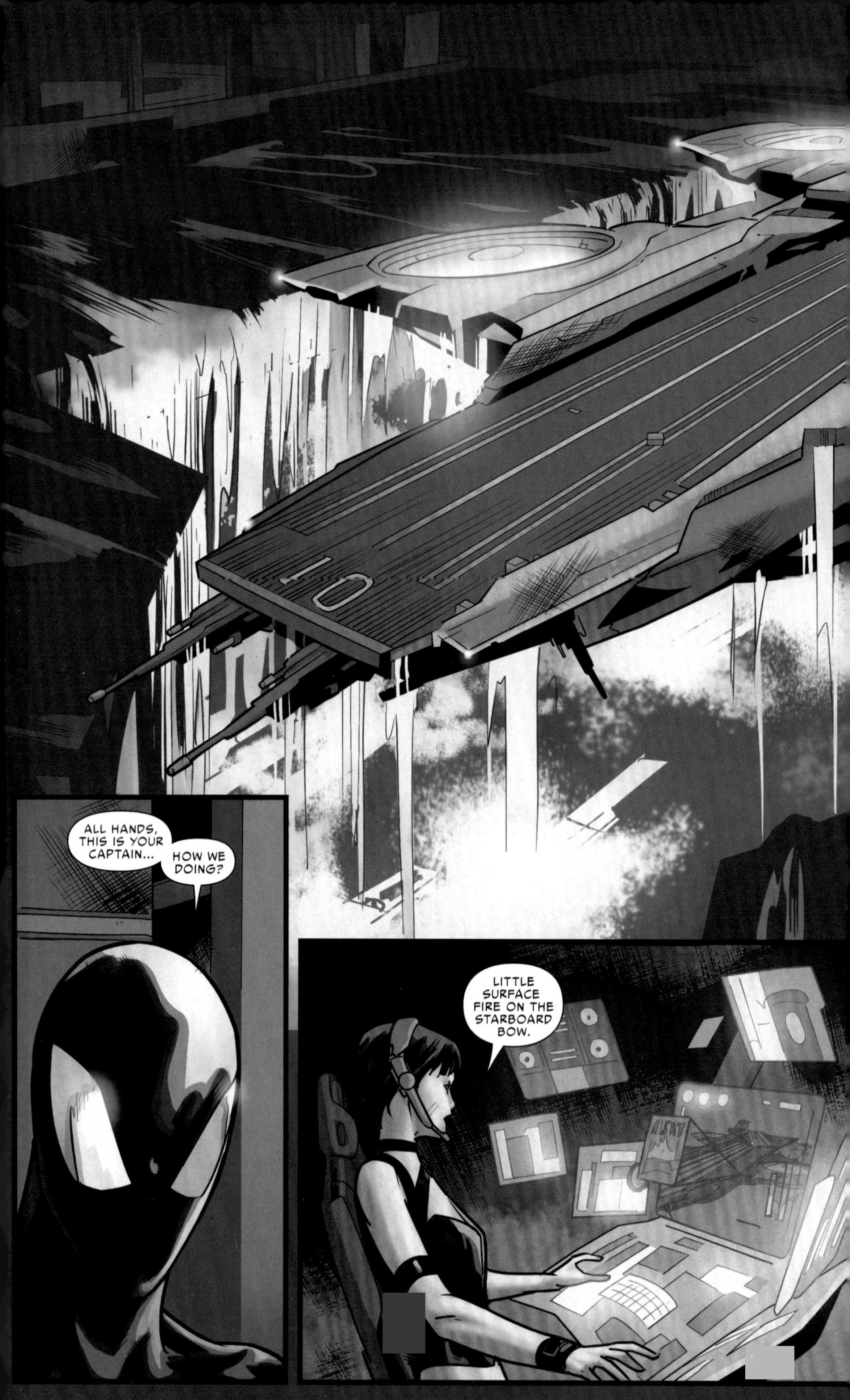
ALL HANDS, THIS IS YOUR CAPTAIN...
HOW WE DOING?
LITTLE SURFACE FIRE ON THE STARBOARD BOW.
ALERT

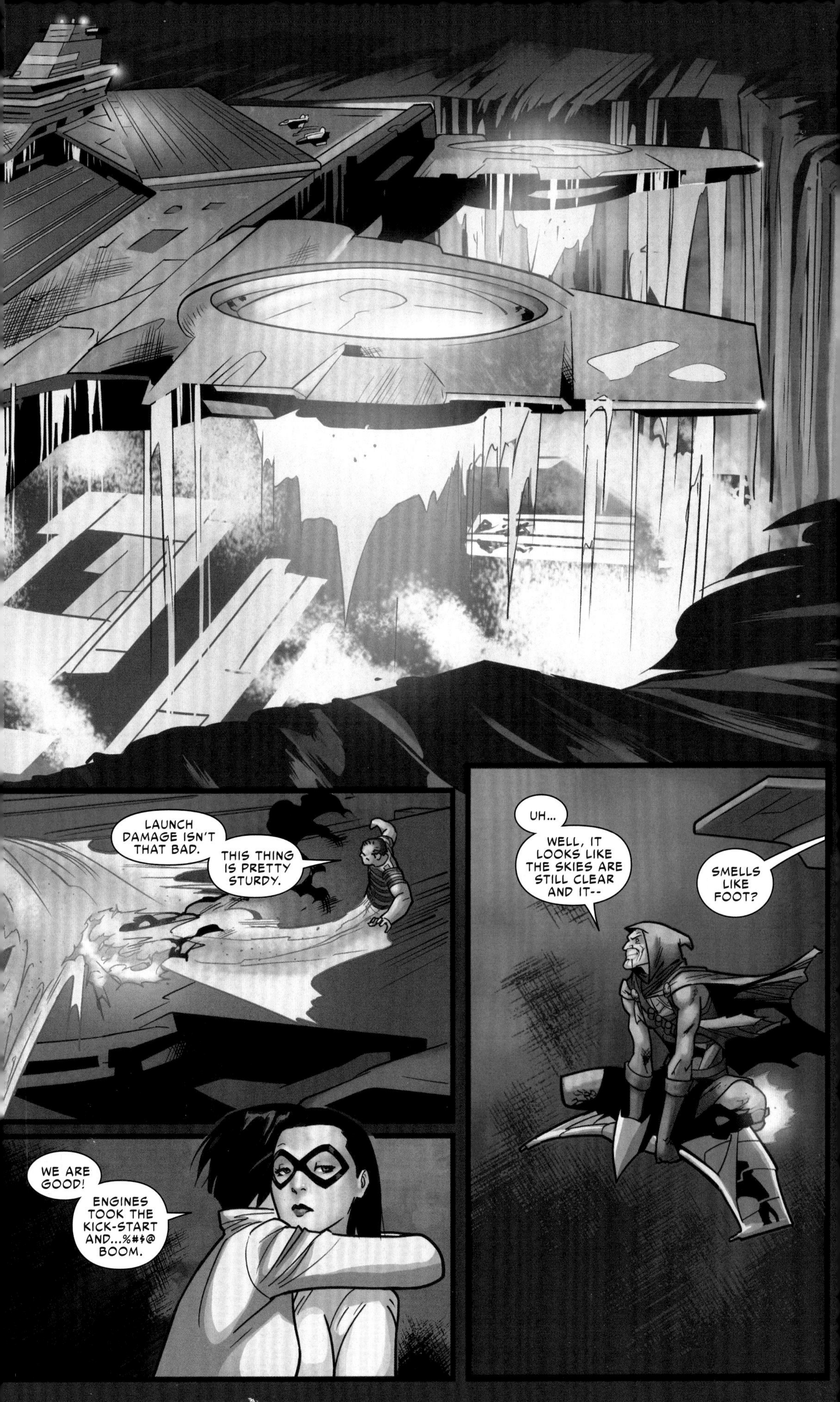
LAUNCH DAMAGE ISN'T THAT BAD.
THIS THING IS PRETTY STURDY.
UH...
WELL, IT LOOKS LIKE THE SKIES ARE STILL CLEAR AND IT--
SMELLS LIKE FOOT?
WE ARE GOOD!
ENGINES TOOK THE KICK-START AND...%#$@ BOOM.

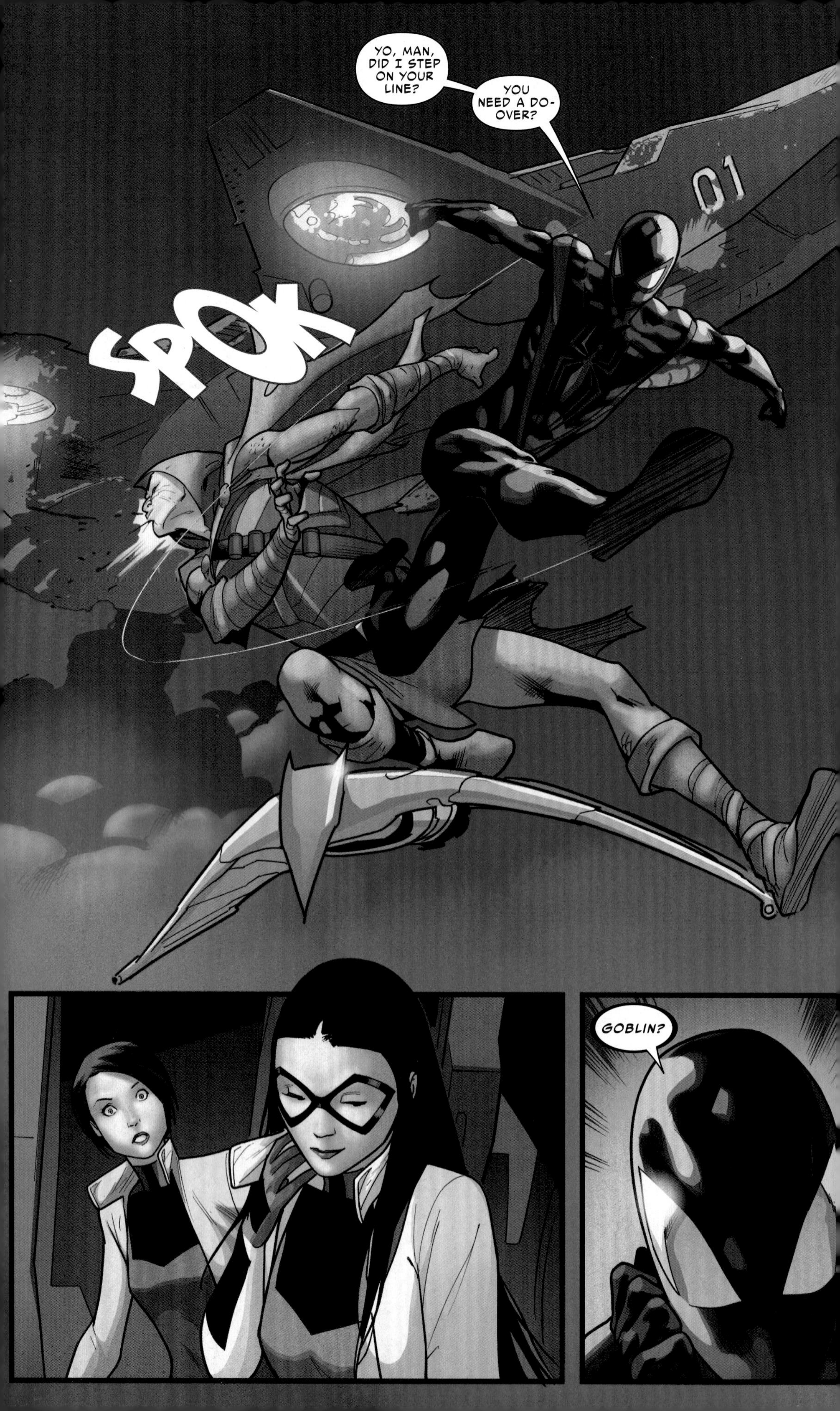
YO, MAN, DID I STEP ON YOUR LINE?
YOU NEED A DO-OVER?
01
SPOK
GOBLIN?

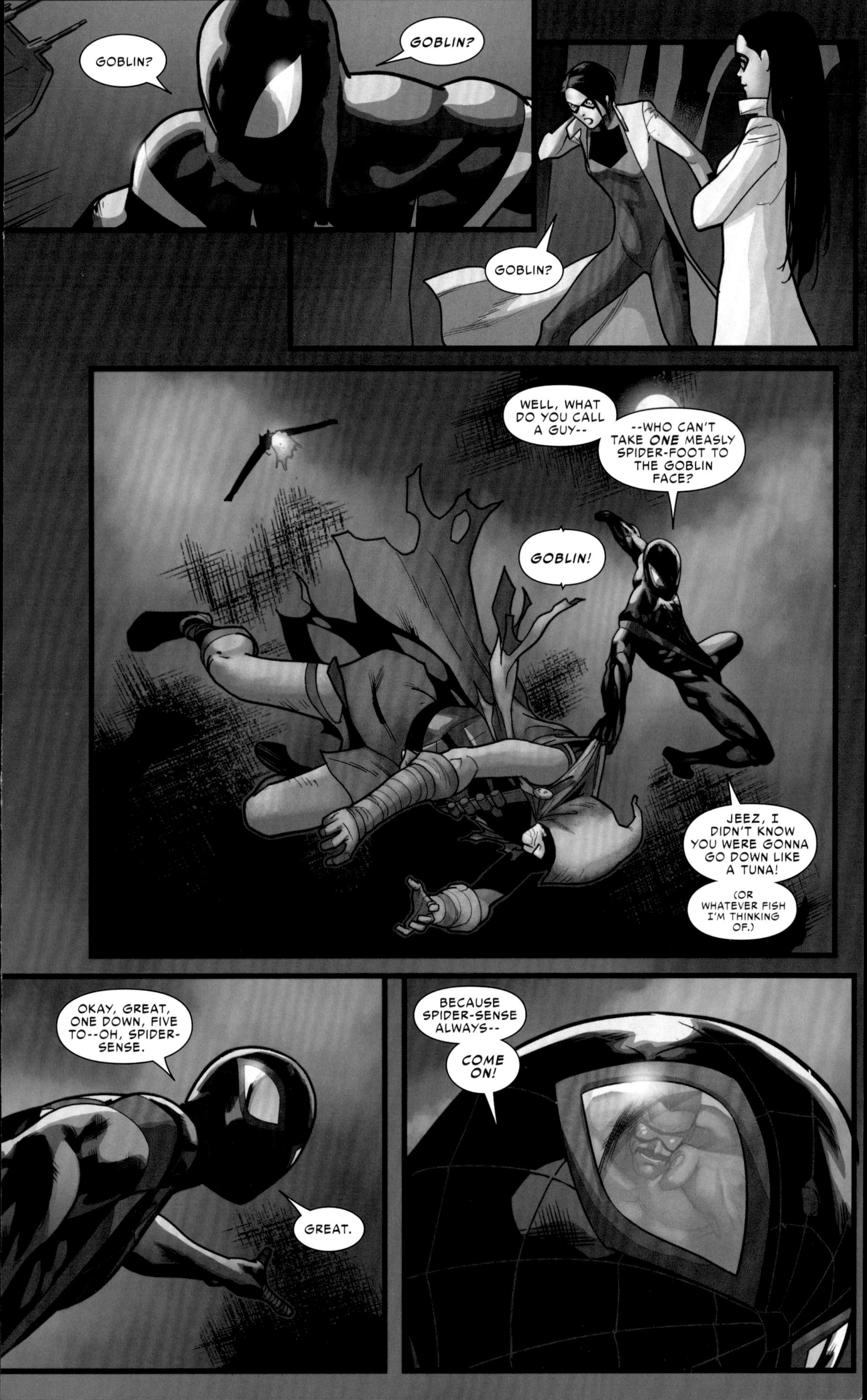
GOBLIN?
GOBLIN?
GOBLIN?
WELL, WHAT DO YOU CALL A GUY--
--WHO CAN'T TAKE ONE MEASLY SPIDER-FOOT TO THE GOBLIN FACE?
GOBLIN!
JEEZ, I DIDN'T KNOW YOU WERE GONNA GO DOWN LIKE A TUNA!
(OR WHATEVER FISH I'M THINKING OF.)
OKAY, GREAT, ONE DOWN, FIVE TO--OH, SPIDER-SENSE.
GREAT.
BECAUSE SPIDER-SENSE ALWAYS--
COME ON!

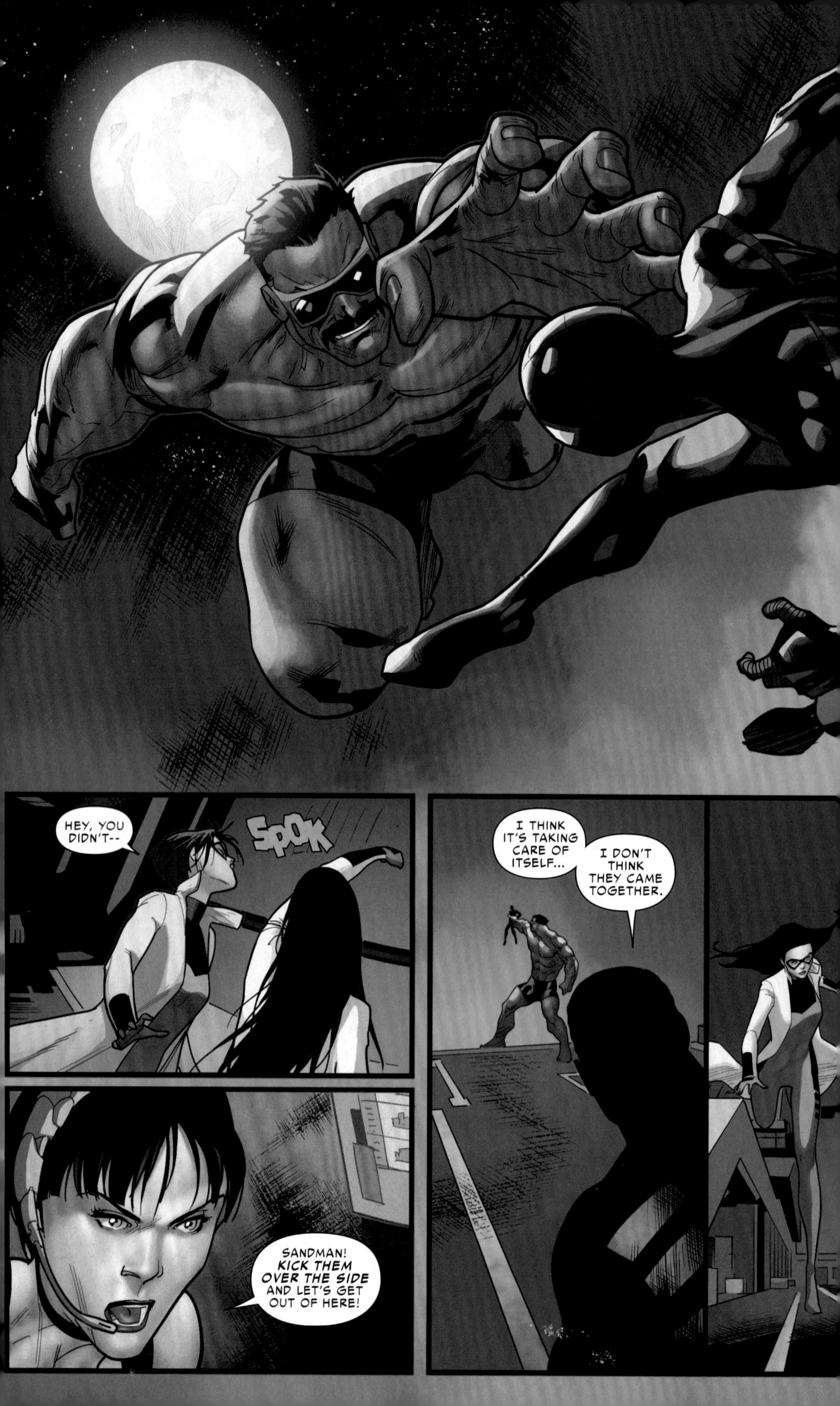
HEY, YOU DIDN'T--
SPOK
SANDMAN! KICK THEM OVER THE SIDE AND LET'S GET OUT OF HERE!
I THINK IT'S TAKING CARE OF ITSELF...
I DON'T THINK THEY CAME TOGETHER.

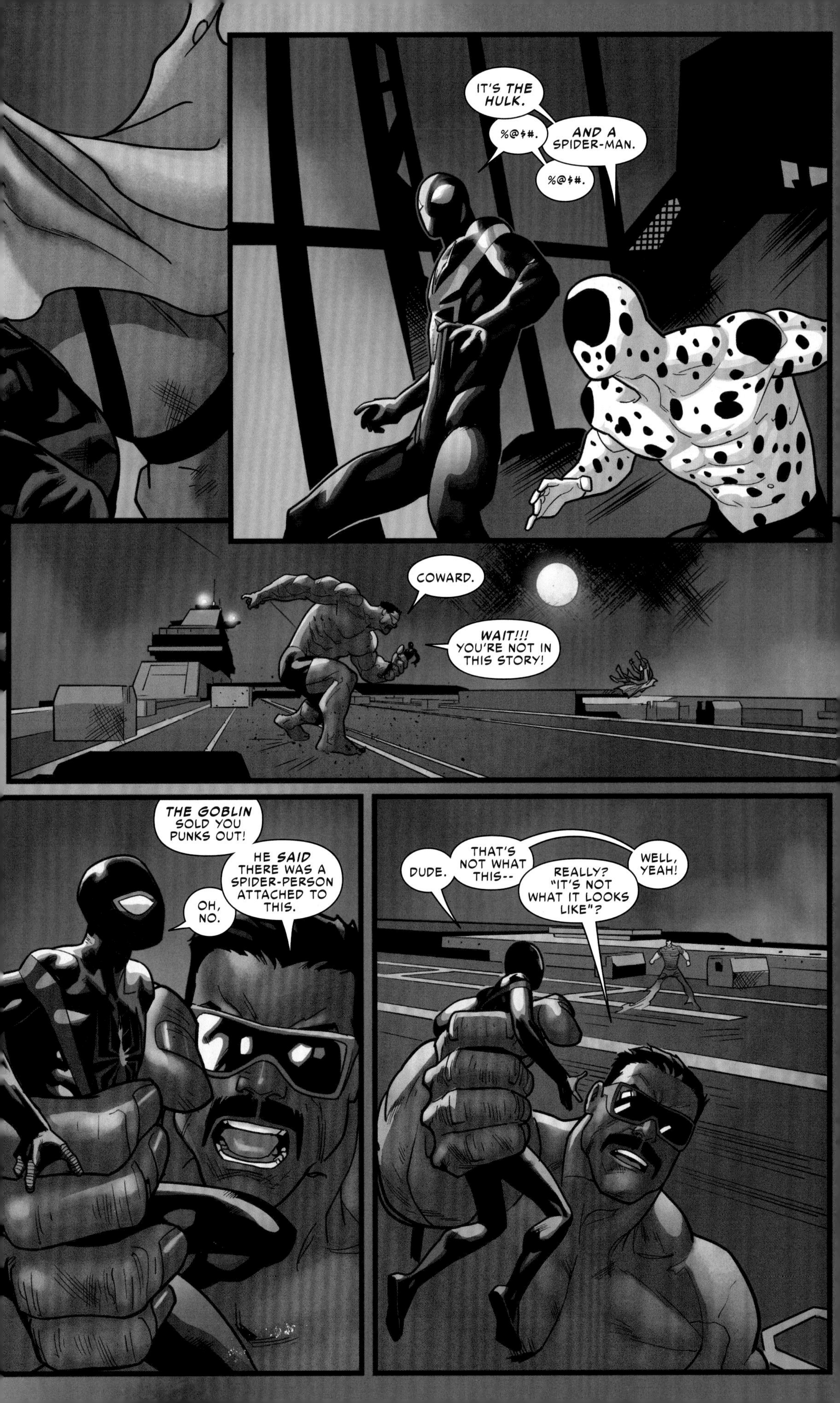

IT'S THE HULK.
%@$#.
AND A SPIDER-MAN.
%@$#.
COWARD.
WAIT!!! YOU'RE NOT IN THIS STORY!
THE GOBLIN SOLD YOU PUNKS OUT!
HE SAID THERE WAS A SPIDER-PERSON ATTACHED TO THIS.
OH, NO.
DUDE.
THAT'S NOT WHAT THIS--
WELL, YEAH!
REALLY? "IT'S NOT WHAT IT LOOKS LIKE"?

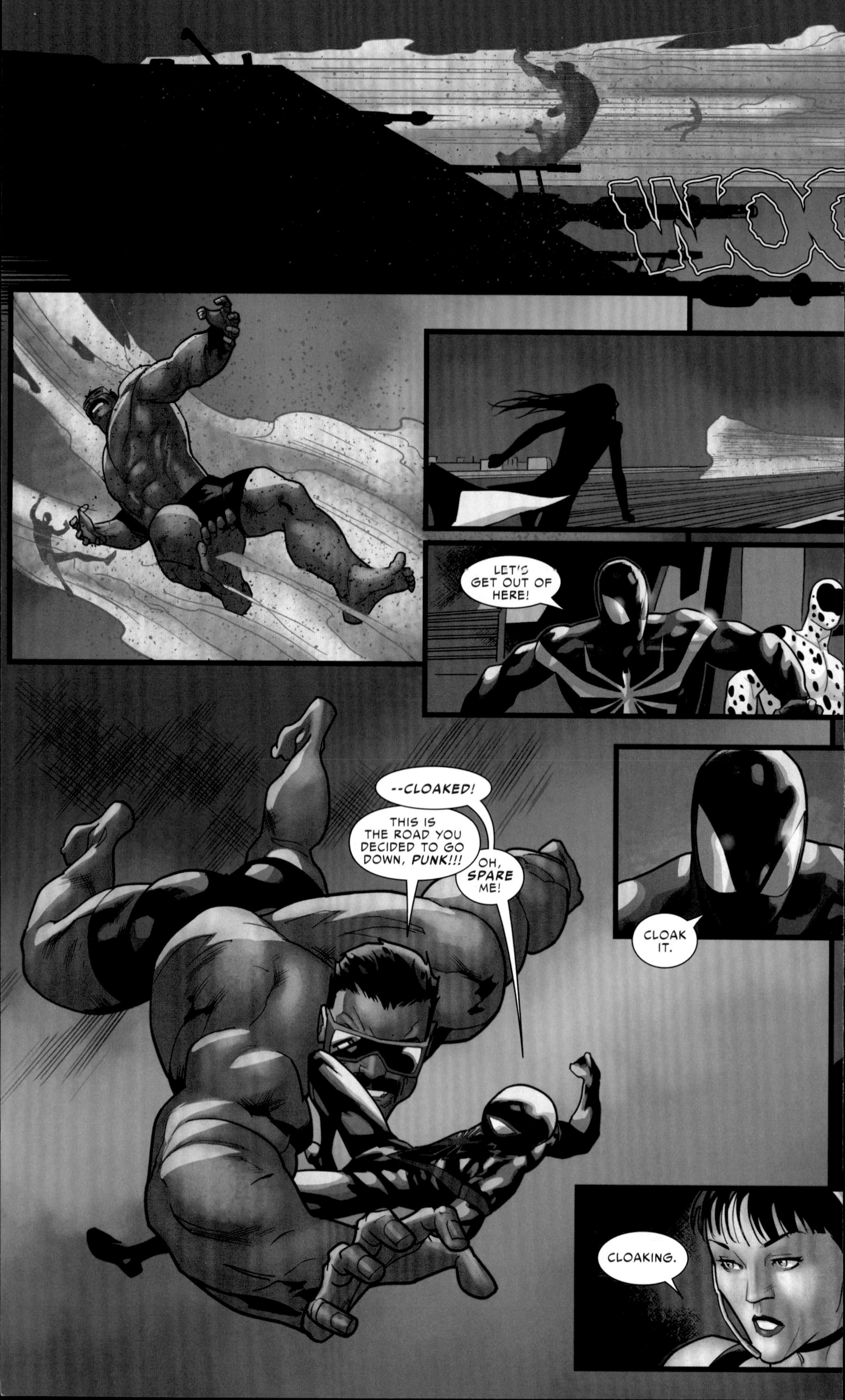
WOO
LET'S GET OUT OF HERE!
--CLOAKED!
THIS IS THE ROAD YOU DECIDED TO GO DOWN, PUNK!!!
OH, SPARE ME!
CLOAK IT.
CLOAKING.

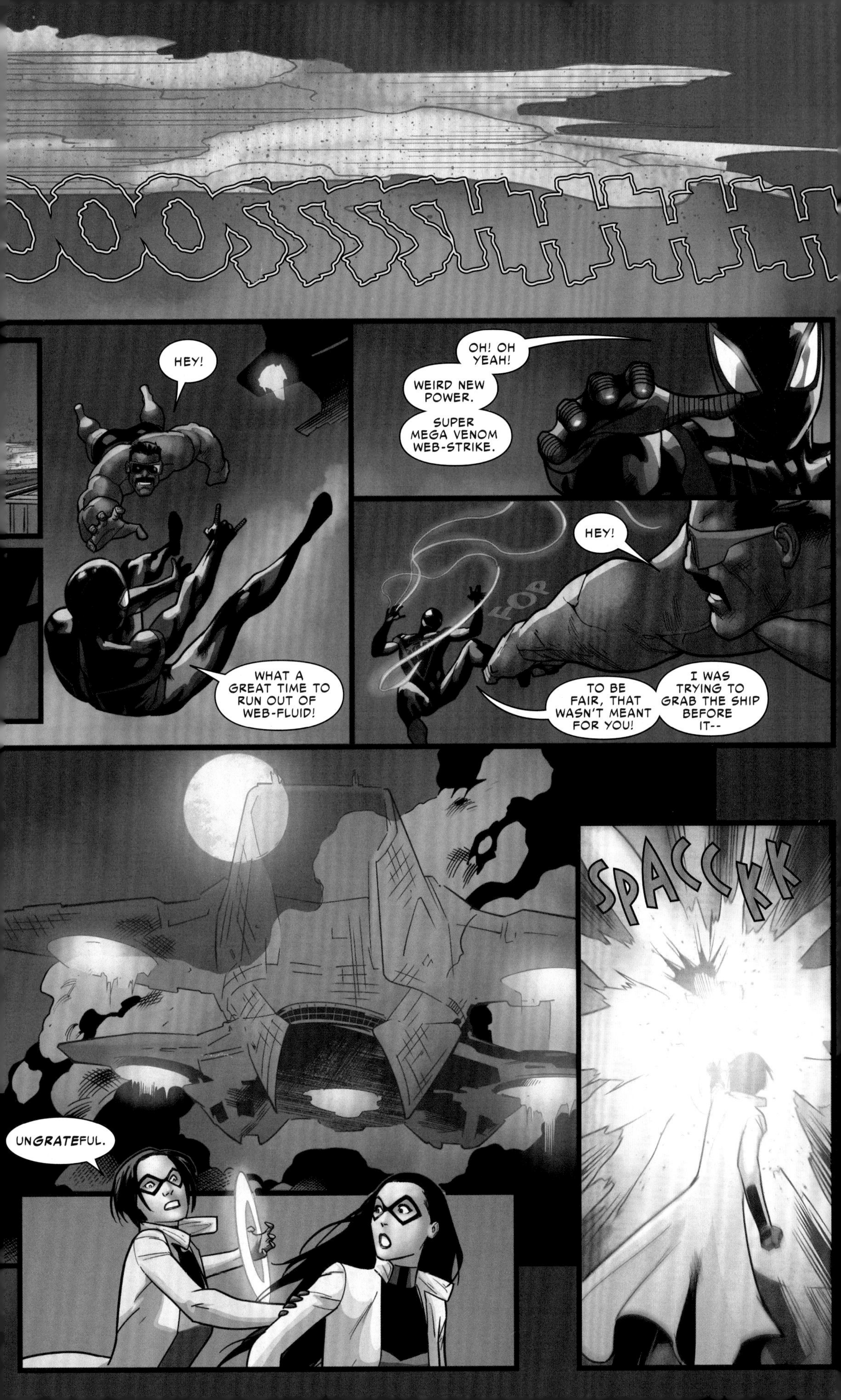

VOOOSSSSHHHHHHH
HEY!
WHAT A GREAT TIME TO RUN OUT OF WEB-FLUID!
OH! OH YEAH!
WEIRD NEW POWER.
SUPER MEGA VENOM WEB-STRIKE.
HEY!
FOP
TO BE FAIR, THAT WASN'T MEANT FOR YOU!
I WAS TRYING TO GRAB THE SHIP BEFORE IT--
UNGRATEFUL.
SPACCKK

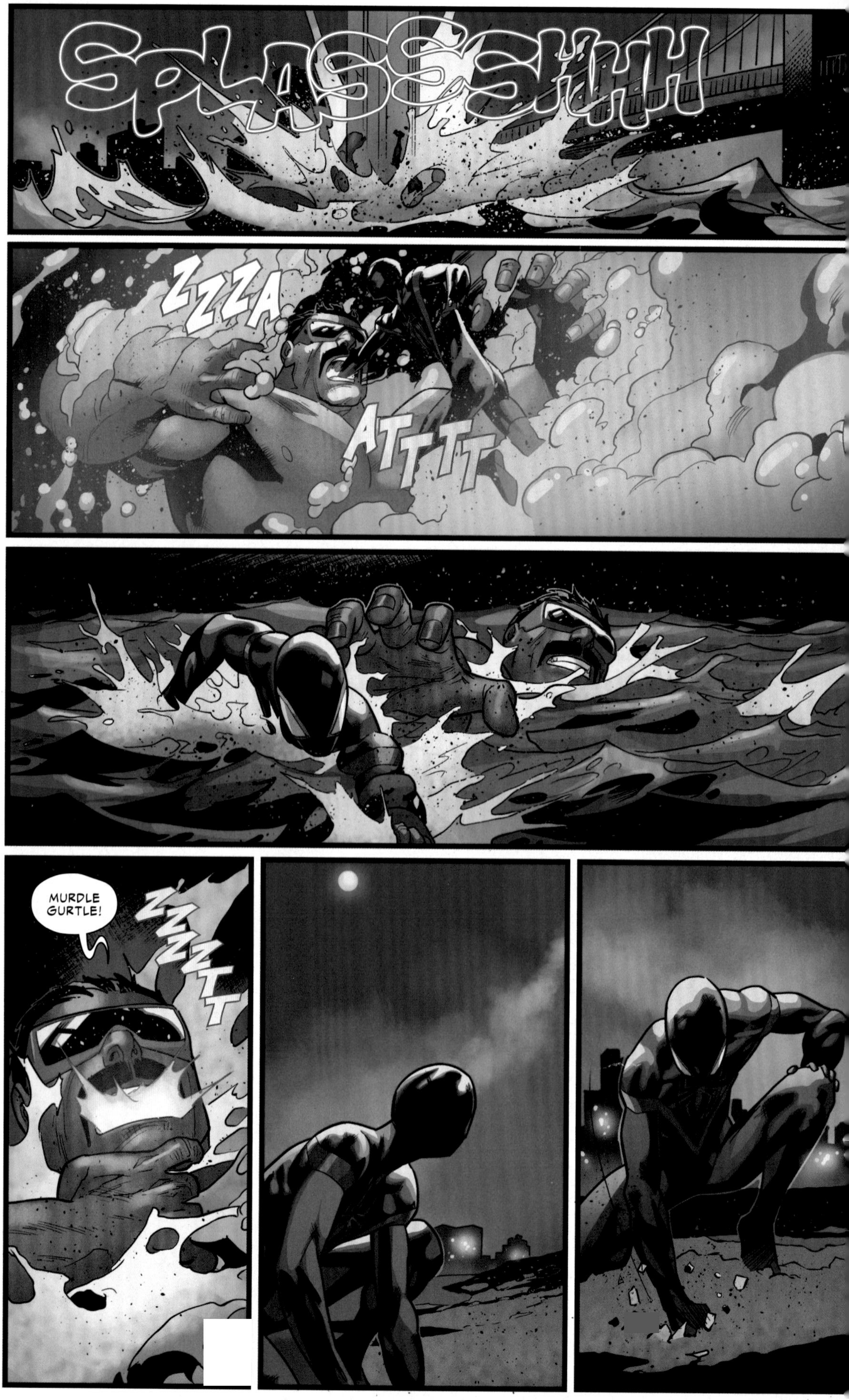
SPLASSSHHH
ZZZA
ATTTTT
MURDLE GURTLE!
ZZZZTTT

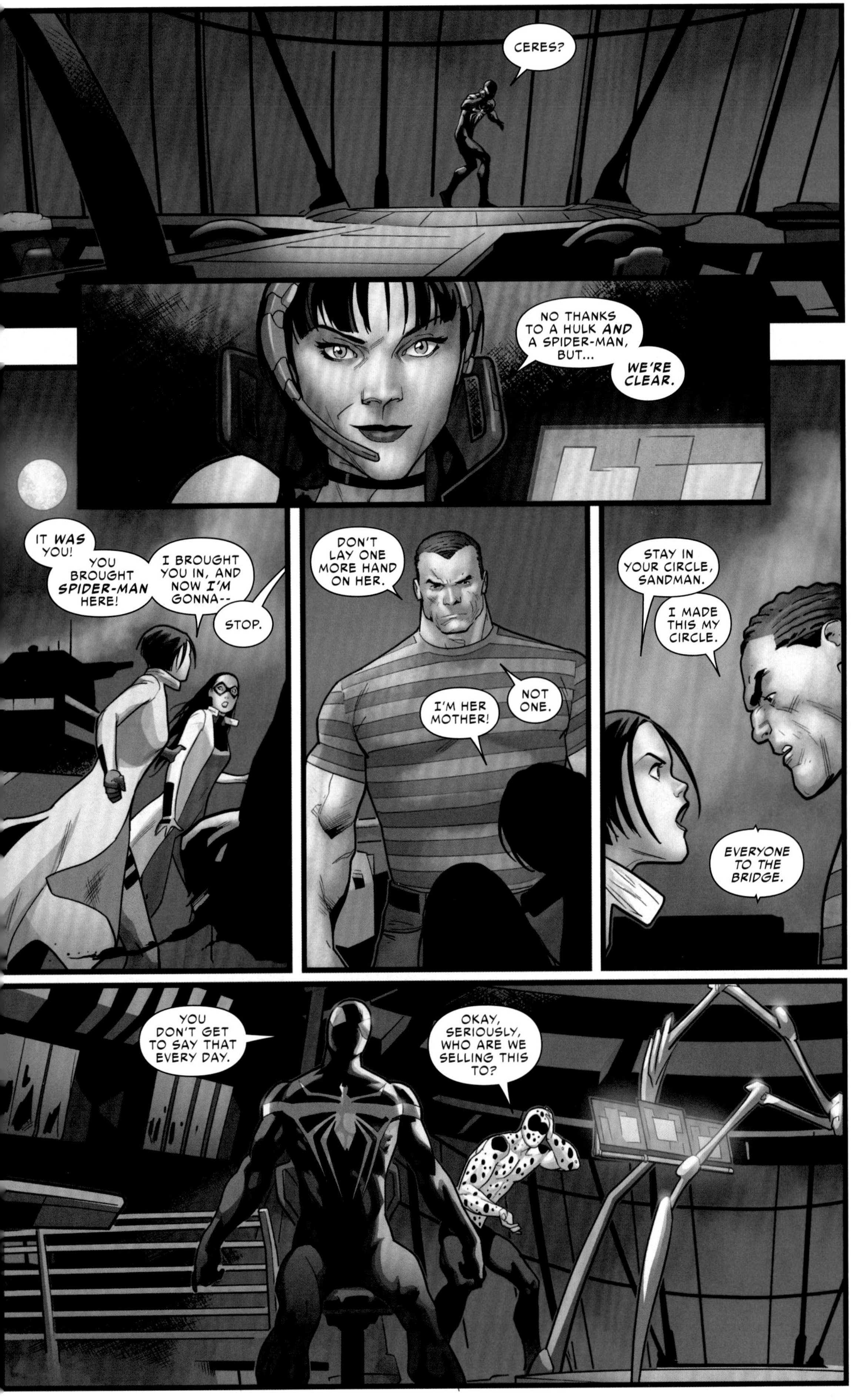
CERES?
NO THANKS TO A HULK AND A SPIDER-MAN, BUT...
WE'RE CLEAR.
IT WAS YOU!
YOU BROUGHT SPIDER-MAN HERE!
I BROUGHT YOU IN, AND NOW I'M GONNA--
STOP.
DON'T LAY ONE MORE HAND ON HER.
NOT ONE.
I'M HER MOTHER!
STAY IN YOUR CIRCLE, SANDMAN.
I MADE THIS MY CIRCLE.
EVERYONE TO THE BRIDGE.
YOU DON'T GET TO SAY THAT EVERY DAY.
OKAY, SERIOUSLY, WHO ARE WE SELLING THIS TO?

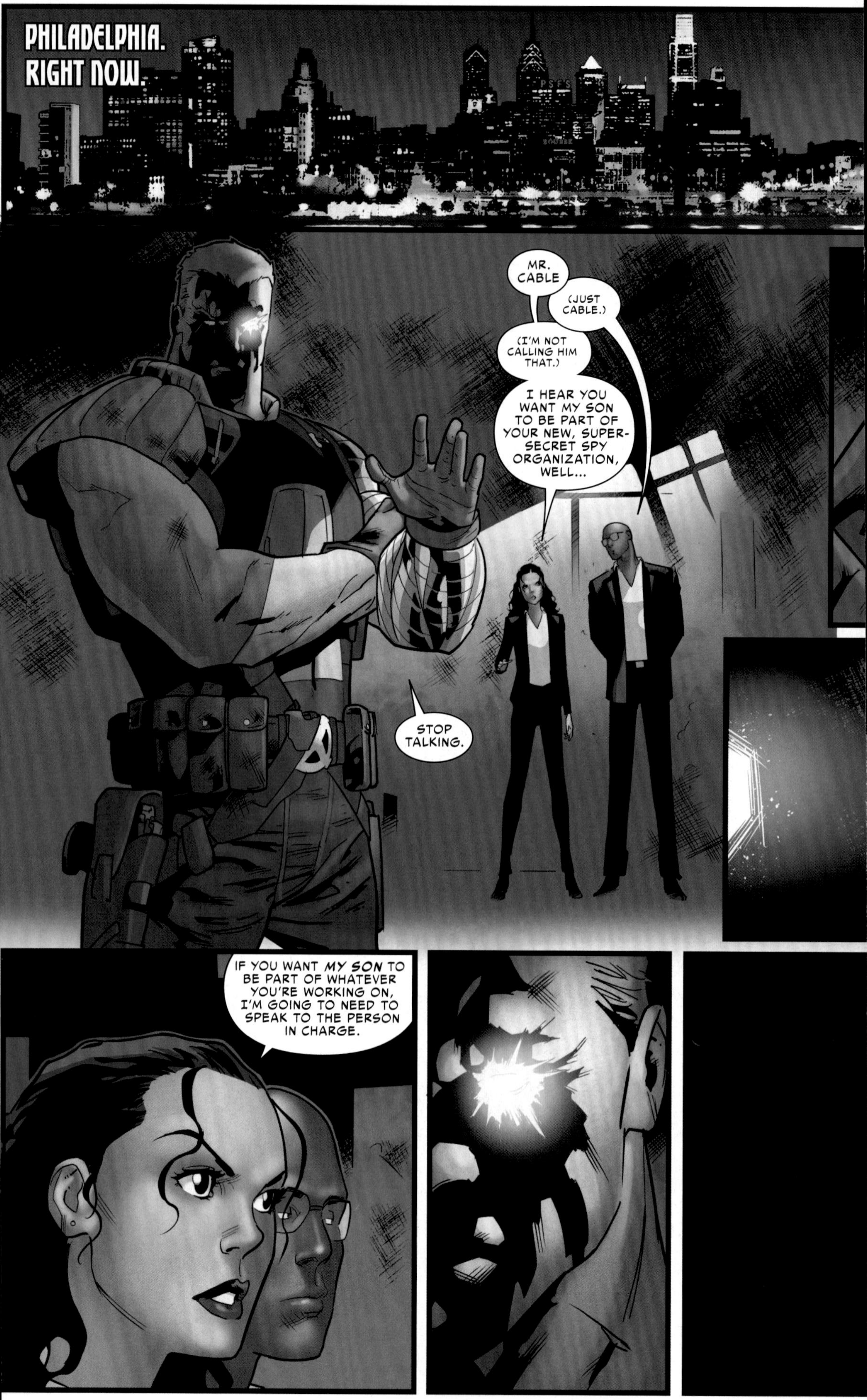
PHILADELPHIA. RIGHT NOW.
MR. CABLE
(JUST CABLE.)
(I'M NOT CALLING HIM THAT.)
I HEAR YOU WANT MY SON TO BE PART OF YOUR NEW, SUPER-SECRET SPY ORGANIZATION, WELL...
STOP TALKING.
IF YOU WANT MY SON TO BE PART OF WHATEVER YOU'RE WORKING ON, I'M GOING TO NEED TO SPEAK TO THE PERSON IN CHARGE.

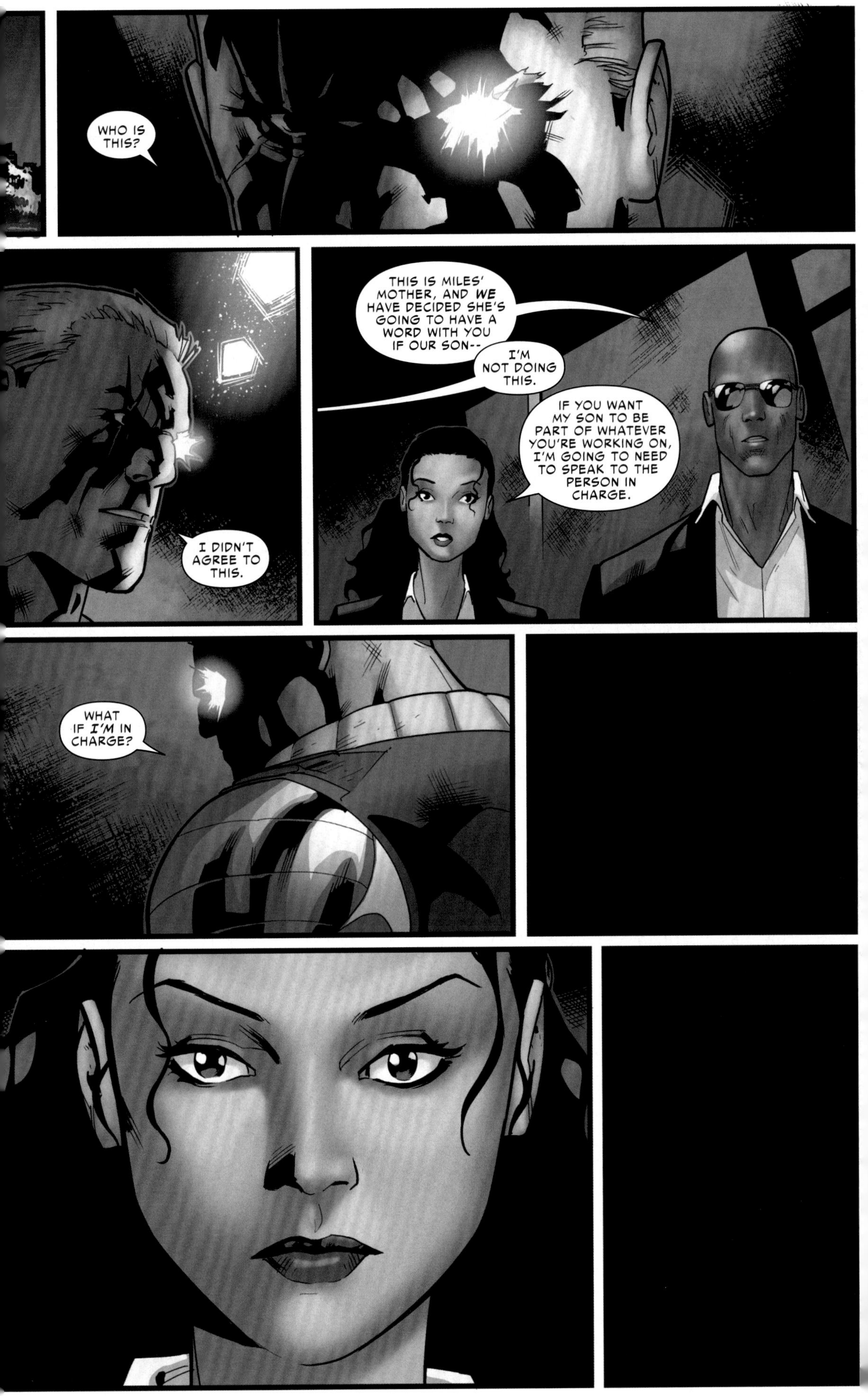
WHO IS THIS?
I DIDN'T AGREE TO THIS.
THIS IS MILES' MOTHER, AND *WE* HAVE DECIDED SHE'S GOING TO HAVE A WORD WITH YOU IF OUR SON--
I'M NOT DOING THIS.
IF YOU WANT MY SON TO BE PART OF WHATEVER YOU'RE WORKING ON, I'M GOING TO NEED TO SPEAK TO THE PERSON IN CHARGE.
WHAT IF *I'M* IN CHARGE?

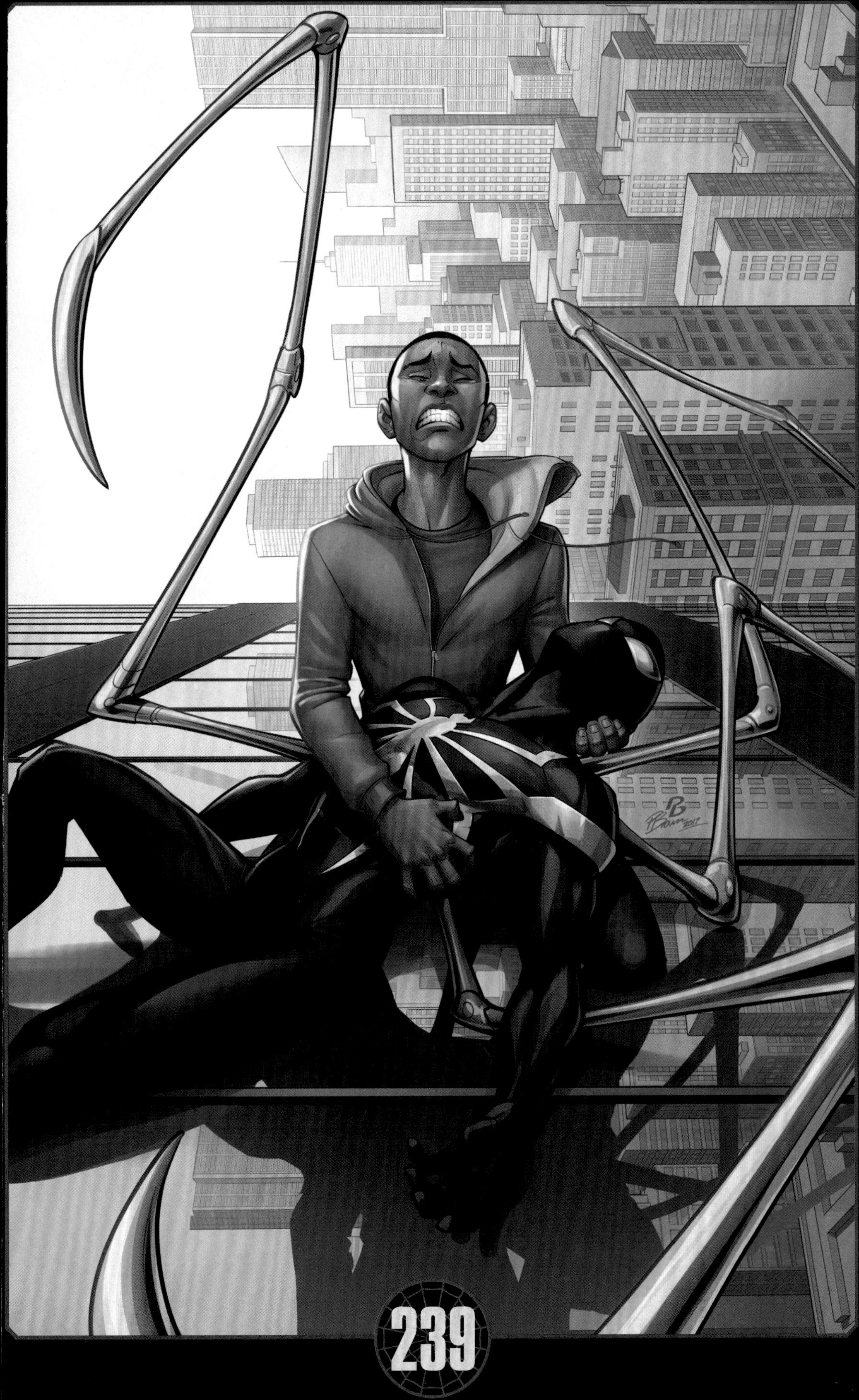
239

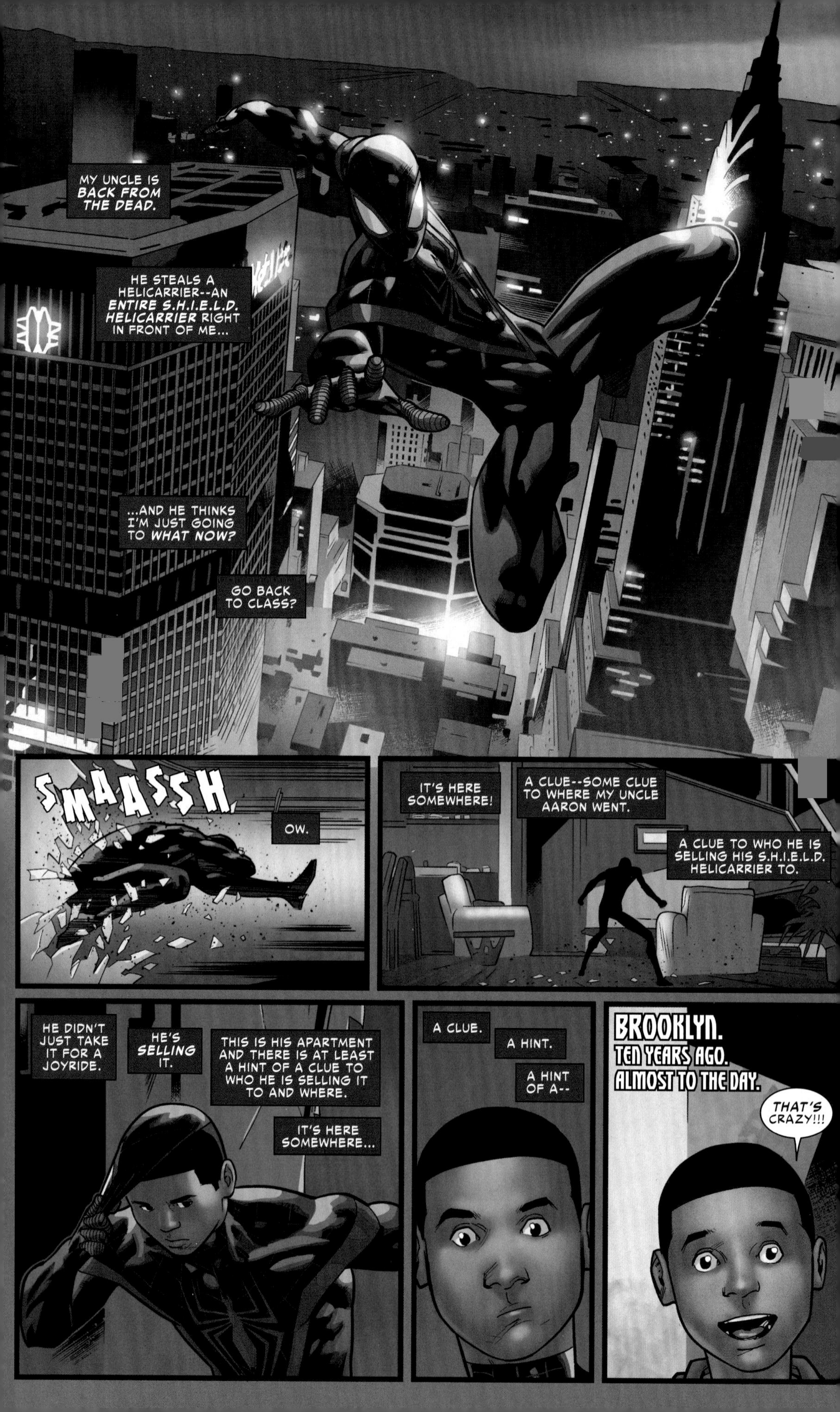
MY UNCLE IS BACK FROM THE DEAD.
HE STEALS A HELICARRIER--AN ENTIRE S.H.I.E.L.D. HELICARRIER RIGHT IN FRONT OF ME...
...AND HE THINKS I'M JUST GOING TO WHAT NOW?
GO BACK TO CLASS?
SMAASSH
OW.
IT'S HERE SOMEWHERE!
A CLUE--SOME CLUE TO WHERE MY UNCLE AARON WENT.
A CLUE TO WHO HE IS SELLING HIS S.H.I.E.L.D. HELICARRIER TO.
HE DIDN'T JUST TAKE IT FOR A JOYRIDE.
HE'S SELLING IT.
THIS IS HIS APARTMENT AND THERE IS AT LEAST A HINT OF A CLUE TO WHO HE IS SELLING IT TO AND WHERE.
IT'S HERE SOMEWHERE...
A CLUE.
A HINT.
A HINT OF A--
BROOKLYN. TEN YEARS AGO. ALMOST TO THE DAY.
THAT'S CRAZY!!!

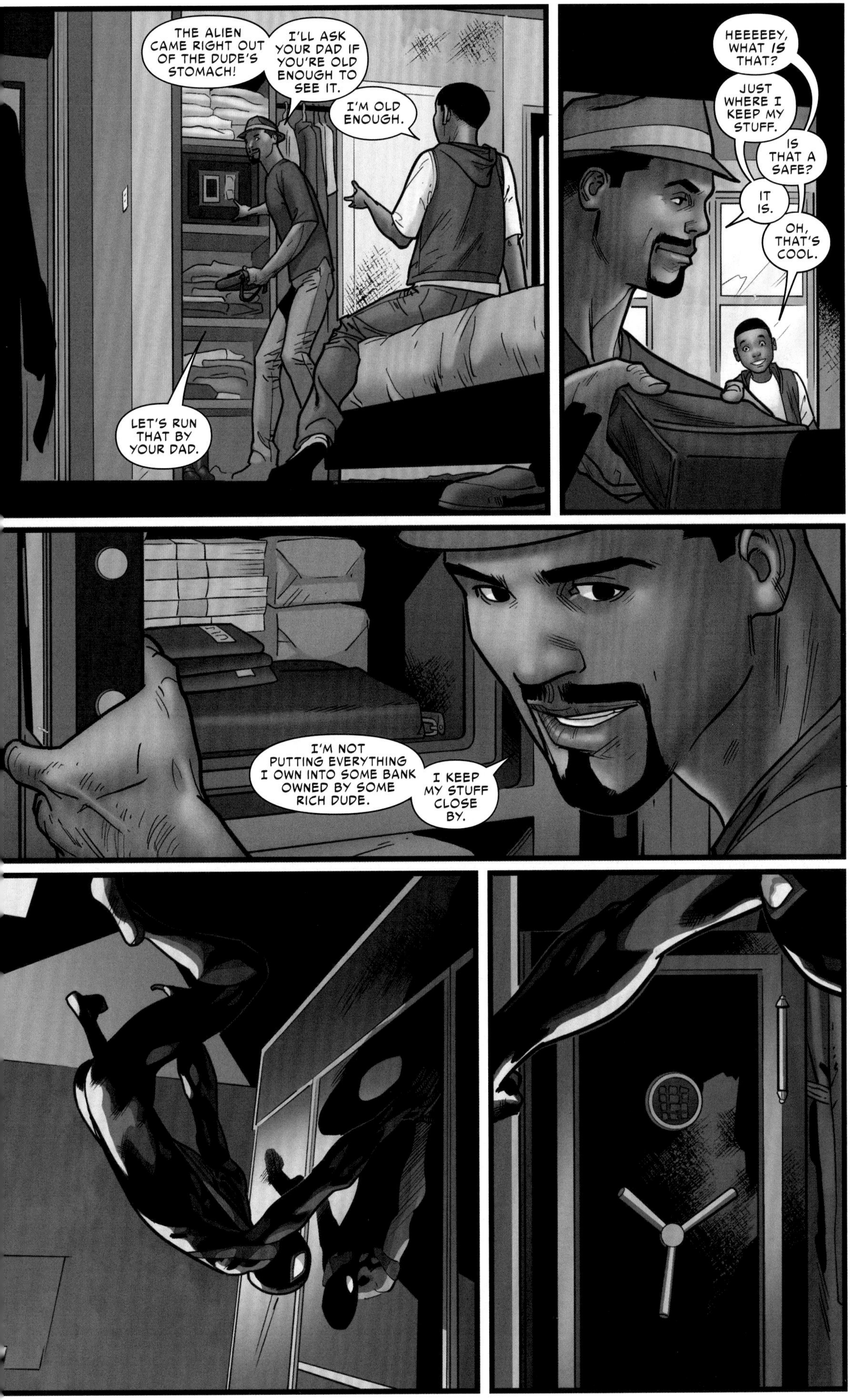
THE ALIEN CAME RIGHT OUT OF THE DUDE'S STOMACH!
I'LL ASK YOUR DAD IF YOU'RE OLD ENOUGH TO SEE IT.
I'M OLD ENOUGH.
LET'S RUN THAT BY YOUR DAD.
HEEEEEY, WHAT *IS* THAT?
JUST WHERE I KEEP MY STUFF.
IS THAT A SAFE?
IT IS.
OH, THAT'S COOL.
I'M NOT PUTTING EVERYTHING I OWN INTO SOME BANK OWNED BY SOME RICH DUDE.
I KEEP MY STUFF CLOSE BY.

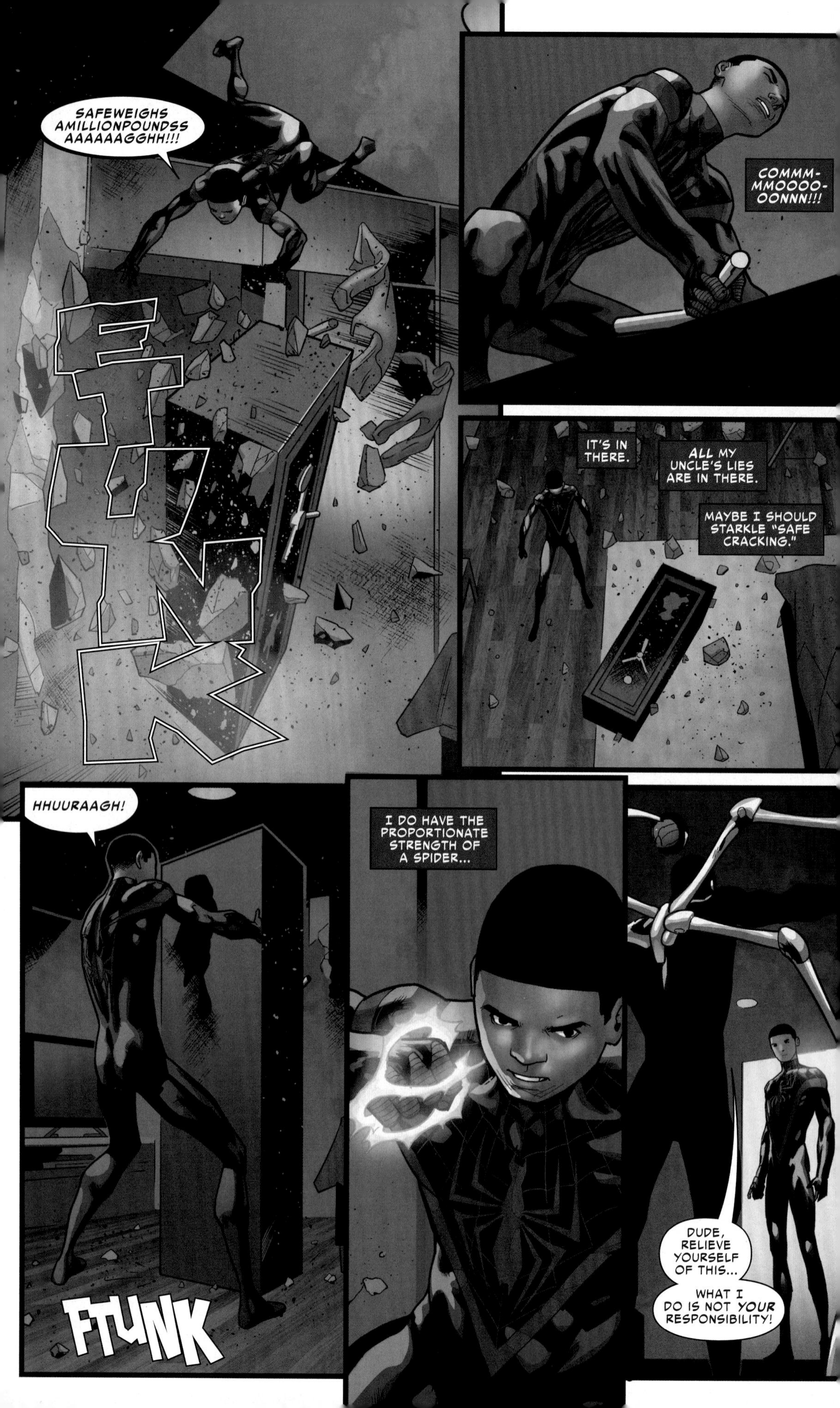
SAFEWEIGHS AMILLIONPOUNDSS AAAAAAGGHH!!!
FTUNK
COMMM-MMOOOO-OONNN!!!
IT'S IN THERE.
ALL MY UNCLE'S LIES ARE IN THERE.
MAYBE I SHOULD STARKLE "SAFE CRACKING."
HHUURAAGH!
FTUNK
I DO HAVE THE PROPORTIONATE STRENGTH OF A SPIDER...
DUDE, RELIEVE YOURSELF OF THIS...
WHAT I DO IS NOT YOUR RESPONSIBILITY!

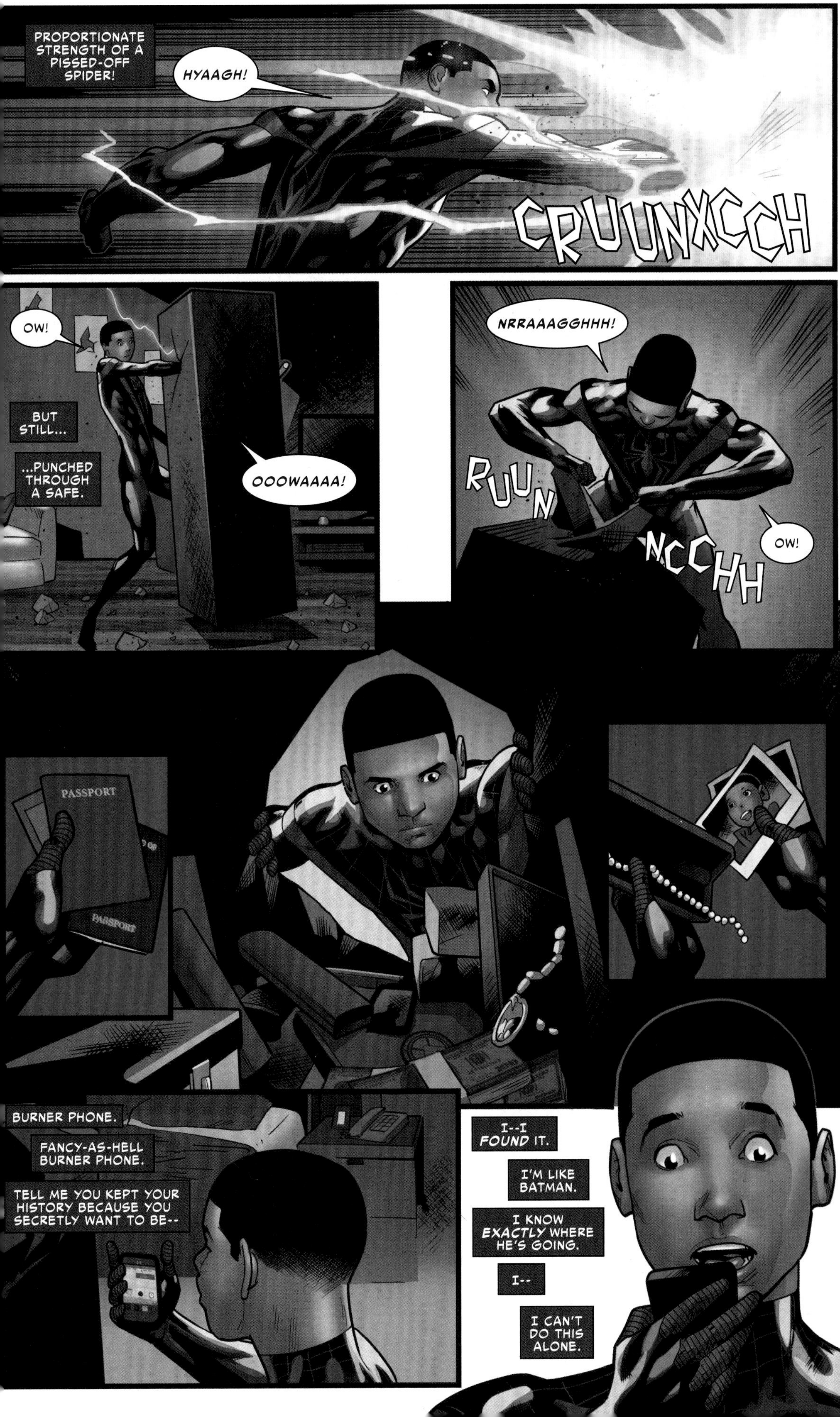
PROPORTIONATE STRENGTH OF A PISSED-OFF SPIDER!
HYAAGH!
CRUUNXCCH
OW!
BUT STILL...
...PUNCHED THROUGH A SAFE.
OOOWAAAA!
NRRAAAGGHHH!
RUUNNCCHH
OW!
PASSPORT
PASSPORT
BURNER PHONE.
FANCY-AS-HELL BURNER PHONE.
TELL ME YOU KEPT YOUR HISTORY BECAUSE YOU SECRETLY WANT TO BE--
I--I FOUND IT.
I'M LIKE BATMAN.
I KNOW EXACTLY WHERE HE'S GOING.
I--
I CAN'T DO THIS ALONE.

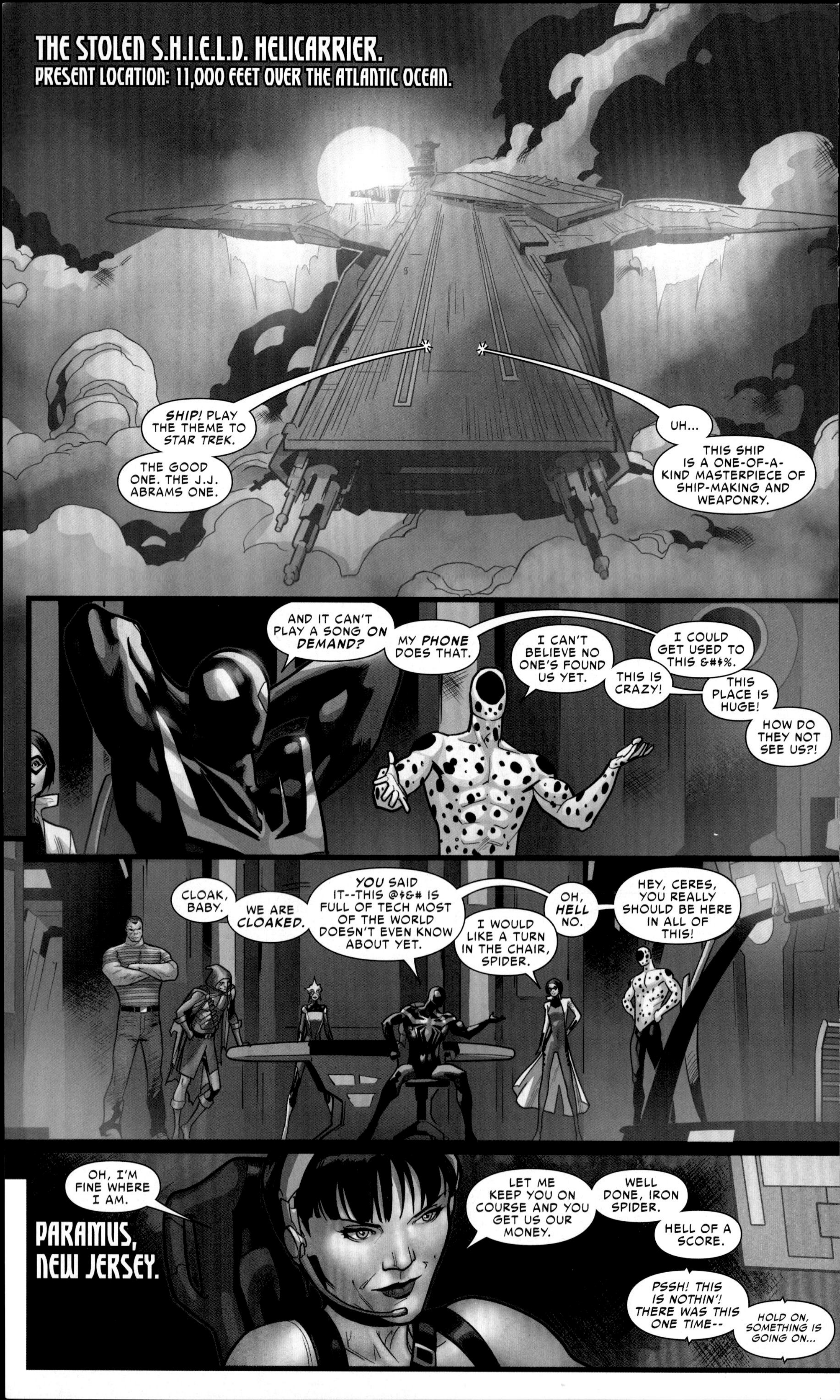
THE STOLEN S.H.I.E.L.D. HELICARRIER.
PRESENT LOCATION: 11,000 FEET OVER THE ATLANTIC OCEAN.
SHIP! PLAY THE THEME TO STAR TREK.
THE GOOD ONE. THE J.J. ABRAMS ONE.
UH...
THIS SHIP IS A ONE-OF-A-KIND MASTERPIECE OF SHIP-MAKING AND WEAPONRY.
AND IT CAN'T PLAY A SONG ON DEMAND?
MY PHONE DOES THAT.
I COULD GET USED TO THIS &#$%.
I CAN'T BELIEVE NO ONE'S FOUND US YET.
THIS IS CRAZY!
THIS PLACE IS HUGE!
HOW DO THEY NOT SEE US?!
CLOAK, BABY.
WE ARE CLOAKED.
YOU SAID IT--THIS @$&# IS FULL OF TECH MOST OF THE WORLD DOESN'T EVEN KNOW ABOUT YET.
I WOULD LIKE A TURN IN THE CHAIR, SPIDER.
OH, HELL NO.
HEY, CERES, YOU REALLY SHOULD BE HERE IN ALL OF THIS!
OH, I'M FINE WHERE I AM.
PARAMUS, NEW JERSEY.
LET ME KEEP YOU ON COURSE AND YOU GET US OUR MONEY.
WELL DONE, IRON SPIDER.
HELL OF A SCORE.
PSSH! THIS IS NOTHIN'! THERE WAS THIS ONE TIME--
HOLD ON, SOMETHING IS GOING ON...

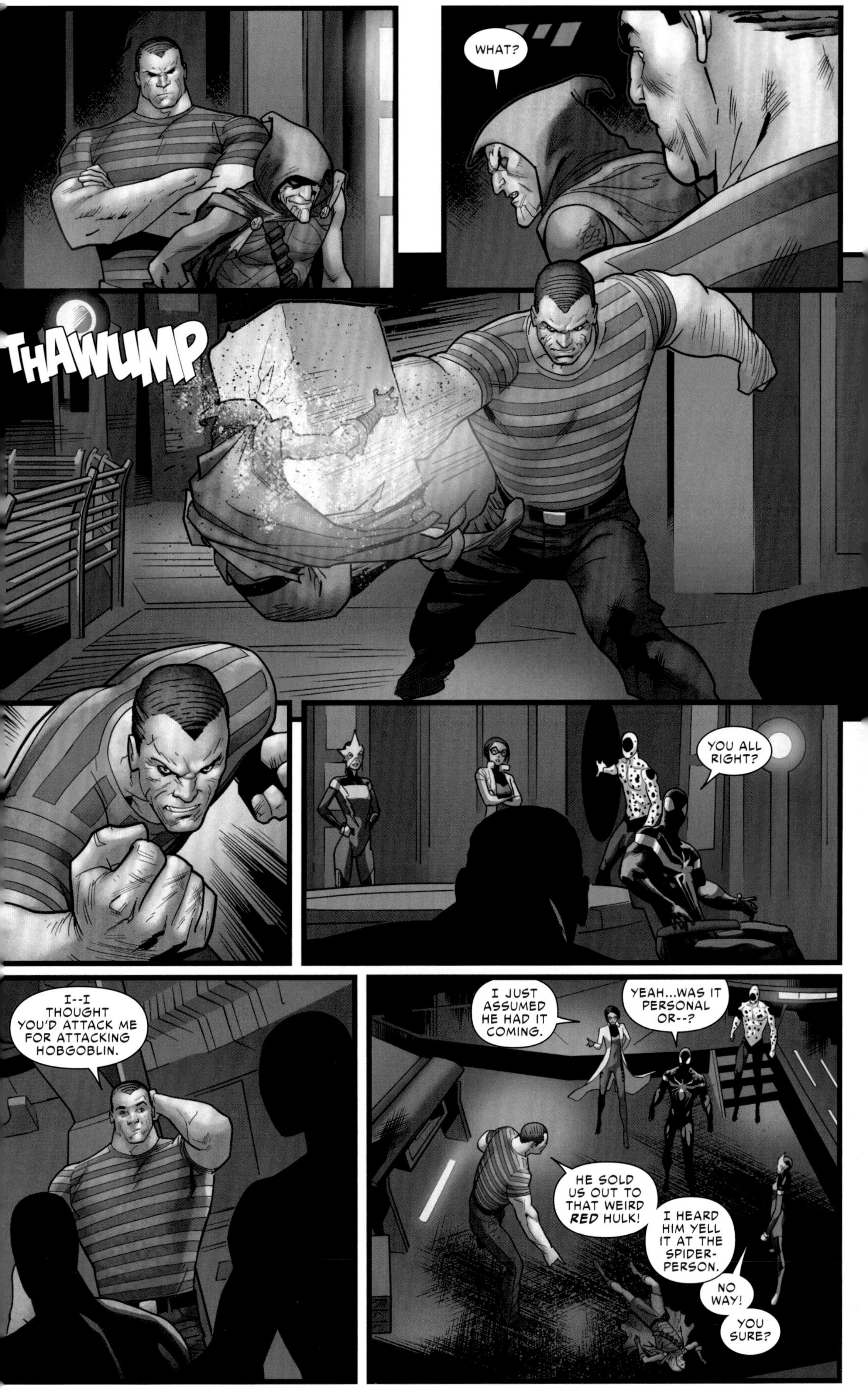
WHAT?
THAWUMP
YOU ALL RIGHT?
I--I THOUGHT YOU'D ATTACK ME FOR ATTACKING HOBGOBLIN.
I JUST ASSUMED HE HAD IT COMING.
YEAH...WAS IT PERSONAL OR--?
HE SOLD US OUT TO THAT WEIRD RED HULK!
I HEARD HIM YELL IT AT THE SPIDER-PERSON.
NO WAY!
YOU SURE?

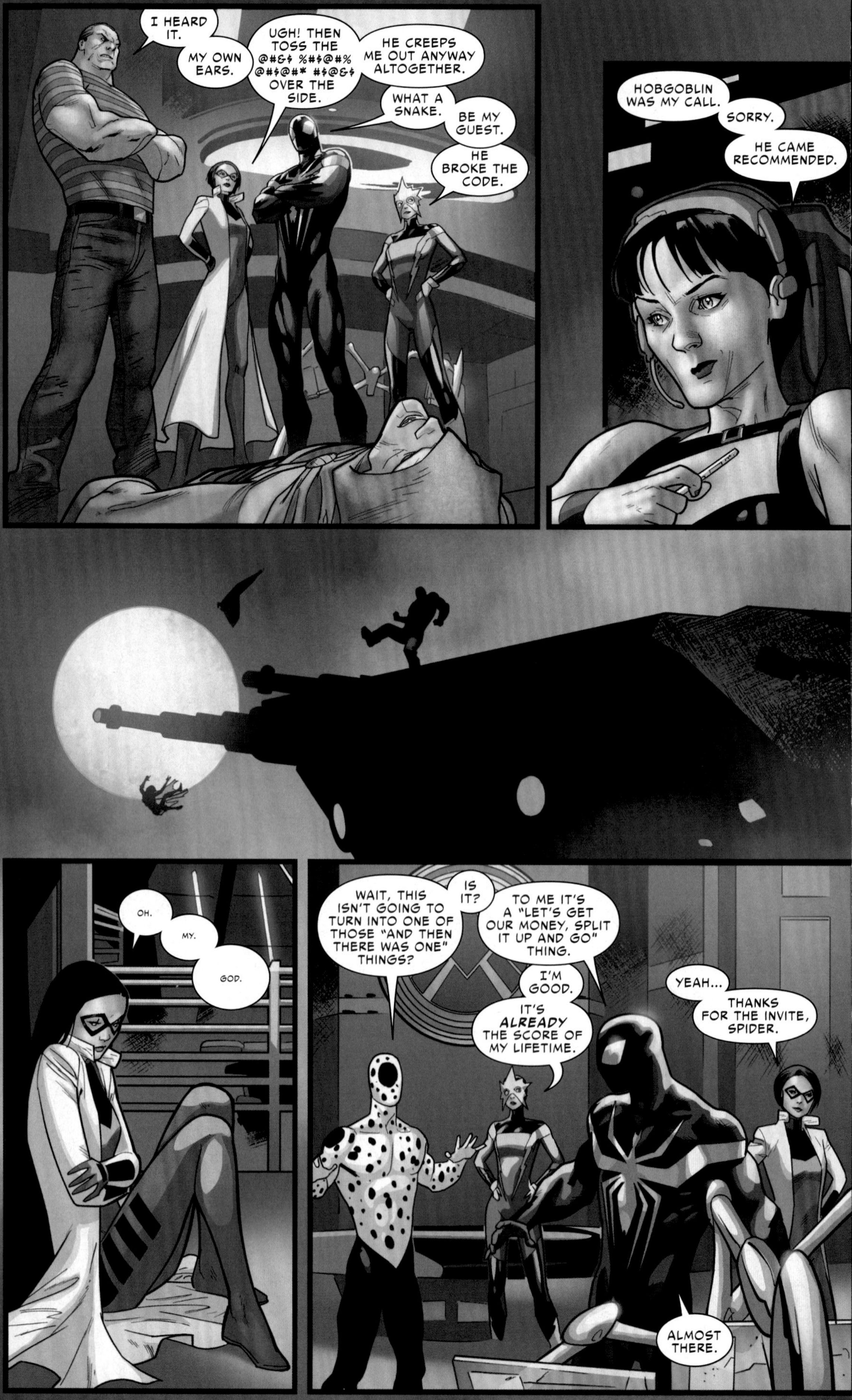
I HEARD IT.
MY OWN EARS.
UGH! THEN TOSS THE @#&$ %#$@#% @#$@#* #$@&$ OVER THE SIDE.
HE CREEPS ME OUT ANYWAY ALTOGETHER.
WHAT A SNAKE.
BE MY GUEST.
HE BROKE THE CODE.
HOBGOBLIN WAS MY CALL.
SORRY.
HE CAME RECOMMENDED.
OH.
MY.
GOD.
WAIT, THIS ISN'T GOING TO TURN INTO ONE OF THOSE "AND THEN THERE WAS ONE" THINGS?
IS IT?
TO ME IT'S A "LET'S GET OUR MONEY, SPLIT IT UP AND GO" THING.
I'M GOOD.
IT'S *ALREADY* THE SCORE OF MY LIFETIME.
YEAH...
THANKS FOR THE INVITE, SPIDER.
ALMOST THERE.

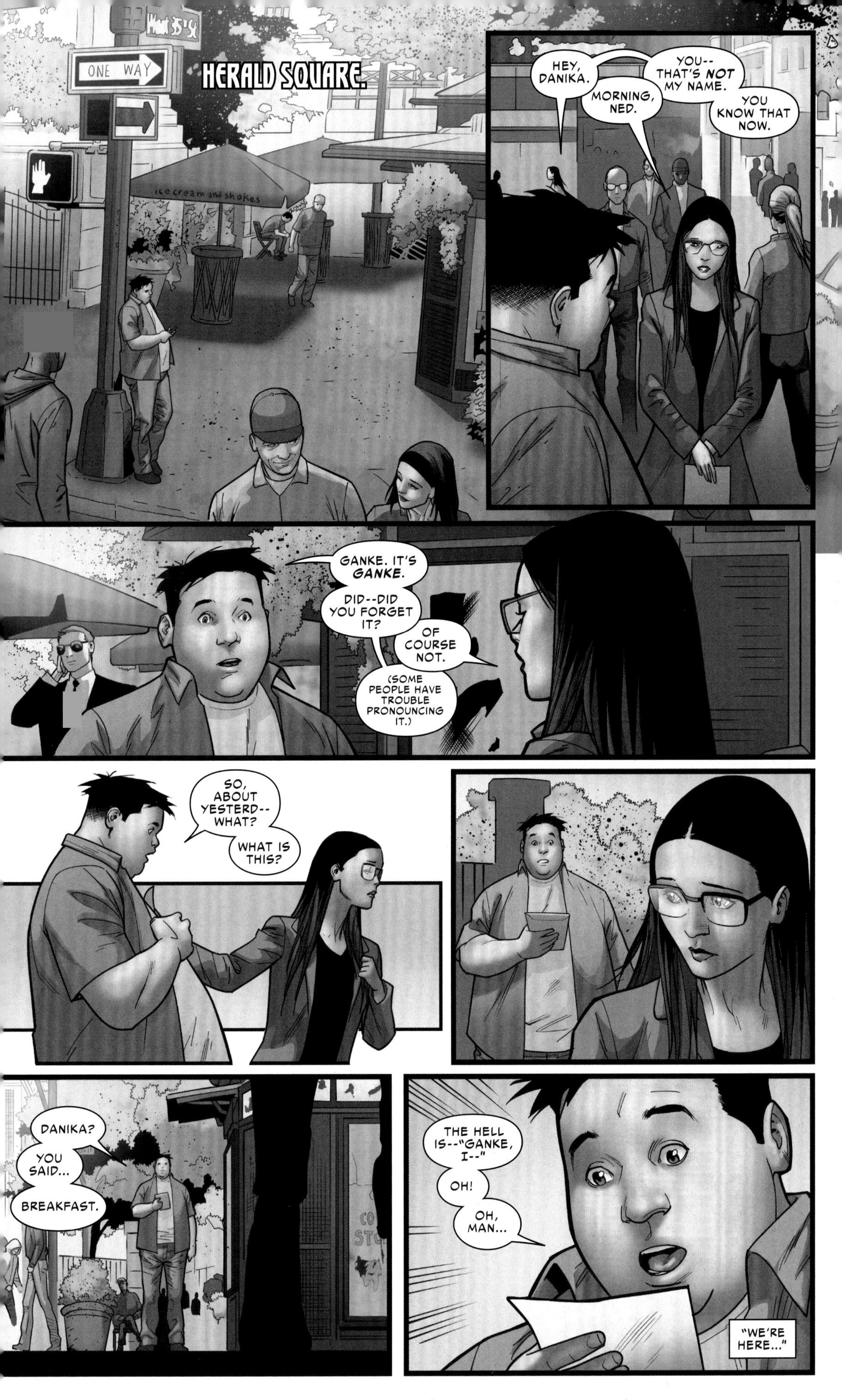

HERALD SQUARE.
ONE WAY
ice cream and shakes
HEY, DANIKA.
MORNING, NED.
YOU-- THAT'S NOT MY NAME.
YOU KNOW THAT NOW.
GANKE. IT'S GANKE.
DID--DID YOU FORGET IT?
OF COURSE NOT.
(SOME PEOPLE HAVE TROUBLE PRONOUNCING IT.)
SO, ABOUT YESTERD-- WHAT?
WHAT IS THIS?
DANIKA?
YOU SAID...
BREAKFAST.
THE HELL IS--"GANKE, I--"
OH!
OH, MAN...
"WE'RE HERE..."

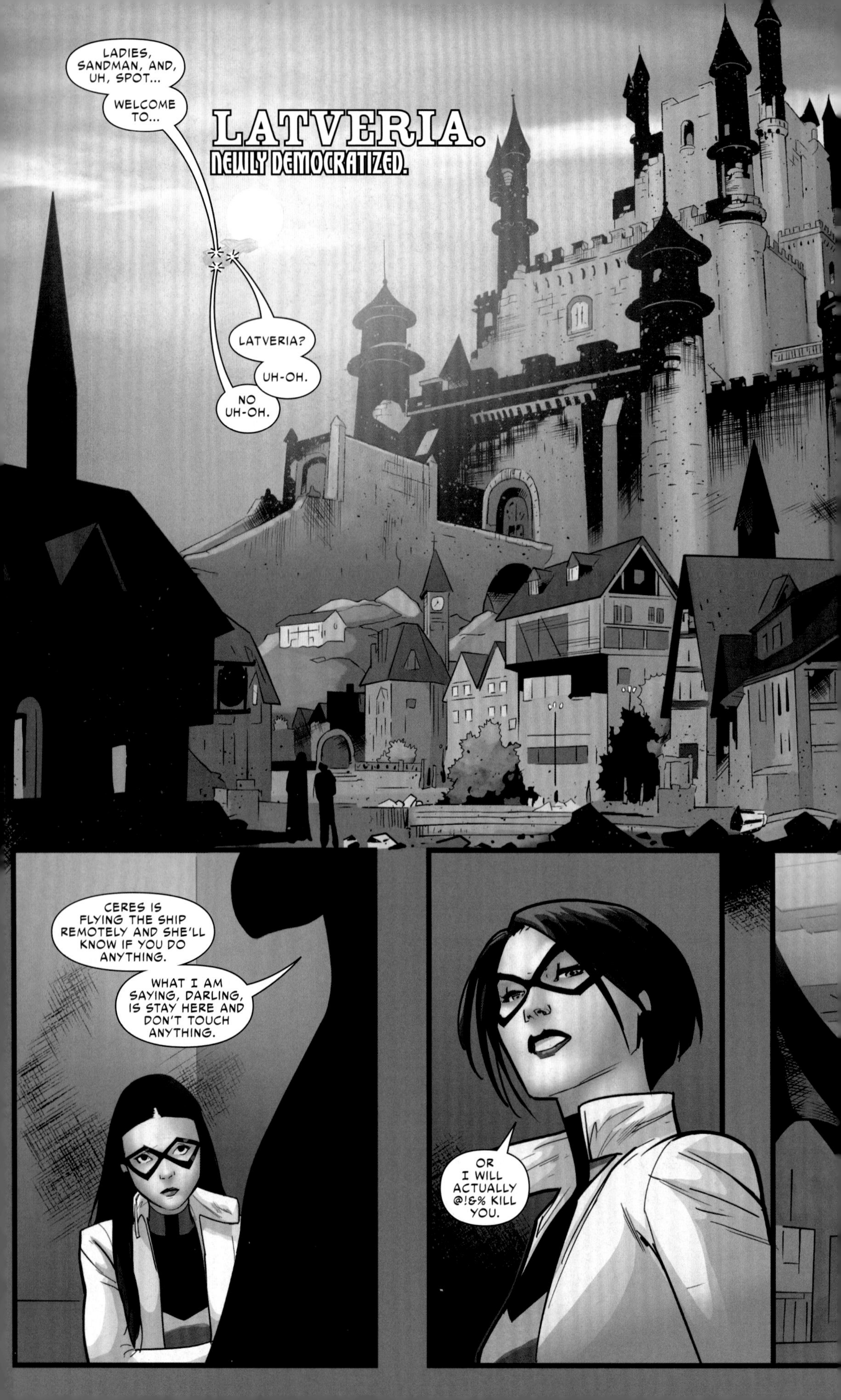
LADIES, SANDMAN, AND, UH, SPOT...
WELCOME TO...
LATVERIA.
NEWLY DEMOCRATIZED.
LATVERIA?
UH-OH.
NO UH-OH.
CERES IS FLYING THE SHIP REMOTELY AND SHE'LL KNOW IF YOU DO ANYTHING.
WHAT I AM SAYING, DARLING, IS STAY HERE AND DON'T TOUCH ANYTHING.
OR I WILL ACTUALLY @!&% KILL YOU.

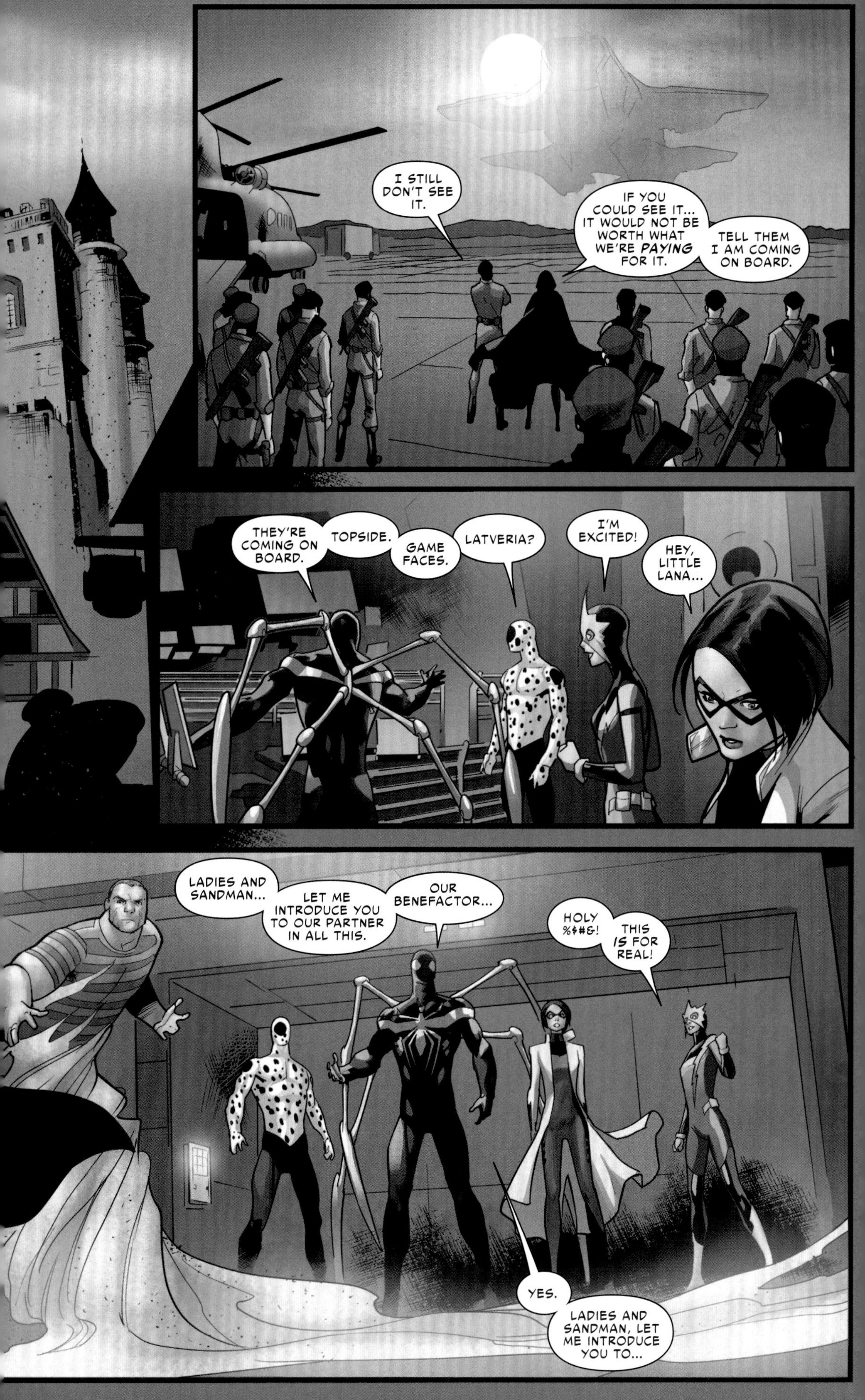
I STILL DON'T SEE IT.
IF YOU COULD SEE IT... IT WOULD NOT BE WORTH WHAT WE'RE *PAYING* FOR IT.
TELL THEM I AM COMING ON BOARD.
THEY'RE COMING ON BOARD.
TOPSIDE.
GAME FACES.
LATVERIA?
I'M EXCITED!
HEY, LITTLE LANA...
LADIES AND SANDMAN...
LET ME INTRODUCE YOU TO OUR PARTNER IN ALL THIS.
OUR BENEFACTOR...
HOLY %$#&!
THIS *IS* FOR REAL!
YES.
LADIES AND SANDMAN, LET ME INTRODUCE YOU TO...

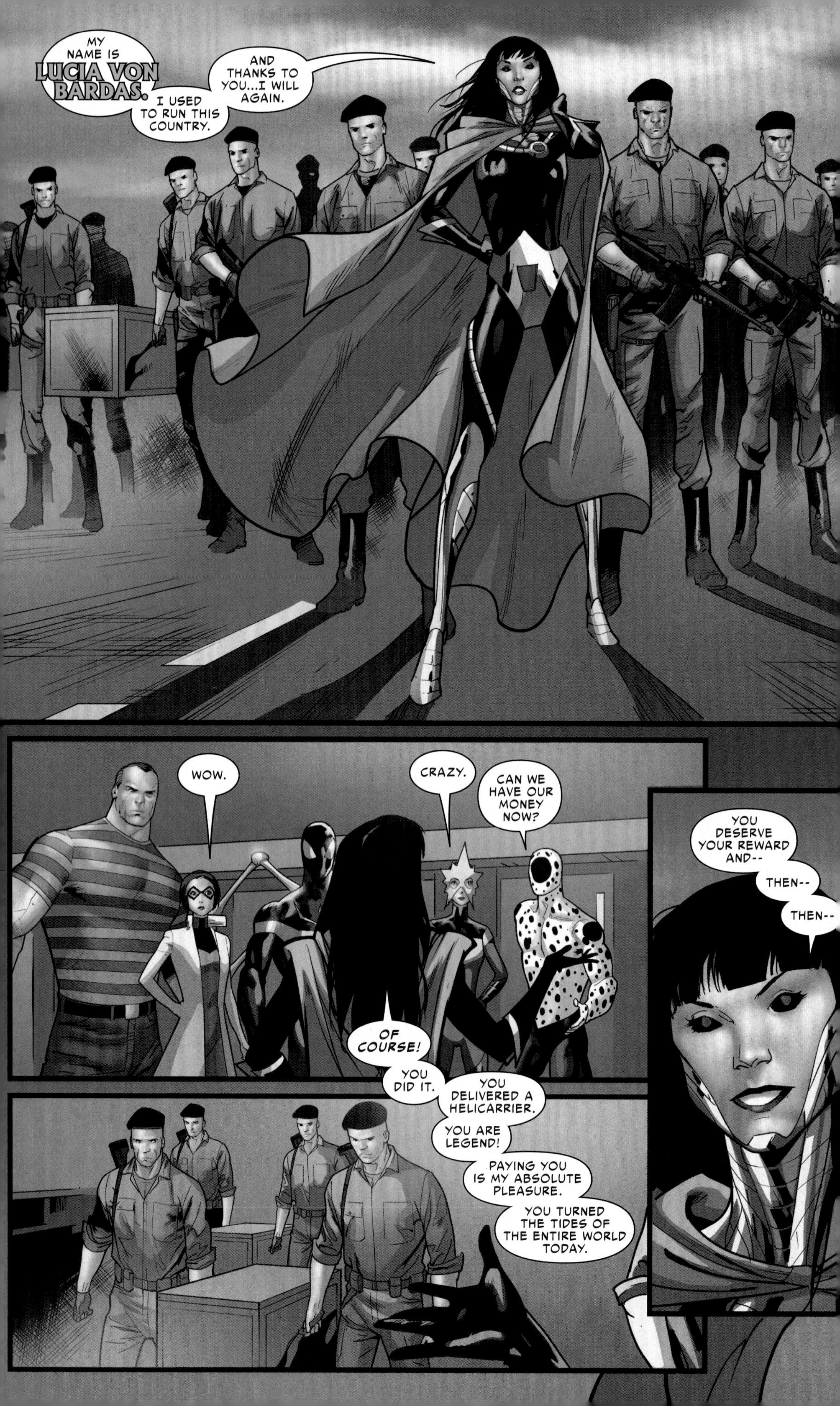
MY NAME IS LUCIA VON BARDAS. I USED TO RUN THIS COUNTRY.
AND THANKS TO YOU...I WILL AGAIN.
WOW.
CRAZY.
CAN WE HAVE OUR MONEY NOW?
OF COURSE!
YOU DID IT.
YOU DELIVERED A HELICARRIER.
YOU ARE LEGEND!
PAYING YOU IS MY ABSOLUTE PLEASURE.
YOU TURNED THE TIDES OF THE ENTIRE WORLD TODAY.
YOU DESERVE YOUR REWARD AND--
THEN--
THEN--

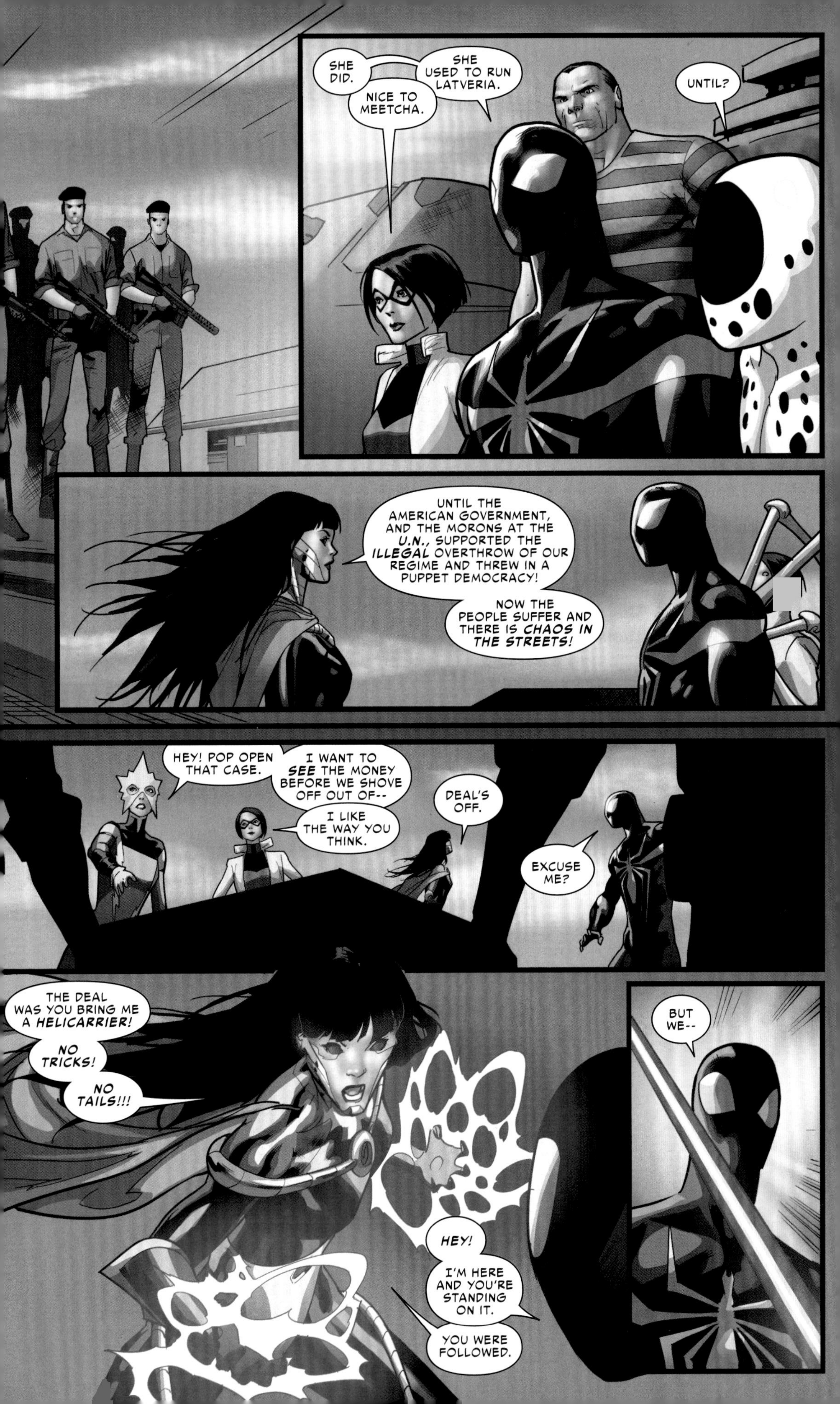

SHE USED TO RUN LATVERIA.
SHE DID.
NICE TO MEETCHA.
UNTIL?
UNTIL THE AMERICAN GOVERNMENT, AND THE MORONS AT THE *U.N.,* SUPPORTED THE *ILLEGAL* OVERTHROW OF OUR REGIME AND THREW IN A PUPPET DEMOCRACY!
NOW THE PEOPLE SUFFER AND THERE IS *CHAOS IN THE STREETS!*
HEY! POP OPEN THAT CASE.
I WANT TO *SEE* THE MONEY BEFORE WE SHOVE OFF OUT OF--
I LIKE THE WAY YOU THINK.
DEAL'S OFF.
EXCUSE ME?
THE DEAL WAS YOU BRING ME A *HELICARRIER!*
NO TRICKS!
NO TAILS!!!
BUT WE--
HEY!
I'M HERE AND YOU'RE STANDING ON IT.
YOU WERE FOLLOWED.

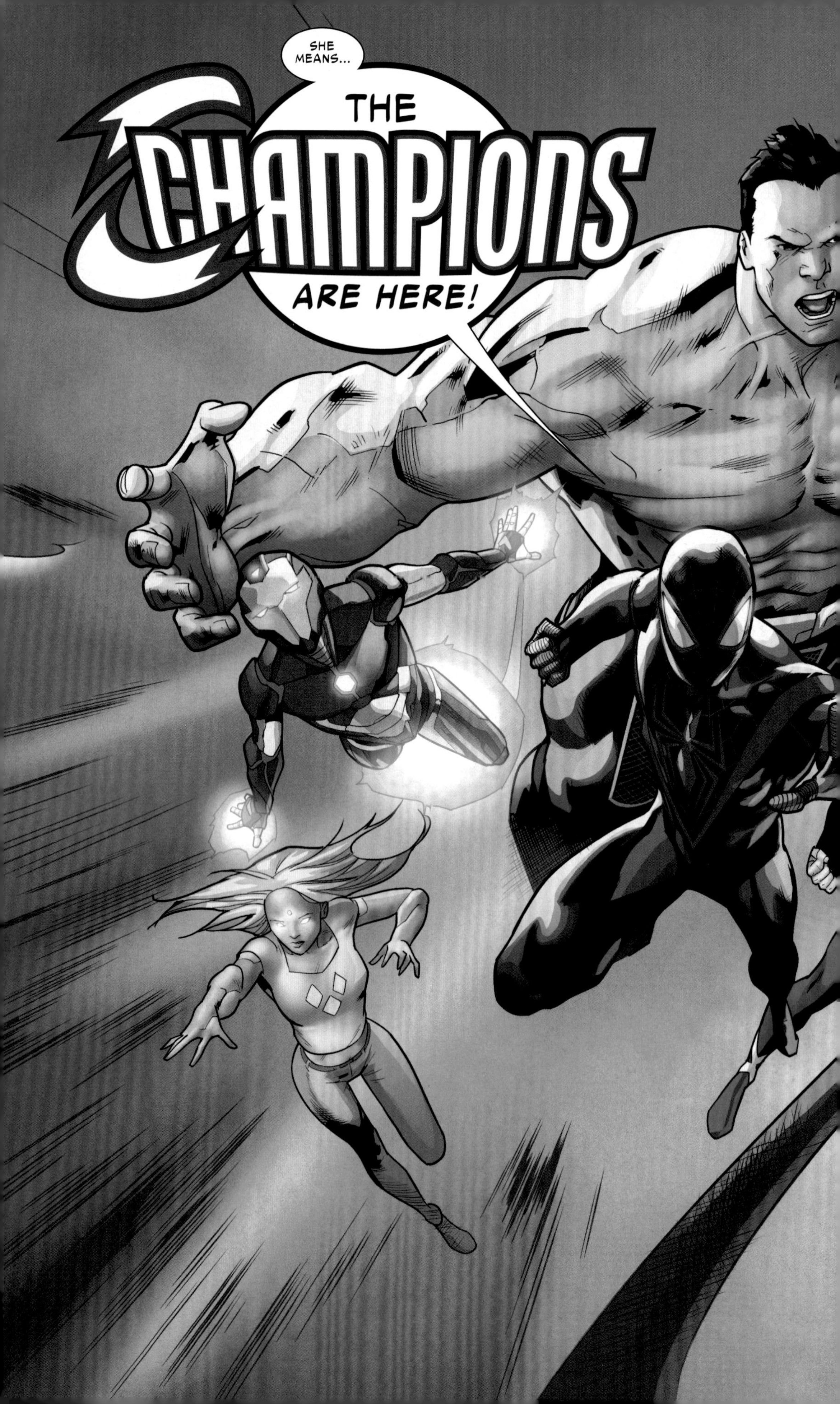
SHE MEANS...
THE CHAMPIONS ARE HERE!

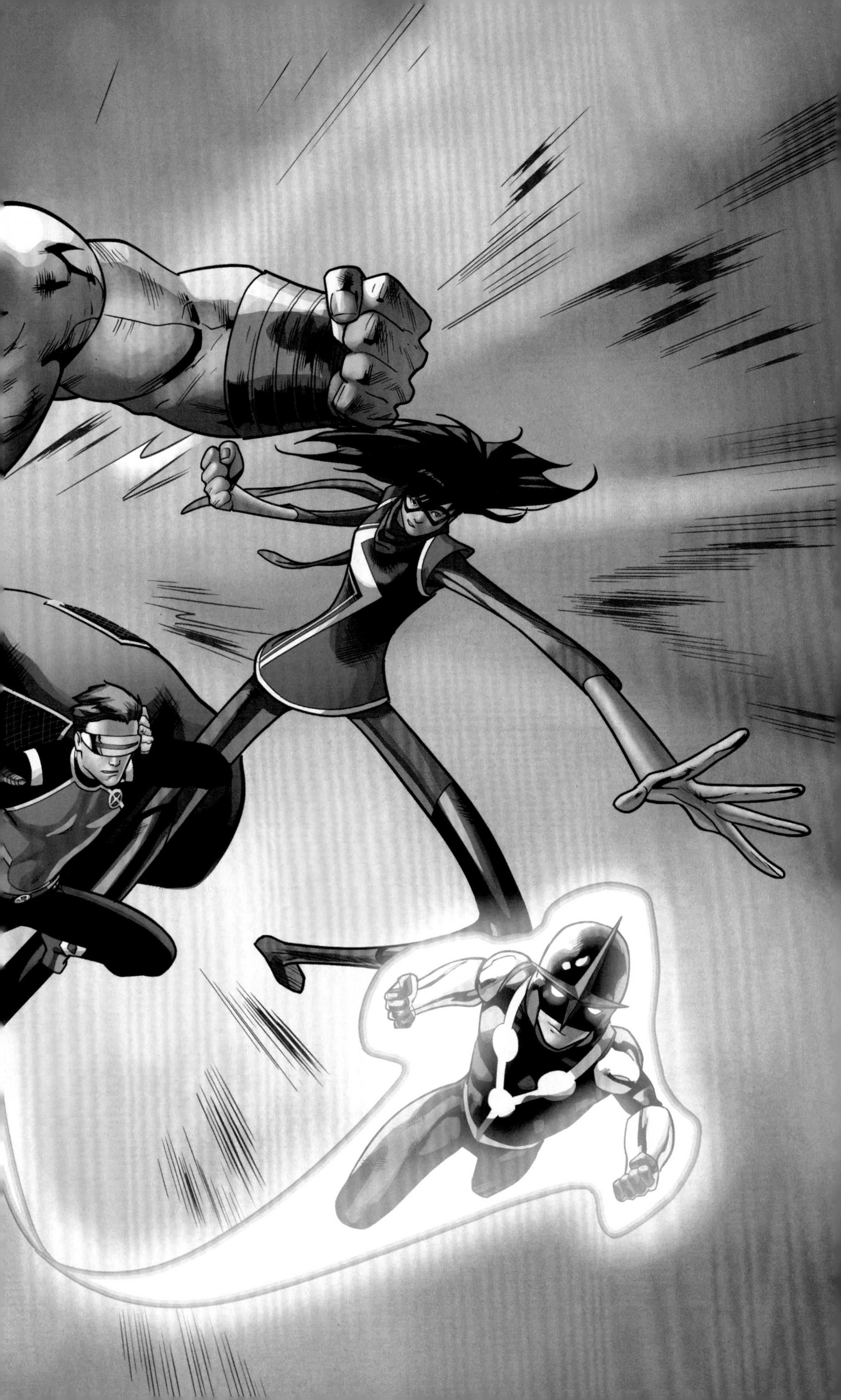

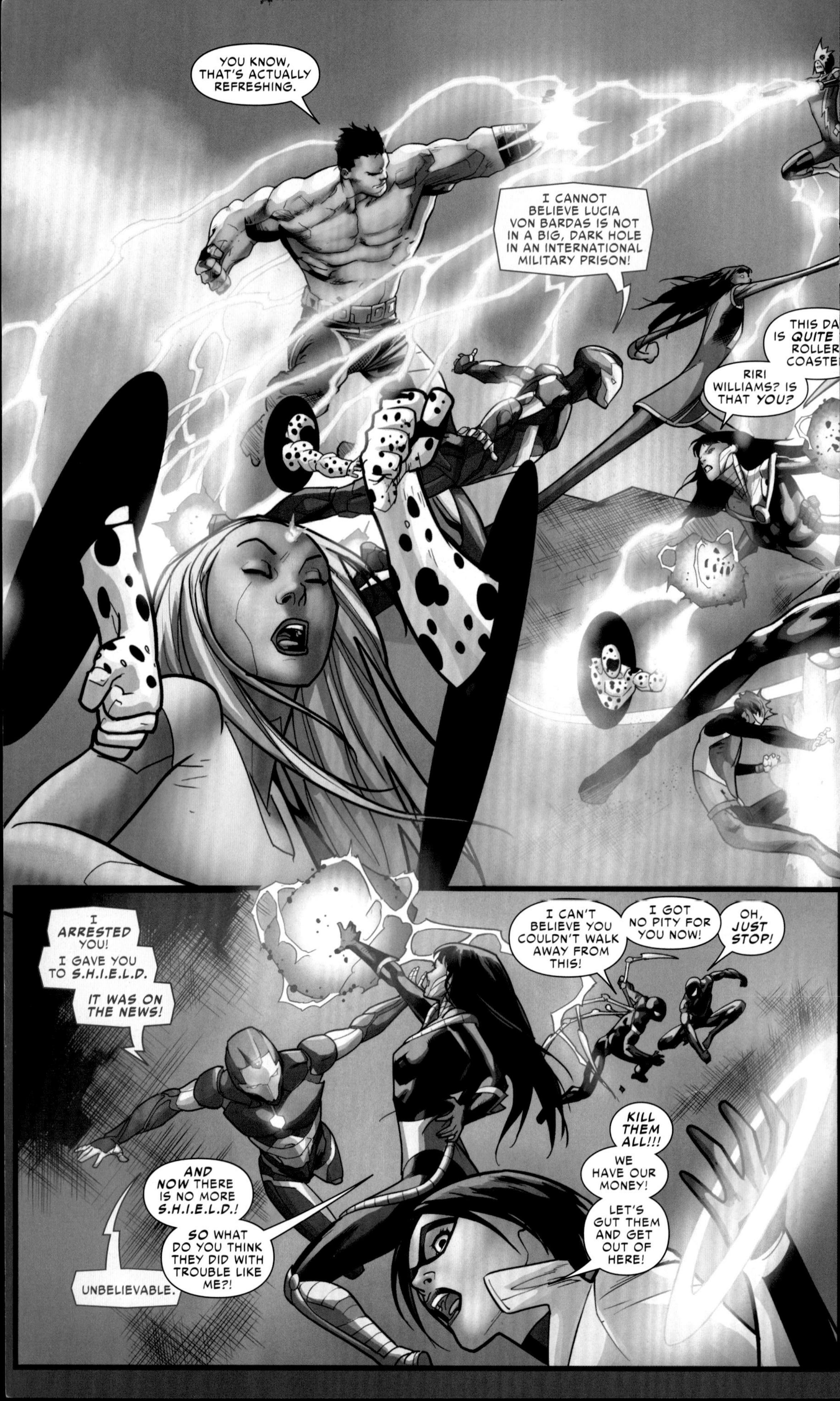

YOU KNOW, THAT'S ACTUALLY REFRESHING.
I CANNOT BELIEVE LUCIA VON BARDAS IS NOT IN A BIG, DARK HOLE IN AN INTERNATIONAL MILITARY PRISON!
THIS DA IS QUITE ROLLER COASTE
RIRI WILLIAMS? IS THAT YOU?
I ARRESTED YOU!
I GAVE YOU TO S.H.I.E.L.D.
IT WAS ON THE NEWS!
I CAN'T BELIEVE YOU COULDN'T WALK AWAY FROM THIS!
I GOT NO PITY FOR YOU NOW!
OH, JUST STOP!
AND NOW THERE IS NO MORE S.H.I.E.L.D.!
SO WHAT DO YOU THINK THEY DID WITH TROUBLE LIKE ME?!
UNBELIEVABLE.
KILL THEM ALL!!!
WE HAVE OUR MONEY!
LET'S GUT THEM AND GET OUT OF HERE!

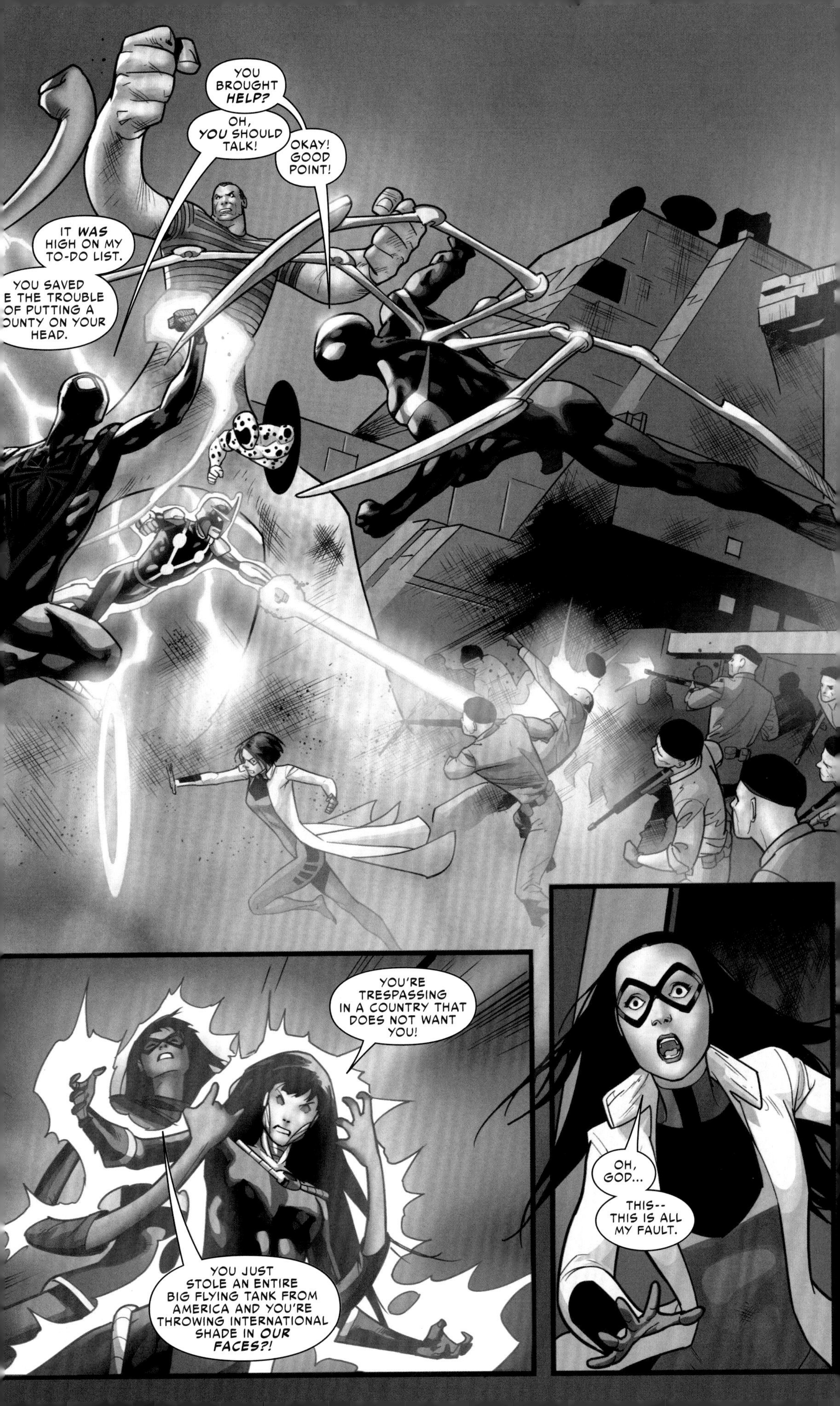
YOU BROUGHT HELP?
OH, YOU SHOULD TALK!
OKAY! GOOD POINT!
IT WAS HIGH ON MY TO-DO LIST.
YOU SAVED E THE TROUBLE OF PUTTING A OUNTY ON YOUR HEAD.
YOU'RE TRESPASSING IN A COUNTRY THAT DOES NOT WANT YOU!
YOU JUST STOLE AN ENTIRE BIG FLYING TANK FROM AMERICA AND YOU'RE THROWING INTERNATIONAL SHADE IN OUR FACES?!
OH, GOD...
THIS-- THIS IS ALL MY FAULT.

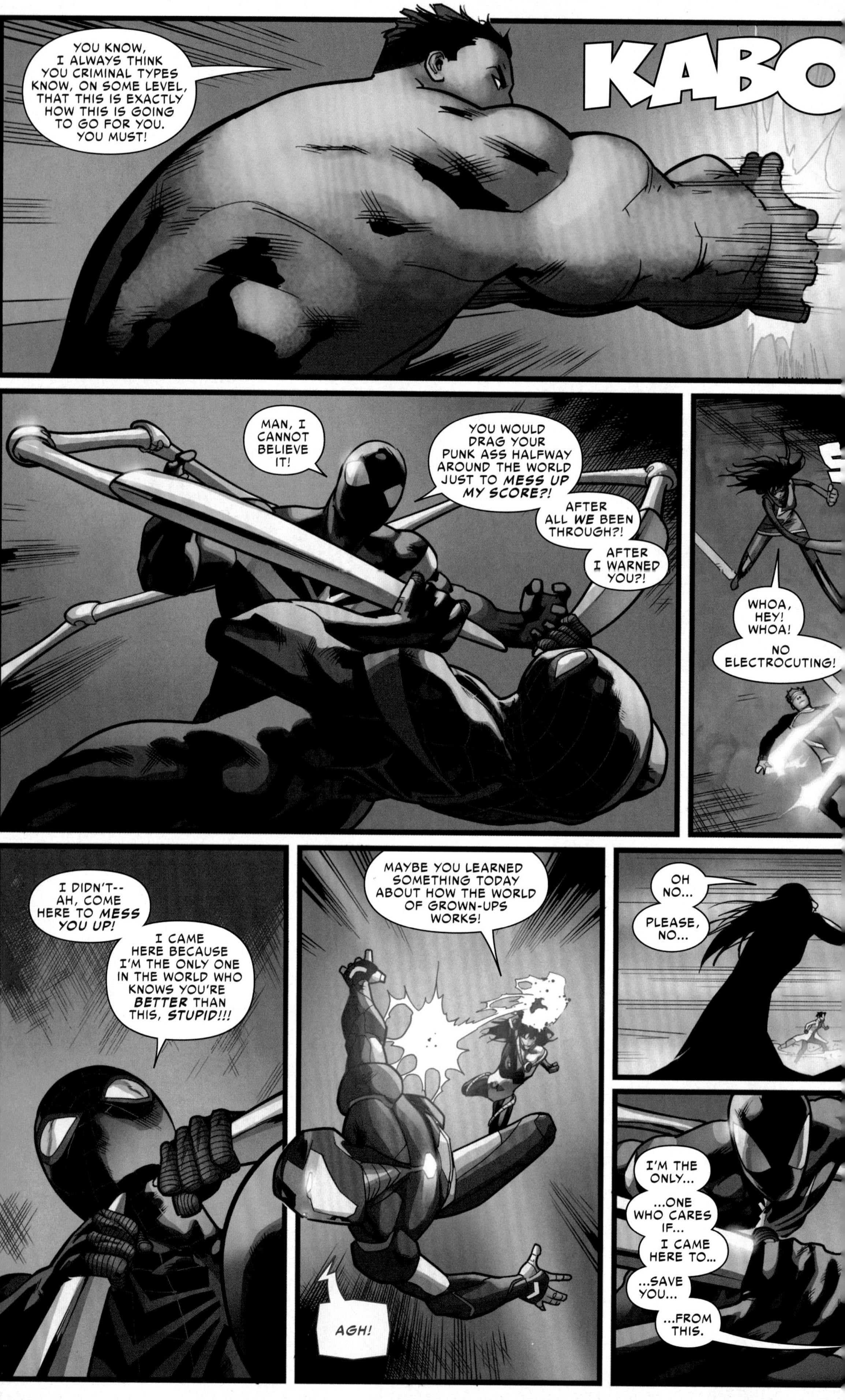

YOU KNOW, I ALWAYS THINK YOU CRIMINAL TYPES KNOW, ON SOME LEVEL, THAT THIS IS EXACTLY HOW THIS IS GOING TO GO FOR YOU. YOU MUST!
KABO
MAN, I CANNOT BELIEVE IT!
YOU WOULD DRAG YOUR PUNK ASS HALFWAY AROUND THE WORLD JUST TO MESS UP MY SCORE?!
AFTER ALL WE BEEN THROUGH?!
AFTER I WARNED YOU?!
WHOA, HEY! WHOA!
NO ELECTROCUTING!
I DIDN'T-- AH, COME HERE TO MESS YOU UP!
I CAME HERE BECAUSE I'M THE ONLY ONE IN THE WORLD WHO KNOWS YOU'RE BETTER THAN THIS, STUPID!!!
MAYBE YOU LEARNED SOMETHING TODAY ABOUT HOW THE WORLD OF GROWN-UPS WORKS!
AGH!
OH NO...
PLEASE, NO...
I'M THE ONLY...
...ONE WHO CARES IF...
I CAME HERE TO...
...SAVE YOU...
...FROM THIS.

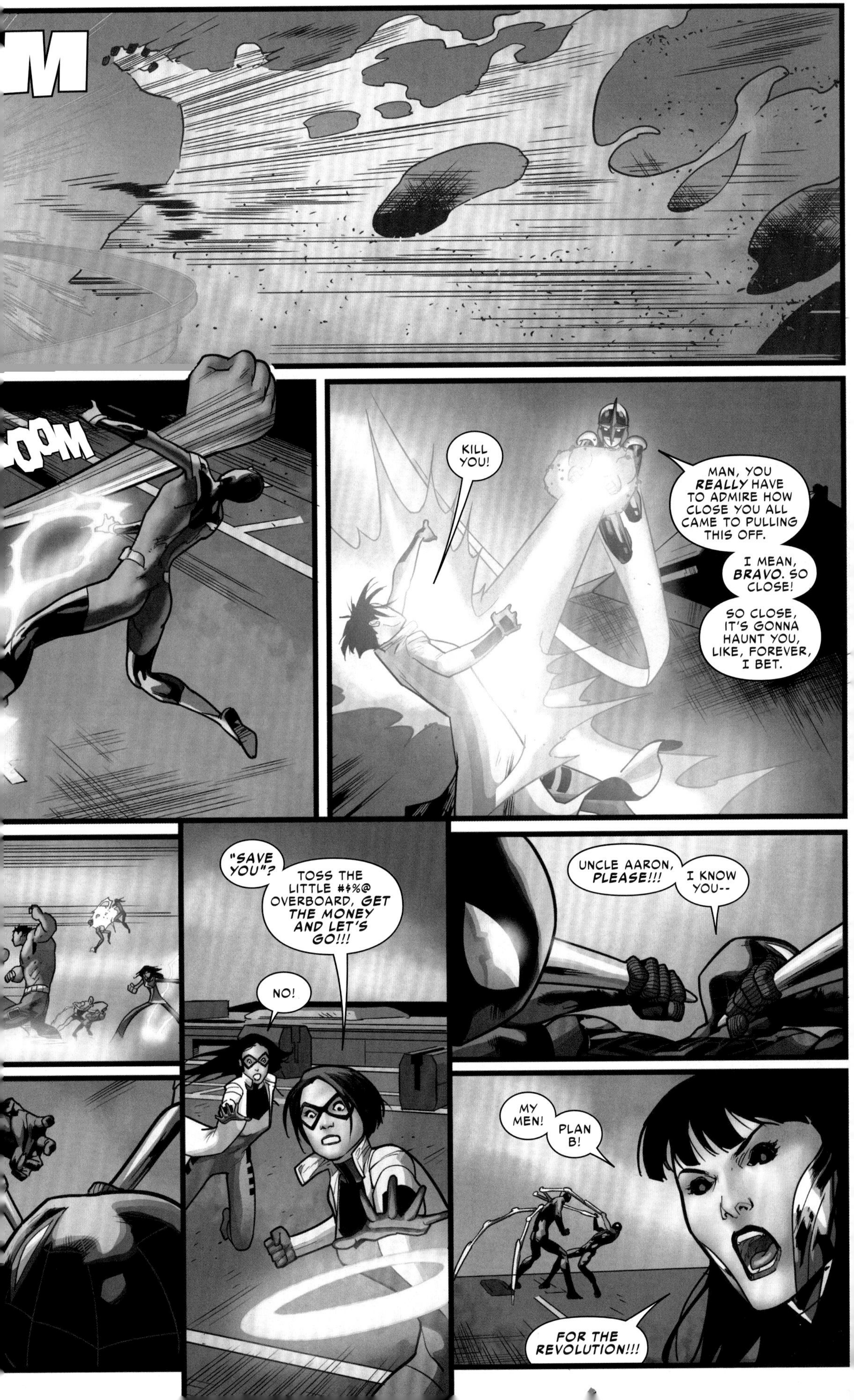
M
OOM
KILL YOU!
MAN, YOU REALLY HAVE TO ADMIRE HOW CLOSE YOU ALL CAME TO PULLING THIS OFF.
I MEAN, BRAVO. SO CLOSE!
SO CLOSE, IT'S GONNA HAUNT YOU, LIKE, FOREVER, I BET.
"SAVE YOU"?
TOSS THE LITTLE #$%@ OVERBOARD, GET THE MONEY AND LET'S GO!!!
NO!
UNCLE AARON, PLEASE!!!
I KNOW YOU--
MY MEN!
PLAN B!
FOR THE REVOLUTION!!!

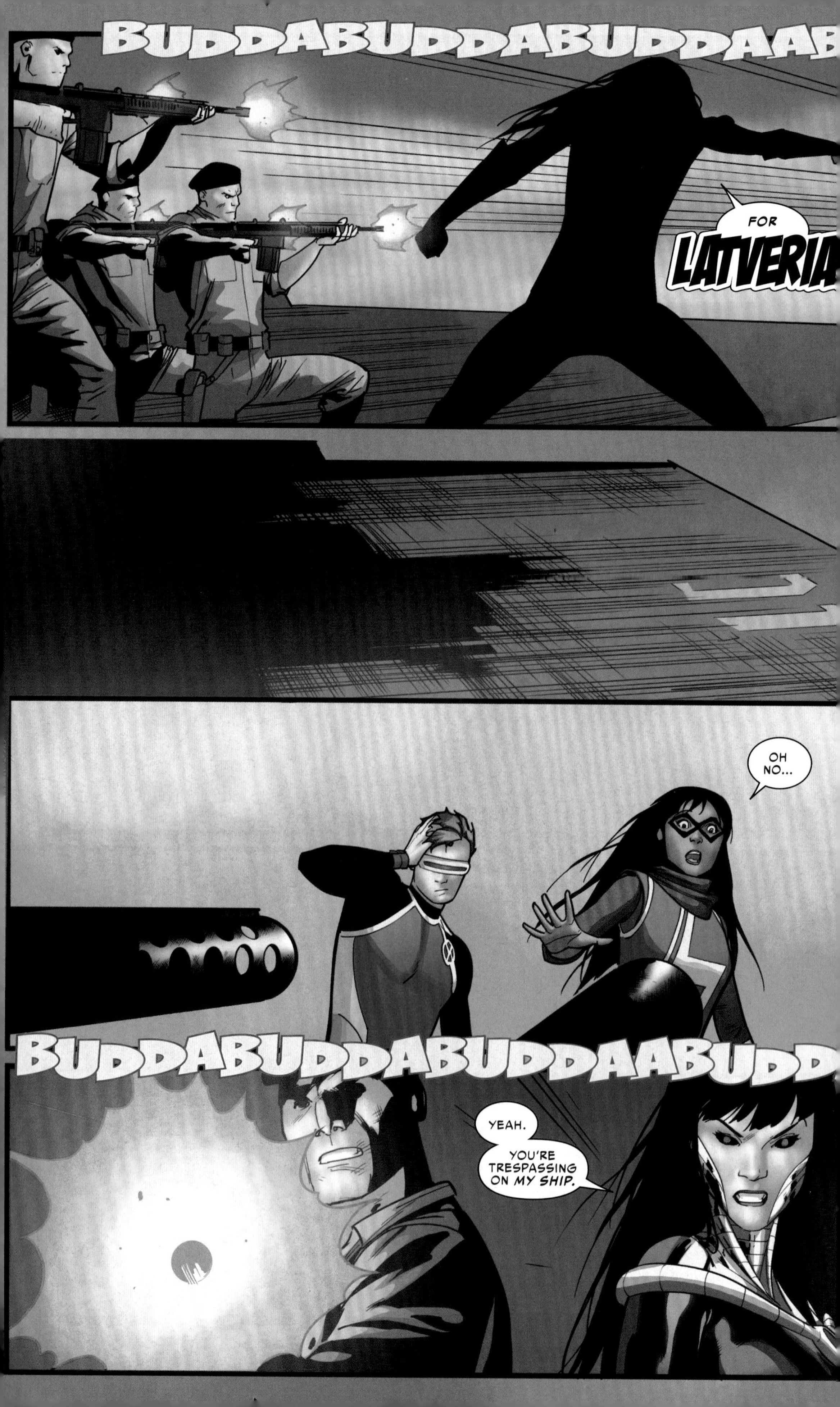
BUDDABUDDABUDDAAB
FOR
LATVERIA
OH NO...
BUDDABUDDABUDDAABUDD
YEAH.
YOU'RE TRESPASSING ON MY SHIP.

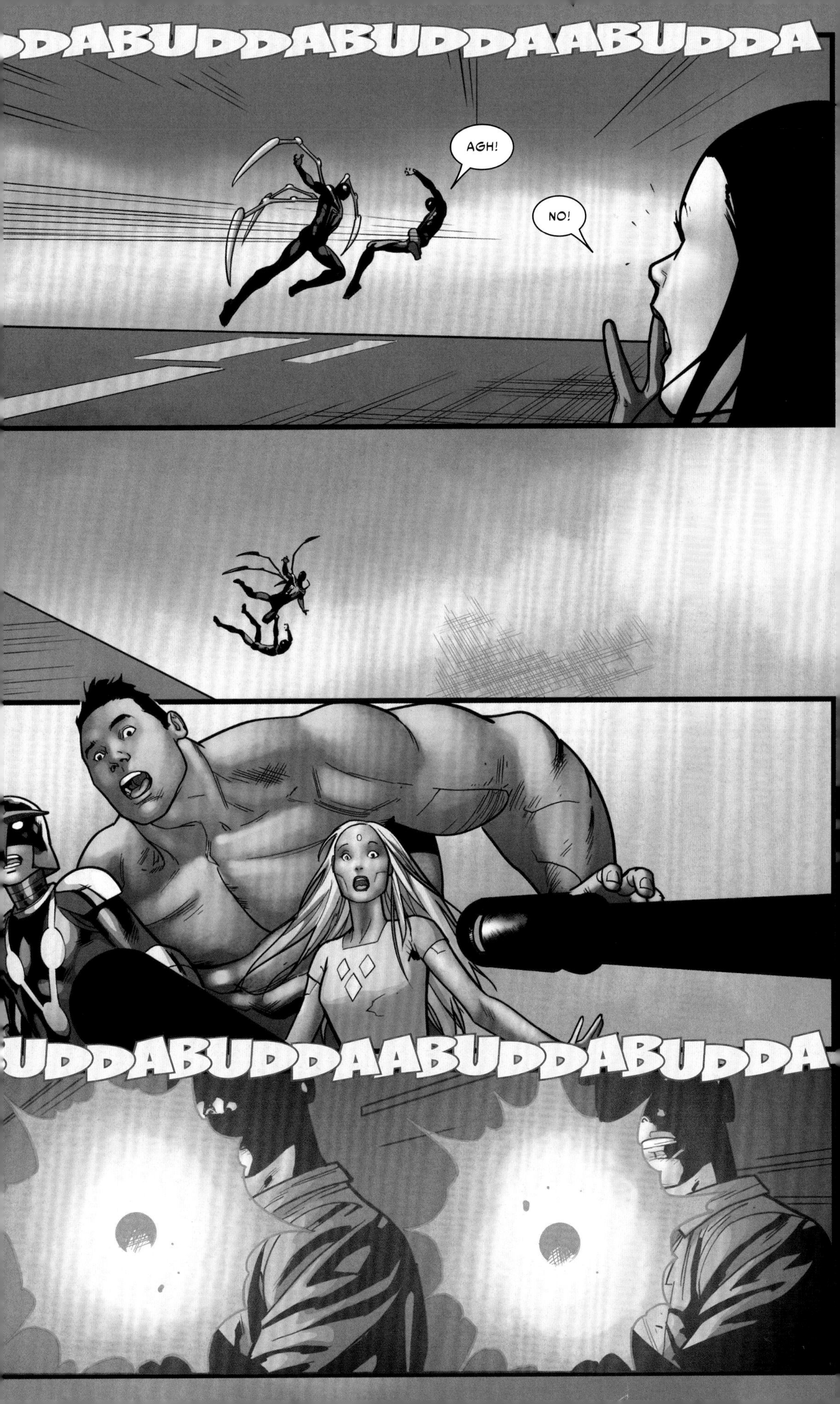
DDABUDDABUDDAABUDDA
AGH!
NO!
UDDABUDDAABUDDABUDDA

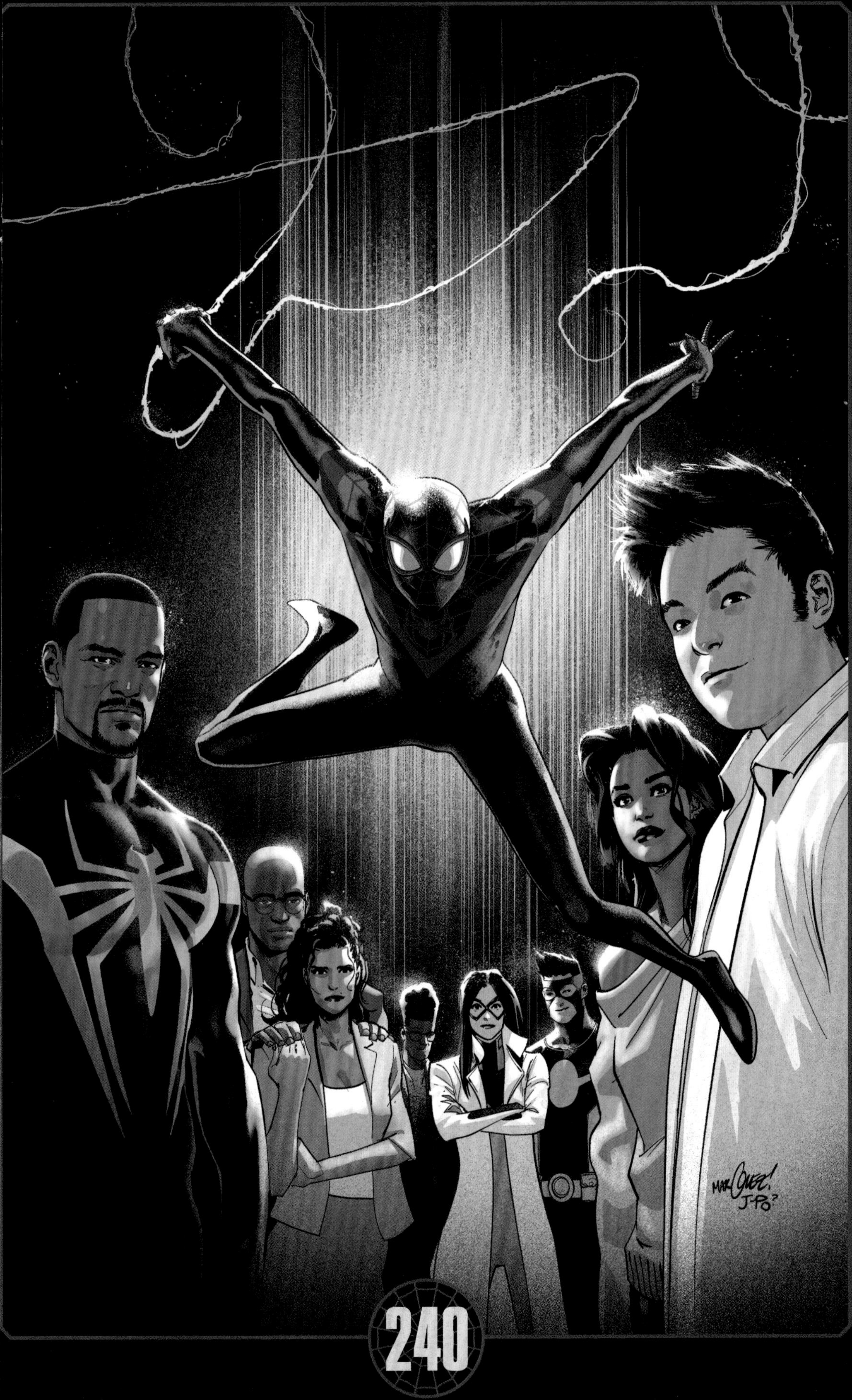
240

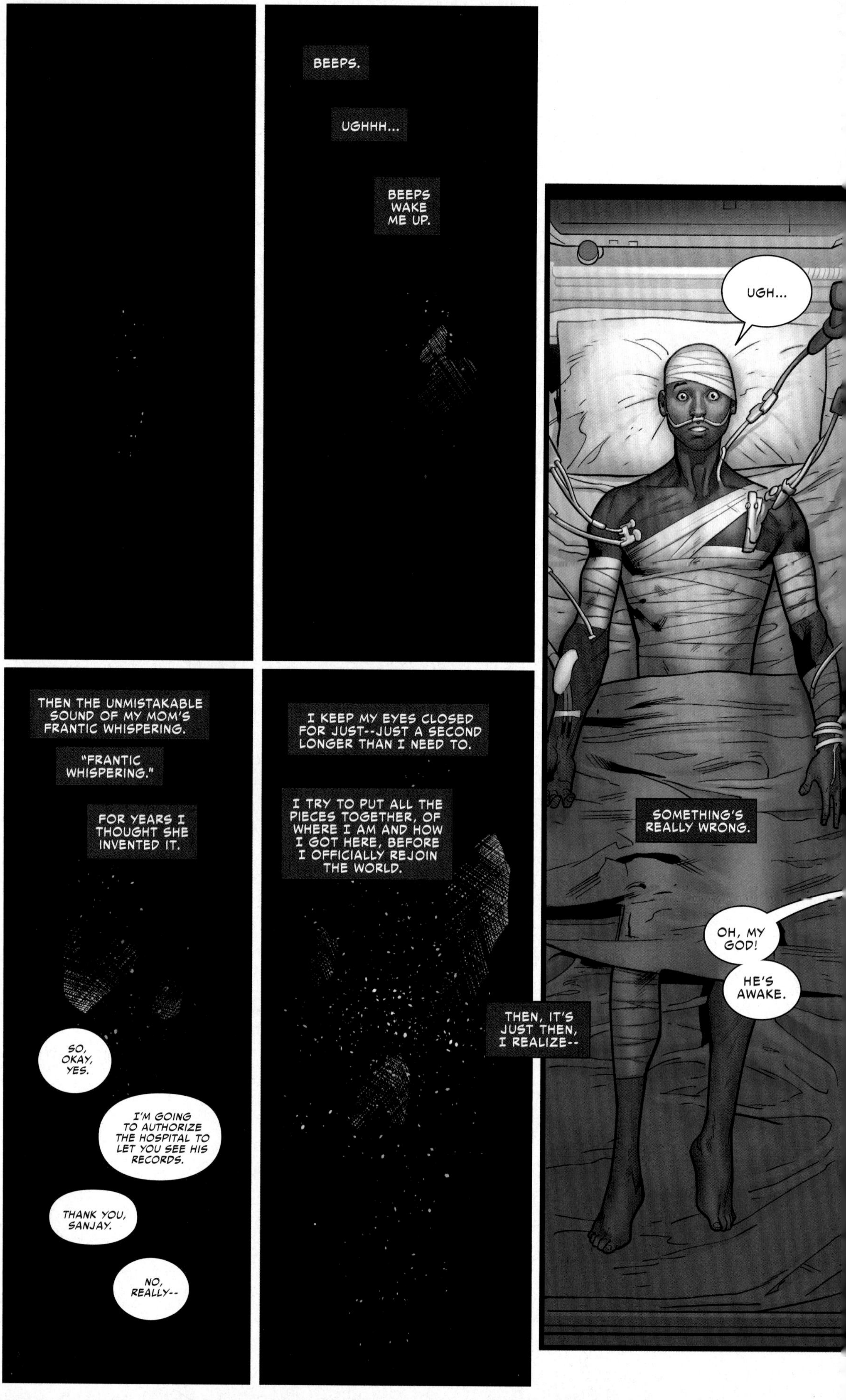

BEEPS.
UGHHH...
BEEPS WAKE ME UP.
THEN THE UNMISTAKABLE SOUND OF MY MOM'S FRANTIC WHISPERING.
"FRANTIC WHISPERING."
FOR YEARS I THOUGHT SHE INVENTED IT.
SO, OKAY, YES.
I'M GOING TO AUTHORIZE THE HOSPITAL TO LET YOU SEE HIS RECORDS.
THANK YOU, SANJAY.
NO, REALLY--
I KEEP MY EYES CLOSED FOR JUST--JUST A SECOND LONGER THAN I NEED TO.
I TRY TO PUT ALL THE PIECES TOGETHER, OF WHERE I AM AND HOW I GOT HERE, BEFORE I OFFICIALLY REJOIN THE WORLD.
THEN, IT'S JUST THEN, I REALIZE--
UGH...
SOMETHING'S REALLY WRONG.
OH, MY GOD!
HE'S AWAKE.

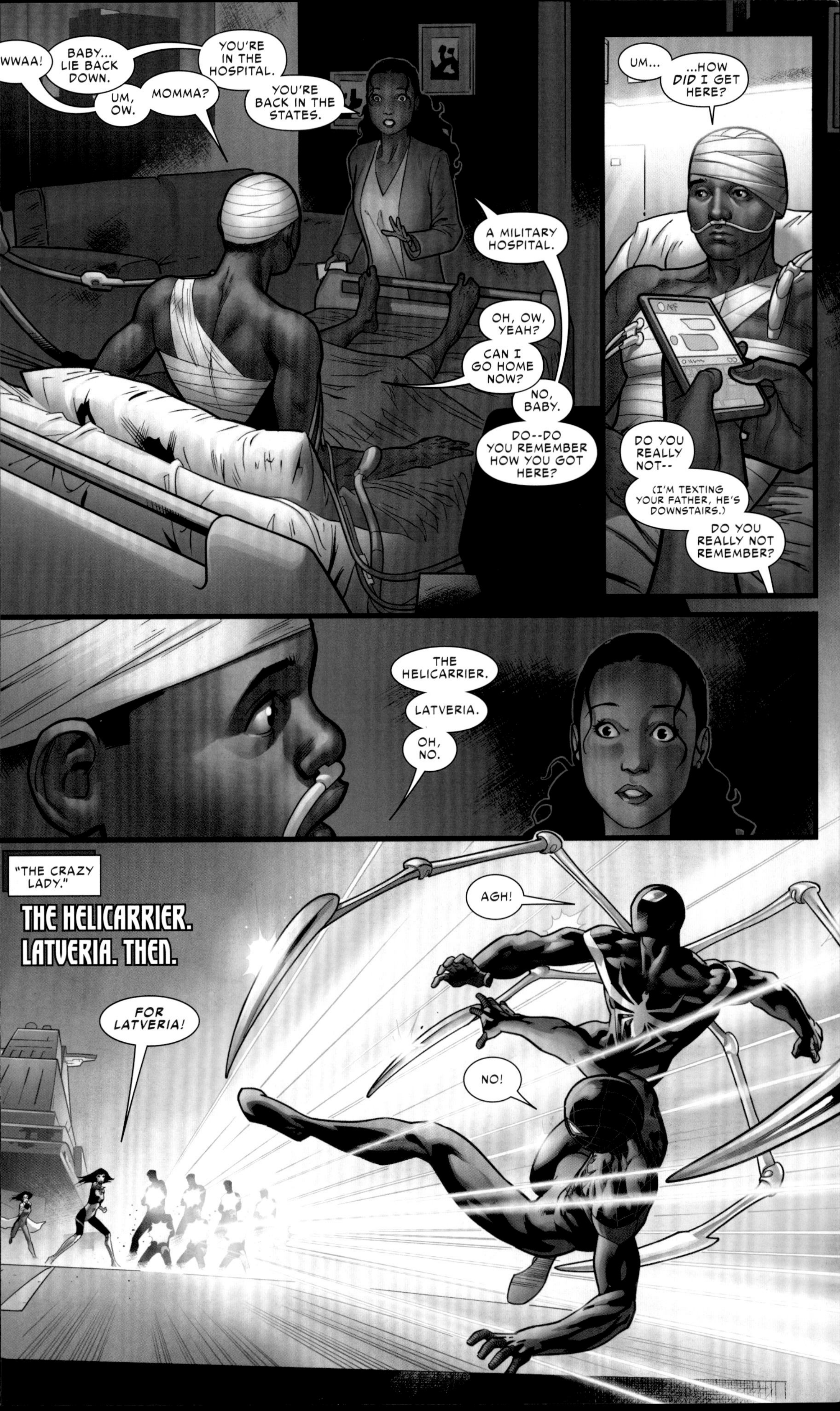
WWAA!
BABY... LIE BACK DOWN.
UM, OW.
MOMMA?
YOU'RE IN THE HOSPITAL.
YOU'RE BACK IN THE STATES.
A MILITARY HOSPITAL.
OH, OW, YEAH?
CAN I GO HOME NOW?
NO, BABY.
DO--DO YOU REMEMBER HOW YOU GOT HERE?
UM...
...HOW DID I GET HERE?
DO YOU REALLY NOT--
(I'M TEXTING YOUR FATHER, HE'S DOWNSTAIRS.)
DO YOU REALLY NOT REMEMBER?
THE HELICARRIER.
LATVERIA.
OH, NO.
"THE CRAZY LADY."
THE HELICARRIER. LATVERIA. THEN.
AGH!
FOR LATVERIA!
NO!

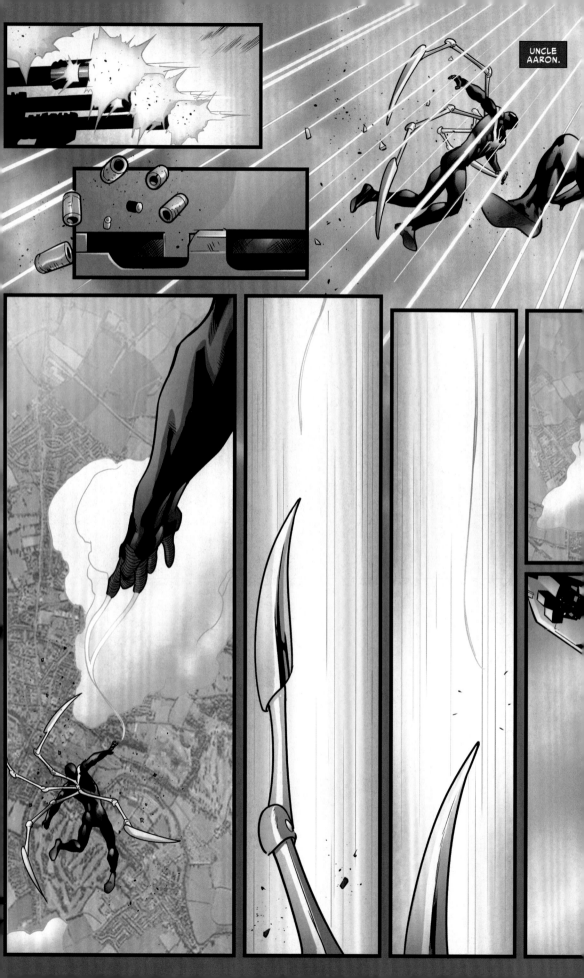

UNCLE
AARON.

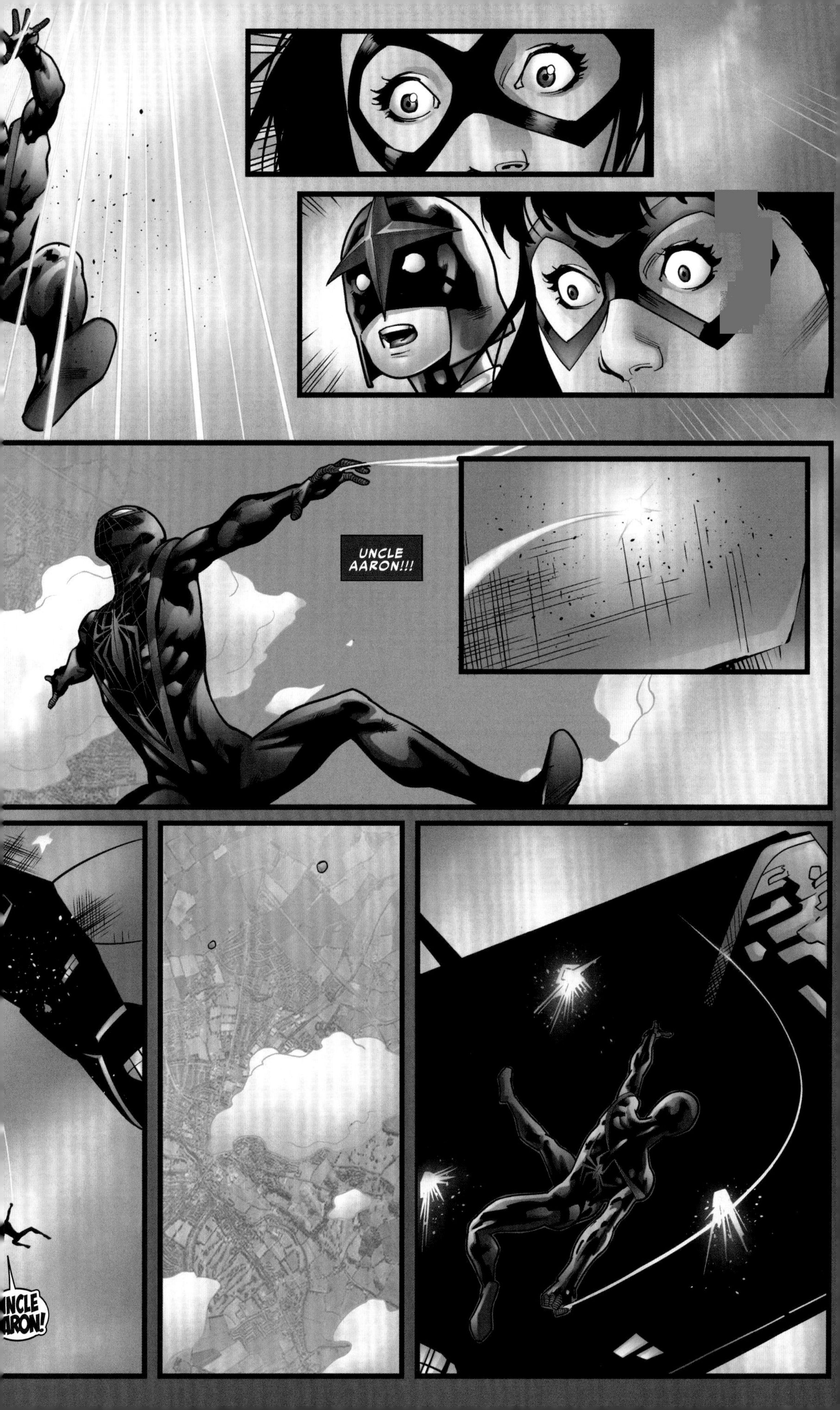
UNCLE AARON!!!

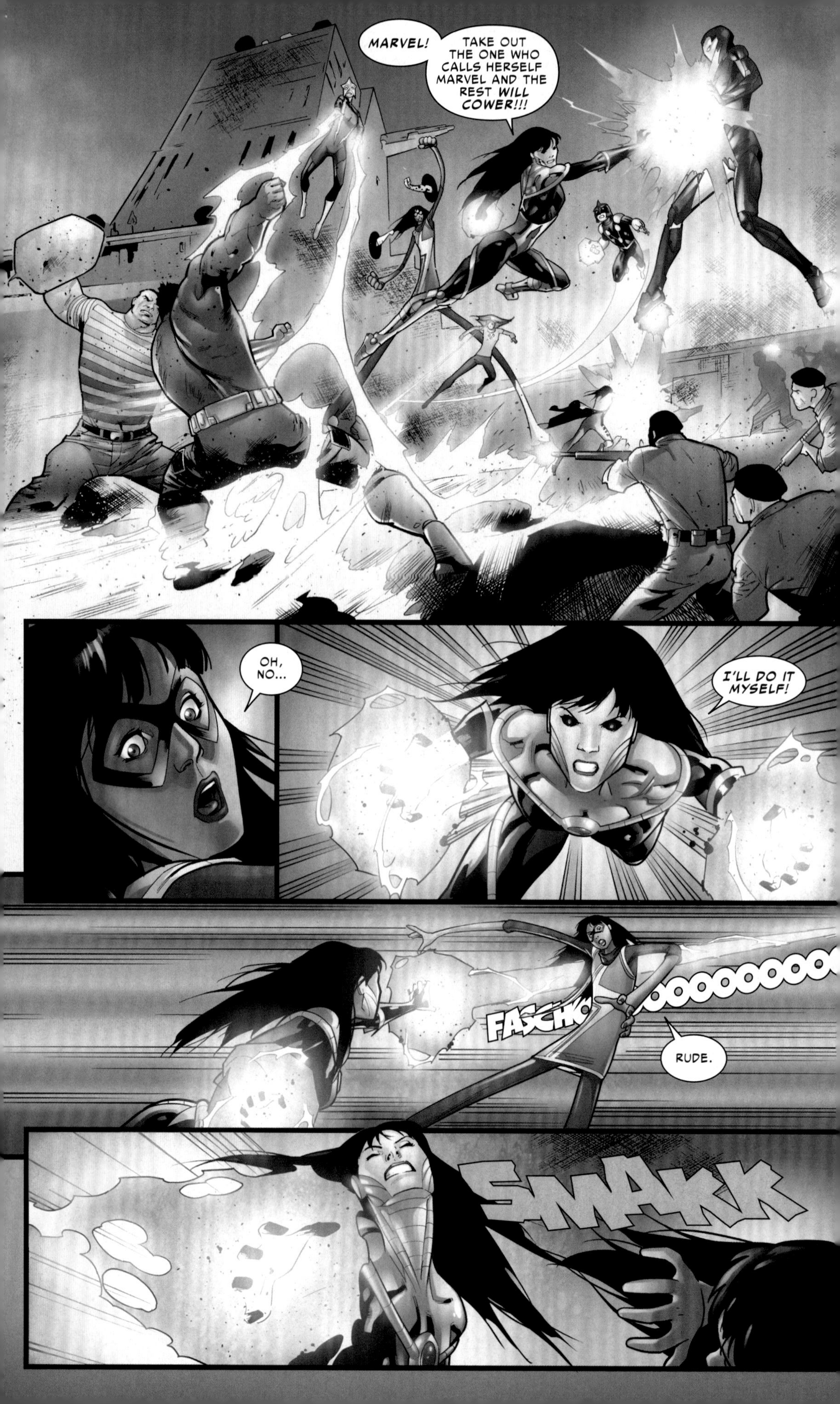
MARVEL!
TAKE OUT THE ONE WHO CALLS HERSELF MARVEL AND THE REST WILL COWER!!!
OH, NO...
I'LL DO IT MYSELF!
FASCHOOOOOOOOOOOOO
RUDE.
SMAKK

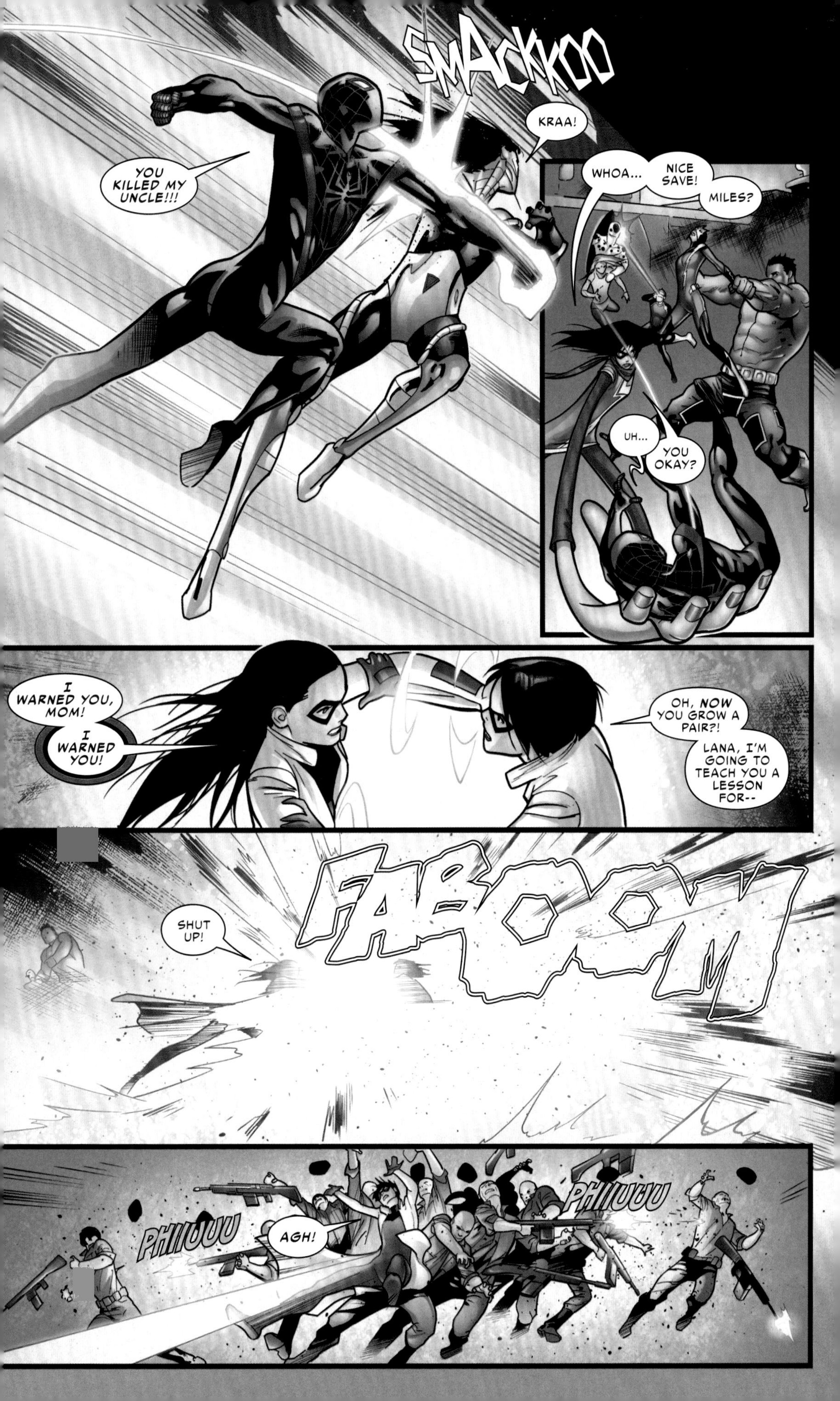
SMACKKOO
YOU KILLED MY UNCLE!!!
KRAA!
WHOA...
NICE SAVE!
MILES?
UH...
YOU OKAY?
I WARNED YOU, MOM!
I WARNED YOU!
OH, NOW YOU GROW A PAIR?!
LANA, I'M GOING TO TEACH YOU A LESSON FOR--
SHUT UP!
FABOOM
PHIIUUU
AGH!
PHIIUUU

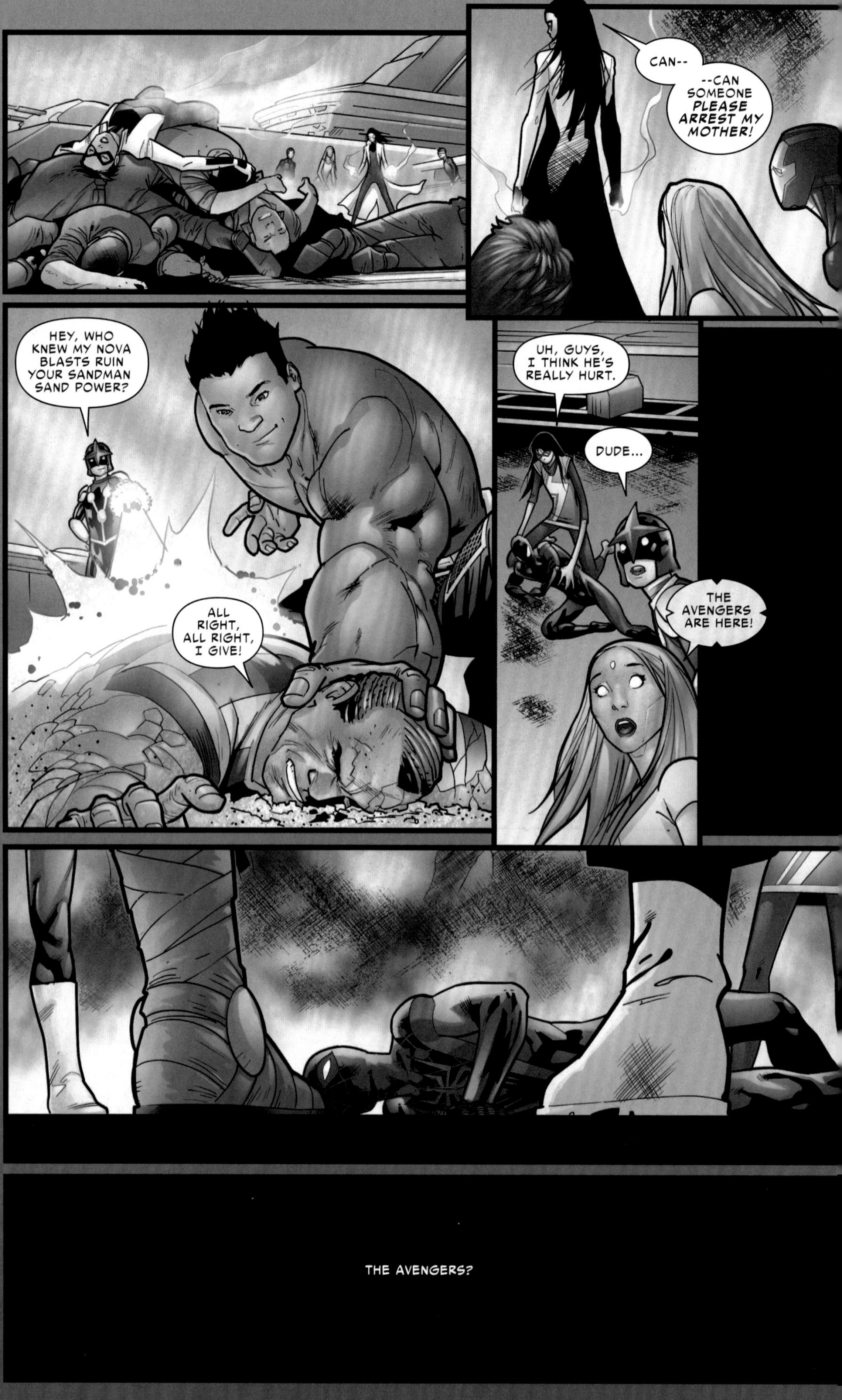
CAN--
--CAN SOMEONE *PLEASE* *ARREST* MY MOTHER!
HEY, WHO KNEW MY NOVA BLASTS RUIN YOUR SANDMAN SAND POWER?
ALL RIGHT, ALL RIGHT, I GIVE!
UH, GUYS, I THINK HE'S REALLY HURT.
DUDE...
THE AVENGERS ARE HERE!
THE AVENGERS?

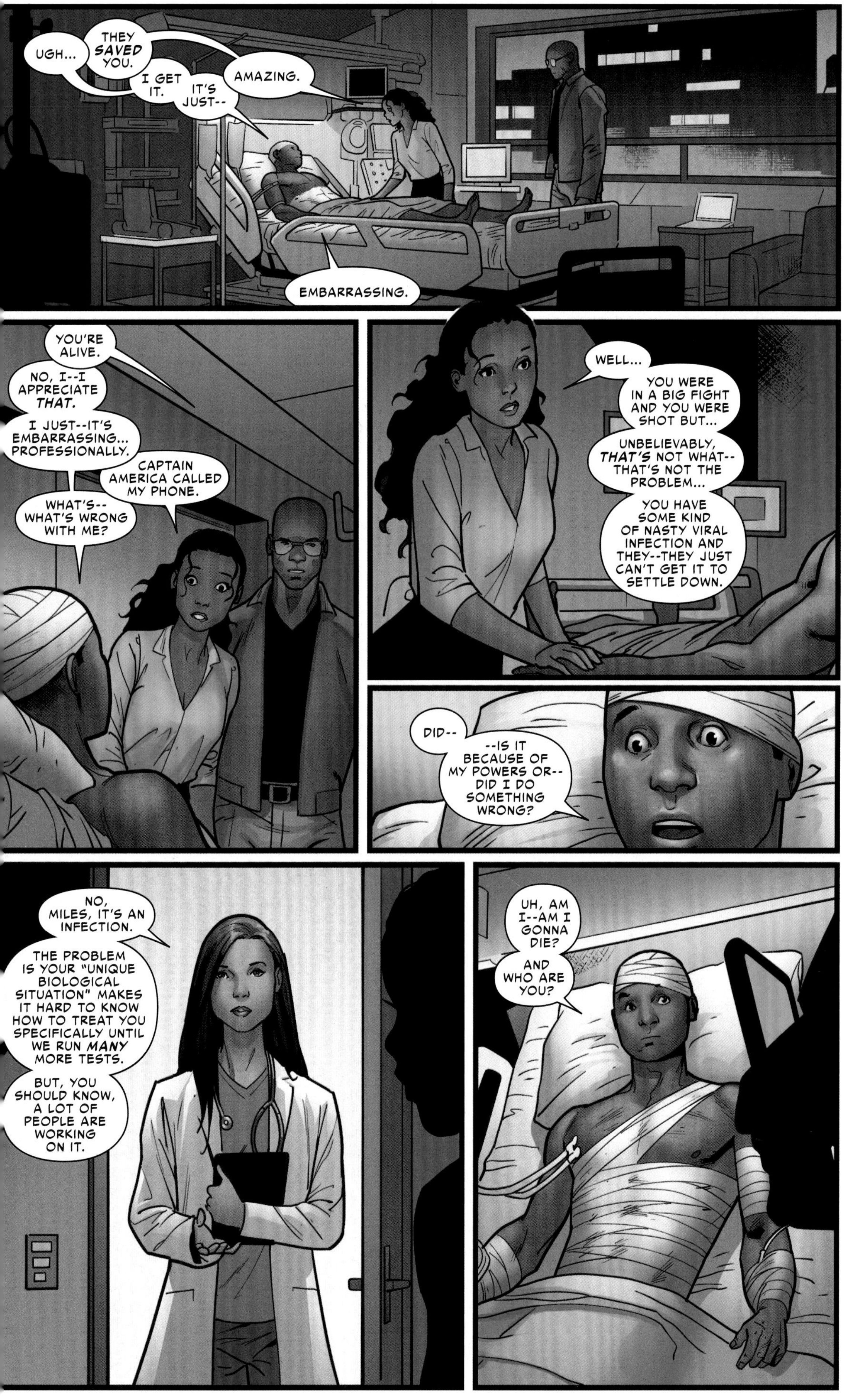

UGH...
THEY SAVED YOU.
I GET IT.
IT'S JUST--
AMAZING.
EMBARRASSING.
YOU'RE ALIVE.
NO, I--I APPRECIATE THAT.
I JUST--IT'S EMBARRASSING... PROFESSIONALLY.
CAPTAIN AMERICA CALLED MY PHONE.
WHAT'S-- WHAT'S WRONG WITH ME?
WELL...
YOU WERE IN A BIG FIGHT AND YOU WERE SHOT BUT...
UNBELIEVABLY, THAT'S NOT WHAT-- THAT'S NOT THE PROBLEM...
YOU HAVE SOME KIND OF NASTY VIRAL INFECTION AND THEY--THEY JUST CAN'T GET IT TO SETTLE DOWN.
DID--
--IS IT BECAUSE OF MY POWERS OR-- DID I DO SOMETHING WRONG?
NO, MILES, IT'S AN INFECTION.
THE PROBLEM IS YOUR "UNIQUE BIOLOGICAL SITUATION" MAKES IT HARD TO KNOW HOW TO TREAT YOU SPECIFICALLY UNTIL WE RUN MANY MORE TESTS.
BUT, YOU SHOULD KNOW, A LOT OF PEOPLE ARE WORKING ON IT.
UH, AM I--AM I GONNA DIE?
AND WHO ARE YOU?

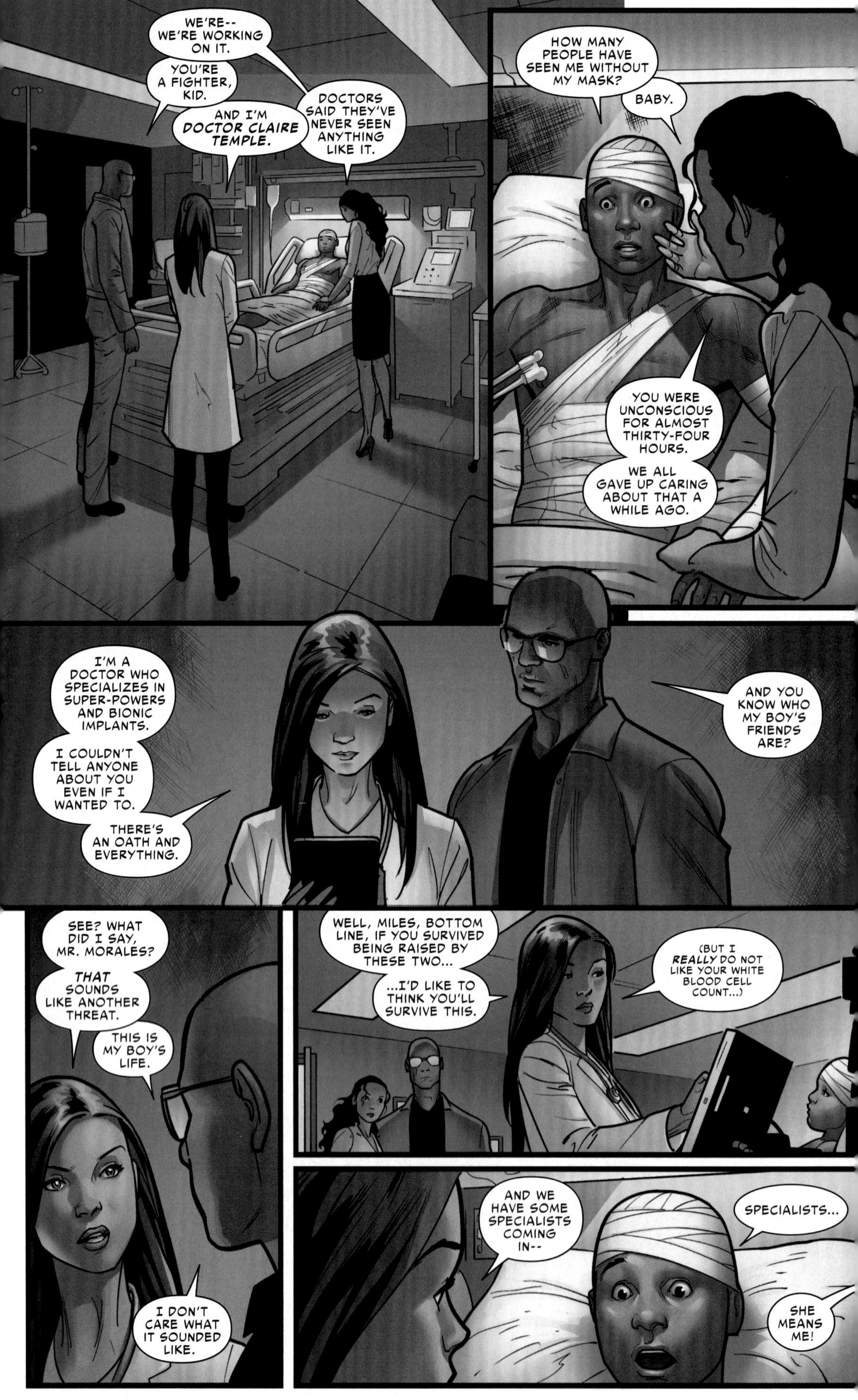

YOU'RE A FIGHTER, KID.
WE'RE-- WE'RE WORKING ON IT.
AND I'M DOCTOR CLAIRE TEMPLE.
DOCTORS SAID THEY'VE NEVER SEEN ANYTHING LIKE IT.
HOW MANY PEOPLE HAVE SEEN ME WITHOUT MY MASK?
BABY.
YOU WERE UNCONSCIOUS FOR ALMOST THIRTY-FOUR HOURS.
WE ALL GAVE UP CARING ABOUT THAT A WHILE AGO.
I'M A DOCTOR WHO SPECIALIZES IN SUPER-POWERS AND BIONIC IMPLANTS.
I COULDN'T TELL ANYONE ABOUT YOU EVEN IF I WANTED TO.
THERE'S AN OATH AND EVERYTHING.
AND YOU KNOW WHO MY BOY'S FRIENDS ARE?
SEE? WHAT DID I SAY, MR. MORALES?
THAT SOUNDS LIKE ANOTHER THREAT.
THIS IS MY BOY'S LIFE.
I DON'T CARE WHAT IT SOUNDED LIKE.
WELL, MILES, BOTTOM LINE, IF YOU SURVIVED BEING RAISED BY THESE TWO...
...I'D LIKE TO THINK YOU'LL SURVIVE THIS.
(BUT I REALLY DO NOT LIKE YOUR WHITE BLOOD CELL COUNT...)
AND WE HAVE SOME SPECIALISTS COMING IN--
SPECIALISTS...
SHE MEANS ME!

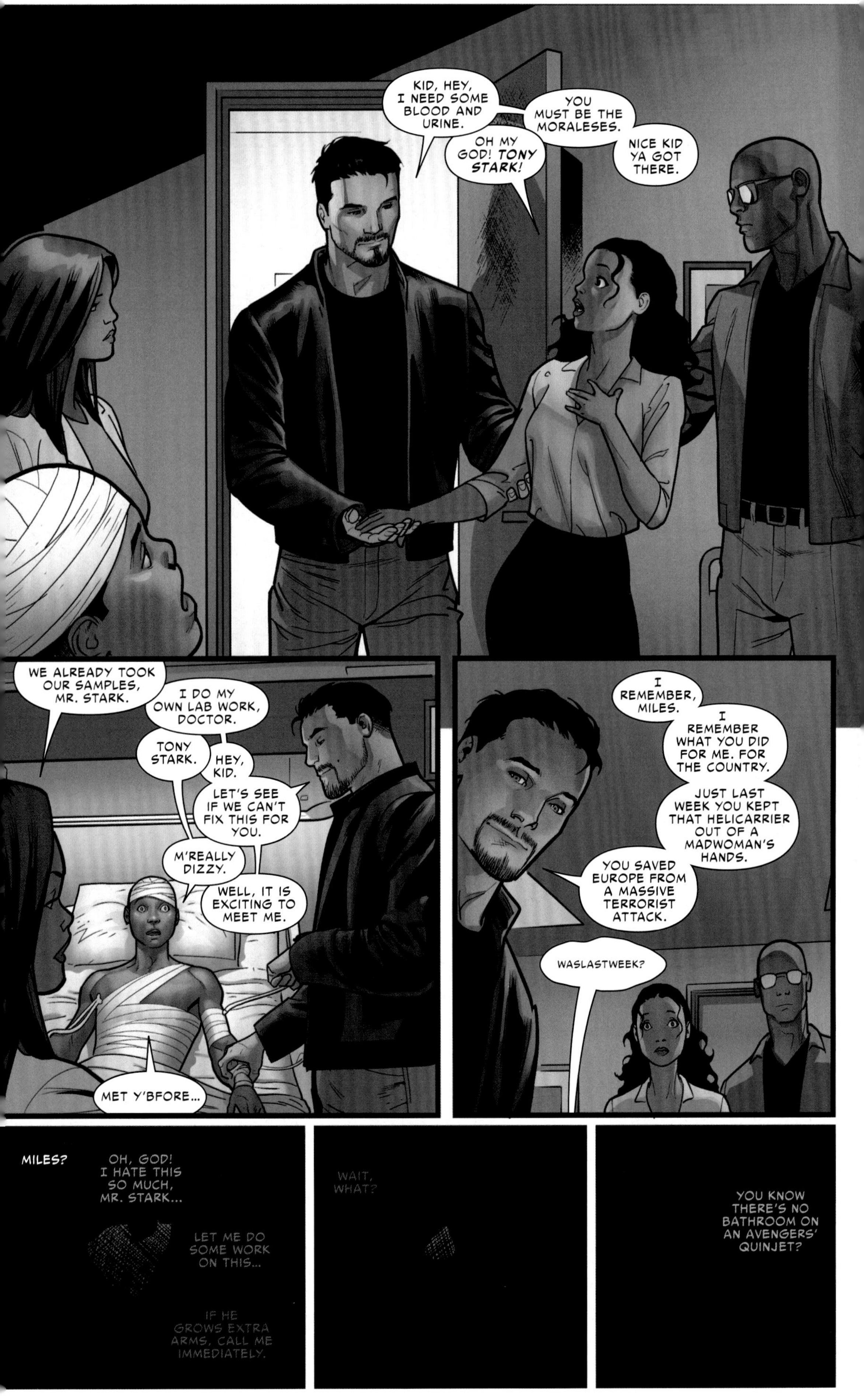

KID, HEY, I NEED SOME BLOOD AND URINE.
YOU MUST BE THE MORALESES.
OH MY GOD! TONY STARK!
NICE KID YA GOT THERE.
WE ALREADY TOOK OUR SAMPLES, MR. STARK.
I DO MY OWN LAB WORK, DOCTOR.
TONY STARK.
HEY, KID.
LET'S SEE IF WE CAN'T FIX THIS FOR YOU.
M'REALLY DIZZY.
WELL, IT IS EXCITING TO MEET ME.
MET Y'BFORE...
I REMEMBER, MILES.
I REMEMBER WHAT YOU DID FOR ME. FOR THE COUNTRY.
JUST LAST WEEK YOU KEPT THAT HELICARRIER OUT OF A MADWOMAN'S HANDS.
YOU SAVED EUROPE FROM A MASSIVE TERRORIST ATTACK.
WASLASTWEEK?
MILES?
OH, GOD! I HATE THIS SO MUCH, MR. STARK...
LET ME DO SOME WORK ON THIS...
IF HE GROWS EXTRA ARMS, CALL ME IMMEDIATELY.
WAIT, WHAT?
YOU KNOW THERE'S NO BATHROOM ON AN AVENGERS' QUINJET?

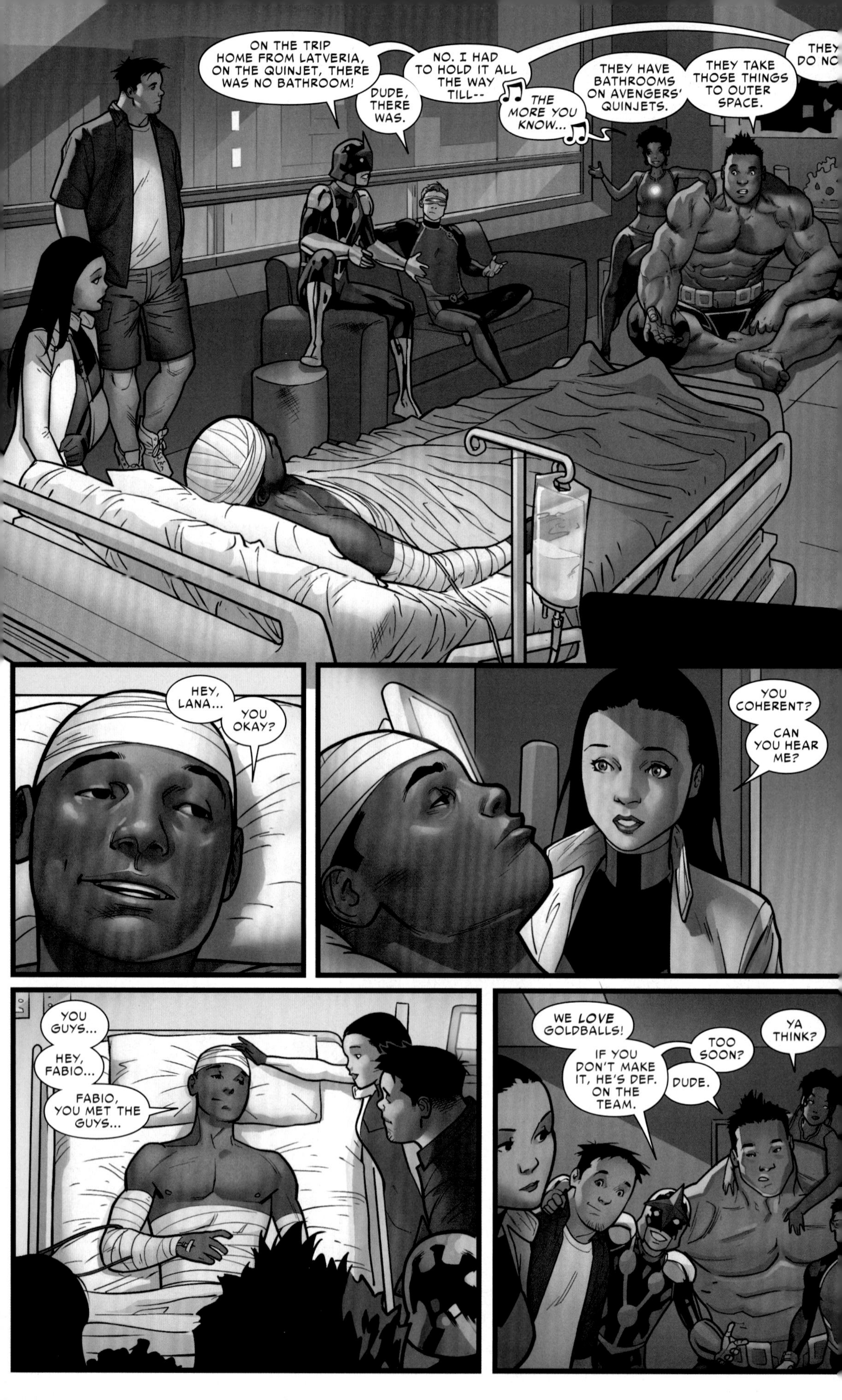

ON THE TRIP HOME FROM LATVERIA, ON THE QUINJET, THERE WAS NO BATHROOM!
DUDE, THERE WAS.
NO. I HAD TO HOLD IT ALL THE WAY TILL--
THE MORE YOU KNOW...
THEY HAVE BATHROOMS ON AVENGERS' QUINJETS.
THEY TAKE THOSE THINGS TO OUTER SPACE.
THEY DO NO
HEY, LANA...
YOU OKAY?
YOU COHERENT?
CAN YOU HEAR ME?
YOU GUYS...
HEY, FABIO...
FABIO, YOU MET THE GUYS...
WE LOVE GOLDBALLS!
IF YOU DON'T MAKE IT, HE'S DEF. ON THE TEAM.
TOO SOON?
DUDE.
YA THINK?

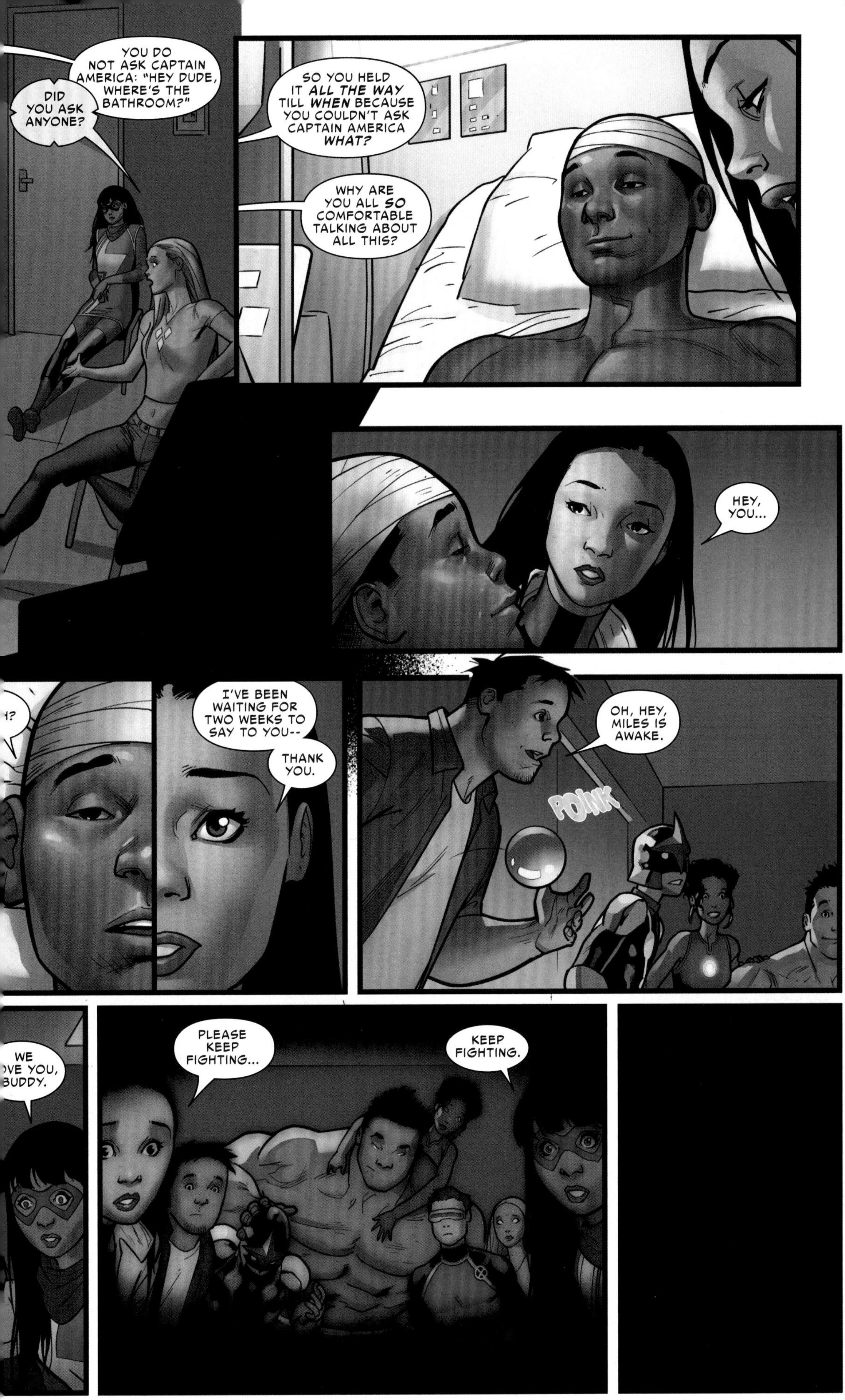
YOU DO NOT ASK CAPTAIN AMERICA: "HEY DUDE, WHERE'S THE BATHROOM?"
DID YOU ASK ANYONE?
SO YOU HELD IT ALL THE WAY TILL WHEN BECAUSE YOU COULDN'T ASK CAPTAIN AMERICA WHAT?
WHY ARE YOU ALL SO COMFORTABLE TALKING ABOUT ALL THIS?
HEY, YOU...
I'VE BEEN WAITING FOR TWO WEEKS TO SAY TO YOU--
THANK YOU.
OH, HEY, MILES IS AWAKE.
POINK
PLEASE KEEP FIGHTING...
KEEP FIGHTING.

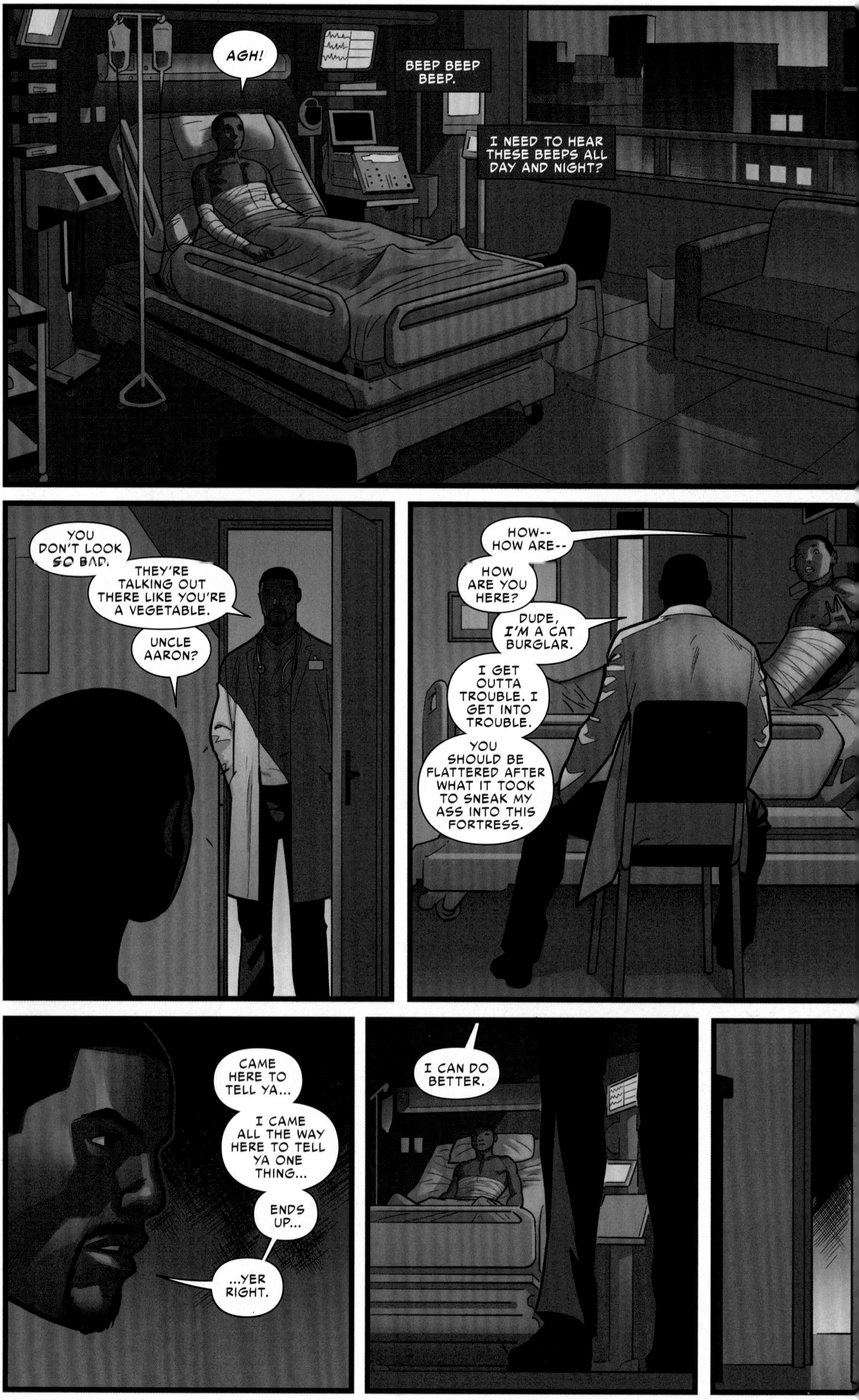

AGH!
BEEP BEEP BEEP.
I NEED TO HEAR THESE BEEPS ALL DAY AND NIGHT?
YOU DON'T LOOK SO BAD.
THEY'RE TALKING OUT THERE LIKE YOU'RE A VEGETABLE.
UNCLE AARON?
HOW-- HOW ARE--
HOW ARE YOU HERE?
DUDE, I'M A CAT BURGLAR.
I GET OUTTA TROUBLE. I GET INTO TROUBLE.
YOU SHOULD BE FLATTERED AFTER WHAT IT TOOK TO SNEAK MY ASS INTO THIS FORTRESS.
CAME HERE TO TELL YA...
I CAME ALL THE WAY HERE TO TELL YA ONE THING...
ENDS UP...
...YER RIGHT.
I CAN DO BETTER.

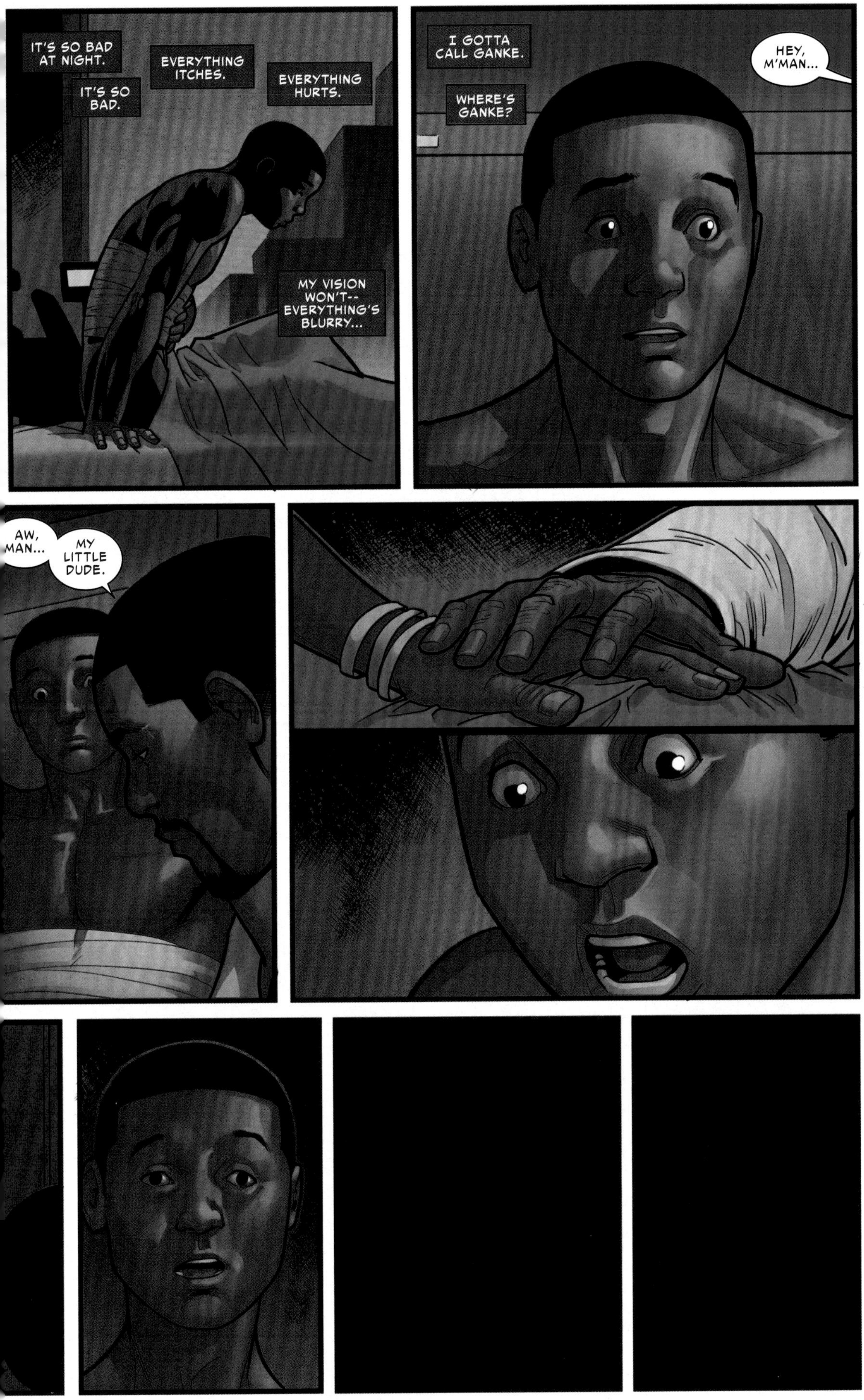

IT'S SO BAD AT NIGHT.
IT'S SO BAD.
EVERYTHING ITCHES.
EVERYTHING HURTS.
MY VISION WON'T-- EVERYTHING'S BLURRY...
I GOTTA CALL GANKE.
WHERE'S GANKE?
HEY, M'MAN...
AW, MAN...
MY LITTLE DUDE.

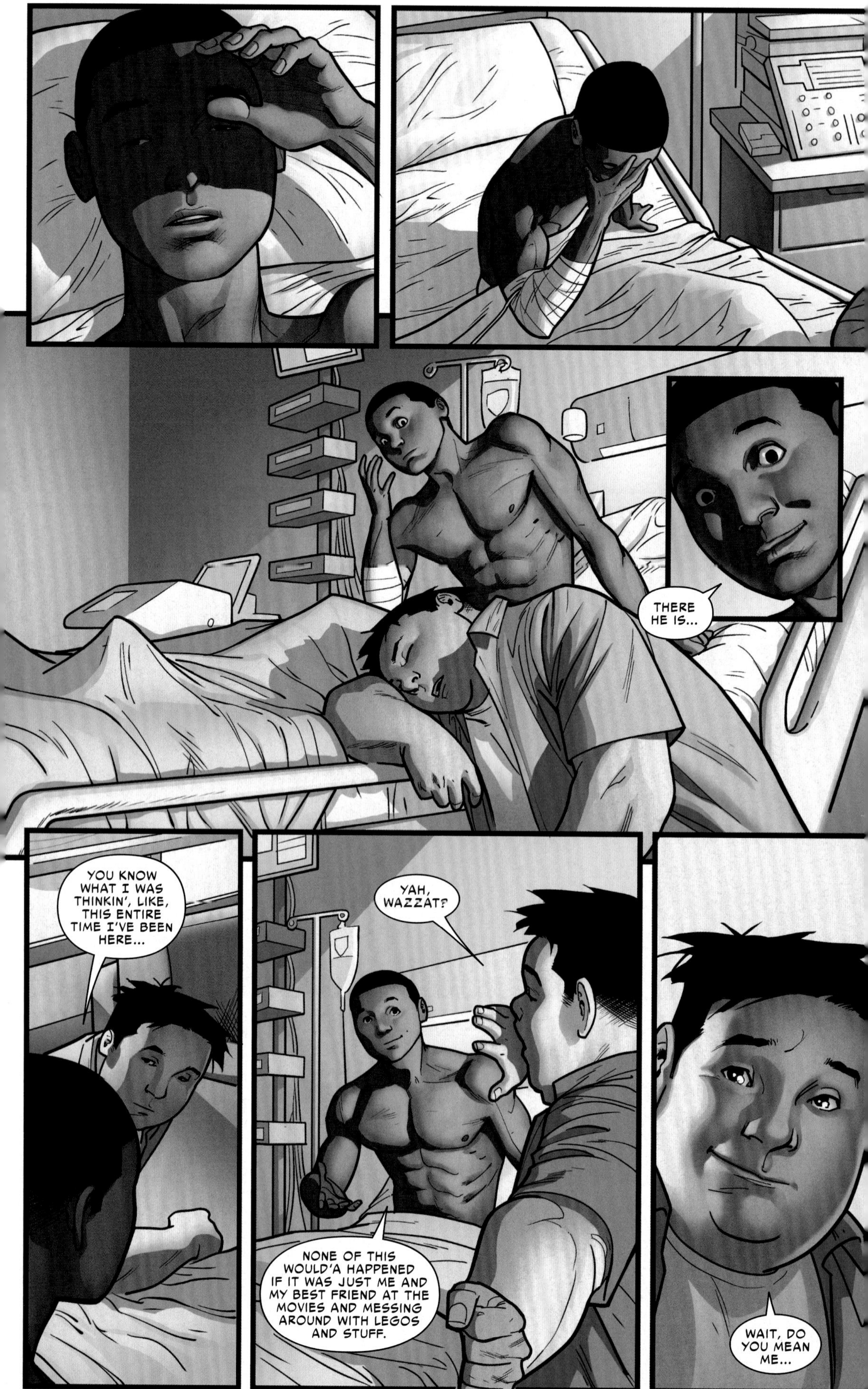
THERE HE IS...
YOU KNOW WHAT I WAS THINKIN', LIKE, THIS ENTIRE TIME I'VE BEEN HERE...
YAH, WAZZAT?
NONE OF THIS WOULD'A HAPPENED IF IT WAS JUST ME AND MY BEST FRIEND AT THE MOVIES AND MESSING AROUND WITH LEGOS AND STUFF.
WAIT, DO YOU MEAN ME...

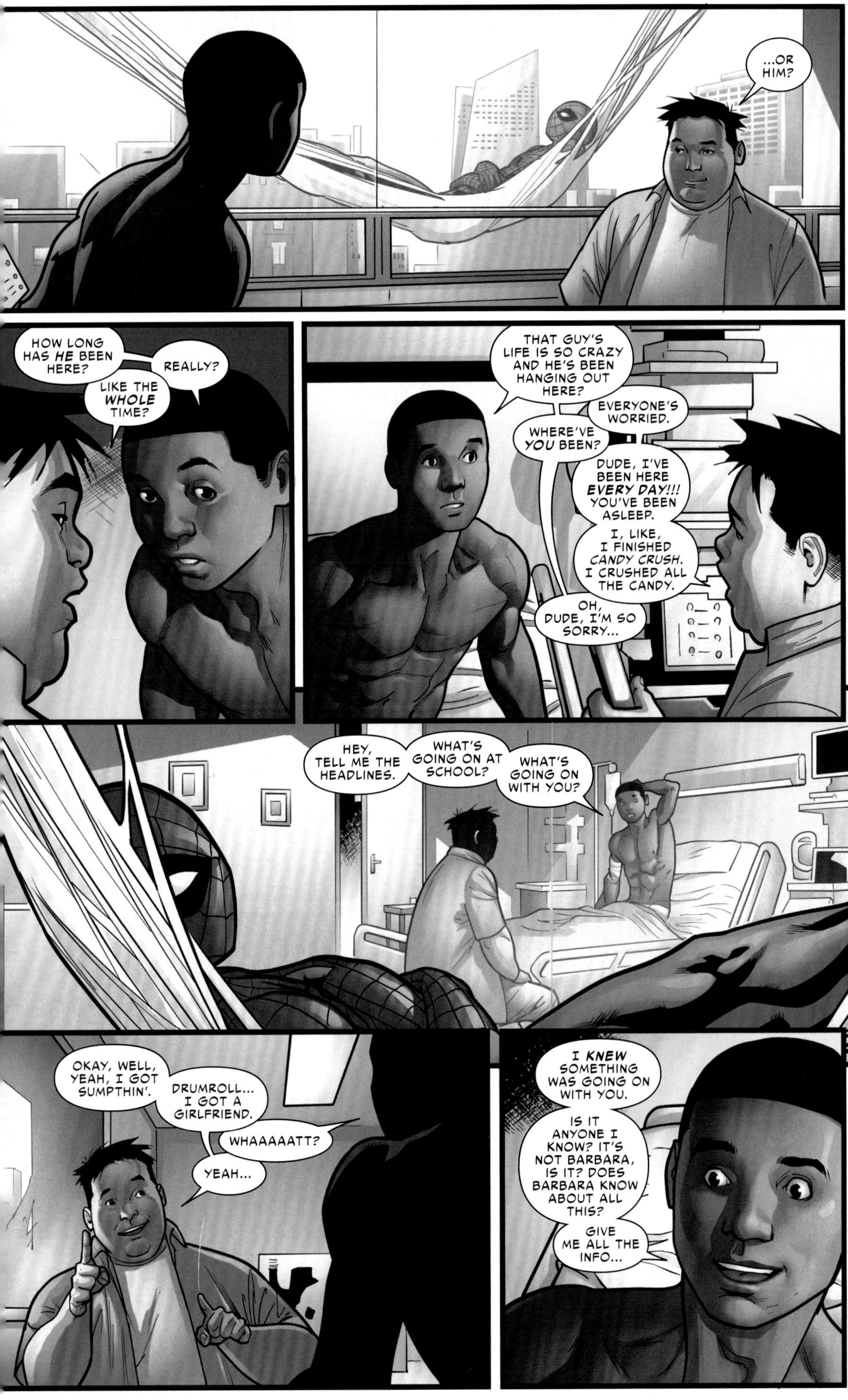
...OR HIM?
HOW LONG HAS HE BEEN HERE?
REALLY?
LIKE THE WHOLE TIME?
THAT GUY'S LIFE IS SO CRAZY AND HE'S BEEN HANGING OUT HERE?
EVERYONE'S WORRIED.
WHERE'VE YOU BEEN?
DUDE, I'VE BEEN HERE EVERY DAY!!! YOU'VE BEEN ASLEEP.
I, LIKE, I FINISHED CANDY CRUSH. I CRUSHED ALL THE CANDY.
OH, DUDE, I'M SO SORRY...
HEY, TELL ME THE HEADLINES.
WHAT'S GOING ON AT SCHOOL?
WHAT'S GOING ON WITH YOU?
OKAY, WELL, YEAH, I GOT SUMPTHIN'.
DRUMROLL... I GOT A GIRLFRIEND.
WHAAAAATT?
YEAH...
I KNEW SOMETHING WAS GOING ON WITH YOU.
IS IT ANYONE I KNOW? IT'S NOT BARBARA, IS IT? DOES BARBARA KNOW ABOUT ALL THIS?
GIVE ME ALL THE INFO...

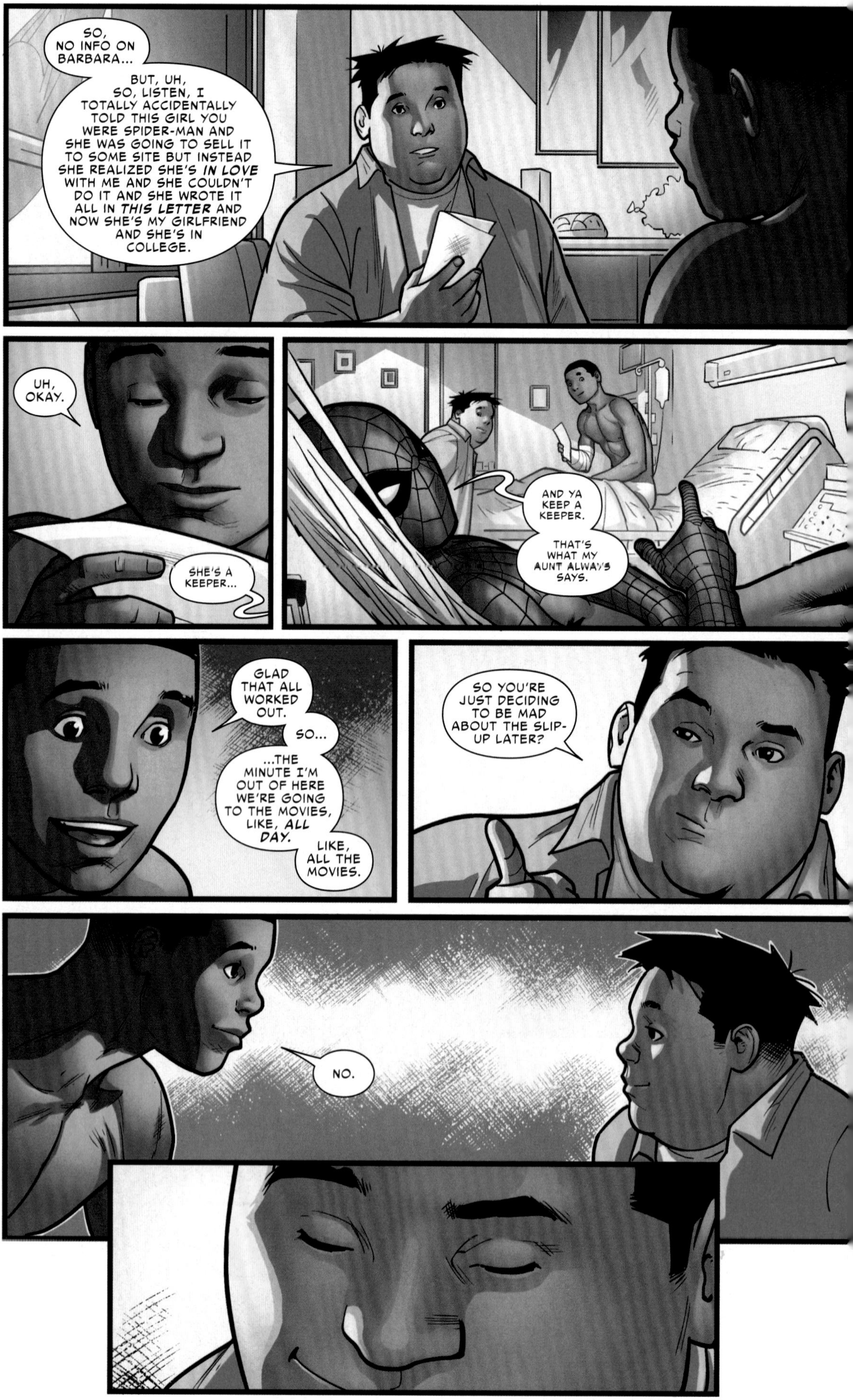

SO, NO INFO ON BARBARA...
BUT, UH, SO, LISTEN, I TOTALLY ACCIDENTALLY TOLD THIS GIRL YOU WERE SPIDER-MAN AND SHE WAS GOING TO SELL IT TO SOME SITE BUT INSTEAD SHE REALIZED SHE'S *IN LOVE* WITH ME AND SHE COULDN'T DO IT AND SHE WROTE IT ALL IN *THIS LETTER* AND NOW SHE'S MY GIRLFRIEND AND SHE'S IN COLLEGE.
UH, OKAY.
SHE'S A KEEPER...
AND YA KEEP A KEEPER.
THAT'S WHAT MY AUNT ALWAYS SAYS.
GLAD THAT ALL WORKED OUT.
SO...
...THE MINUTE I'M OUT OF HERE WE'RE GOING TO THE MOVIES, LIKE, *ALL DAY.*
LIKE, ALL THE MOVIES.
SO YOU'RE JUST DECIDING TO BE MAD ABOUT THE SLIP-UP LATER?
NO.

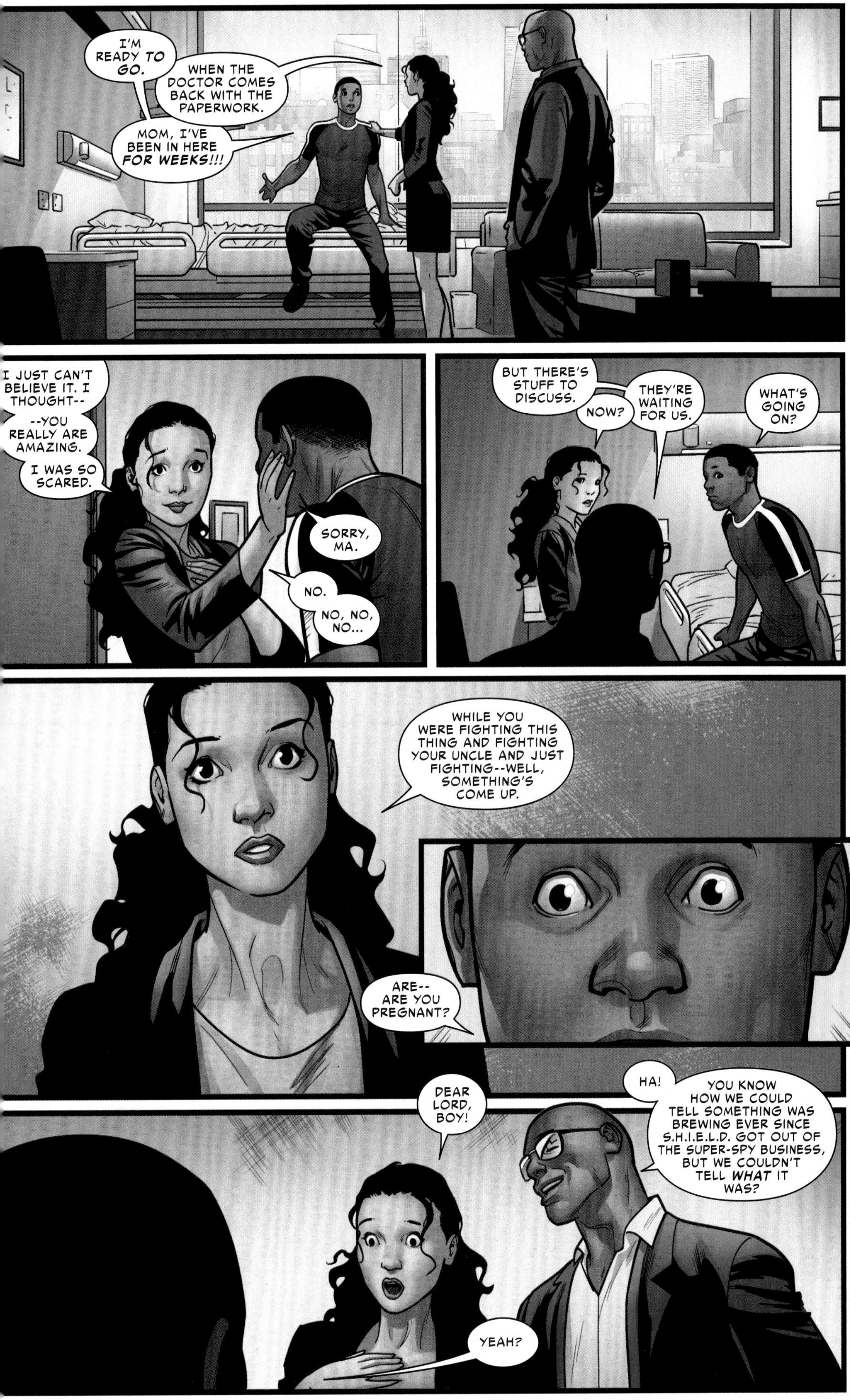
I'M READY TO GO.
WHEN THE DOCTOR COMES BACK WITH THE PAPERWORK.
MOM, I'VE BEEN IN HERE FOR WEEKS!!!
I JUST CAN'T BELIEVE IT. I THOUGHT--
--YOU REALLY ARE AMAZING.
I WAS SO SCARED.
SORRY, MA.
NO.
NO, NO, NO...
BUT THERE'S STUFF TO DISCUSS.
NOW?
THEY'RE WAITING FOR US.
WHAT'S GOING ON?
WHILE YOU WERE FIGHTING THIS THING AND FIGHTING YOUR UNCLE AND JUST FIGHTING--WELL, SOMETHING'S COME UP.
ARE-- ARE YOU PREGNANT?
DEAR LORD, BOY!
HA!
YOU KNOW HOW WE COULD TELL SOMETHING WAS BREWING EVER SINCE S.H.I.E.L.D. GOT OUT OF THE SUPER-SPY BUSINESS, BUT WE COULDN'T TELL WHAT IT WAS?
YEAH?

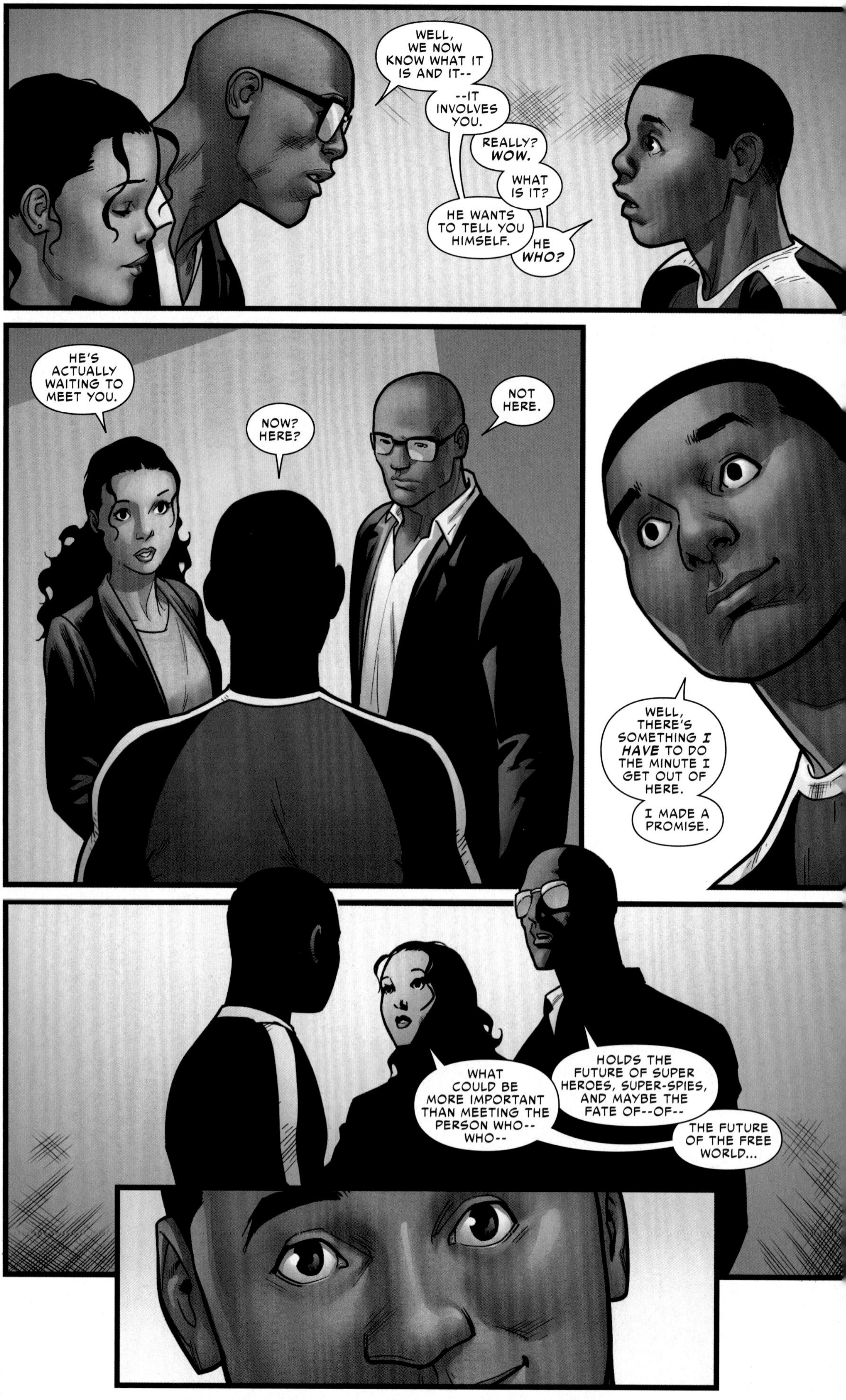
WELL, WE NOW KNOW WHAT IT IS AND IT--
--IT INVOLVES YOU.
REALLY? WOW.
WHAT IS IT?
HE WANTS TO TELL YOU HIMSELF.
HE WHO?
HE'S ACTUALLY WAITING TO MEET YOU.
NOW? HERE?
NOT HERE.
WELL, THERE'S SOMETHING I HAVE TO DO THE MINUTE I GET OUT OF HERE.
I MADE A PROMISE.
WHAT COULD BE MORE IMPORTANT THAN MEETING THE PERSON WHO-- WHO--
HOLDS THE FUTURE OF SUPER HEROES, SUPER-SPIES, AND MAYBE THE FATE OF--OF--
THE FUTURE OF THE FREE WORLD...

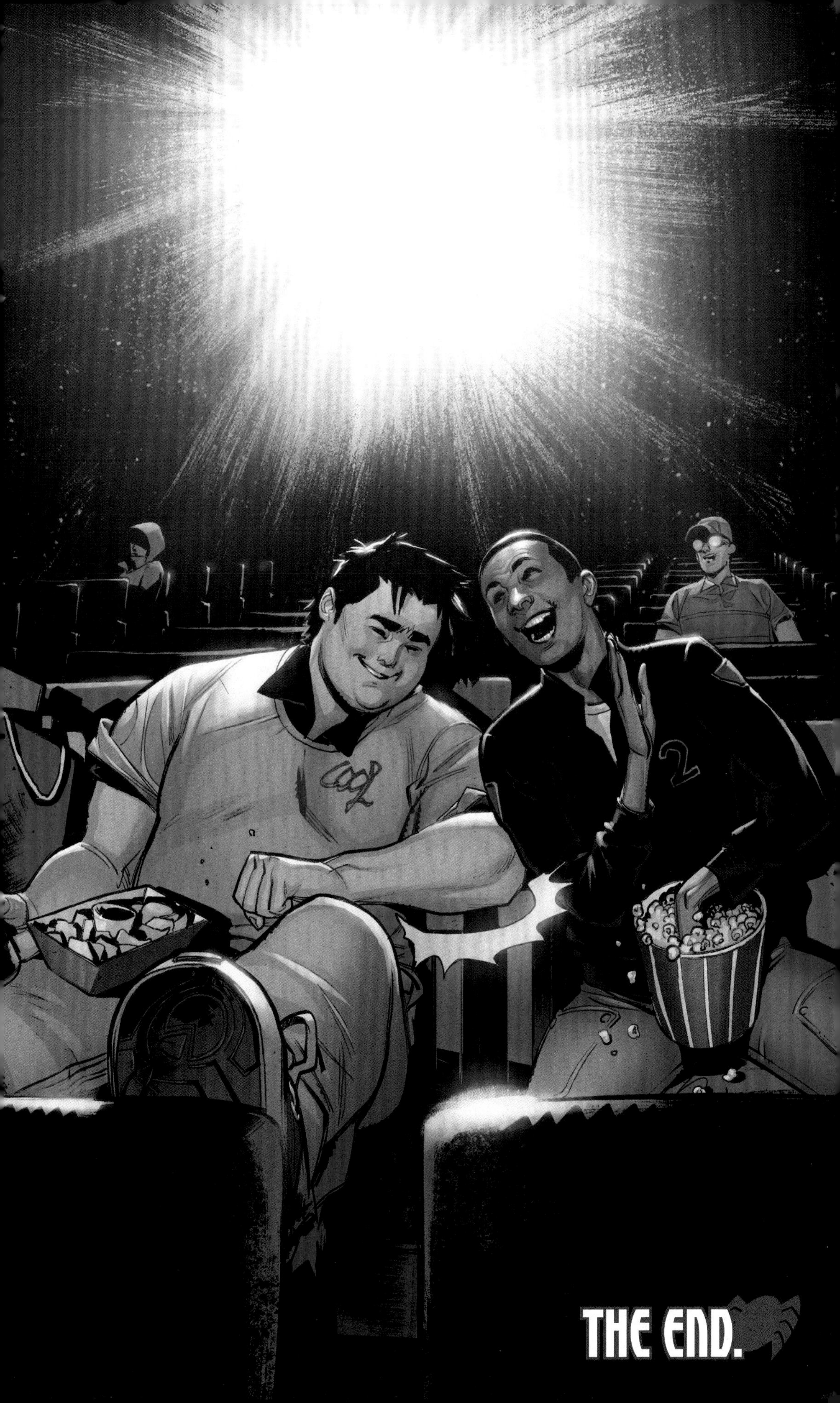
THE END.

"Bye, Spider-Man"
By Brian Michael Bendis

Hi! Hey! I'm Brian, the co-creator of Miles Morales. And if you are just tuning in, you missed a lot! But the headline today is--after eighteen-plus years, 240 issues, over 300 if you count minis, specials, annuals, and events, and I do :)--I am done.

I am moving on. This is my last issue of Spider-Man. Maybe ever. Eighteen years!

I didn't see any of this coming. I did not see Miles Morales becoming a "thing." I did not see him leaping from comics to cartoons to toy shelves and now...movies! And even if I did, maybe, sometimes, dream about it in my quietest of moments, I certainly didn't imagine it all happening while I was still alive and certainly not while I was still on the book. This stuff, if it happens, usually happens decades later. It took X-Men forty years to make it to the big screen. Miles did it in seven! That's crazy!

Okay. A little context into Miles' history…

I've said this so many times and people think I'm being coy, but I'm really not --Miles should not have worked. I know enough about pop culture. I'd fancy myself a professor of popular culture if you all wouldn't make fun of me. I know enough to know that Miles should not have worked. Peter Parker wasn't broken. Spider-Man never has and never will need "fixing." The world wasn't clamoring for someone to come along and fix Spider-Man already.

But what Spider-Man had subtly done over the years is grow beyond itself. Quite a few things were happening in the comics. First off, we launched this comic, then called ULTIMATE SPIDER-MAN which chronicled the TEEN exploits of Peter Parker as if they happened today instead of 1960-something. Now there were different Spider-Man titles doing very well. Then, over in AMAZING SPIDER-MAN, quite a few supporting or "legacy" characters became very popular. Popular enough to get their own comics and toys. Before you knew it Spider-Man was more than a character. He had become his own universe. Here come the cartoons and games and...

A Spider-Verse is born. If you will...

Nick Lowe, editor of this book on and off for most of its ENTIRE run, is more than partly responsible for the Spider-Verse. It's a tribute to his abilities as an editor that it thrives and surprises so much so often in so many formats.

FLASHBACK! At Marvel, we have frequent get-togethers called "retreats" where we just sit around and talk about everything you'd think nerds of our caliber would talk about. One of the subjects was ULTIMATE SPIDER-MAN. We talked about what we would do differently today. We talked about his universal appeal. His unique global appeal. We talked about how Spider-Man, if you look at the basic building blocks of his origin, where he's from, what motivated him, there's really nothing that said this character should be Caucasian. In fact, you could argue there's very little that says he should be. Is that part of his unique appeal?

Could Spider-Man BE someone else? Who? Why?

Well, those ideas scared the hell out of me. So I did what you do when something scares the hell out of you creatively. You do it. You do it in spite of.

Co-created by Sara Pichelli, the artist of ULTIMATE SPIDER-MAN, with a great deal of input and inspiration from Marvel Chief Creative Officer Joe Quesada, Miles Morales was born.

We created a brand-new Spider-Man. But none of it was easy. Should he be created from scratch or should he be something out of the ULTIMATE SPIDER-MAN story? Should Miles be motivated by Peter Parker or should he be motivated by his own situation? Both? Should they EVER meet? Is the world ready for a new kind of Spider-Man? Does the world want this?

And was this really Ganke's story the entire time?

All good questions. All scary questions.

I sat on this for a while. I needed that extra-special magic connection in my brain. Between Miles and Peter? Between myself and the character? A couple months later, on a long bike ride, the simple, elegant idea finally found its way to the surface: if Peter Parker dies heroically enough, he could be the "Uncle Ben" character to this new Spider-Man. Then he continues the legacy of Peter, which is the legacy of Uncle Ben, which is the legacy of "with great power there must also come great responsibility." This new character can feel the words from his new perspective. Now we have a Spider-Man that means something to the legacy of Spider-Man but takes it in a completely different direction.

And then, yada yada yada... They made a Miles Build-a-Bear!

And here we are, you and I, at the end of the run. How do you say goodbye to an audience filled with those who may have just joined you (every comic is someone's first) and others who have been with us since the beginning? Well, I had been thinking about THAT for months. Once I knew my time at Marvel

was done I asked myself: How do yo wrap up such a thing? What does a "las story after eighteen years feel like? Ho does a story sum up everything yo want to say about the franchise, th characters and your personal feeling about all things Spider-Man?

Well, last December I caught a MRS infection that went septic. I was in th hospital for most of December. It's th worst thing that ever happened to me. flat out almost died three times. No jok My wife saved my life for real. I spent mo of December in and out of consciousnes as my body held on.

But every time I woke up in the hospita one or some or all of my friends were the in my room. Some of them are, of cours famous comic book people whose name you might know. Others are big-tim doctors you don't know, but if you like m world you should salute them. They a why I am still here.

If you didn't know, Portland, Orego where I live, is lousy with comics creator Almost to a ridiculous degree. Most of u all know and hang out with each othe Some of these people I consider family.

I kept waking up to see Matt Fractio asleep in a chair only to find out fro others he hadn't left the chair for day Every day Greg Rucka came in wit Hanukah cookies from a local old-scho bakery. I woke up once to David Walke Mike Oeming, Taki Soma, and Dav Marquez each trying to top each other poop-related horror stories. They didr even see me wake up because they we having such a good time.

Hey, this sounds a lot like what you ju read! Yeah, you're getting it. Every tim I opened my eyes...friendship and lov Every time. So as I thought about what wanted to leave you with it was obviou that the world had shown me how to en this run. So we made this. I left you wit a Marvel version of what I felt like in th hospital. Warmth. Love. Friendship. It how you always made me feel when yo bought this book.

Two weeks before, I decided to take th biggest chance in my adult life and leav Marvel for the Distinguished Competitio Not because I am mad at Marvel, b because the mountain had been climbed

My old friends at Marvel, when the heard I got sick, had literally stoppe the presses. Even though I had polite quit, given notice, jumped ship to th competition, Joe Quesada, Tom Brevoo and the others...didn't care. They sai "Get better and finish your work, we wait!" That's why people love Marv comics so much. The people that mak these comics are good people, mostly who live by the codes they write and dra about. (Again, mostly, but WAY more tha you'd guess. It's kind of amazing.)

This was my childhood dream job. Actually, my dream job was to have written A Spider-Man comic. I leave behind the longest running Spider-Man run ever. Dan Slott only missed by 100 issues. :)

2000. 1999, actually. I was first teamed up with Mark Bagley. It was a blind date. We were thrust together. We did the first 111 issues together. In retrospect, the entirety of my over-the-top success at Marvel is due to my calm and compassionate friend Mark Bagley being nothing but calm and compassionate with me in those early days.

And then, in relation to how many comics we're talking about, a VERY elite group of artists joined us. Stuart Immonen and David Lafuente did amazing runs with me. I am so proud of them and all the other artists who have dropped by for a one-shot or pin-up or cover.

Then came a couple of very special collaborators.

First, the aforementioned Sara Pichelli. She came to ULTIMATE SPIDER-MAN early in her career. C.B. Cebulski, my old friend and now EDITOR IN CHIEF (!) discovered her fashion-infused brilliant work and I bore witness to her fast artistic evolution right here on this book. She joined me in the creation on Miles, Ganke, Rio, etc. She was such an amazing collaborator on the two SPIDER-MEN series and then GUARDIANS OF THE GALAXY...but that meant she wasn't drawing this book.

Now, with some collaborators, you work well but have no actual relationship, while with others you can strike a deep, long friendship.

Enter Texas-born David Marquez. He came to the book and my life after doing just a little work at Marvel but it was so clear he was about to explode. And he did. It was awesome. And then we tricked him into moving to Portland. David has been an amazing friend and partner. Buy whatever book you see his name on. He is the real damn deal. If Sara is Miles' Steve Ditko, David is Miles' John Romita. Google it, it's a phenomenal reference. :)

David and Sara? Man, that is two HUGE careers out of one book!

But this last book is dedicated to my friend and longest collaborator on so many, many books...Justin Ponsor. Justin has been on this book for over a decade. He brought his masterful blend of cinematic palette to everything and everyone from Bagley on up to our most recent collaborator, the lovely Oscar Bazaldua.

As some of you may know, Justin fell ill, too. We are all hoping he pulls through. The only reason he is not coloring this issue, which was written with him in mind, is because he can't at the moment. The amazing Laura Martin has stepped in for him and in tribute to his amazing contribution to this book.

Eighteen years! Hundreds of issues! It is so difficult to thank everyone. And I haven't even thanked Oscar. Oscar, you have made my last years on this book a blessing. I am truly sorry to be breaking up this team because, like Sara and David before him, it has been so fun to watch you pop. Every issue is better than the last and the last was amazing. Oscar, thank you. Call me.

So take a minute and read the fine print on this book's credits. Every single person really hunkered down to make every issue special. We all knew how important Miles and company are to the readers and we all worked VERY hard to make every issue honest.

Every letterer, colorist, penciler, inker, and editor that graced our pages... thank you.

To the creators now entrusted with Miles, Ganke, Lana, Rio and Jefferson... thank you. Take good care of them, but, and I am saying this publicly, don't be nice to them. Give them good stories that challenge the hell out of them. Do stuff I NEVER would have done. Nothing would make me happier.

So this is it. The end of the run. Everything about my life has changed in that time. I was a feisty up-and-comer living in Cleveland when I got this book. Now I'm married with four kids in Portland and I got my "veteran comics creator" ID card when I finished my X-MEN run. This book has taken me around the world, to Japan, Bolivia, London, Paris, and even Detroit! I have met fans who have lovingly and painstakingly stitched together their own cosplay so it looks EXACTLY like Bagley drew it. People made Miles costumes for years before you could buy them. Just this last ECCC, a kick-ass female fan came cosplaying as KONG. And he hasn't been in the book in years.

I could write a long, memory-filled dissertation on every single issue, that's how much I have to say and feel about this life-altering opportunity. There were times where my world had crumbled to the point of nothing and this book, crafting and writing these characters, got me through it. I figured out who I wanted to be while writing this book.

I once got to tell Stan Lee that and, to my delight, he quietly admitted that the same thing happened to him.

Miles, I miss you already. I actually

have a book at DC that I know you'd be perfect for, but Marvel said no. But I tried.

Ganke, Ned, whatever your name is... Don't tell anyone, I'm going to miss you most of all.

I was going to say I was going to miss you, the reader, most of all, but I feel like when Letterman switched networks. It's sad, but I'm still going to be on the stands on Wednesday. I hope I'll see you over there. But meanwhile, please continue to support this book in whatever form it takes. The creators have my full blessing and support. I have had long talks with them. I'm excited. You and I get to read this book together for the first time.

And I am consulting on, and have seen, the *Spider-Verse* movie starring Miles. It's so good. December!

Joe Quesada and Bill Jemas originally hired me for this job and they pretty much let me do whatever I wanted the entire time, including ignoring the fact that it was a six-issue miniseries (true story) and then I got to write the cartoons and the video games... Thank you.

And as I think of all the joy this book has given me on so many levels. The best? It brought me to you. The best fans. When you see me at a show say you read this. You get a hug.

This offer is good for life.

Thank you.

Thank you, thank you, thank you.

BENDIS!

We here in the Spidey-Office and at Marvel in general want to add our thanks on top of Brian's to everyone who's worked on this Spider-Man saga and the creation of Miles and his world. And we want to add a huge note of thanks to Brian Michael Bendis himself. Those of us who've worked on this book know how much of Brian's heart and soul are in this book and character and world. Brian and Mark and Stuart and David L. and Sara and David M. and Oscar all did incredible work to make some of the best comics ever. And on a more personal note, Brian was one of the first writers I worked with as an editor, and from day one when I called him to talk about DAREDEVIL lettering notes to the days on ULTIMATE SPIDER-MAN to our time on ALL-NEW X-MEN this very series, Brian always went out of his way to listen and collaborate. It didn't matter if I was a green assistant editor or an executive editor. That's not every collaborator, people. That makes a special person, and I feel lucky to call Brian a friend and am very sad to see him go. We'll always have ULTIMATE SPIDER-MAN #66 and #67, Brian.

Sincerely,
Nick

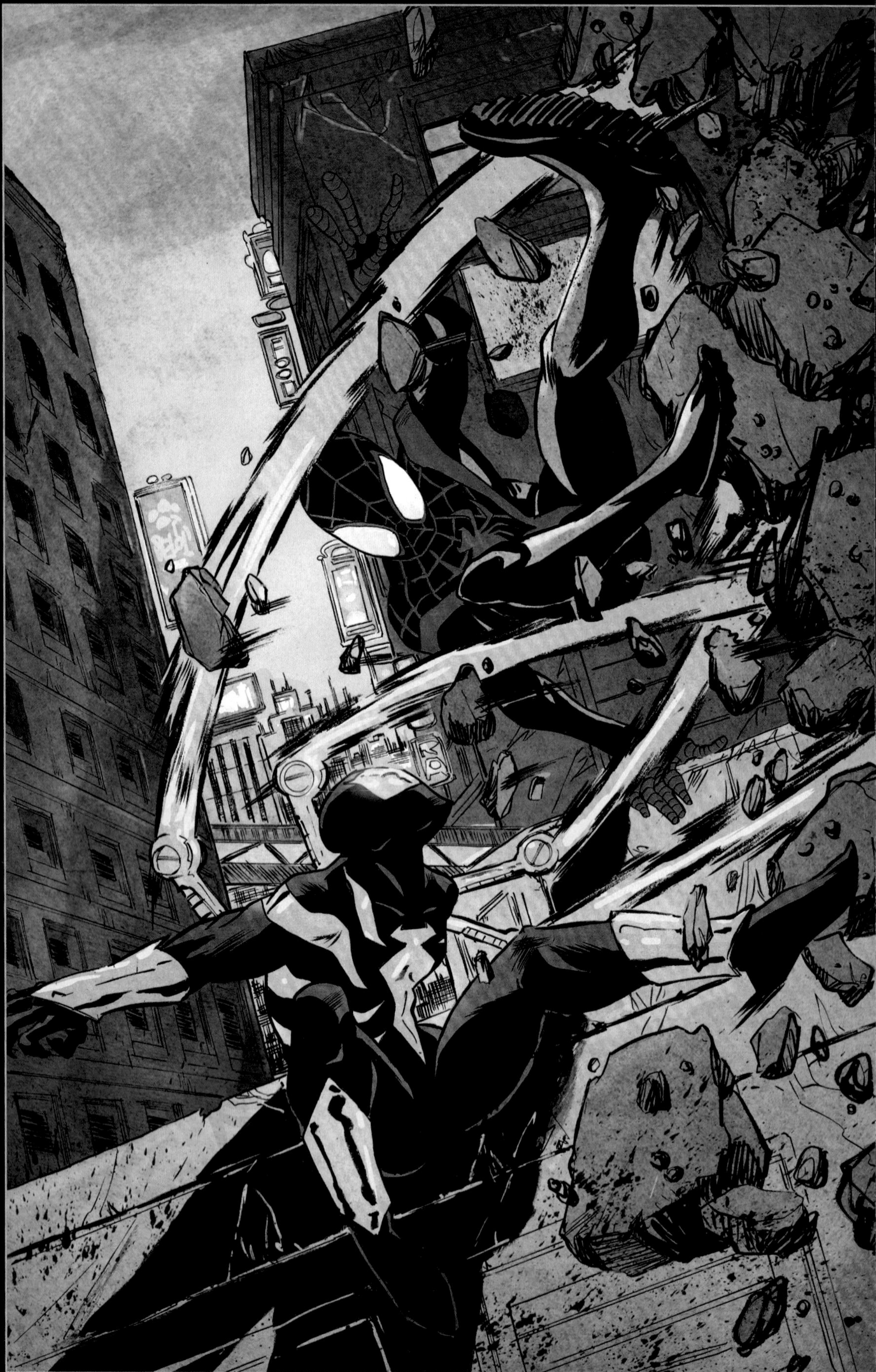

SANFORD GREENE
#234 VARIANT

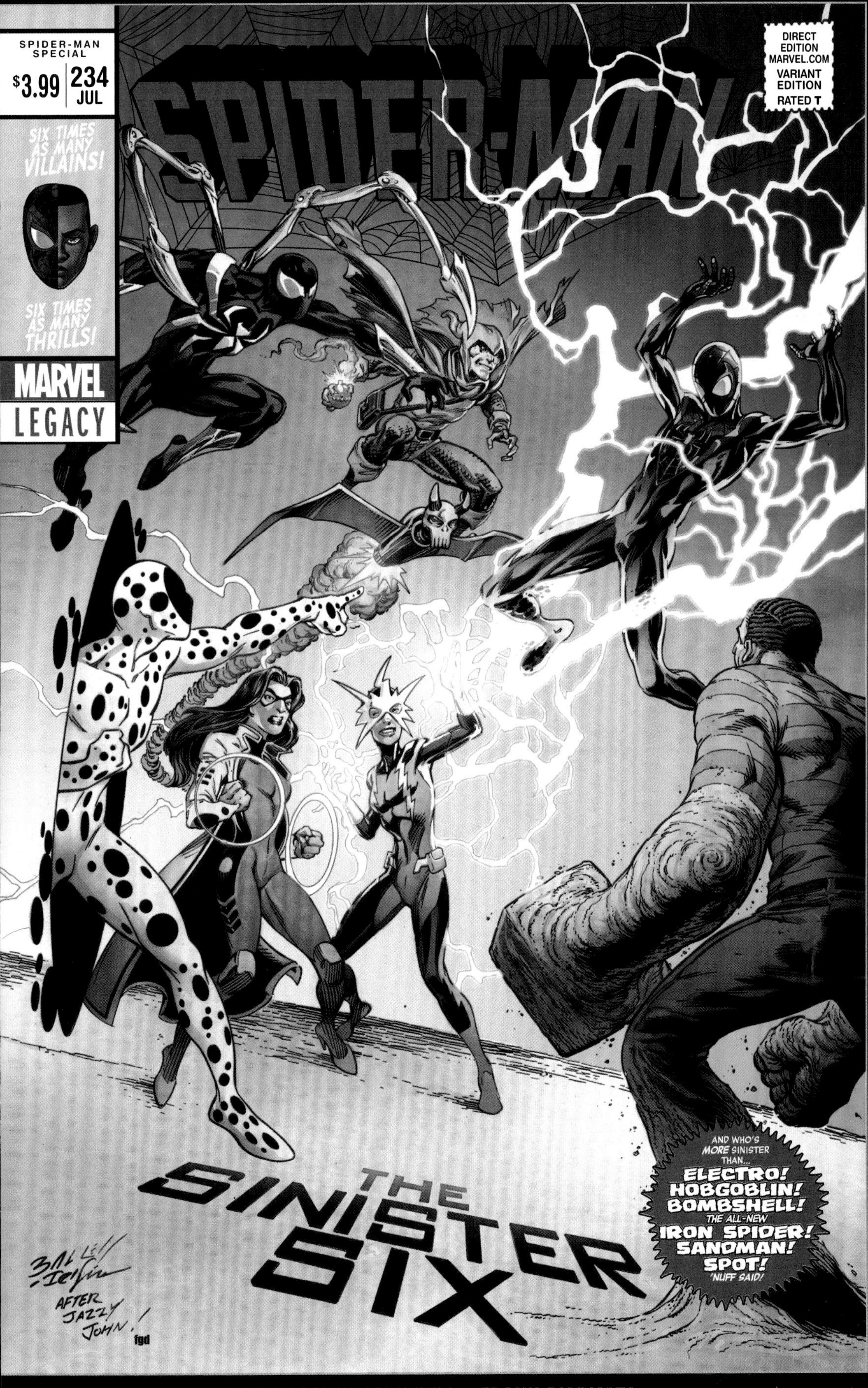
SPIDER-MAN SPECIAL
$3.99
234
JUL
SPIDER-MAN
DIRECT EDITION
MARVEL.COM
VARIANT EDITION
RATED T
SIX TIMES AS MANY VILLAINS!
SIX TIMES AS MANY THRILLS!
MARVEL
LEGACY
THE SINISTER SIX
AND WHO'S MORE SINISTER THAN...
ELECTRO!
HOBGOBLIN!
BOMBSHELL!
THE ALL-NEW
IRON SPIDER!
SANDMAN!
SPOT!
'NUFF SAID!
AFTER JAZZY JOHN!
fgd

MARK BAGLEY, JOHN DELL & FRANK D'ARMATA

#234 VARIANT

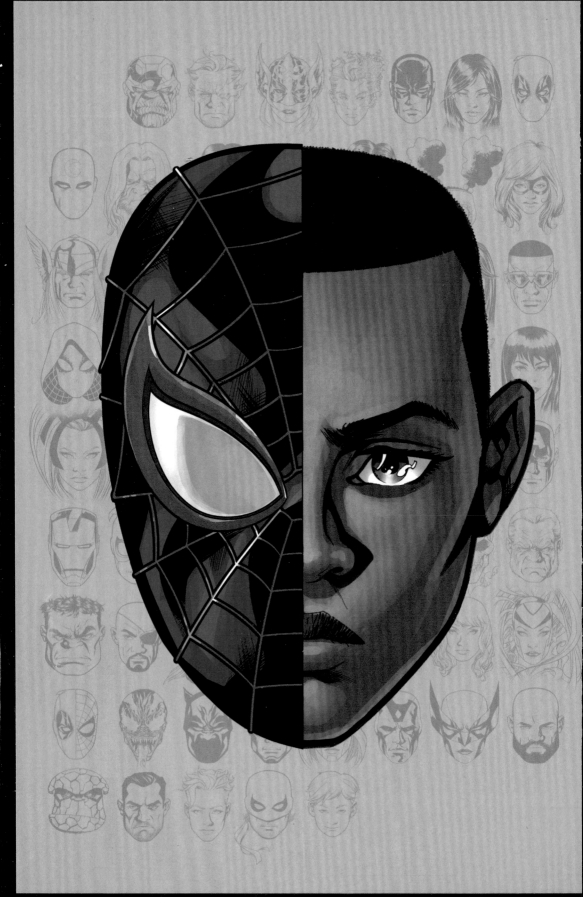

MIKE McKONE & ANDY TROY
#234 LEGACY HEADSHOT VARIANT